T0221040

Quantum Computing

Quantum Computing

A New Era of Computing

Kuldeep Singh Kaswan
Galgotias University
Uttar Pradesh, India

Jagjit Singh Dhatterwal
KL Deemed to be University
Andhra Pradesh, India

Anupam Baliyan
Chandigarh University
Punjab, India

Shalli Rani
Chitkara University Institute of Engineering
and Technology, Chitkara University
Punjab, India

IEEE PRESS

WILEY

Library of Congress Cataloging-in-Publication Data:

Names: Kaswan, Kuldeep Singh, author. | Dhatterwal, Jagjit Singh, author. |
    Baliyan, Anupam, 1976- author. | Rani, Shalli, author.
Title: Quantum computing : a new era of computing / Kuldeep Singh Kaswan,
    Galgotias University, Uttar Pradesh, India, Jagjit Singh Dhatterwal, PDM
    University, Haryana, India, Anupam Baliyan, Chandigarh University,
    Punjab, India, Shalli Rani, Chitkara University Institute of
    Engineering, India.
Description: First edition. | Hoboken, New Jersey : John Wiley & Sons, Inc,
    [2023] | Includes index.
Identifiers: LCCN 2023002835 (print) | LCCN 2023002836 (ebook) | ISBN
    9781394157815 (hardback) | ISBN 9781394157822 (adobe pdf) | ISBN
    9781394157839 (epub)
Subjects: LCSH: Quantum computing.
Classification: LCC QA76.889 .K37 2023 (print) | LCC QA76.889 (ebook) |
    DDC 006.3/843–dc23/eng/20230201
LC record available at https://lccn.loc.gov/2023002835
LC ebook record available at https://lccn.loc.gov/2023002836

Cover Design: Wiley
Cover Image: © AniGraphics/Getty Images

Set in 9.5/12.5pt STIXTwoText by Straive, Chennai, India

Contents

Preface

In the twenty-first century, it is reasonable to expect that some of the most important developments in science and engineering will come about through interdisciplinary research. Already in the making is surely one of the most interesting and exciting development we are sure to see for a long time, *quantum computation*. A merger of computer science and physics, quantum computation came into being from two lines of thought. The first was the recognition that *information is physical*, which is an observation that simply states the obvious fact that information can't exist or be processed without a physical medium. At the present time, quantum computers are mostly theoretical constructs. However, it has been proved that in at least some cases, quantum computation is much faster in principle than any done by classical computer. The most famous algorithm developed is Shor's factoring algorithm, which shows that a quantum computer, if one could be constructed, could quickly crack the codes currently used to secure the world's data. Quantum information processing systems can also do remarkable things not possible otherwise, such as teleporting the state of a particle from one place to another and providing unbreakable cryptography systems.

Our treatment is not rigorous nor is it complete for the following reason: this book is aimed primarily at two audiences, the first group being undergraduate physics, math, and computer science majors. In most cases these undergraduate students will find the standard presentations on quantum computation and information science a little hard to digest. This book aims to fill in the gap by providing undergraduate students with an easy-to-follow format that will help them grasp many of the fundamental concepts of quantum information science. This book is also aimed at readers who are technically trained in other fields. This includes students and professionals who may be engineers, chemists, or biologists. These readers may not have the background in quantum physics or math that most people in the field of quantum computation have. This book aims to fill the gap here as well by offering a more "hand-holding" approach to the topic so that readers can learn the basics and a little bit on how to do calculations in quantum computation.

Finally, the book will be useful for graduate students in physics and computer science taking a quantum computation course who are looking for a calculational oriented supplement to their main textbook and lecture notes.

The goal of this book is to open up and introduce quantum computation to these nonstandard audiences. As a result, the level of the book is a bit lower than that found in the standard quantum computation books currently available. The presentation is informal, with the goal of introducing the concepts used in the field and then showing through explicit examples how to work with them. Some topics are left out entirely and many are not covered at the deep level that would be expected in a graduate level quantum computation textbook. An in-depth treatment of adiabatic quantum computation or cluster state computation is beyond this scope of this book. However, it will give readers who are new to the field a substantial foundation that can be built upon to master quantum computation. While an attempt was made to provide a broad overview of the field, the presentation is weighted more in the physics direction.

Dr. Kuldeep Singh Kaswan

Author Biography

Dr. Kuldeep Singh Kaswan is presently working in School of Computing Science & Engineering, Galgotias University, Uttar Pradesh, India. His contributions focus on BCI, Cyborg and Data Sciences. His Academic degrees and thirteen years of experience working with global Universities like, Amity University, Noida, Gautam Buddha University, Greater Noida and PDM University, Bahadurgarh, has made him more receptive and prominent in his domain. He received Doctorate in Computer Science from Banasthali Vidyapith, Rajasthan. He Received Doctor of Engineering (D. Eng.) from Dana Brain Health Institute, Iran. He has obtained Master Degree in Computer Science and Engineering from Choudhary Devi Lal University, Sirsa (Haryana). He has supervised many UG and PG projects of engineering students. He has supervised 2 PhD graduates and presently is supervising 4 PhD. He is also Member of Computer Science Teacher Association (CSTA), New York, USA, International Association of Engineers (IAENG), Hong Kong, IACSIT (International Association of Computer Science and Information Technology, USA, professional member Association of Computing Machinery, USA, and IEEE. He has number of publications in International/National Journal and Conferences. He is an editor/author, and review editor of Journals and Books with IEEE, Wiley, Springer, IGI, River etc.

Dr. Jagjit Singh Dhatterwal is presently working as an Associate Professor, Department of Artificial Intelligence & Data Science Koneru Lakshmaiah Education Foundation, Vaddeswaram, AP, India. He completed Doctorate in Computer Science from Mewar University, Rajasthan, India. He received Master of Computer Application from Maharshi Dayanand University, Rohtak (Haryana). He has also worked with Maharishi Dayanand University, Rohtak,

Haryana. He is also Member of Computer Science Teacher Association (CSTA), New York, USA, International Association of Engineers (IAENG), Hong Kong, IACSIT, USA, professional member Association of Computing Machinery, USA, IEEE. His area of interests includes Artificial Intelligence, BCI and Multi-Agents Technology. He has numbers of publications in International/National Journals and Conferences.

Dr. Anupam Baliyan is working as an Additional Director (Computer Science & Engineering) in Department of Computer Science and Engineering, Chandigarh University, Ghraun, Mohali, Punjab(India). He has more than 22 Years of Experience in Academic. He is MCA from Gurukul kangari University, MTech(CSE) and Phd(CSE) from Banasthali University. He published more than 30 Research papers in various International Journal indexed at Scopus and ESI. He is Life time member of CSI and ISTE. He has been chaired many sessions in International Conferences across the India. He also published some edited books and chapters. He is also the Asst. Editor of some Journals those are Scopus indexed. His Research Area is Algorithms, Machine learning, Wireless networks and AI.

Dr. Shalli Rani is pursuing postdoctoral from Manchester Metropolitan University from July, 2021. She is Associate Professor in CSE with Chitkara University Institute of Engineering and Technology, Chitkara University, Punjab, India. She has 18+ years teaching experience. She is pursuing postdoctoral fellowship from Manchester Metropolitan University, UK. She received MCA degree from Maharishi Dyanand University, Rohtak in 2004 and the MTech degree in Computer Science from Janardan Rai Nagar Vidyapeeth University, Udaipur in 2007 and PhD degree in Computer Applications from Punjab Technical University, Jalandhar in 2017. Her main area of interest and research are Wireless Sensor Networks, Underwater Sensor networks and Internet of Things. She has published/accepted/presented more than 70+ papers in international journals /conferences (SCI+Scopus) and edited/authored five books with international publishers. She is serving as the associate editor of IEEE Future Directions Letters. She is serving as a guest editor in IEEE Transaction on Industrial Informatics and Elsevier IoT Journals. She has also served as reviewer in many repudiated journals of IEEE, Springer, Elsevier,

IET, Hindawi and Wiley. She has worked on Big Data, Underwater Acoustic Sensors and IoT to show the importance of WSN in IoT applications. She received a young scientist award in February 2014 from Punjab Science Congress, Lifetime Achievement Award and Supervisor of the year award from Global Innovation and Excellence, 2021.

1

Introduction of Quantum Computing

1.1 Introduction

A significant advancement in computer science may take the form of a new algorithm that significantly outperforms the state of the art, or it may provide theoretical evidence that the state of the art cannot be significantly improved. The latter condition imposes a fundamental limit on the complexity of problems that any given computer can solve in a given amount of time. Increasing the computer's processing speed is the only way to increase the number of problems that can be solved. According to Moore's Law, the size of semiconductors (and, by extension, computing capability) has approximately doubled every two years since the 1960s. It is clear that, despite the fact that this development has been going on for decades, it cannot go on forever because of a number of basic physical constraints. As a result, quantum weirdness will dominate the behavior of the circuitry by 2020, and by 2050, the circuits will have achieved the lowest size at which knowledge can be permanently contained [1].

The results of this study have piqued the public's interest in how quantum theory may affect the future of computing over the next several decades. Is it possible, for instance, to make circuits immune to the influence of quantum effects? As an alternative, may quantum phenomena be exploited to do arithmetic? In order to do calculations, quantum computers take advantage of quantum phenomena. However, a quantum computer is not only a device with enhanced performance because of the faster speed of quantum-scale circuits. It is of more interest to the software programmer than to the theoretical physicist. After all, the computational complexity of algorithms executed on a certain CPU remains the same regardless of the CPU's clock speed. Different algorithms may provide better complexity in terms of the new variable P if the computer's architecture is altered

Quantum Computing: A New Era of Computing, First Edition.
Kuldeep Singh Kaswan, Jagjit Singh Dhatterwal, Anupam Baliyan, and Shalli Rani.
© 2023 The Institute of Electrical and Electronics Engineers, Inc. Published 2023 by John Wiley & Sons, Inc.

to include some number P of processors. We may able to reduce the greatest feasible complexity for solving a specific problem from O(N) to O(N/P), if we have a good parallel extraction of processors. However, not all algorithms can be broken down into O(P)-independent portions that can be incorporated and enforced during the algorithm's operating time, therefore obtaining an O(P) complexity reduction is not always possible. To store and manipulate data, for instance, analog hardware and programmable real numbers may replace a discrete set of symbols, which would need a more radical redesign. It is possible that this design will prove to be far more powerful than the classic Turing machine. Because of the limitless precision with which a single physical value may be measured, it is possible to analyze massive amounts of data in parallel by treating them as a single unit cost. This is, of course, completely hypothetical since it assumes infinite precision can be maintained throughout those operations, and there is no reason to believe that such an infrastructure is physically conceivable. The potential of a quantum computer, which relies on the preservation of real, complex values, is underutilized [2].

1.2 What Is the Exact Meaning of Quantum Computing?

Large, complex datasets are no match for the speed with which quantum computers can process them. They use the foundations of quantum physics to speed up the process of doing complex computations. Quantum computers' ability to break cryptography and encrypted electronic communications is already changing portions of cybersecurity, and their usage in simulators with a practically endless quantity of variables has implications across fields, from biology to economics. The next large electronics race has already started [3], with some of the biggest names in industry, including Google, Microsoft, Intel, IBM, and Alibaba, exploring quantum computing to improve rates and other applications. Although Google has been studying quantum computing to speed up internet searches since at least 2009, the market for commercialized quantum entanglement is still in its infancy, and it is not yet obvious who will emerge as the market leader.

1.2.1 What Is Quantum Computing in Simple Terms?

Figure 1.1 depicts the interactions of matter in the universe at the level of fundamental particles, which provide the basis for special relativity, upon which quantum computing is founded. Bits can only be encrypted in classical computers if they have a value of 1 or 0.

Figure 1.1 David Deutsch father of quantum computing. Source: Lulie Tanett (https://images.app.goo.gl/CQBoMf7JqWzXfr6r9).

1.3 Origin of Quantum Computing

Some types of computations now baffle today's computers and will continue to do so even if Moore's Law is extended indefinitely, although quantum computers may give a stronger correlation boost. Just imagine you have a phone book and need to find a certain number. A conventional computer would have to go through each listing in the phone book to find and provide the appropriate contact information. In theory, a computer system might scan an entire phone book in a fraction of a second, evaluating each line simultaneously and returning the result far faster than a modern computer [4]. The term "complex mathematical optimizing" is often used to describe the process of finding the best possible combination of elements and answers to a problem. Consider the costs of building the tallest building in the world, including machinery, food, labor, and permits. The challenge is in figuring out how to optimally allocate resources like money, time, and manpower. As a result, we may be able to plan for major projects with more efficiency with the aid of quantum computing if these factors are taken into account. Software development, supply chain management, finance, internet-based research, genomics, and other fields all face optimization challenges. The most challenging optimization problems in these fields are inherently well-suited for solution on a quantum machine [4] but stump conventional computers. In contrast to classical

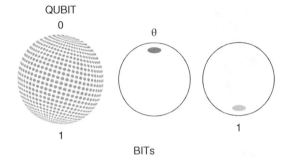

Figure 1.2 Structure of bits and Qbits. Source: Adapted from https://images.app.goo.gl/ DeYCU9A7TeJvV5c16 Last accessed 25 Oct 2022.

computers, which rely almost entirely on technological advances in transistors and microchips, quantum computers may evolve in ways that classical computers cannot. In quantum computers, transistors are not utilized (or classical bits). Substituting qubits for bits. In a quantum algorithm, qubits serve as the basic building blocks for pattern recognition. The example is shown in Figure 1.2.

Qubits may take on the characteristics of either a 0 or a 1, or they can have both at the same time. More choices exist to get accurate results quickly while doing computations. In addition, quantum entanglement and superposition are two important states of matter on which quantum computers depend. When applied to computing, these physical properties have the potential to greatly increase our ability to do very large computations [5].

Although Rigetti Computing's 19-qubit devices are the most powerful in the field of quantum computing, but after 2019, the business is moving on 128-qubit circuit. But as can be seen in Table 1.1, the race to build the most advanced quantum computer with the most qubits has been going on since at least the late 1990s.

Table 1.1 Quantum computing getting more powerful.

Year	Labs	Q-bits
1998	IBM, Oxford, Berkeley, Stanford, MIT	2
2000	Technical University of Munich	7
2006	Institute for Quantum Computing	12
2008	D-Wave System	28
2016	IBM	50
2018	Google	72
2020	Rigetti	128

1.4 History of Quantum Computing

Conjugate coding was first developed in the 1960s by Stephen Wiesner. In the 1970s, James Park established the no-cloning theorem using his formulation. Alexander Holevo proved what is now known as Holevo's theorem, or Holevo's bound, in a paper that was published in 1973. This theorem states that even though n qubits may store more relevant data than n classical bits, only n conventional bits are obtainable. This is despite the fact that n qubits may store more information than n classical bits.

Research conducted by Charles H. Bennett demonstrates that it is feasible to carry out computing in a backward-compatible manner.

- In 1975, R. P. Poplavskii published (in Russian) thermodynamical models of information processing. This work highlights the computational difficulties of reproducing quantum systems on classical computers owing to the fact that the superposition principle is at play.
- In 1976, the Polish mathematician and physicist Roman Stanislaw Ingarden published Quantum Information Theory in the journal *Reports on Mathematical Physics*. Ingarden's paper "1976 Quantum Information Theory." This study, which was one of the early efforts to build quantum synchronization theory, demonstrates that the traditional Shannon communication theory cannot simply be translated into the quantum situation. This was one of the earliest attempts to establish quantum entanglement theory. However, a quantum entanglement theory, which is a wide expansion of Shannon's theory, is possible to construct within the representation of an expanded subatomic particles of open systems and a generalized idea of explanatory variables that is both broad and imprecise (the so-called semi-observables).

Paul Benioff is credited with developing the very first computer model based on quantum physics in the 1980s. In this paper, Benioff paved the way for further research in quantum computing by laying the groundwork for future work in the field by proposing a Schrodinger equation description of Turing machines. This demonstration showed that a computer could operate in accordance with the rules of quantum physics. The work was first shown to the public in June 1979, and four months later, in April 1980, it was published. Yuri Manin presents a synopsis of the field of quantum computing in this article.

The reversible Toffoli gate, with the NOT and XOR gates, forms the foundation of a universal set that is used for bidirectional classical computing.

In May 1980, the Massachusetts Institute of Technology (MIT) played host to the First Conference on the Physics of Computation. At this conference, prominent figures in the field of computing, such as Paul Benioff and Richard Feynman, explored quantum computing. Benioff's current investigation is an expansion of his earlier work from 1980, which demonstrated the possibility that a computer may function in line with the principles of quantum physics. Quantum mechanical Hamiltonian models of discrete processes that delete their own histories: application to Turing machines," the talk's title said. During his presentation, Feynman said that it seemed to be difficult to properly mimic the evolution of a quantum particle on a regular computer. In addition to that, he laid the foundation for the contemporary quantum algorithm.

Paul Benioff continued to develop his concept of a Turing machine that was based on quantum modeling in 1982. William Wootters, Wojciech Zurek, and Dennis Dieks all independently rediscovered the no-cloning theorem at around the same time.

In 1984, Charles Bennett and Gilles Brassard resort to Wiesner's conjugate coding in order to distribute cryptographic keys in an uncompromised manner.

In 1985, while working at Oxford University, David Deutsch was the first person to conceptualize a universal quantum computer. A universal quantum computer, much like a multiclass support vector machine, has the potential to successfully imitate any other quantum computer with just a polynomial amount of latency (Church–Turing thesis).

Yoshihisa Yamamoto and K. Igeta, two physicists, developed the first practical implementation of a quantum algorithm in 1988. Their algorithm utilized Feynman's CNOT gate as one of its components. Their system utilizes both atoms and photons, which positions it as a forerunner of present quantum computing and networking protocols. These protocols employ photons to transport qubits, while atoms are utilized to carry out two-qubit operations. Gerard J. Milburn demonstrates a quantum-optical variant of the Fredkin gate in his presentation.

- In 1989, researchers at the Saha Institute of Nuclear Physics in Kolkata, led by Bikas K. Chakrabarti, proposed that particle physics activity could be used to learn to navigate rough energy environments by tunneling (rather than trying to climb over using thermal vibrational modes) to escape from local minima of crystalline form systems with tall but thin barriers. This was done in an effort to break free from the local optimal solution of crystallized systems with large but small barriers.
- In 1991, Artur Ekert of the University of Oxford expanded upon the idea of entanglement-based encrypted communication proposed by David Deutsch.
- David Deutsch and Richard Jozsa proposed a number of problems in 1992 that could be quickly solved on a quantum system with the assistance of the predetermined Deutsch–Jozsa automated system, but for which there are no feasible categorical imperatives using classical methodology. This problem was referred to as the "Deutsch–Jozsa algorithm problem." It was the possible first discovery of its kind in the realm of quantum computing, and it demonstrated that qubits

are capable of doing a particular computing job more rapidly and precisely than any conventional computer.

- In 1993, Dan Simon, a professor at the University of Montréal, thought of the concept of an "oracle scenario," in which a computer program would be able to do calculations at a rate that is geometrically faster than a typical computer. The enhancements that were made to Peter were based, in large part, on the core principles that are provided in this method.
- Peter Shor of AT&T's Bell Labs in New Jersey discovered a crucial method via his factorization algorithm. A quantum computer can now quickly factor very large numbers using this method. As a bonus, it also solves the discrete log issue and the factoring problem. Many modern cryptosystems may be vulnerable to Shor's algorithm. Following its discovery, enthusiasm for quantum computers skyrocketed.

In the fall, the first federal government workshop on quantum computing will be held in Gaithersburg, Maryland, hosted by the National Institute of Standards and Technology (NIST).

Isaac Chuang and Yoshihisa Yamamoto, both of whom are physicists, believe that the most effective implementation of Deutsch's method would be to use a quantum computer that was instantiated via quantum optics. A new method of dual-rail encoding for photonic qubits was developed as a consequence of their research.

During the month of December, Ignacio Cirac of the University of Castilla-La Mancha in Ciudad Real and Peter Zoller of the University of Granada got together.

Researchers from Innsbruck University have suggested the controlled-NOT gate as a potential use in the real world. In order to make the gate function properly, the researchers recommend using cold trapped ions.

Three US Army scientists, Charles M. Bowden, Jonathan P. Dowling, and Henry O. Everitt, planned the first US Department of Defense training course in electromagnetism and cryptography in February 1995 at the University of Arizona in Tucson.

Peter Shor is credited with having suggested some of the early quantum error-correcting algorithms.

At the NIST in Boulder, Colorado, Christopher Monroe and David Wineland used trapped ions and the Cirac–Zoller principle to construct the first quantum logic gate. This gate was called the controlled-NOT gate. In 1996, at Bell Labs, Lov Grover developed the first approach that might be considered practically useful for exploring quantum databases. Compared to a quadratic speedup, a factorization, discrete log, or linear speedup comes up more prominently.

Simulations of the physical world are one example. Having said that, the approach may be used to address a far larger range of issues. This speedup by a factor of four is available for use in any activity that can gain an advantage by doing a random brute-force search (in the number of search queries).

The federal government of the United States has just released its first call for research ideas on quantum computing. This request is the result of a collaborative effort between the National Security Agency and the Army Research Office, which is now a branch of the Army Research Laboratory. Steane codes are a kind of error-correcting code that was developed by Andrew Steane. IBM's David P. DiVincenzo sets out the fundamentals that have to be in place before one can build a quantum computer. These fundamentals are required in order to build a computational model.

In 1997 David Cory, Amr Fahmy, Timothy Havel, Neil Gershenfeld, and Isaac L. Chuang were all working at MIT at the same time when they published the first publications establishing gates for subatomic particles based on bulk nuclear spin-responsive or thermal ensembles. These works were published simultaneously. This method makes use of a device known as a nuclear magnetic resonance (NMR) machine, which is relatively similar to magnetic resonance scanners used in the medical field.

Alexei Kitaev has presented topological quantum computing as one technique for lowering the risk of decoherence occurring in a quantum system.

The electrons contained within quantum dots serve as qubits in the Loss–DiVincenzo quantum computer, which was suggested by Daniel Loss and David P. DiVincenzo. Each electron has its own spin-1/2 degree of freedom.

In 1998, a quantum algorithm was successfully realized for the first time in an experimental setting. Jonathan A. Jones and Michele Mosca of Oxford University and Isaac L. Chuang of IBM's Watson Research Center employed a two-qubit NMR quantum computer to answer the issue that was presented by Deutsch. The problem was solved by the computer. Researchers from the Almaden Research Center, directed by Mark Kubinec, collaborated with colleagues from Stanford University and MIT. An NMR computer that has, for the first time, a data storage capacity equal to three qubits. Bruce Kane has developed a computational model for nuclear spins in silicon. In this model, the nuclear spins of certain phosphorus atoms in silicon serve as qubits, while donor electrons are responsible for mediating qubit coupling. The first time Grover's method was ever put into action, it was on an NMR computer. Researchers at the Tokyo Institute of Technology, headed by Hidetoshi Nishimori, have shown that quantum annealing is better than more traditional types of simulated annealing. Daniel Gottesman and Emanuel Knill, two different researchers, separately demonstrate that classical resources may successfully simulate a subset of quantum processes (the Gottesman–Knill theorem).

Isaac Chuang and Yoshihisa Yamamoto, who are both physicists, think that the use of a quantum algorithm that was created by the application of quantum optics would be the way that would result in the most successful application of Deutsch's method. As a direct result of their investigation, a novel approach to dual-rail encoding for photonic qubits was conceived and created.

Ignacio Cirac and Peter Zoller, both from the University of Castilla-La Mancha in Ciudad Real, and Peter Zoller, from the University of Granada, joined together during the month of December.

The controlled-NOT gate has been proposed as a possible use in the real world by a group of researchers from Innsbruck University. The researchers suggest using cold ions that are confined in a vacuum in order to ensure that the gate operates correctly.

The first United States Department of Defense training course on electromagnetism and cryptography is scheduled to take place at the University of Arizona in Tucson in February 1995. The course is being planned by three scientists who are employed by the United States Army: Charles M. Bowden, Jonathan P. Dowling, and Henry O. Everitt. Henry O. Everitt, Charles M. Bowden, and Jonathan P. Dowling are the authors of this work.

Peter Shor is widely acknowledged as having proposed some of the first quantum error-correcting algorithms.

Christopher Monroe and David Wineland built the first quantum logic gate at the NIST in Boulder, Colorado, by using trapped ions and the Cirac–Zoller principle. This gate was known as the controlled-NOT gate at one point in time. In 1996, Lov Grover created the first method that might be regarded as realistically viable for browsing quantum datasets at Bell Labs. This method was the first of its kind. A factorization, discrete log, or linear speedup shows a more significant increase when compared to a quadratic speedup.

One example of this would be simulations of the physical world. Having said that, the strategy may be used to solve a far wider variety of problems than I've mentioned here. This increase in speed by a factor of four is accessible for use in any endeavor that can benefit from carrying out a random brute-force search (in the number of search queries).

The United States federal government has officially issued its first request for ideas pertaining to research on quantum computing. The National Security Agency and the Army Research Office, which is now a part of the Army Research Laboratory, are working together to put out this call for proposals. This request is the result of their joint effort. Steane codes are a kind of error-correcting code that was invented by Andrew Steane. Steane codes were developed in the 1960s. David P. DiVincenzo of IBM lays out the principles that have to be in place before one can develop a quantum computer. These fundamentals are necessary in order to build a quantum computer. To construct a computational model, you will need to have a firm grasp of these foundations.

In 1997, when David Cory, Amr Fahmy, Timothy Havel, Neil Gershenfeld, and Isaac L. Chuang published the first works defining gates for subatomic particles based on bulk nuclear spin-sensitive or thermal ensembles, they were all working at MIT at the same time. These pieces appeared in publications at the same time. This technique makes use of a machine that is referred to as an NMR machine, which is somewhat comparable to magnetic resonance scanners that are used in the area of medicine.

Alexei Kitaev has proposed topological computational methods as a method that may reduce the likelihood of decoherence taking place in a quantum system.

The Loss–DiVincenzo quantum computer, which was proposed by Daniel Loss and David P. DiVincenzo, uses the electrons that are housed inside quantum dots as qubits. Every electron has a degree and a half of spin-dependent freedom individually.

It was not until 1998 that a quantum algorithm was effectively implemented in an experimental environment for the very first time. Jonathan A. Jones and Michele Mosca of Oxford University and Isaac L. Chuang of IBM's Watson Research Center used a two-qubit NMR quantum computer to answer the question that was posed by Deutsch. Deutsch was the one who posed the question. The issue was resolved as a result of the computer's efforts. Researchers from Stanford University and MIT worked with their counterparts at the Almaden Research Center, which is managed by Mark Kubinec. A first-of-its kind NMR computer with a data storage capacity equivalent to three qubits. An innovative computational model for nuclear spins in silicon was created by Bruce Kane. Donor electrons are responsible for mediating qubit coupling in this paradigm. The qubits themselves are the nuclear spins of certain phosphorus atoms in silicon. The NMR computer was the platform on which Grover's approach was first implemented for the first time in history. Researchers at the Tokyo Institute of Technology led by Hidetoshi Nishimori have found quantum annealing to be superior to more conventional kinds of simulated annealing. Both Daniel Gottesman and Emanuel Knill, who are scholars in their own right, show that classical resources may effectively imitate a subset of quantum processes in their own respective studies (the Gottesman–Knill theorem).

In 2007, the development of a waveguide with a sub-wavelength light signal. Creation of an optical fiber-based single-photon emitter. We construct a six-photon, single-direction multicore computer. There is a new suggested material for use in quantum computers. There is now a server for spontaneous emission from a single atom. This is the first instance of Deutsch's algorithm being implemented on a quantum computer with a cluster state. An electron quantum pump has been developed at Cambridge University. Better qubit coupling methods have been developed. Demonstration of qubits with a connection that can be controlled. An important step forward in incorporating spin-based electronics with silicon-based devices. The quantum states of light and matter are shown to exchange with one another by scientists. Making a quantum register out of a diamond. In this scenario, we use a controlled NOT to activate quantum gates implementation of two superconducting quantum bits in a three-dimensional array, scientists may hold and analyse hundreds of individual atoms. The bucky-ball molecule, which contains nitrogen, is used in quantum computing. Several hundreds of electrons have established quantum connections. The spin-orbit coupling of electrons was quantified. Laser-light-based atomic manipulation at the quantum level. Electronic spins are controlled by pulsing light. Over a range of tens of nanometers, quantum effects have been shown. The evolution of quantum computers is being hastened by the use of light pulses. Plans for quantum random-access memory are now public knowledge. Development of a prototype quantum transistor. Proof of long-range entanglement has been shown. Photonic quantum computing was used to factor numbers in two separate labs. The quantum bus was developed in a joint effort between two separate laboratories. Construction of a quantum cable using superconducting technology. An example of qubit transfer is shown. The development of high-quality qubit material is a major achievement. Electronic memory have single qubit space in the disk. Quantum memory via Bose–Einstein condensation has been realized. D-Wave Systems showcases a 28-qubit processor in action. By decreasing deco-herence and increasing interaction distance, a novel cryonic technique improves the efficiency of quantum computers. A proof-of-concept for a photonic quantum computer has been shown. The use of graphene quantum dots as spin qubits has been suggested [6].

In 2008, researchers were able to store a quantum bit in graphene quantum dots, demonstrate three-dimensional qubit–qutrit entanglement, and establish analog quantum computing. Controlling quantum tunneling led to the creation of entan-gled memory, the invention of a superior NOT gate, the discovery of an optical fiber quantum logic gate, the development of qutrits, and the creation of a better Hall as a result, we may infer that the spin states of quantum dots are stable for a considerable amount of time. A quantum memory based on molecular magnets has been proposed.

The possibility of a reliable quantum computer is improved by the existence of quasiparticles.

It is possible that qubit storage is preferable than image storage.

- Quantum entangled pictures.
- Modified the quantum state of a molecule on purpose.

Microwave photons are pumped into a silicon circuit with the help of a super-conducting electronic circuit.

D-Wave Systems claim that it has designed a computer chip with 128 qubits; however, this has not been independently validated.

In 2009, the purity of carbon-12 was improved, which should result in increased coherence over longer periods of time.

Entanglement of the six-photon graph state is used in order to simulate the fractional statistics of anyons that are situated in synthetic spin-lattice models.

Quantum computing: create a photon grenade launcher the development of a quantum algorithm for use with differential equation systems – Presentation of the world's first quantum system, which has completely digital control hardware as well as software. Scientists are able to change the atoms and molecules of electrons using electromagnetic energy. Google, in collaboration with D-Wave Systems, presented a technique for synchronizing the characteristic features of several linked CJJ rf-SQUID flux qubits with a low distribution of electronic resistivity due to manufacturing differences. The spectrum response of hydrogen and helium was correctly calculated by an optical quantum computer with three qubits in 2010; the first semiconductor materials laser brings us closer to electro-optical computing systems. Ions were captured via an optical trap in 2010.

The transmission of subatomic particles across a quantum communications channel may be sped up by architectures that use multiplexing. Quantum state in macroscopic object. Innovative strategy for the cooling of quantum computers. Quantum contact between a single photon and a single atom has been shown to exist using microfabricated planar ion traps in the research. Quantum bits (or "qubits") are handled using electrical current rather than magnets.

Electron quantum states are electrically controlled by scientists.

- A technique for synchronizing the characteristics of several connected CJJ rf-SQUID flux qubits with a minimal spread of electrical characteristics owing to manufacturing variances was shown by Google in collaboration with D-Wave Systems.
- Realization of Universal Ion Trap Quantum Computation with Decoherence Free Qubits 2010
- Ion trapped in optical trap
- Optical quantum computer with three qubits calculated the spectral response of hydrogen and helium with high precision
- First semiconductor materials laser brings us closer to electro - optic computer systems
- Single electron qubit established
- Quantum state in macroscopic object
- New quantum computer cooling method developed
- Quantum interface between a single photon and a single atom proven
- LED quantum entanglement established
- Multiplexed design speeds up quantum information transfer across a quantum communications channel
- Planar ion traps that have been microfabricated Qubits are controlled electricity

In a solid-state spin ensemble, what exactly is meant by the term "entanglement"? In a quantum semiconductor technology that makes use of superconductivity, light from the near-outer radiation (NOON) is used. Quantum antennas are due to multimode quantum interference.

- Atomic racing dual
- Quantum pen

D-Wave one product claims that it discovered quantum annealing. The company claims its product is the world's first quantum computer accessible for purchase. It has been demonstrated that a quantum processor can perform repetitive error correction, that a diamond can be used as a storage medium for a quantum computer, that Modes can be established, that DE coherence can be suppressed, that controlled operations can be streamlined, and that ions can be entangled using microwaves.

- Repetitive error correction performed in a quantum processor
- Diamond quantum computer storage exhibited
- Qmodes established
- DE coherence suppressed
- Simplification of controlled operations
- Ions entangled using microwaves
- Practical error rates attained Quantum Entanglement might aid in the development of photonic processors.

It was reported that a quantum simulator with 300 qubits or particles had been successfully built.

A topologically protected qubit that is entangled with eight photons provides a safe and secure approach to the implementation of real quantum computing [7].

In the beginning, there was 1QB Information Technologies (1QBit). The first software firm in the world to exclusively concentrate on quantum computing. Developed the first system for repeating quantum operations that does not depend on quantum memory.

At room temperature, the use of a laser to manipulate carbon-13 atoms briefly and for a period of two seconds reduced decoherence.

The development of a revolutionary, low-overhead approach for building fault-tolerant quantum logic, which is referred to as lattice surgery. This method is developed on the concept of Bell-based unpredictable expansion and makes a more moderate assumption of measurement being independent.

In 2013, 39-minute coherence times have been measured for ensembles of impurity-spin qubits in isotopically linked systems while the temperature was maintained at room temperature (and three hours at cryogenic temperatures).

The amount of time that a qubit remains in a superimposed state has been multiplied by 10 in order to account for the change.

In 2014, the first ever evaluation of this kind was constructed for factoring in order to determine whether or not it would be possible to implement a large-scale quantum algorithm with explicit fault-tolerant and error-correcting protocols.

The NSA's Penetrating Hard Targets program, which is constructing a computer program for the purposes of cryptanalysis, has received backing as a result of the disclosures that were made public by Edward Snowden.

In a first-of-its-kind development anywhere in the world, researchers from Japan and Austria have made public the designs for a huge quantum computer based on diamonds. Researchers at the University of Innsbruck accomplish quantum numerical computations on a qubit that is topologically encapsulated and password protected in linked states that are scattered among seven trapped-ion qubits.

Using neutrino oscillation, scientists have succeeded in sending data across a distance of 10 feet (3.048 m) with no discernible delay. Percent of inaccuracies, a significant achievement on the way to the construction of a quantum network. Nike Dattani and Nathan Bryans have set a new record for the number 56 153 that can be factored using a quantum device.

In 2015, nuclear spins in a solid, which can have their coherence examined optically, may have coherence periods of up to six hours. A quantum process known as transcription makes use of straightforward electrical pulses, and a quantum error detection code is based on a square lattice of four superconducting qubits as its fundamental building block. On June 22, D-Wave Systems Inc. made the announcement that the company has reached a breakthrough of 1,000 qubits. A silicon logic gate with two qubits has been designed and tested satisfactorily. By simulating its behavior after that of a classical computer and replicating quantum states such as quantum superposition and entanglement using a traditional analog web browser, it is possible to develop a completely classical framework that behaves like a real quantum computer. This is made possible by designing its behavior after that of a quantum computer.

Researchers headed by Rainer Blatt and Isaac Asimov used an ion-trap-based quantum computer to solve the problem. In 2016, Chuang at MIT was successful in running the algorithm developed by Shor. The online interface for IBM's superconducting systems, known as the Quantum Experience, has been made available. After that, the system is put to use in the propagation of cutting-edge techniques in digital signal processing. In order to replicate a hydrogen molecule, Google makes use of an array consisting of nine superconducting qubits. This array was built by the Martinis group at UCSB. In 2017, researchers from Japan and Australia created a quantum version of the communications system known as Sneakernet. D-Wave Systems Inc., claims that the D-Wave 2000Q quantum annealed is now readily accessible for widespread usage in business settings. This apparatus is capable of storing 2000 qubits of information. The blueprint for a quantum computer that operates by entrapping ions in microwaves has been made available to the public. A novel approach to evaluating IBM's 17-qubit quantum computer has been made public by the company. Scientists have devised a device that can produce two entangled qubits, each of which may exist in one of ten distinct states consisting of a hundred different dimensions Visual Studio now comes equipped with Q Sharp, the newest quantum software platform developed by Microsoft. For the purpose of program execution, there is accessibility to both a local 32-qubit simulator and a cloud-based 40-qubit simulator. Intel recently claimed in a news release that it had produced a superconducting test circuit with 17 qubits. The device was used for testing purposes. IBM demonstrates for the very first time a functional model of a quantum computer that has 50 qubits and has the ability to maintain its physical phenomenon for 90 microseconds [8].

In 2018, researchers from MIT discovered evidence of a previously undiscovered kind of light that is composed of three independent photons. The group from Oxford used a technique known as trapped ions. In order to produce logic gates that are 20–60 times speedier than those that are traditionally used, the researchers used a method in which they entangled and superposed two charged atoms obtaining a level of precision of 99.8% in 1.6 milliseconds. QuTech achieves positive results in its testing of a silicon-based two-spin-qubit processor. Google has revealed that it has developed a Bristlecone quantum gadget with a whopping 72 qubits, setting a new record in the process. Intel has started building a silicon-based spin-qubit computer processor at its D1D Fab in Oregon. Tangle Lake, Intel's superconducting test chip with 49 qubits, has been finished, and the company has made the formal announcement. Researchers in Japan have demonstrated holonomic quantum gates that are reliable in every environment. An integrated photonic platform may be useful for quantum systems that rely on a dependent variable. This past Monday, December 17 2018, is the relevant date. The first commercialized trapped-ion functional prototype has been presented by IonQ. This prototype has more than 60 two-qubit gates, 11 fully linked qubits, 55 addressable pairs, and an error rate of 0.03% for one-qubit gates and 1% for two-qubit gates. The National Quantum Initiative Act was signed into law by President Trump on December 21 2018, and it provides an overview of the objectives and prerequisites for a ten-year plan. The objective is to hasten the development of new technologies in the United States that are founded on the study of quantum information.

In 2019, Nike Dattani and his colleagues deciphered the architecture of the D-Pegasus Wave and made it open to the public. IBM also introduced the IBM Q System One, the company's first commercial quantum computer, which was established by the UK's Map Project Office and Universal Design Studio and manufactured by Goppion. Both of these organizations are based in the United Kingdom. Researchers in Austria have demonstrated self-verifying hybrid and variational quantum simulations of lattice structures in crystalline materials and high-energy physics by using a feedback loop between a computing environment and a quantum coprocessor. These simulations are hybrid, self-verifying, and self-variational. At room temperature, the phenomenon of quantum Darwinism may be seen operating in diamonds. In a study that was released at the end of September 2019, the research team working on quantum computing at Google said that the company's project had established itself as the industry leader. IBM has just unveiled its most cutting-edge quantum computer to date, which is comprised 53 qubits. The introduction of the system will officially take place in October of 2019.

In the 2020s, a method for producing "hot qubits," also known as quantum gadgets, that may operate at temperatures as low as 1.5 °C has been developed by researchers at UNSW Sydney. Researchers from Griffith, UNSW, and UTS, in addition to seven other institutions in the United States, have developed a method using pattern recognition to cancel out background noise in quantum bits, thereby reducing quantum device noise to zero. This method was developed in collaboration with researchers from seven institutions in the United States. Researchers at the University of New South Wales have found a way to command subatomic particles inside electronic circuits by using electric nuclear recombination. This feat was accomplished by the researchers. In order to overcome the difficulties associated with experimental wiring, a two-dimensional framework for qubits has been designed and validated by researchers from the University of Tokyo and Australia. This kind of architecture is realizable with the integrated circuit technology of the present day and has far less cross-talk [9].

On the 16th of January, 2019, researchers in theoretical physics said that they have successfully accomplished the first direct dissection of a photon into its constituent pieces. Applications are conceivable in the field of quantum technology, which makes use of spontaneous programmable down-conversion.

It was announced on February 11 that engineers working in the area of quantum computing claim to have built artificial atoms in silicon nanoparticles. These engineers believe that atoms containing more electrons than were previously considered conceivable may be more stable qubits. If silicon-based quantum mechanics can be enabled, there will be a number of benefits, one of which is the potential to reuse traditional manufacturing techniques for computer system chips.

The 14th of February saw the development of a revolutionary single-photon source by quantum scientists. This source might open the way for semiconductor-based quantum machines to communicate with photons by translating the state of an electrostatic interactions. They show that it is possible to generate just a single photon in a controllable environment, without having to resort to completely at random manufactured quantum dots or structural flaws in diamonds.

On February 25, scientists will imagine quantum instrumentation by taking pictures of ion states at separate moments during standard measure by conjugating a trapped ion to the photon environment. They demonstrate that differences in the degrees of superposition, and thus the likelihood of the occurrence of states after measurement, can be observed.

On March 2, scientists revealed repeated quantum inspections of an electron's spin in a silicon quantum dot. These are inspections that do not affect the electron's spin in any way.

The effective manipulation of the nucleus of a single atom using just electric fields was disclosed by quantum engineers on March 11th. The year 1961 marks the beginning of this concept, which might one day be used to study quantum mechanics in silicon. It may have far-reaching ramifications for nanodevices, accurate sensors of electric and magnetic fields, and basic investigations of quantum nature if experiments without oscillating magnetic fields are conducted using single-atom spins.

Researchers at a US Army unit published their experiment on the responsiveness of a Rydberg sensor to different electric fields at frequencies ranging from zero to tens of hertz (the spectrum to 0.3 mm wavelength) on March 19. The Rydberg sensor shows promise as a tool for detecting information components due to its superior performance when compared to other specified electric field wearable sensors such as electro-optic crystallites and dipole antenna-coupled passive electronics. This is due to the Rydberg sensor's ability to detect parts of an organization in a more accurate manner.

On March 23, researchers revealed that they had discovered a method to compensate for signal loss in an early version of a quantum computer. Prototype quantum computer node capable of capturing, storing, and entangling quantum bits. Their proposals might be put into action as essential components of quantum repeaters in quantum networks, which would result in an increase in the potential range of the networks.

Scientists unveiled a proof-of-concept silicon quantum processor unit cell that operates at a temperature of 1.5 kelvin on April 15. This temperature is several times higher than that of commonly constructed quantum computers. It is likely that it will make it feasible to integrate the qubit array with more traditional control electronics, which will result in a large margin reduction in the total price. One of the most challenging obstacles facing the industry is said to be the cooling requirements that must be met by quantum computers.

On April 16, researchers demonstrated that the Rashba effect may be seen in perovskites that are produced in bulk. Despite the fact that it is thought to be related to the material's exceptional electrical, magnetic, and optical capabilities, which make it a regularly used material for solar cells and quantum electronics, this phenomenon has not yet been evidenced in the material. This is despite the fact that it has yet to be made clear in the material.

On the 8th of May, scientists explained their plans to employ quantum phenomena and microwaves to develop a "concrete proof quantum radar." This kind of radar might be important in the development of future radar technology, surveillance scanning, and computed tomography.

Using femtosecond X-ray laser pulses, a team of researchers has discovered a method that allows them to selectively modify the spin state of connected electrons in a multilayer manganite (May 12). As a result, the use of changes in orbital orientations, known as orbitronics, has the potential to work as the basic bit stream in cutting-edge information technology devices.

On the 19th of May, scientists made the exciting announcement that they had successfully manufactured the first silicon on-chip with integrated circuitry. In order to function properly, high-throughput quantum optical communications need just a single, low-noise piece of evidence.

This report on the evolution stage of rubidium Bose–Einstein gaseous hydrocarbons that took place on June 11 at the Cold Atom Laboratory of the International Space Station might be beneficial to investigations into BECs and quantum mechanics, the rules of which are scaled to macroscopic sizes in BECs. This may be of assistance in the ongoing research and pursuit of few-body physics, as well as in the encouragement of the adoption of strategies for atom-wave electric potential between atoms and maybe other benefits.

On June 15, researchers announced the achievement of the world's smallest traditional chemical complex machine. It is comprised 12 atoms and a rotor that is comprised 4 atoms, and it is capable of being obtained by an electromotive force and beginning to rotate even with very low magnitudes of electricity, as revealed by searching transmission electron microscopy light imaging technology in relation to perturbation theory. This discovery was made possible by scanning electron microscope and light microscopy, which were done in relation to quantum tunneling.

On June 17, quantum scientists made public their development of a system that entangles two-photon quantum communication nodes by means of a microwave cable. This enables information to be transferred between the nodes without the photons themselves ever having to travel through or populate the wire. They announced on June 12 that they had employed a technique called delayed-choice quantum erasure to entangle two phonons and remove data from their measurement.

On August 1, it was announced that global coherence protection had been accomplished in a solid-state spin qubit. This is a tweak that will enable quantum systems to preserve their functioning (or coherence) for 10,000 times longer than was previously achievable.

On the 26th of August, researchers suggested that ionizing radiation, which can come from both naturally radioactive elements and cosmic rays, may have a significant impact on the phenomenon known as quantum tunneling.

On June 17, quantum physicists revealed that they had constructed a system that entangles two-photon quantum communication nodes across a microwave cable. This system is capable of conveying information between the nodes even if the photons never travel through or fill the wire. They announced on June 12 that they had employed a technique called delayed-choice quantum erasure to entangle two phonons and remove data from their measurement.

On August 13, it was announced that global coherence protection has been accomplished in a solid-state spin qubit. This is a tweak that will enable quantum systems to preserve their functioning (or coherence) for 10,000 times longer than was previously achievable.

According to research written by experts and published on August 26, the possibility exists that ionizing radiation from cosmic rays and other radioactive elements in the environment may have a significant impact.

1.5   Quantum Communication

The possibility of developing a computing model capable of running Shor's algorithm for large numbers is a driving force in the advancement of quantum communication. For a fuller picture of quantum computers, it is important to keep in mind that these machines will bring about significant time savings for just a subset of all possible jobs. Scientists are working to develop techniques to demonstrate that some problems are indeed susceptible to quantum speedups and are also attempting to learn whether or not such problems exist. As optimization plays crucial roles in fields as diverse as the military and the currency markets, it stands to reason that computers would be of considerable help in solving related problems. Several other applications for qubit systems are being actively researched, but they are beyond the scope of this overview since they are not directly related to computation or modeling. Quantum networks and telephony may lead to new, creative methods of exchanging information [10], while quantum detection and measurement leverage qubits' exceptional sensitivity to the environment to realize sensing much beyond the conventional shot noise limit.

1.6   Build Quantum Computer Structure

Quantum computers are incredibly challenging to build. Although there are many possible qubit systems in the subatomic particle range, physicists, engineers, and materials scientists who seek to conduct quantum operations on these systems are always challenged by competing requirements. Qubits must first be protected from outside influences that may otherwise destroy the fleeting quantum states necessary for computation. If a qubit can maintain its ground state for a longer period of time, its coherence time will be longer. In this setting, seclusion plays an important role. Second, qubits need to be entangled, movable across physical structures, and programmable on demand so that algorithms may be carried out. These procedures benefit from increased accuracy. It is difficult to achieve the necessary isolation and interaction, but after decades of research, a number of promising systems are emerging as potential candidates for large-scale quantum systems [11].

In order to build a quantum computer, some of the most promising technologies to use include superconducting innovations, trapped molecule ions, and semiconductors. With respect to consistency, accuracy, and, most importantly, scalability to large systems, each has advantages and disadvantages. However, it is obvious that all of these platforms will need some type of error-correcting mechanism in order to be powerful enough to execute large calculations, and how to design and implement these mechanisms is a huge topic of study in and of itself. For a more in-depth introduction of quantum entanglement and its applications in the real world, see [12].

All calculations that make use of subatomic particles have been lumped together under the umbrella term "quantum computing" for the purposes of this chapter. Different types of dynamic programming exist. It is safe to say that logical, gate-based quantum computing is the most well-known kind. Depending on the kind of qubit, they are created in starting states and then put through a series of gate operations, such as current or laser pulses. Similar to AND, OR, and NOT gates in classical computing, the qubits are placed in the quantum mechanical state, entangled, and used in logical operations. Following this, the qubits are measured, and results are obtained.

The study of complicated qubits is also fundamental to the measurement-based computing paradigm. Then, instead of messing with several qubits, a single qubit is measured, locking it into a predetermined state. The outcomes of these tests on additional qubits inform further measurements, which are conducted until a solution is discovered [13].

Finally, a topological computing framework is built on quasiparticles and their intertwining operations, which are the basis for qubits and processes. Theoretically protected against noise that degrades the coherence of other qubits, topological quantum computer chips are intriguing despite the fact that the first demonstration of this technology has yet to be shown.

Quantum simulators, like Feynman's analog computers, are the last option. Emulators of quantum systems are quantum computers designed for this specific purpose. This knowledge might help them solve issues with high-temperature superconductors, the reactions of certain chemicals, or the construction of materials with desired properties.

1.7 Principle Working of Quantum Computers

Because quantum computers can determine the state of an item based on its probability rather than just its binary value, they can handle far more information than traditional computers.

Computing devices of the past were able to execute arithmetic and logic on the fixed coordinates of physical objects. Binary systems rely on just two possible locations for their operations, and this limits them to a limited set of uses. To put it simply, a bit is a binary digit.

Instead, a quantum bit (qubit) is created by using an object's quantum state in quantum computing methods. Prior to their discovery, properties like an object's temperature or the spin of its electrons had no name. A photon's polarization.

Quantum states that cannot be measured are not located in one particular place but rather exist in a "superposition," much like a coin that spins in the air before landing in your hand [14].

Since the outcomes of one set of superposition's might get entangled with those of another, we can infer that the quantities associated with the results of both sets of superposition's are related, even if we do not know what those sets of superposition's are.

The complicated mathematics behind these unstable states of entangled "spinning coins" may be fed into novel algorithms to tackle problems that would take a conventional computer a very long time to calculate, if it could compute them at all.

These algorithms might be used to predict the outcomes of complex chemical reactions, create secure passwords, or solve tough mathematical problems.

1.7.1 Kinds of Quantum Computing

Different varieties of quantum mechanics exist. How much computing power (qubits) is needed, how well they can be put to use, and how long it will take for them to become commercially viable are all different for each kind.

What is quantum annealing? When dealing with optimization problems, quantum annealing is the most efficient approach. In other words, scientists are looking for the best possible configuration by testing out many possibilities. Recently, Volkswagen (VW) has been experimenting with quantum technology in an effort to improve traffic flow in Beijing, the most populous city in China. Google and D-Wave Systems worked together to do the research.

If the technology is successful in choosing the optimum route for each vehicle, it might drastically reduce traffic, according to VW. In order to find the most economical travel and logistics solutions for everyone, it may be worthwhile to conduct this research on a global scale, optimizing every aircraft route, airport schedules, weather data, fuel prices, and passenger comfort. A typical computer would need thousands of years to provide a best guess at the solution to such a problem. Quantum computers might potentially complete the task in a few hours or less as the number of qubits per computer increases [15].

A wide range of industrial problems may be addressed by annealing. For instance, in 2015, Airbus, a multinational aerospace and defense company best known for producing both military and civilian aircraft, established a quantum information unit at its Newport, United Kingdom, manufacturing facility. The company is looking into the potential applications of quantum annealing in digital modeling and materials science. A classical computer could replicate every subatomic particle of air flowing over a wing at different angles and speeds in a matter of hours or days, allowing for the identification of the best or most effective raked wingtips in a fraction of the time it now takes researchers. The most basic and restricted kind of quantum computing is known as quantum annealing. According to experts, modern supercomputers can handle optimization problems just as well as the quantum annealed devices shown in Figure 1.3.

Quantum modeling: for problems in quantum physics that cannot be solved by traditional means, researchers are turning to computer simulations. Quantum entanglement's potential use in simulating intricate quantum processes is among its most intriguing applications. Simulation of the response of many subatomic particles to a condition that becomes true, or inorganic chemistry, is an exciting area of study (Figure 1.4).

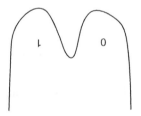

Figure 1.3 Structure of quantum annealing. Source: Adapted from https://images.app .goo.gl/DeYCU9A7TeJvV5c16 Last accessed 25 Oct 2022.

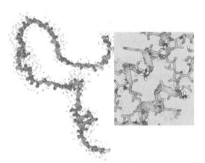

Figure 1.4 Structure of quantum simulation. Source: Vivien Marx 2021/Springer nature.

Protein folding is a challenging problem in biochemistry that could be replicated with quantum simulations. Researchers testing potential therapeutics for diseases like Alzheimer's and Parkinson's must use stochastic mathematical models to determine which drugs cause reactions for each protein.

Some scientists estimate that it would take longer than the duration of the universe for a protein to fold into its optimal shape if they had to choose among all of the possible drug-induced consequences. If the protein folding sequences could be accurately mapped, it would be a major scientific and medical breakthrough that might ultimately save lives. The vast number of possible protein folding configurations may be calculated with the use of quantum computers, which can speed up the discovery of new and improved pharmaceuticals. In the future, fast designer testing techniques will be possible thanks to quantum algorithms that account for every possible protein–drug interaction.

Quantum computing for all: the most effective and generally applicable kind of computing is quantum, yet it is also the most challenging to build. Some estimates put the minimum number of qubits required for a truly ubiquitous quantum computer at one million. Keep in mind that the current ceiling on available qubits is much below 128 [16].

One of the main ideas underlying the universal quantum system is that it might be put to work on any really difficult problem and quickly provide an answer. Some examples of such work are the solution of the annealing equations stated above and the modeling of quantum events. For a long time now, scientists have been working on algorithms that would need a universal quantum computer to run. Two of the most well-known algorithms are Grover's algorithm for quickly solving equations and Shor's technique for quickly multiplying integers (which may be used for complex code cracking), exploring massive and unstructured data sets (to be used for advanced internet search, etc.)

At now, at least fifty unique algorithms have been developed for implementation on a universal quantum computer. In the distant future, universal quantum computing may radically alter the field of artificial intelligence (AI). It is possible that quantum AI might allow machines to learn at a faster rate than classical computers. While recent research has produced algorithms that might form the basis for quantum machine learning, the hardware requirements need to fully realize quantum AI remain as foreign to us as a general quantum system themselves [17].

1.8 Quantum Computing Use in Industry

Despite the hype in Table 1.2, commercial usage of quantum computers is still in its infancy, with just a handful of private enterprises in the sector having raised at least $50 million (and an even smaller number having raised more than $100 million).

Table 1.2 Company funding in quantum technology.

Country	Quantum technology	Funding in dollars ($)
Canada	D-Wave	210
USA	Rigetti	119
Australia	Silicon Quantum Computing	66
UK	CQC	50

Table 1.3 Year-wise investing.

Years	Dollars
2013	10
2014	40
2015	100
2016	40
2017	200+
2018	125

D-Wave, the most well-funded private quantum computing startup, has raised $210 million to date, followed by Rigetti Computing ($119 million), Silicon Quantum Computing ($66 million), and Cambridge Quantum Computing (CQC) ($50 million).

Notably, since 2013, 70% of all industry capital has gone toward acquisitions by just these four companies. Table 1.3 also shows that 2018 was the year with the highest volume of sales to private quantum computing companies.

With a six-year increase of more than 200%, from seven in 2013 to twenty-four in 2018, the total number of deals has increased significantly. This year's biggest deal, a $50 million Series C round for Rigetti Computing, closed in August.

With over $200 million invested across 14 deals, 2017 was a record year for funding quantum computing companies. In 2017, Silicon Quantum Computing, Rigetti, 1QBit, IonQ, and D-Wave were the only companies to raise over $20 million in investment.

1.9 Investors Invest Money in Quantum Technology

The ecosystem that facilitates the birth of such businesses has been growing in tandem with the increased attention paid to it. Private quantum computing startups have already attracted the attention of major investors in the form of venture capital firms and large enterprises. Investment from Google Ventures (GV), Amazon, and others has helped IonQ toward its goal of developing general-purpose quantum mechanics capable of handling a wide variety of applications. Quantum Circuits, Inc., was backed by the prestigious venture capital company Sequoia Capital (QCI). Rigetti Computing has received a sizeable investment from Andreessen Horowitz (a16z), whereas D-Wave Systems has received many investments from Draper Fisher Jurvetson (DFJ) [18].

In February 2018, South Korean mobile phone carrier SK Telecom entered the fray, joining Germany's Deutsche Telekom in exploring the potential of quantum computing to deliver secure communications. In the wake of a few months for $65 million and a minority stake in the business, the telecom companies have acquired ID Quantique, a provider of quantum-based multi-protocol network cryptography for securing communications. Even the largest companies in the world have their own internal quantum computing projects. An advanced quantum computer made by D-Wave Systems is located at Google's Quantum Artificially Intelligent Lab (QuAIL). The lab is located at NASA's Ames Research Center in Mountain View, California, and is cohosted by NASA and the Universities Space Research Association.

The Alibaba Quantum Computing Laboratory was established in Shanghai, China, in July 2015 by the Chinese Academy of Sciences and Alibaba's Aliyun cloud service. The lab's current focus is on developing quantum data encryption for use in online commerce and data storage facilities. IBM presented the world's first commercial quantum computer at the Consumer Electronics Show (CES) in January 2019. The Q System One from IBM uses 20 qubits and combines classical and quantum features. IBM Q systems are designed to one day overcome difficulties that are presently regarded as being too sophisticated and exponential in nature for conventional systems to handle, but the company's announcement made it clear that commercialized quantum computers would take time to surpass today's conventional machines. Hewlett-Packard, Intel, and Microsoft aren't the only tech giants curious about quantum computing. Companies like Booz Allen Hamilton, Lockheed Martin, and Raytheon, which specialize in the production and development of weapons, have also placed bets on quantum computing as a potential business advantage. The governments of the European Union (EU), the United States (US), Australia (AU), and China (China) are all providing financing for quantum computing research and development [19], in addition to money from corporations.

In the United States, organizations including Los Alamos National Laboratory, the National Security Agency, and NASA are all engaged in quantum computing research and development. Table 1.4: The Chinese government established the first-ever quantum observatory in 2016 to facilitate the development of further methods of secure communication.

Table 1.4 Companies investing in quantum computing.

Companies	Quantum technology
SK Telecom	ID Quantique
Deutsche Telecom	ID Quantique
Sequoia	Quantum Circuit
Amazon	Ion Q
DFJ	D-Wave System
Goldman Sachs	D-Wave System, QC Wave
Andreessen Horowitz	Rigetti Computing

1.10   Applications of Quantum Computing

- As the price of quantum computing resources decreases, more commercial players will emerge. As more companies join the market, the widespread use of quantum computing will increase, especially in situations where conventional computers are inefficient.
- Its effects are already being seen in many other fields.
- Now is the dawn of the quantum information age. To the best of our knowledge, we are on the cusp of delivering capabilities that are beyond the reach of conventional computers. This sort of computer has this kind of impact in pretty much every field. Vern Brownell, CEO of D-Wave Systems.
- Some potential fields of use for quantum computing range from the medical to the agricultural.
- Healthcare: By analyzing the correlations and effects of numerous medications on a wide range of diseases, quantum computers may facilitate the process of identifying the most effective pharmaceuticals. Furthermore, genetic advancements might be used in conjunction with quantum computing to design individualized treatment plans for each patient. Data generated by next-generation sequencing is so large that it requires a lot of computing power and storage space to represent a single human's whole DNA strand. Although businesses are rapidly decreasing the time and money needed to evaluate genomic data, the use of a quantum computer may make genome sequencing more efficient and scalable on a global scale. An entire generation's worth of sequencing work may be completed in half the time with a quantum computer building and filtering through all possible gene variants simultaneously, discovering all nucleotide pairs swiftly [20]. We may be able to sequence the whole human genome in a single day using the latest rapid quantum generation sequencing technology.

Figure 1.5 Quantum computing use in healthcare. Source: Bartek Wróblewski/Adobe Stock.

Using quantum computers, we might synthesize patterns in the world's DNA data to learn more about our genetic make-up and maybe even uncover previously unknown illness occurrences, as shown in Figure 1.5.

- The financial sector often uses algorithms constructed from probability and assumptions on future market and investment performance. The use of quantum computing has the potential to help in the eradication of data blind spots and the avoidance of losses brought on by incorrect financial assumptions. In particular, the optimization of investment performance and biometric identification are two areas where quantum teleportation shows the greatest promise for the financial sector. If hundreds of assets with complex relationships are available, quantum computing might be utilized to more efficiently identify fraudulent patterns and build enticing investment portfolios [21].

- Cybersecurity is a concern since quantum computers may be used to decipher the encryption protocols now used to protect sensitive data and documents stored digitally. However, quantum cryptography, which may be performed on quantum computers, might be used to safeguard information from quantum hacking. Quantum cryptography is the idea of securing contact by sending pairs of quantum-entangled particles of light (entangled photons) across long distances in a technique called quantum key distribution (QKD). The most important point is that the encryption system will quickly show signs of failure if quantum encrypted communications are identified, signaling that the interaction is not secure. The reasoning for this is based on the fact that constant observation of a quantum system renders it useless. This is the "measurement effect," as seen in Figure 1.6.

- Agriculture: Fertilizer production might benefit from the use of quantum computers. Almost all fertilizers that are used to grow food for people include

Figure 1.6 Quantum computing use in satellite for cyber security.

ammonia. Reduced costs and lower energy consumption in fertilizer production would arise from a more efficient means of producing ammonia (or a suitable alternative). Improved access to fertilizers may help both the environment and the world's growing population. Little progress has been made in perfecting the process since there are an infinite number of possible catalyst combinations to create or replace ammonia. Basically, the Haber–Bosch approach, which was created in the 1900s, is necessary for any kind of deliberate imitation of the process. Extreme heat and pressure are needed to convert nitrogen, hydrogen, and iron into ammonia. Digitally testing for the optimal catalysis combination to create ammonia would take years to solve with today's supercomputers. Ammonia production is best optimized with the help of a quantum computer, which can quickly analyze chemical catalytic processes and identify the most effective catalyst combinations. As a matter of fact, we know that tiny bacteria in plant roots perform this same action every day, using a chemical called nitrogenize to do so with a little energy expenditure. Our most powerful supercomputers cannot represent this molecule, but a quantum computer can, as shown in Figure 1.7.

- The cloud: The field of quantum cloud computing is maturing into a commercially relevant field. Access to quantum devices might be made more affordable and programming for them simplified with the help of quantum cloud platforms. QC Ware is a startup in the process of creating a cloud-based quantum computing platform. Investors in QC Ware include Airbus Ventures and Goldman Sachs. Massive corporations like IBM, Google, and Alibaba are all working on quantum cloud computing projects right now.

Figure 1.7 Ammonia use in agriculture.

1.11 Quantum Computing as a Solution Technology

Quantum computers are particularly well-suited to solving problems with an infinite number of variables, encoding and decoding data in a secure manner, and accurately duplicating quantum processes and molecular behavior. To this end, almost all commercially available technology focuses on finding answers to these problems. Notably, security requirements engineering techniques may hold the key to safeguarding our digital future with the help of quantum computers. Automobile and airplane piloting, healthcare provision, economic decision-making, and many other activities are becoming more software dependent. Problems in a codebase may be found and fixed before they have a chance to impact the user experience, thanks to real-time analysis by computer algorithms. Finding bugs in the software that supports these life-or-death processes is becoming more important. Any issue involving nanomaterials can be better tackled with the help of a quantum computer. Potentially, almost any material might be designed using quantum computers. Transportation, building, sensing, the armed forces, medical tools, and many more fields may all benefit. Ultimately, the building blocks of these industries are molecules and atoms, each with its own unique set of quantum mechanical and physical characteristics and linkages.

1.11.1 Quantum Artificial Intelligence

In the far future, quantum computers might be used to hasten the development of AI. AI that can carry out complex tasks in a more efficient and human-like manner may one day be created via quantum machine learning. For instance, it enables humanoid robots to make the best possible decisions at the moment, despite the fact that they face uncertainty. The use of quantum computers for AI training might significantly advance the state of the art in several areas, including computer vision, pattern recognition, voice recognition, and computational linguistics. The commercial use of quantum AI is still in its infancy. Zapata Computing, Xanadu, and Qindom are just a few examples of the many companies working to advance the state of the industry via research and innovation.

1.11.2 How Close Are We to Quantum Supremacy?

We say that quantum computers have "quantum supremacy" when they can solve problems that classical computers cannot. Keep in mind that the perfect quantum computer would be one that could be used everywhere and would have superior performance to existing computers. Several organizations, some of their government agencies, have claimed to have a quantum computer powerful enough to achieve quantum supremacy. For instance, in March 2018, Google claimed that their 72-qubit processor solved a specially chosen problem faster than conventional computers. Shortly after the announcement, Alibaba's researchers said that they had solved the same issue using conventional methods. This debate exemplifies the critical nature of the race among the world's largest enterprises to become quantum dominant first. Hybrid classical quantum services from companies like D-Wave Systems, Alibaba, IBM, and Rigetti Quantum Computing are at the forefront of today's most advanced quantum computing systems. That is to say, they provide not just robust classical systems but also exceptional quantum capabilities. But things are changing quickly in this industry. By 2030, most industry experts predict, quantum computers will have caught up to, or perhaps surpassed, their classical counterparts in terms of performance. There are still numerous technical obstacles that need to be resolved before computer technology can realize its full potential. Distributing and making available quantum computing power will need the development of more robust hardware, commercial software programming interfaces, and cloud processing capacity.

1.12 Conclusion

This chapter addressed the development of quantum computing and suggested that exponential growth in hardware technology is a fair (though not guaranteed) assumption. A quantifiable database documenting successes in the application of quantum computing by various businesses for reasons of security, including the largest physical qubit count and the lowest average two-qubit gate error rates. Consistent with the idea that both measurements are in conflict at a particular stage of technological development, there is a link between the highest qubit counts and the lowest error rates across all technologies.

References

1 Nielsen, M. and Chuang, I. (2000). *Quantum Computation and Quantum Information*. Cambridge University Press.

2 Devoret, M.H. and Schoelkopf, R.J. (2013). Superconducting circuits for quantum information: an outlook. *Science* 339 (6124): 1169–1174.

3 Pednault, E., Gunnels, J.A., Nannicini, G., Horesh, L., and Wisnieff, R. (2019). *Leveraging Secondary Storage to Simulate Deep 54-qubit Sycamore Circuits*.

4 Arute, F. et al. (2019). Quantum supremacy using a programmable superconducting processor. *Nature* 574 (7779): 505–510.

5 Alon, N., Dao, P., Hajirasouliha, I. et al. (2008). Biomolecular network motif counting and discovery by color coding. In: *Proceedings 16th International Conference on Intelligent Systems for Molecular Biology (ISMB)*, 241–249.

6 Miller, D.M., Wille, R., and Sasanian, Z. (2011). Elementary quantum gate realizations for multiple-control Toffolli gates. In: *International Symposium on Multiple-Valued Logic*, 288–293.

7 Amy, M., Maslov, D., Mosca, M., and Roetteler, M. (2013). A meet-in-the-middle algorithm for fast synthesis of depth-optimal quantum circuits. *IEEE Transactions on Computer-Aided Design of Integrated Circuits and Systems* 32 (6): 818–830.

8 Wille, R., Soeken, M., Otterstedt, C., and Drechsler, R. (2013). Improving the mapping of reversible circuits to quantum circuits using multiple target lines. In: *Asia and South Pacific Design Automation Conference*, 145–150.

9 IBM. Quantum Information Software Kit (QISKit). https://qiskit.org/.

10 Siraichi, M.Y., Santos, V.F.D., Collange, S., and Pereira, F.M.Q. (2018). Qubit allocation. In: *International Symposium on Code Generation and Optimization*, 113–125.

11 Matsuo, A., Hattori, W., and Yamashita, S. (2019). Reducing the overhead of mapping quantum circuits to IBM Q system. In: *International Symposium on Circuits and Systems*, 1–5.

12 Zulehner, A., Paler, A., and Wille, R. (2019). An efficient methodology for mapping quantum circuits to the IBM QX architectures. *IEEE Transactions on Computer-Aided Design of Integrated Circuits and Systems* 38 (7): 1226–1236.

13 Zulehner, A. and Wille, R. (2019). Compiling SU(4) quantum circuits to IBM QX architectures. In: *Asia and South Pacific Design Automation Conference*, 185–190.

14 Wille, R., Burgholzer, L., and Zulehner, A. (2019). Mapping quantum circuits to IBM QX architectures using the minimal number of SWAP and H operations. In: *Design Automation Conference*.

15 Selinger, P. (2013). Quantum circuits of T-depth one. *Physical Review A* 87 (4): 042302.

16 Sisodia, M., Shukla, A., de Almeida, A.A.A., Dueck, G.W., and Pathak, A. (2019). Circuit optimization for IBM processors: a way to get higher fidelity and higher values of nonclassicality witnesses. Technical Report arXiv:1812.11602 [quant-ph], ArXiV.

17 Kjaergaard, M., Schwartz, M.E., Braumüller, J., Krantz, P., Wang, J.I., Gustavsson, S., and Oliver, W.D. (2019). Superconducting qubits: current state of play. Technical Report arXiv:1608.02792 [cs.IT], ArXiV.

18 Steffen, M., DiVincenzo, D.P., Chow, J.M. et al. (2011). Quantum computing: an IBM perspective. *IBM Journal of Research and Development* 55 (5): 13.

19 Tannu, S.S. and Qureshi, M.K. (2019). Not all qubits are created equal: a case for variability-aware policies for NISQ-Era quantum computers. In: *International Conference on Architectural Support for Programming Languages and Operating Systems*, 987–999.

20 Patterson, A.D. et al. (2019). Calibration of the cross-resonance two-qubit gate between directly-coupled transmons. Technical Report arXiv:1905.05670 [quant-ph], ArXiV.

21 Botea, A., Kishimoto, A., and Marinescu, R. (2018). On the complexity of quantum circuit compilation. In: *International Symposium on Combinatorial Search*, 138–142.

2

Pros and Cons of Quantum Computing

2.1 Introduction

If superpositions are never used, quantum technology is effectively a regular computer implementation. Quantum information systems will ultimately be able to execute all conventional algorithms, regardless of whether quantum sequencing is employed on a large scale or in some instances. The reason for this is because the size of the logic gates has a more significant effect on the outcome of quantum events [1].

We stated that the quantum computing (QC) paradigm absorbs the conventional computing (CC) architecture [2]. The realization that, in some cases, all quantum registrations hold perturbation theory comprising a single element, such as, may help to solidify this connection by allowing CC algorithms to be executed on a supercomputer.

$$|R\rangle = |00\rangle \tag{2.1}$$

In this chapter, we will examine the advantages and disadvantages of a highly automated system. Furthermore, we will investigate several computational restraints that arise while developing a quantum algorithm using a stripped-down quantum computer.

2.2 Quantum as a Numerical Process

The mathematical features of intelligent technology architecture are superior to those of classical computing.

$$CC \subseteq QC \tag{2.2}$$

Anything a conventional computer can accomplish, and maybe much more, a quantum computer can do as well. A computer model is as capable computationally as a regular computer [3].

Quantum Computing: A New Era of Computing, First Edition.
Kuldeep Singh Kaswan, Jagjit Singh Dhatterwal, Anupam Baliyan, and Shalli Rani.

It has been shown, however, that a regular computer may (sometimes) mimic a computational model. That is, a classical algorithm may reproduce any quantum method provided CC is augmented by a simple mathematical formula; nevertheless, the classical technique may need geometrically more computing resources. This means that there is not much difference between classical and QC in terms of numerical methodologies or the feasibility of a given computational task.

Similarly, a function that can be calculated by a computer processor may be evaluated by a quantum algorithm [4].

When a classical computer fails to solve a problem, a quantum computer will also fail.

It has been shown, for instance, that the freezing problem faced by traditional computers cannot be solved using a quantum algorithm.

For computer programmers, the critical distinction between QC and CC is that QC is more cost-effective than CC for specific jobs. Because of this, the Church–Turing thesis [5] holds that every function that can be computed efficiently by intuition can also be calculated by a Turing machine.

However, QC demonstrates that the robust version of the hypothesis cannot be accurate; any functions traditionally thought to be computable may have their consistency improved by QC. Specific problems cannot be modeled efficiently on a computer fast enough for a recurrent neural network to tackle.

Due to the contradiction of the strong Church–Turing Thesis [6], new important classes of complexity for the supercomputing model may be created.

2.3 Quantum Complexity

Remember that in computer science, complexity classes label problems as either easy or hard to solve. Classifications of time and space difficulty are made independently of the hardware used to solve each unique problem. Therefore, complexity classifications are studied to evaluate the challenges of a set of concerns rather than the efficiency of a computer system [7].

The most important categories of deterministic and stochastic computing are as follows:

- P = Type of issue that can be solved by a computer algorithm in polynomial time [8].

    The notation NP refers to a set of issues for which a computer can provide mathematical proof that a solution exists.

    The BPP categorizes problems that can be solved by applying a probability algorithm to a traditional computer. A mathematical computer has a probability of at least one-third.

Figure 2.1 Structure of quantum computing complexity class.

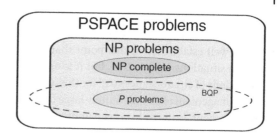

- EQP = Cases where a quantum computer may provide an answer with a probability of 1 in polynomial time [9].
- BQP = A category of problems that can be solved by a quantum computer in combinatorial optimization problems with a statistical approach of at least 1/3.

It's essential to remember that the one-third factor in these categories is entirely made up. Any number greater than zero and less than one was acceptable as per the class specification. The logic is that the probability of success may be increased by repeating the algorithm several times. This allows for the possibility of errors to be reduced to an infinitesimal fraction. For example, if you have two n-bit values that you need to add or perform some other arithmetic and logical operations on, you have a problem that falls within the primary division of P and should be solved using $O(n)$ computational steps. On the other hand, the computational complexity of an n-bit integer is NP-hard; the best-known traditional approach takes logarithmic time to compute a solution, but the result may be verified in polynomial time. However, in QC, decomposition may be accomplished mathematically [10]. Thus, in Figure 2.1, factorization is a problem for both NP and BQP.

However, there are problems with both NP and BQP, and it is not shown that every NP problem also exists in BQP. Strangely, in the early years of quantum entanglement [11], NP was anticipated to be a part of BQP. A problem from NP may not be in BQP if its structure is like that of the issues in NPBQP. It is presently known what systems correspond:

$$P \subseteq BPP \subseteq BQP \tag{2.3}$$

$$P \subseteq EQP \subseteq BQP \tag{2.4}$$

Based on the available evidence, the two most pressing issues in complexity theory are:

$$NP \subseteq P? \tag{2.5}$$

$$NP \subseteq BQP? \tag{2.6}$$

The question therefore becomes whether a conventional computer can effectively solve all NP problems. In other words, can all NP problems be solved by a simulation environment? Experts in systems theory have come to the same conclusion in answer to both questions.

It is well established at this point that QC is superior to CC for dealing with certain situations. This is true, but it is up to the computer scientist to determine what kinds of circumstances call for this. Quantum concurrency, the maintenance and management of an indefinitely large number of countries in superposition and entanglement, is the only proven approach for simplifying QC.

2.4   The Pros and Cons of the Quantum Computational Framework

To better understand the scope and limitations of particle physics, one may use a quantum register to keep track of a miniature replica of the cosmos. If all the information ever gathered about the universe, from the Big Bang to the current day, was divided into a grid with cells measuring the Planck scale (1.61035 m), then there would be around 2800 bits of data.

That much data might potentially be processed using just 800 qubits.

A description of the whole world in fractional order should be stored in an 800-qubit microscopic memory, and this memory should also be able to be modified in $O(1)$ time. To rephrase, all 2800 coordinates may be changed by the same amount, U, at the same time. This raises the question of whether a traditional computer can successfully replicate a virtual environment. The following points, however, show how inadequate the QC framework is and hence support the negative verdict.

Our plaything model of the universe is a grid with cells containing the limits of our knowledge as the initial condition. Each of the 2800 cells must be given the value 0 or 1 to define the state. It would take billions and trillions of thousands of years to do 2800 explicit reassignment transactions on the quantum registers to achieve this goal. Another option is to use a function $f(x)$ to assign values to all cells compiled by the x-measurement in $O(1)$ time (assuming that the calculation of f is linear) (x). As little as $O(1)$ clock ticks per cell is required [12].

As an independent function $f(x)$ may be used to activate all cells simultaneously, so too can a function be used to transform all cells simultaneously. It seems like the evolution of the cosmos may be modeled using Markov processes. Unfortunately, with QC, it is not possible to apply a function to a condition that depends on other elements in a combination. Take the function $f(x, y)$ as an example; in this case, x and y represent two separate parallel processing cells. To rephrase, changes to any one state must be made permanently, or else separate configurations must be stored and made available. In the former scenario, we are restricted to very dull models, whereas in the latter, we are forced to store an infeasible $O(2800)$ worth of classical information [13].

- Manufacturing – Without reading the location of the dynamic registration, we will not be able to gain any information from the simulation, no matter how beneficial our techniques for initializing and growing our universe modeling may be. The aggregation disintegrated at that point, and the register recorded the disassembled state of one of the 2800 cells. We can, in effect, imitate the growth of 2800 states, but we can only visit one. We are restricted to transmitting no more than 800 data items. The simulations may be performed again to test other scenarios. The fact, however, is that any relevant statistics will need $2800/O(1)$ computations. Since the optimal QC computation of the mean of N states in a superposition takes time, an infeasibly large number of simulations would be required (about 2400 for our toy universe model), as will be demonstrated in Chapter 1.

This simple, maybe unrealistic example highlights how the key benefit of quantum mathematical expressions is the inherent operational synchronization of the underlying mathematical calculation across an ever-larger computing area (Rules 4 and 6). Disadvantages of the quantum paradigm include its inability to replicate itself and the destructive nature of quantum experiments [14].

I: print a;

II: c = b;

III: f(a);

IV: f(b);

V: f(c);

2.5 Further Benefits of Quantum Computing

Quantum computers can do any job more quickly than classical ones. This is because the particles used in a quantum computer may move far more swiftly than those in a traditional computer. If the qubit is in a superposition state, then the quantum computer may do an exponentially larger number of calculations in a shorter amount of time. The second advantage of QC is that it is equally adept at doing classical and quantum calculations. The best illustration of a quantum algorithm is Peter Shor's quantum factorization method from AT&T Bell Labs. Accelerating medical research using a quantum computer would assist the chemical industry and may aid in the fight against climate change. Quantum computers have the potential to advance radar concealment techniques. In this regard, Peter Shor's algorithm is illustrative. According to this notion, quantum algorithms might be useful in developing new medicines. Quantum computers have the potential to improve security in the realm of cryptography. Utilizing quantum computers, one can foresee the weather. In the stock market, quantum computers may be used to detect problems before they become widespread. Quantum physics has the potential to be used in mathematics for superior optimization. Quantum computers may be used by Google's search engine to provide the most relevant results for users' requests.

2.6 Further Drawbacks to Quantum Computing

The main disadvantage of a quantum computer is its high price tag. It is possible that a small company would not be able to afford such a costly piece of machinery. There are not enough infrastructures in place to construct a quantum computer at this moment. This is because the electron, a crucial part of QC, is easily damaged by its surroundings.

A new research study claims that all computers on Earth, including nuclear codes, will be vulnerable to QC. Let us say it gets into the wrong hands.

For this technology to reach its full potential, a plethora of novel quantum algorithms is needed. Without quantum algorithms, a classical computer will have no benefit over a regular computer, just as a computer scientist can only operate as a conventional computer without these methods. If the outcome of the calculation is not at the starting point, the answer is too complicated to grasp.

Several companies claim to have built quantum computers, with IBM and D-Wave being the most well-known. Even if quantum computers exist, we lack the necessary knowledge to effectively use them. Complex puzzles like sudoku can be solved just as easily by a traditional computer as by a quantum one. Quantum computers are inefficient unless they are kept at very low temperatures (as low as 460 °C).

2.7 Integrating Quantum and Classical Techniques

As has been hypothesized, all computer hardware will one day consist of quantum circuits. The more pressing question is whether quantum concurrency will have a major effect on algorithm design. The advantages of quantum parallelism may only be applicable to a subset of real-world problems in particular cases. When used in conjunction with other tools, such as vector processors, it has the potential to boost the performance of many different algorithms.

The term "hybrid computing" refers to the practice of developing algorithms that make use of a quantum register as a supplementary dedicated hardware component to accelerate certain operations. This approach is narrower than letting researchers create new algorithms for all of quantum logic. However, the difficulty of developing new algorithms is greatly reduced if attention is instead focused on extracting value from existing, general-purpose solutions. In traditional algorithm design, this is how you would go about creating an algorithm like a binary search to solve a certain issue.

The need to speed up the development of algorithms for quantum systems inspired the creation of the hybrid computing paradigm. In this way, computer scientists may tap into the power of QC in the same way they have traditionally used software libraries. Hybrid algorithm development differs from full quantum optimization techniques in that its major purpose is to find the best possible algorithmic solutions based on a given set of conventional and quantum building elements. With the whole architecture of the quantum algorithm system in mind, it is feasible to create product key components that cannot be explained in terms of earlier building blocks/primitives [15].

2.8   Framework of QRAM

The QRAM hybrid architecture is used to specify that the quantum processor is dedicated to certain algorithms, or computational kernels. Figure 2.2 depicts the QRAM design's master/slave connection between classical and quantum processors. In this scenario, the conventional code invokes the quantum processor. An appropriate quantum code is constructed to deliver further instructions. Therefore, the classical computer feeds information and orders to the quantum

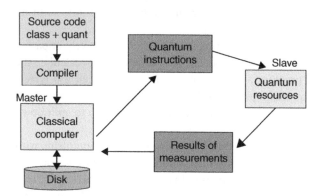

Figure 2.2   Structure of QRAM architecture.

processors. The traditional computer, which originally got the instructions, will need certain measures to be carried out to obtain this data. This method may be pipelined endlessly, allowing for infinite iterations [16].

There is no question that the quantum processor, in its current configuration, is constrained by the same constraints as more traditional enhancements, such as vector and graphics processors, for example, in terms of additional data transfer costs. It is possible that the quantum computer will introduce even more problems. Depending on how the quantum register is built, there might be a limit on how long a quantum superposition can be maintained. This computational time restriction is unprecedented in the development of classical algorithms.

2.9 Computing Algorithms in the Quantum World

A quantum algorithm that only depends on nontrivial quantum superpositions is bound to fail because of the seeming constraints on cloning and deleting observations. However, the algorithmic foundation of QC is beyond the scope of a basic superposition algorithm. Since there is an issue with algorithmic balance, the quantum software developer will need to determine which sections of his code may benefit from quantum acceleration.

To create functional quantum algorithms, it is necessary to consider a number of architectural and evolutionary algorithm considerations.

The theoretical speed of the first generation of quantum computers, to provide just one example, has not yet been specified. However, quantum computers will undoubtedly be a lot slower than their classical counterparts. In 2025, classical computers will likely operate at gigahertz speeds, whereas quantum processors will operate at megahertz speeds, at best. To prevent the slow quantum hardware from negating the algorithmic benefits of the quantum model, quantum software engineers must strike a delicate balance [17].

As was previously noted, the quantum processor might be negatively impacted by brief periods of decoherence. As a result, the programmers must calculate the expected lifetime of the program and guarantee that it is less than the typical decoherence time of the quantum processor they are employing. To prevent decoherence from interfering with the operation, it may be necessary to split down large computations into smaller ones.

Note that in the QRAM design, the normal processor must communicate with the quantum block and provide data and instructions to it, and vice versa. This process will incur some data transport expenses. In large datasets, this savings may disappear altogether due to the time needed to transport massive volumes of data through quantum acceleration.

Due to its I/O features, the QC paradigm also raises algorithmic concerns. Evidently, property #8 proves that the 0 states are the only viable starting point for a quantum computer. Gates may be used by the programmer to set the 0 states to whatever they want them to be initially. If the initial state is unspecified, finding the reversible unitary gate that does the desired transformation may involve $O(\text{poly}(2^n))$ computation steps. Another factor that might reduce the quantum model's potential advantage in computational speed.

Most quantum algorithms need a uniform superposition as their initial state. It's feasible to use n Hadamard gates, as we saw in Chapter 1. This means that these algorithms incur an $O(1)$ startup cost (n). Future quantum computers may be able to use Hadamard gates in more than one dimension. As a result, the architecture of the machine will determine how much strain this has. This layout would be more effective since the time required for initialization may be reduced to $O(1)$.

Due to the increasing destructive power of quantum measurement, no component of a superposition can be output. As the reader will remember, there is a possibility that we will arrive at a certain condition. An n-qubit register containing 2^n states can only output n-bits of logical information. While performing the algorithm, it is possible that some information may be lost. The user may rerun the same process more than n times to extract more than n pieces of classical knowledge. Although, once again, this procedure has the potential to quickly outpace the processing advantage afforded by quantum acceleration.

However, there may also be issues with memory addressing methods. Let us check out an n-qubit quantum register. Dereferencing an address needs $O(n)$ computation steps and employs $O(2^n)$ switching gates in the most basic memory addressing system, which is a binary tree that traverses a quantum register's states. The inefficiency and complexity of the model lead to a waste of these materials. Quicker implementations, however, have been proposed.

Moreover, it is unrealistic to expect QC to work effectively with processed data. When we have an n-qubit register that refers to 2^n states and we need to fill it with data stored somewhere on disc space, the number of operations required to move the data from the disc to memory is $O(2^n)$. To do such a task on a machine with 800 qubits is just unrealistic.

Consequently, it seems that QC is well-suited for dealing with data sets that are generated on the fly. Precomputed data stored in two different locations inside the computer may remain in their current locations. The fact that the whole dataset cannot be exported is the source of the problem here.

Therefore, it will be challenging for quantum software engineers to identify which portions of a classical program may benefit from quantum acceleration. They will have to basically start again in most circumstances. As a result, they are working to perfect hybrid programs before the usage of quantum computers poses a serious challenge. However, the same issue affects reconfigurable supercomputing that relies on FPGAs.

2.9.1 Programming Quantum Processes

There are numerous ground rules to follow while designing quantum algorithms:

To be efficient, a quantum program has to make use of the QC's parallelism and massive expansion of the available computing area.

So, we should stay away from anything that requires us to read or copy information from the registers.

The importance of considering probabilities and recycling options cannot be overstated.

Think about the algorithmic issues that arise from using a certain kind of QC hardware, such as QRAM.

Finally, we need to demonstrate that quantum efficacy outperforms the most popular classical method.

The development of a workable quantum algorithm is no easy task. Perhaps it should not come as a surprise that just a small number of useful quantum algorithms have been detailed in the open literature, given all the hurdles that must be overcome.

2.10 Modification of Quantum Building Blocks

Recent studies suggest that the quantum process provides considerable benefits over the most popular classical alternatives in six key algorithmic domains.

The amplitude of a measurement is amplified to make it easier to measure a quantum system in which several states are equally probable. An amplitude amplifier may be used as a generic tool for finding optimal solutions to a variety of search and optimization problems.

The quantum Fourier transform (QFT) may compute some types of Fourier transformation data at a time that is sublinear to the size of the dataset. To get the most effective classical algorithm, you will need a time-consuming algorithm.

When a standard method of statistical estimation fails, quantum random walks (QRW) may be employed to get the job done. When it comes to programming, a comprehensive introduction to QRW is available.

With quantum error correction (QEC), qubit errors are harder to identify and fix than with regular bit flips. It is implemented in QRAM rather than being employed in the creation of hybrid algorithms.

Despite their limited practicality, cryptographic algorithms are a vital area of study for the QRAM computer architecture.

It is not surprising that quantum equipment can simulate quantum phenomena more effectively than classical equipment. Feynman's studies in QC were motivated by this application. A new wave of adiabatic quantum algorithms has emerged to tackle tough problems in bioinformatics, such as protein docking and folding.

From a purely formal perspective, this application is not especially interesting, even though quantum computers promise huge breakthroughs in a broad variety of scientific and technological domains. The evolution of a physical system being compared to the evolution of a quantum computer is like trying to represent the dynamics of the ocean with a water tank. The first three factors mentioned above have a significant impact on the development of algorithms.

The ability to do tasks in parallel with a growing superposition is the primary advantage of the QC concept. Quantum superpositions cannot be precisely recreated, and measuring procedures are destructive; therefore, the applicability of this paradigm is restricted. The computational power of quantum computers is severely hampered by these two characteristics, yet there are significant advantages to exploiting quantum information for encrypted communications. Since measurements are destructive, snoops are easily uncovered, and the no-cloning theorem states that quantum superpositions cannot be falsified.

Consequently, the efficiency of any quantum algorithm is certain to be affected by several factors, such as the specific architecture used in developing the corresponding computing model. When designing quantum algorithms, it's important to consider the time costs of I/O operations, cognitive processing, and initialization.

The most important foundations for creating quantum algorithms are the QFT, QRW, and amplitude amplification techniques.

References

1 Preskill, J. (2018). Quantum computing in the NISQ era and beyond. *Quantum* 2: 79. https://doi.org/10.22331/q-2018-08-06-79.

2 Moll, N., Barkoutsos, P., Bishop, L.S. et al. (2018). Quantum optimization using variational algorithms on near-term quantum devices. *Quantum Science and Technology* 3 (3): 030503. https://doi.org/10.1088/2058-9565/aab822

3 Preskill, J. (2012). *Quantum Computing and the Entanglement Frontier*. Cornell University.

4 Arute, F., Arya, K., Babbush, R. et al. (2019). Quantum supremacy using a programmable superconducting processor. *Nature* 574 (7779): 505–510. doi: 10.1038/s41586-019-1666-5. Epub 2019 Oct 23. PMID: 31645734.

5 Pednault, E., Gunnels, J., Maslov, D. et al. (2019). Quantum Computing. On "Quantum Supremacy". IBM Research Blog. Retrieved from https://www.ibm.com/blogs/research/.

6 Zhong, H.S., Hui, W., Yu-Hao, D. et al. (2020). Quantum computational advantage using photons. *Science* 370 (6523): 1460–1463.

7 Feynman, R.P. (1982). Simulating physics with computers. *International Journal of Theoretical Physics* 21: 467–488.

8 Peruzzo, A., Jarrod, M., Peter, S. et al. (2014). A variational eigen solver on a photonic quantum processor. *Nature Communications* 5 (4213): 1–7.

9 Zardoshti, A. (2021). *The Impacts of Quantum Computing on Insurance*. Lloyd's Lab.

10 Chen, H., Vasmer, M., Breuckmann, N.P., and Grant, E. (2019). *Machine Learning Logical Gates for Quantum Error Correction*. Cornell University.

11 Niu, M.Y., Boixo, S., Smelyanskiy, V.N., and Neven, H. (2019). Universal quantum control through deep reinforcement learning. *npj Quantum Information* 5 (1): 33.

12 Usman, M., Wong, Y.Z., Hill, C.D., and Hollenberg, L.C. (2020). Framework for atomic-level characterization of quantum computer arrays by machine learning. *npj Computational Materials* 6 (1): 19.

13 Quantum Machine Learning (2019). Quantum machine learning – 41 – guest lecture by Seth Lloyd. YouTube, Vol 574, 505–510.

14 Mari, A., Thomas, R.B., Josh, I. et al. (2020). *Transfer Learning in Hybrid Classical-Quantum Neural Networks*. Cornell University.

15 Giovannetti, V., Lloyd, S., and Maccone, L. (2008). *Quantum Random Access Memory*. Cornell University.

16 Harrow, A.W. (2020). *Small Quantum Computers and Large Classical Data Sets*. Cornell University.

17 Shor, P.W. (1997). Polynomial-time algorithms for prime factorization and discrete logarithms on a quantum computer. *SIAM Journal on Computing* 26 (5): 1484–1509.

3

Methods and Instrumentation for Quantum Computing

It is important to lay the groundwork for quantum communication theory, which is what we will do in this chapter. The major focus of this course will be on developing skills in making educated value estimates. For this purpose, we will use entropy, a measure of disorder in physics. We will look at how uncertainty, the antidote to sickness, may be used to evaluate the quality of a signal and the number of bits needed to deliver it reliably. Quantum cryptography will soon include these ideas. This chapter will provide a high-level overview of several current topics in computer science and investigate the potential advantages of using classical computers. This chapter will teach you the fundamentals of programming, but it will not prepare you for a career as a computer system or network administrator.

3.1 Basic Information of Quantum Computing

In order to learn new ways for the brain to process information, quantum computing is being used. In addition to the contemporary methods of computation and data analysis that you are accustomed to, historical information . Let us take a brief look at how data are stored and used on personal computers for the benefit of individuals who are not acquainted with them. A bit is the simplest data unit since it merely stores a binary value – a yes or no answer to a question. Since our technology operates on a binary system, the terms "base 2" or "binary" may be used to describe it. Each bit in a binary number may take one of two values: 0 or 1. To effectively integrate a bit (binary 1), an electrical circuit may be connected to binary 0 for ground/zero volts and binary 1 for, say, +5 V.

For the sake of brevity, we will not go into the inner workings of a computer in this chapter, but will instead focus on the mathematical operations principles upon which computers are built [1]. We may start our exploration of binary numbers by

Quantum Computing: A New Era of Computing, First Edition.
Kuldeep Singh Kaswan, Jagjit Singh Dhatterwal, Anupam Baliyan, and Shalli Rani.
© 2023 The Institute of Electrical and Electronics Engineers, Inc. Published 2023 by John Wiley & Sons, Inc.

delving into the details of the base-2 system. It is important to keep in mind that the following formula may be used to estimate the amount of bits needed to describe an object. Let us pretend for a moment that some amount q may exist in any one of M states [2]. Then

$$2p \geq q \tag{3.1}$$

That was a n – here's another one. In order to encode or represent a given quantity, it is necessary to know the smallest n for which this is true.

To demonstrate this, you may use the binary representation of the numbers 0 through 3 to write them down. There are 22 components, which is 4. This necessitates a representation using two bits. The information is graphically shown in Table 3.1. The numbers 0 through 7 can only be represented using three bits.

The first seven digits of the numbers 0 through 7 are represented in binary in Table 3.2.

Table 3.1 Decimal to binary representation (4 numbers).

Decimal number	Binary number
0	00
1	01
2	10
3	11

Table 3.2 Decimal to binary representation (4 numbers).

Decimal number	Binary number
0	000
1	001
2	010
3	011
4	100
5	101
6	110
7	111

3.2 Signal Information in Quantum Computing

We can start to think about characterizing data now that we know how to transform it. If we have a message m, how much information does it really contain?

Look at Table 3.1 to gain an understanding of how to measure things. If we take out the assignment operator [3], we can get the base two logarithms of both edges. Therefore, let us start with

$m = 2n$

By using a base-2 logarithmic comparison, we are able to make this observation.

$$\log_2 m = n \tag{3.2}$$

It was not until 1927, when Ralph Hartley first introduced Eq. (1.2), that it gained widespread attention. To our knowledge, this was the first effort at quantifying the information contained in a communication. According to (1.2), it is possible to store m separate messages using n data bits. Note this for the purpose of clarity:

$\log_2 8 = 3$

Eight different messages may be encoded in three bits. Table 3.2 displays the eight secret codes (0–7) that make up the coded communications. In comparison, the code may represent anything, with eight possible meanings [4].

You have undoubtedly already familiarized yourself with your computer's storage requirements. A byte is the smallest unit of information that may be used as a word. The byte, an eight-bit integer, is the lowest unit of storage for information. Now

$\log_2 256 = 8$

Therefore, a single byte may store up to 256 unique data bits. The fact that logarithms are progressive makes it feasible to quantify knowledge in support of trigonometric functions.

3.3 Quantum Data Entropy

The Hartley method may be used to describe the information carried by a signal. However, the work of another scientist, Claude Shannon, has shown that we may go much farther in our comprehension of the information contained in a signal. With the simple question, "How likely is it that this information will be seen?" Shannon made great progress. This finding has allowed us to quantify the information gained from a signal [5].

We do not learn very lot more when we come across likely-to-occur communication. However, when we become aware of a message whose possibility of occurrence is minimal, we gain a great deal of insight. Let us look at an example to see how this works in practice. In 1812, a major earthquake hit the St. Louis area. Though earthquakes are less prevalent there than they are in California, they nonetheless occur [6].

This means that most people in Missouri are not ready for an earthquake. There is a very small chance of an earthquake happening in Missouri, and the chances of one happening are much lower. If we know there will not be any earthquakes in Missouri tomorrow, an enhanced probability message does not tell us anything new. There have been no earthquakes in Missouri during the last 200 years. If tomorrow's earthquake prediction holds true, this is devastating news for folks in Missouri. They get a lot of knowledge from this experience, so it is important to them.

Shannon calculated the probability that a given message would be sent using logarithms with a base of 2. The information in a message is indicated by I, and the likelihood of its occurrence is denoted by p.

$$I = -\log_2 p \tag{3.3}$$

The usage of negative numbers indicates that the message's source credibility decreases as its optimism increases, and vice versa for the information's value. Say later today that there is a 0.995% chance of an earthquake in St. Louis. Even a single fact contains a wealth of information.

$$I = -\log_2 0.995 = 0.0072$$

The probability of earthquakes occurring tomorrow is 0.005%. There is a tremendous amount of data in this report.

$$I = -\log_2 0.005 = 7.6439$$

Logarithms provide a convenient way to describe the data in a signal, as seen below.

Due to the low probability of an occurrence, a great deal of detail is often given in an unlikely message.

The informational value of a communication is low if its occurrence is very probable.

More detail on the definition is required. One interpretation of X is as a probabilistic random variable with associated uncertainty [7].

Chances $p_1, p_2, ..., p_n$ for each possible x value. When conditions like these are there, possibilities may be realized.

The complexity of X is quantified by its Shannon entropy.

$$H(X) = -\sum_i p_i \log_2 p_i \tag{3.4}$$

$$H(n) = -\Sigma_{P_j} \log_2 P_i$$

If the chance of an xj is zero, we use the formula $0 \log 0 = 0$. It is possible to see the Shannon entropy function, which quantifies the degree of randomness or uncertainty in a signal, as the natural logarithm of the probability of x.

It is possible to make the following observations regarding communications in transit: If our signal always sends a 2, we will call it the sequence 22 222 222 222. The entropy in this situation looks like what? Entropy, sometimes known as the degree of disorganization, may be defined as

$$H = -\log_2 1 = 0$$

Since a signal with a low Shannon entropy retains the same properties throughout, it may be reliably predicted.

Now, let us do something completely out of the ordinary. The signal would look like this: 1112122212121212221121211112... with around 50% 1s and 50% 2s if the odds of obtaining a 1 were 50% and the odds of getting a 2 were 50%. What does the entropy look like in this case? It is

$$H = -1/2 \log_2 1/2 - \tfrac{1}{2} \log_2 = \tfrac{1}{2} + 1/2 = 1$$

Assuming three possible outcomes have been generated. If this were true, we would be in a different position.

$$H = -\frac{1}{3} \log_2 \frac{1}{3} - \frac{1}{3} \log_2 \frac{1}{3} = 0.528 + 0.528 + 0.528 = 1.585$$

It has become less clear what characters will appear in the following part of the message as the unpredictability of the communications has increased in every scenario we have examined here. One way of looking at Shannon entropy is as a measure of how unpredictable or uncertain a signal is. To clarify, once we decipher the message, the Shannon entropy will be identical to zero. More Shannon entropy means more uncertainty about the future. This is a short definition of Shannon entropy. An increase in knowledge lessens worry. Boost the randomness by raising the entropy of the system. A total of I_i bits are required to adequately describe a set of x_i. The greatest bit rate required to encode X is

$$R_x = \sum_{i=1}^{n} I_i p_i \tag{3.5}$$

The average bit rate cannot be decreased below the Shannon entropy.

$$H(X) \leq R_x \tag{3.6}$$

Since we know the least about uniform distributions, they represent the worst-case scenario.

Again, let us pretend that there are n parts. In a normal distribution, the probability of locating any given x_i is $1/n$. Sequences have entropy if and only if the probability of each element occurring in the sequence is $1/n$. Based on this, it is reasonable to infer that there is a maximum value for the Shannon entropy [8].

$$0 \leq H(X) \leq \log_2 n \tag{3.7}$$

The volatility of two random variables is p/q if their probability density curves are proportionate to one another.

$$H(X\|Y) = \sum p \log_2 \frac{p}{q} = -H(X) - \sum p \log_2 q \tag{3.8}$$

Let us assume we take any given y_i from Y and multiply it by Y. Given what we do know about X, we may write the range of probable outcomes for X as $(X|y_i)(y_i)$. Then

$$H(X|Y) = -\Sigma p(x_j|y_i) \log_2 (p(x_j|y_i)) \tag{3.9}$$

This behavior is known as unrestricted entropy. Conditioned multiplicity fulfills all of the requisites.

$$H(X|Y) \leq H(X) \tag{3.10}$$

To obtain equality in (3.10), the variables X and Y must be independent. So, we are now in a position to define mutual information of the variables X and Y. In words, this is the difference between the entropy of X and the entropy of X given knowledge of what value Y has assumed, that is,

Because X and Y have created a shared understanding, we can explain it. When the value of Y is unknown, the unpredictability of X is equal to the disparity between the initial and current entropies of X, or.

$$I(X|Y) = H(X) + H(X|Y) \tag{3.11}$$

$$I(X|Y) = H(X) - H(X|Y) \tag{3.12}$$

It is possible to write this as

$$I(X|Y) = H(X) + H(Y) - H(X, Y) \tag{3.13}$$

3.4 Basics of Probability in Quantum Computing

As a result, if we want X and Y to be on equal footing, we cannot have them linked together (3.10).

X and Y have generated a body of knowledge that can be characterized now that it exists. As the entropy of X equals the difference between its initial and current states when Y is unknown, this property is equivalent to a measure of uncertainty.

$$0 \leq p_i \leq 1 \tag{3.14}$$

To sum up the two poles of this scale, we may say that if something is impossible, then it has zero probability of occurring. For each given event, the chance is 1. This range encompasses all other possible outcomes.

A situation's likelihood may be roughly estimated by looking at how often it occurs in comparison to similar situations. For the sake of argument, let us say n is the total number of occurrences and j is the number of times the nth event happens. Thus, the likelihood of the jth event occurring is

$$P_j = n_j/n \tag{3.15}$$

Given that 1 is the combined result of all probability, we may deduce:

$$\sum_{J=1}^{\infty} P_j = \sum_{j=1}^{\infty} \frac{n_j}{n} = \frac{1}{n} \sum_{j=1}^{\infty} n_j = \frac{n}{n} = 1 \tag{3.16}$$

The following equation is commonly used in quantum theory to calculate the amount of a dispersion. According to what people understand,

$$\sum_{j=1}^{\infty} \frac{jn_j}{n} = \frac{1}{n} \sum_{j=1}^{\infty} jp_j \tag{3.17}$$

One such expression for the variance of a distribution is

$$\langle(\Delta_j)\rangle = \langle j^2 \rangle - \langle j \rangle^2 \tag{3.18}$$

Example 3.1 The students in the class are handed a test. There is a set of students associated with each score.

Score	Students
95	1
85	3
77	7
71	10
56	3

Where do you anticipate arriving? The average, or what can we anticipate to pay, is.

Solution

To begin, let us just add up how many pupils there are.

$$N = \sum n_j = 1 + 3 + 7 + 10 + 3 = 24$$

The chance of getting a 95 is 1/100.

$$p_i = \frac{n_1}{n} = \frac{1}{24} = 0.04$$

That similar process is applied to the remaining choices. This has been the most probable result, with a chance of 71.

$$p_4 = \frac{n_4}{n} = \frac{10}{24} = 0.42$$

By dividing by (3.17), we get the anticipated value.

$$\langle j \rangle = \sum j\, p_j = 95(0.04) + 85(0.13) + 77(0.29) + 71(0.42) + 56(0.13) = 74.3$$

3.5   Quantum Theorem of No-Cloning

In the market for knowledge packaging, duplication of data is routine practice. Most people assume that a file saved in a word processor or a music file may be duplicated indefinitely [9]. Because a qubit may exist in a combination, a classical computer is tremendously powerful, as we have demonstrated.

It is feasible to construct clone of any qubit those information have been given. The ultimate verdict was disappointingly unfavorable. The full proof of Wooters and Zurek's no-cloning theorem from 1982 is presented. It is useful to consider two extremes: Consider the possibility of a unique operator U, in the sense that

$$U(|\psi\rangle \otimes |\chi\rangle) = |\psi\rangle \otimes |\psi\rangle$$
$$U(|\phi\rangle \otimes |\chi\rangle) = |\phi\rangle \otimes |\phi\rangle \tag{3.19}$$

with a target in mind by combining the left-hand sides of (13.19) and (3.2), we can calculate the derivative of the function and, with the help of the fact that $UU = I$, derive

$$((\langle\psi| \otimes \langle\chi|U^\dagger)(U|\phi\rangle \otimes |\chi\rangle) = \langle\psi|\phi\rangle\langle\chi|\chi\rangle = \langle\psi|\phi\rangle \tag{3.20}$$

On the other hand, if we take the kernel function of the right-hand sides of (3.19) and (3.20), we obtain

$$(\langle\psi|\emptyset\rangle)^2 \tag{3.21}$$

We can get the equation by comparing these two outcomes.

$$\langle\psi|\emptyset\rangle = (\langle\psi|\emptyset\rangle)^2 \tag{3.22}$$

There are simply two potential outputs to this exponential distribution: the states are complementary in this circumstance.

This suggests that any given quantum state cannot be duplicated using the universal unitary operator U.

Another example, this time via inconsistency, is offered here. We apply linear functions in mathematical mechanics. Therefore, U must be a straight line, as shown.

$$U(\alpha|\psi\rangle \oplus |\chi\rangle) = \alpha(U(|\psi\rangle \oplus |\chi\rangle)) = \alpha|\psi\rangle \oplus |\chi\rangle \tag{3.23}$$

On the other hand, if we allow and apply (3.23), we get

$$U(|\omega\rangle \oplus |\chi\rangle) = |\omega\rangle \oplus |\omega\rangle = \alpha|\psi\rangle \oplus \alpha|\chi\rangle = \alpha^2|\psi\rangle \oplus |\psi\rangle \tag{3.24}$$

Disagreement arises when (3.6) is contrasted with (3.7). Worldwide cloning is impossible at this time. Since it is impossible to make an exact copy of an entangled photon, we could wonder how close together the various quantum states really are. Produce imperfect carbon copies [10].

3.6 Measuring Distance

If it is impossible to recreate an exact copy of a quantum state, the next question is whether or not an approximation can be built. First, we need to know what resources we have before we can assess the degree of similarity between two circumstances.

We will start by examining the trace distance. Multiplication of intensities by two matrices will be denoted as. The separation of two vertices is denoted by the symbol (,) in the notation of the trace distance.

$$\delta(P_\sigma) = \frac{1}{2}T_\gamma|\rho_{-\sigma}| \tag{3.25}$$

Please take note of it. We might, for instance, want to draw a line between the equally likely scenarios of and. Standardized performance is on average.

$$P_\gamma = \frac{1}{2} + \frac{1}{2}\delta(\rho, \sigma) \tag{3.26}$$

The trace distance may be thought of as a universal measure in Hilbert space. Evidence for this may be seen in the fact that the trace velocity is positive.

$$0 \leq \delta(\rho, \sigma) \tag{3.27}$$

When and are equal, both and have the same value. The distance along the trace is a symmetrical function.

$$\delta(\rho, \sigma) = \delta(\sigma, \rho) \tag{3.28}$$

When the triangle inequalities is met

$$\delta(R\sigma) \leq \delta(\rho, \vartheta) + \delta(\vartheta, \sigma) \tag{3.29}$$

If $\rho = |\psi\rangle\langle\psi|$ is a pure state, then $\delta(\rho, \sigma)$ is given by

$$\delta(\rho_\sigma) = \sqrt{1 - \langle\psi|r|\psi\rangle} \tag{3.30}$$

A presumption of $[\rho, \sigma] = 0$ as long as the primary components of are r_i and s_i, and that and communicate with respect to some basis,

$$\delta(\rho\sigma) = \frac{1}{2}T_\gamma \left| \sum_i (\gamma_i - s_i)|_{v_i} x \bigcup_i 1 \right| \tag{3.31}$$

Example 3.2 Compute the trace distance between [13]

$$P = \frac{3}{4}|0\rangle\langle0| + \frac{1}{4}|1\rangle\langle1|$$

$$\sigma = \frac{2}{3}|0\rangle\langle0| + \frac{1}{3}|1\rangle\langle1|, \pi = \frac{1}{8}|0\rangle\langle0| + \frac{7}{8}|1\rangle\langle1|$$

Solution

All of these places are under the microscope. Since greater emphasis has been placed on the first element, the values of and should be closer together.

$$\rho - \sigma = \frac{3}{4}|0\rangle\langle0| + \frac{1}{4}|1\rangle\langle1| - \left(\frac{2}{3}|0\rangle\langle0| + \frac{1}{3}|1\rangle\langle1|\right)$$

$$= \frac{1}{12}|0\rangle\langle0| - \frac{1}{12}|1\rangle\langle1|$$

The trace is complicated, so let us go through a few specifics. Being a straight line, + the trace again inverts the outer product to the inner product.

$$\text{Tr}(|\psi\rangle\langle\psi|) \geq \psi|\psi >$$

so we can write

$$\delta(\rho, \sigma) = \frac{1}{2}\text{Tr}|\rho - \sigma|$$

$$= \frac{1}{2}\text{Tr}\left|\frac{1}{12}|0\rangle\langle0| - \frac{1}{12}|1\rangle\langle1|\right|$$

$$= \frac{1}{2}\left(\frac{1}{12}\right)(\text{Tr}(|0\rangle\langle0|) + \text{Tr}(|1\rangle\langle1|)) = \frac{1}{2}\left(\frac{1}{12}\right)(\langle0|0\rangle + \langle1|1\rangle)$$

$$= \frac{1}{2}\left(\frac{1}{12}\right)(2) = \frac{1}{12}$$

Now let us see what the trace distance $\delta(\rho, \pi)$ is. We have

$$\rho - \pi = \frac{3}{4}|0\rangle\left\langle0| + \frac{1}{4}|1\right\rangle\langle1| - \left(\frac{1}{8}|0\rangle\langle0| + \frac{7}{8}|1\rangle\langle1|\right)$$

$$= \frac{5}{8}(|0\rangle\langle0| - |1\rangle\langle1|)$$

We find that

$$\delta(\rho, \pi) = \frac{1}{2}\text{Tr}|\rho - \pi|$$

$$= \frac{1}{2}\text{Tr}\left|\frac{5}{8}\left(|0\rangle\langle 0| - |1\rangle\langle 1|\right)\right|$$

$$= \frac{1}{2}\left(\frac{5}{8}\right)\left(\text{Tr}\left(|0\rangle\langle 0|\right) + \text{Tr}\left(|1\rangle\langle 1|\right)\right) = \frac{1}{2}\left(\frac{5}{8}\right)\left(\langle 0|0\rangle + \langle 1|1\rangle\right)$$

$$= \frac{1}{2}\left(\frac{5}{8}\right)(2) = \frac{5}{8}$$

We have $\delta(\rho, \pi) \, \delta(\rho, \sigma)$ as predicted, because and are more highly weighed. State and are more similar to each other than state and.

Be sure to jot down the matrix notations for $\rho = \frac{3}{4}|0\rangle\langle 0| + \frac{1}{4}|1\rangle\langle 1|, \sigma = \frac{2}{3}|0\rangle\langle 0| + \frac{1}{3}|1\rangle\langle 1|$, and $\pi = \frac{1}{8}|0\rangle\langle 0| + \frac{7}{8}|1\rangle\langle 1|$. Check Example 3.2 outcome.

The trace distance may be readily calculated using the (ρ, σ) matrix's eigenvalue, where lambda I is the notation for the eigenvalues, which is the trace distance.

$$\delta(\rho, \sigma) = \frac{1}{2}\sum_i |\lambda_i| = \frac{1}{2}\sum_i \sqrt{\lambda_i * \lambda_i} \tag{3.32}$$

The trace distance may be simply computed if we are both familiar with the Bloch vectors of each density matrix. Let us pretend $\vec{r}$ is the Bloch vector of ρ and $\vec{s}$ is the Bloch vector of σ. This allows us to get the formula for the ρ, σ trace distance:

$$\delta(\rho, \sigma) = \frac{1}{2}|\vec{r} - \vec{s}|$$

Write

$$\rho = \frac{3}{4}|0\rangle\left\langle 0\left|+\frac{1}{4}\right|1\right\rangle\left\langle 1\right|, \sigma = \frac{2}{3}|0\rangle\left\langle 0\left|+\frac{1}{3}\right|1\right\rangle\langle 1| \tag{3.33}$$

Example 3.3 Find the trace distance between the states [13]

$$\rho = \begin{pmatrix} \frac{5}{8} & \frac{i}{4} \\ \frac{-i}{4} & \frac{3}{8} \end{pmatrix}, \sigma = \begin{pmatrix} \frac{2}{5} & \frac{-i}{8} \\ \frac{i}{8} & \frac{3}{5} \end{pmatrix}$$

Solution

Let us do it using (13.8) first. We have

$$\rho - \sigma = \begin{pmatrix} \frac{5}{8} & \frac{i}{4} \\ \frac{-i}{4} & \frac{3}{8} \end{pmatrix} - \begin{pmatrix} \frac{2}{5} & \frac{i}{8} \\ \frac{i}{4} & \frac{3}{5} \end{pmatrix} = \begin{pmatrix} \frac{9}{40} & \frac{i^3}{8} \\ \frac{-i^3}{4} & \frac{-9}{40} \end{pmatrix}$$

Now $(\rho - \sigma)^\dagger = \rho - \sigma$, so

$$(\rho - \sigma)^\dagger (\rho - \sigma) = \begin{pmatrix} \dfrac{9}{40} & \dfrac{i3}{8} \\ \dfrac{-i3}{4} & \dfrac{-9}{40} \end{pmatrix} \begin{pmatrix} \dfrac{9}{40} & \dfrac{i3}{8} \\ \dfrac{-i3}{4} & \dfrac{-9}{40} \end{pmatrix} = \begin{pmatrix} \dfrac{153}{800} & 0 \\ 0 & \dfrac{153}{800} \end{pmatrix}$$

Next, we find

$$|\rho - \sigma| = \sqrt{(\rho - \sigma)^\dagger (\rho - \sigma)} = \sqrt{\begin{pmatrix} \dfrac{153}{800} & 0 \\ 0 & \dfrac{153}{800} \end{pmatrix}} = \frac{1}{20}\begin{pmatrix} 3\sqrt{\dfrac{17}{2}} & 0 \\ 0 & 3\sqrt{\dfrac{17}{2}} \end{pmatrix}$$

Hence

$$\delta(\rho, \sigma) = \frac{1}{2}\left(\frac{1}{20}\right)(2)\left(3\sqrt{\frac{17}{2}}\right) \approx 0$$

The Bloch vector for ρ was found in Example 3.13:

$$S_x = \text{Tr}(X\rho) = \text{Tr}\left[\begin{pmatrix} 0 & 1 \\ 1 & 0 \end{pmatrix}\begin{pmatrix} \dfrac{5}{8} & \dfrac{i}{4} \\ \dfrac{-i}{4} & \dfrac{3}{8} \end{pmatrix}\right] = \text{Tr}\begin{pmatrix} \dfrac{-i}{4} & \dfrac{3}{8} \\ \dfrac{5}{8} & \dfrac{i}{4} \end{pmatrix} = 0$$

$$S_y = \text{Tr}(Y\rho) = \text{Tr}\left[\begin{pmatrix} 0 & -i \\ i & 0 \end{pmatrix}\begin{pmatrix} \dfrac{5}{8} & \dfrac{i}{4} \\ \dfrac{-i}{4} & \dfrac{3}{8} \end{pmatrix}\right] = \text{Tr}\begin{pmatrix} \dfrac{-1}{4} & \dfrac{-i^3}{8} \\ \dfrac{i5}{8} & \dfrac{-1}{4} \end{pmatrix} = \frac{-1}{2}$$

$$S_z = \text{Tr}(Z\rho) = \text{Tr}\left[\begin{pmatrix} 1 & 0 \\ 0 & -1 \end{pmatrix}\begin{pmatrix} \dfrac{5}{8} & \dfrac{i}{4} \\ \dfrac{-i}{4} & \dfrac{3}{8} \end{pmatrix}\right] = \text{Tr}\begin{pmatrix} \dfrac{5}{8} & \dfrac{i}{4} \\ \dfrac{i}{4} & \dfrac{-3}{8} \end{pmatrix} = \frac{1}{4}$$

Exercise 3.11 yielded the following Bloch vector for the parameter:

$$\vec{s} = \frac{1}{4}\vec{y} - \frac{1}{5}\vec{z}$$

Therefore,

$$\vec{\gamma} - \vec{s} = -\frac{3}{4}\hat{y} + \frac{9}{20}z$$

The amplitude of this arrow's magnitude is

$$|\vec{r} - \vec{s}| = \sqrt{\left(-\frac{3}{4}\right)^2 + \left(\frac{9}{20}\right)^2} = \frac{\sqrt{306}}{20}$$

Hence,

$$\delta(\rho, \sigma) = \frac{1}{2}|\vec{r} - \vec{s}| = \frac{1}{2}\frac{\sqrt{306}}{20} \approx 0\cdot437$$

Example 3.4   A system is in the pure state [13]

$$\rho = \frac{3}{4} |+\rangle\langle+| + \frac{1}{4}|-\rangle\langle-|$$

Find the trace distance between ρ and $\sigma = |\psi\rangle\langle\psi|$, $\sigma = |\psi\rangle\langle\psi|$ where

$$|\psi\rangle = \frac{1}{\sqrt{5}}|0\rangle + \frac{2}{\sqrt{5}}\langle1|$$

Solution

The foundation for both intensity matrices must be the same. Rewriting in terms of computation is the first step. Experiment 5.6 revealed what we discovered:

$$\rho = \frac{3}{4} |+\rangle\left\langle+| + \frac{1}{4}|-\right\rangle\langle-|$$

$$= \left(\frac{3}{4}\right)\left(\frac{1}{2}\right)(|0\rangle\langle0| + |0\rangle\langle1| + |1\rangle\langle0| + |1\rangle\langle1|$$

$$+ \left(\frac{1}{4}\right)\left(\frac{1}{2}\right)(|0\rangle\langle0| + |0\rangle\langle1| + |1\rangle\langle0| + |1\rangle\langle1|$$

$$= \frac{1}{2}|0\rangle\left\langle0| + \frac{1}{4}|0\rangle\langle1| + \frac{1}{4}|1\rangle\left\langle0|\frac{1}{2}|1\right\rangle\langle1|$$

Density operators are represented in a matrix form.

$$\rho = \frac{1}{4}\begin{pmatrix} 2 & 1 \\ 1 & 2 \end{pmatrix}$$

Now for

$$|\psi\rangle = \frac{1}{\sqrt{5}}|0\rangle + \frac{2}{\sqrt{5}}|1\rangle$$

We found in Example 3.5 that

$$\sigma = |\psi\rangle\langle\psi| = \left(\frac{1}{\sqrt{5}}|0\rangle + \frac{2}{\sqrt{5}}|1\rangle\right)\left(\frac{1}{\sqrt{5}}|0\rangle + \frac{2}{\sqrt{5}}\langle1|\right)$$

$$= \frac{1}{5}|0\rangle\left\langle0| + \frac{2}{5}|0\rangle\langle1| + \frac{2}{5}|1\rangle\left\langle0|\frac{4}{5}|1\right\rangle\langle1|$$

The matrix representation is

$$\sigma = \begin{pmatrix} \dfrac{1}{5} & \dfrac{2}{5} \\[2mm] \dfrac{2}{5} & \dfrac{4}{5} \end{pmatrix}$$

The matrix $\rho - \sigma$ is given by

$$\rho - \sigma = \frac{1}{20}\begin{pmatrix} 6 & -3 \\ -3 & -6 \end{pmatrix}$$

This matrix has two eigenvalues, namely

$$\lambda_1 = -\frac{3}{4\sqrt{5}}, \lambda_2 = \frac{3}{4\sqrt{5}}$$

Using (3.15), we find the trace distance to be

$$\delta(\rho, \sigma) = \frac{1}{2}\sum_i |\lambda_i| = \frac{1}{2}\left(\left|-\frac{3}{4\sqrt{5}}\right| + \left|\frac{3}{4\sqrt{5}}\right|\right) = \frac{3}{4\sqrt{5}}$$

3.7 Fidelity in Quantum Theory

Similarity between two states may be evaluated using the statistical method of "fidelity" [9], which measures the degree of similarity between two distributions. Let us pretend for a moment that we are once again concentrating operators. Precision is guaranteed by

$$F(\rho, \sigma) = \mathrm{Tr}\left(\sqrt{\sqrt{\rho}\,\sigma\sqrt{\rho}}\right) \tag{3.34}$$

When two quantum states are integrated into one, they generate a concept called fidelity. Then there will be two states. The probability of finding the system in a given state may be calculated using the inner product, and vice versa if the system's presence in the state is known in advance. Therefore, this gives a method for evaluating the similarity between the two states. The density operators and make the assumption that they are pure states in the space of all possible variations. Due to the nature of the only pure states, $2 = 1, 2 = 2$, etc. Then

$$F(\rho, \sigma) = \mathrm{Tr}\left(\sqrt{\sqrt{\rho}\,\sigma\sqrt{\rho}}\right) = \mathrm{Tr}_r \sqrt{(|\psi\rangle\langle\psi|)(|\phi\rangle\langle\phi|)(|\psi\rangle\langle\psi|)}$$
$$= \mathrm{Tr}\sqrt{(|\langle\phi|\psi\rangle|)^2\,(|\psi\rangle\langle\psi|)} = |\langle\phi|\psi\rangle|\sqrt{(|\psi\rangle\langle\psi|)} = |\langle\phi|\psi\rangle| \tag{3.35}$$

You can learn about the essential features of loyalty in (13.18). Keep in mind, to begin with, that genuineness is a numeric value between 0 and 1.

$$0 \le F(\rho, \sigma) = \mathrm{Tr} \le 1 \tag{3.36}$$

Since the condition and the state do not overlap, the value is 1. As a result of (13.18) we know that two pure states are the same, even though their faithfulness is the same. That is to say, in most cases, this holds true.

$$F(\rho, \sigma) = F(\sigma, \rho) \tag{3.37}$$

Under unilateral computations, the faithfulness is even more invariant.

$$F(U\rho U^\dagger, U\sigma U^\dagger) = F(\rho, \sigma) \tag{3.38}$$

If both coefficients are located diagonally in the same foundation, then we may describe the fidelity in terms of their principal components. Let us assume that. When both are true

$$F(\rho, \sigma) = \sum_i \sqrt{r_i s_i} \tag{3.39}$$

Example 3.5 Compute the fidelity between [13]

$$\rho = \frac{3}{4}|0\rangle\langle 0| + \frac{1}{4}|1\rangle\langle 1|$$

and each of

$$\sigma = \frac{2}{3}|0\rangle\langle 0| + \frac{1}{3}|1\rangle\langle 1|, \pi = \frac{1}{8}|0\rangle\langle 0| + \frac{7}{8}|1\rangle\langle 1|$$

Can (3.18) or (3.22) be used to determine fidelity?

Solution

First, we compute

$$\sigma^2 = \begin{pmatrix} \frac{3}{4} & 0 \\ 0 & \frac{1}{4} \end{pmatrix} \begin{pmatrix} \frac{3}{4} & 0 \\ 0 & \frac{1}{4} \end{pmatrix} = \begin{pmatrix} \frac{9}{16} & 0 \\ 0 & \frac{1}{16} \end{pmatrix}$$

This is due to the fact that $Tr(2) = 10/161$ is not a deterministic state of the variable. Similar calculations show that $Tr(2) = 5/91$ and $Tr(2) = 50/641$, demonstrating that $Tr(2)$ does not contain any mixed states. That is because the diagonal nature of the combinatorial framework makes it possible for all three density operators to exist (3.22). Consider that [10].

$$\rho\sigma = \begin{pmatrix} \frac{3}{4} & 0 \\ 0 & \frac{1}{4} \end{pmatrix} \begin{pmatrix} \frac{2}{3} & 0 \\ 0 & \frac{1}{3} \end{pmatrix} = \begin{pmatrix} \frac{1}{2} & 0 \\ 0 & \frac{1}{12} \end{pmatrix}$$

$$\sigma\rho = \begin{pmatrix} \frac{2}{3} & 0 \\ 0 & \frac{1}{3} \end{pmatrix} \begin{pmatrix} \frac{3}{4} & 0 \\ 0 & \frac{1}{4} \end{pmatrix} = \begin{pmatrix} \frac{1}{2} & 0 \\ 0 & \frac{1}{12} \end{pmatrix}$$

Therefore $[\rho, \sigma] = 0$. Using (3.22), we find that the fidelity is

$$F(\rho, \sigma) = \sum_i \sqrt{r_i s_i} = \sqrt{\left(\frac{3}{4}\right)\left(\frac{2}{3}\right)} + \sqrt{\left(\frac{1}{4}\right)\left(\frac{1}{3}\right)} = \frac{1}{\sqrt{2}} + \frac{1}{\sqrt{12}}$$

$$= \frac{1 + \sqrt{6}}{\sqrt{12}} = 0.996$$

Since the ration of love to commitment is so close to 1, we can assume that the two states are very similar to one another. Since there is not too much "distance" between the two states in Example 3.2, where the trace distance is just 1/12, we may draw that conclusion. Accordingly, states that are qualitatively near to one another have a small trace distance [11].

Concerning the second state, we find that:

$$F(\rho, \pi) = \sum_i \sqrt{r_i s_i} = \sqrt{\left(\frac{3}{4}\right)\left(\frac{1}{8}\right)} + \sqrt{\left(\frac{1}{4}\right)\left(\frac{7}{8}\right)} = \sqrt{\frac{3}{32}} + \sqrt{\frac{7}{32}}$$

$$= \frac{\sqrt{3} + \sqrt{7}}{\sqrt{32}} = 0.774$$

This suggests that the boundary between these two states is much more porous than it was between the two preceding ones. In Example 3.2, the tracing distance was 5/8 of an inch. Whenever there is less of a connection between states, fidelity drops and trace distance rises.

One possible way to look at loyalty is as a distribution of probabilities based on some other criterion. The % chance of that happening is also given.

$$\Pr(\rho \to \sigma) = (F(\rho, \sigma))^2 \tag{3.40}$$

Example 3.6 Do you know the likelihood for each of the states in the above example to develop into the other two? [13]

Solution
The probability that ρ evolves in to σ is

$$\Pr(\rho \to \sigma) = (F(\rho, \sigma))^2 = (0.996)^2 = 0.992$$

The probability that ρ evolves into π is

$$\Pr(P \to \Pi) = (1 = (p, \Pi))^2 = (0.774)^2 = 0.599$$

Quantum distance metrics based on the accuracy of the analytical method are known as Bures accessibility. The statement is true.

$$d_B^2(p, \sigma) = 2(1 - F(p, \sigma_\sigma)) \tag{3.41}$$

Quantum distance metrics based on the accuracy of the analytical method are known as Bures accessibility. The statement is true.

$$d_B^2(p, \sigma) = 2(1 - F(\rho, \sigma)) \tag{3.42}$$

Example 3.7 Example 3.5 shows that the Bures separation around and is substantially greater than the Bures distance between and.

Solution

In the first case we find that

$$d_{\mathrm{B}}^2(p\ \sigma) = 2(1 - F(p, \sigma)) = 2(1 - 0.996) = 0.008$$

For the other two states we have

$$d_{\mathrm{B}}^2(p\ \sigma) = 2(1 - F(p, \sigma)) = 2(1 - 0.774) = 0.452$$

$$d_{\mathrm{B}}^2(\rho, \pi) \gg d_{\mathrm{B}}^2(\rho, \sigma)$$

The above equation shows common value of particular equation.

Finding the minimum achievable quality on a given channel is important in a variety of contexts. This is due to the fact that, in the absence of knowledge of the quantum state, a study of a given frequency channel in the worst-case scenario may be calculated by computing the least fidelity [12].

Example 3.8 The probability of a bit-flip error on a given quantum channel is $p = 1/9$. In this case, how much accuracy can the bit flip channel keep? In this scenario, we will pretend that the system starts off in a pristine state.

$$\rho = |\psi\rangle\langle\psi|$$

Solution

In this chapter, the bit-flip channel was explained. While it is possible that the qubit does not experience any change, it has a greater than one-to-one likelihood of making a mistake (1ρ). It is called a quantum action because

$$\rho' = \phi(\rho) = p\rho + (1 - p)X\rho X$$

The fidelity between this state and $\rho = |\psi\rangle\langle\psi|$ is given by

$$F(\rho, \rho') = F(\rho', \rho) = \mathrm{Tr}(\sqrt{\sqrt{\rho'\rho}\sqrt{\rho'}}) = Tr\sqrt{\sqrt{\rho'}\,(|\psi\rangle\langle\psi|)\,\sqrt{\rho'}}$$

Using simplifies the fidelity to

$$F(\rho', \rho) = \sqrt{\langle\psi|(p\rho + (1 - p)X\rho X)|\psi\rangle}$$

$$= \sqrt{\langle\psi|(p|\psi\rangle\langle\psi| + (1 - p)X|\psi\rangle\langle\psi|X)|\psi\rangle}$$

$$= \sqrt{p + (1 - p)\langle\psi|X|\psi\rangle\langle\psi|X|\psi\rangle}$$

$$= \sqrt{p + (1 - p)\langle\psi|X|\psi\rangle^2}$$

Finding the condition in which F is maximal will help us identify the worst-case scenario. As it is obvious that, the corresponding value will be used for when. Therefore, we must determine the location where.

Notice that if

$$|\psi\rangle = \frac{|0\rangle + i|1\rangle}{\sqrt{2}}$$

Then,

$$\langle \psi | X | \psi \rangle = \left(\frac{|0\rangle - i\langle 1|}{\sqrt{2}} \right) X \left(\frac{|0\rangle + i\langle 1|}{\sqrt{2}} \right) = \left(\frac{|0\rangle - i\langle 1|}{\sqrt{2}} \right) \left(\frac{|1\rangle + i\langle 0|}{\sqrt{2}} \right)$$

$$= \frac{i\langle 0|0\rangle - i\langle 1|1\rangle}{2} = 0$$

Let us verify that $|\psi\rangle$ is a pure state. We find that

$$\rho = |\psi\rangle\langle\psi| = \frac{1}{2} \begin{pmatrix} 1 & -i \\ i & 1 \end{pmatrix}$$

$$\rho^2 = \frac{1}{4} \begin{pmatrix} 2 & -2i \\ 2i & 2 \end{pmatrix}$$

So, we have $\text{Tr}(\rho^2) = \frac{1}{4}(2 + 2) = 1$ and this is a pure state. So, the minimum fidelity occurs when $\langle \psi | X | \psi \rangle = 0$, in which case

$$F(\rho, \rho') = \sqrt{p}$$

For the case where $p = 1/9$ the minimum fidelity is $F_{\min} = \sqrt{1/9} \approx 0.33$.

3.8 Quantum Entanglement

This section revisits the topic of examining the interference of two qubits. When describing a state, how much attachment does it have, and how much entanglement is required to establish a certain state? One method for describing entanglement is via the calculation of concordance. Formal network computations might help us estimate the energy and time commitment associated with achieving entanglement.

Let us start by taking a look at how widespread the consensus is. Essentially, it is a way to quantify the degree to which the boundaries of two states meet. Plus a country:

$$C(\varphi) = |\langle \varphi | \tilde{\psi} \rangle| \tag{3.43}$$

In what location is the state's Fourier transform not to be found? Alternatively, the density operator may be used to determine concurrence by considering the amount.

Example 3.9 Entanglement and coincidence are related to one another. Concentrate on the end result.

$$|\varphi\rangle = |0\rangle \oplus |1\rangle$$

demonstration that there is no concordance at all.

So there is absolutely no consensus. By describing the operators using matrices, we can see how concurrency vanishes. So, this is a start.

This state's density operator is given below

Hence

$$\rho(Y \otimes Y)\rho^{\dagger}(Y \otimes Y)$$

$$= \begin{pmatrix} 0 & 0 & 0 & 0 \\ 0 & 1 & 0 & 0 \\ 0 & 0 & 0 & 0 \\ 0 & 0 & 0 & 0 \end{pmatrix} \begin{pmatrix} 0 & 0 & 0 & -1 \\ 0 & 0 & 1 & 0 \\ 0 & 1 & 0 & 0 \\ -1 & 0 & 0 & 0 \end{pmatrix} \begin{pmatrix} 0 & 0 & 0 & 0 \\ 0 & 1 & 0 & 0 \\ 0 & 0 & 0 & 0 \\ 0 & 0 & 0 & 0 \end{pmatrix} \begin{pmatrix} 0 & 0 & 0 & -1 \\ 0 & 0 & 1 & 0 \\ 0 & 1 & 0 & 0 \\ -1 & 0 & 0 & 0 \end{pmatrix}$$

$$= \begin{pmatrix} 0 & 0 & 0 & 0 \\ 0 & 1 & 0 & 0 \\ 0 & 0 & 0 & 0 \\ 0 & 0 & 0 & 0 \end{pmatrix} \begin{pmatrix} 0 & 0 & 0 & -1 \\ 0 & 0 & 1 & 0 \\ 0 & 1 & 0 & 0 \\ -1 & 0 & 0 & 0 \end{pmatrix} \begin{pmatrix} 0 & 0 & 0 & 0 \\ 0 & 0 & 1 & 0 \\ 0 & 0 & 0 & 0 \\ 0 & 0 & 0 & 0 \end{pmatrix}$$

$$= \begin{pmatrix} 0 & 0 & 0 & 0 \\ 0 & 0 & 0 & 0 \\ 0 & 0 & 0 & 0 \\ 0 & 0 & 0 & 0 \end{pmatrix}$$

The match might be established by inspecting the matrix's principal components. This matrix has zero eigenvalues, meaning that the entries do not coincide. The key elements of the matrices may also be used to describe concurrency.

$$R = \sqrt{\sqrt{p}P\sqrt{p}} \qquad (3.44)$$

which are denoted by $\lambda_1, \lambda_2, \lambda_3, \lambda_4$. The concurrence is

$$C(9) = \max\{0, \lambda_1 - \lambda_2 - \lambda_3 - \lambda_4\} \qquad (3.45)$$

where $\lambda_1 \geq \lambda_2 \geq \lambda_3 \geq \lambda_4$. In the next two cases, we will look at how entanglement entities may coexist.

Example 3.10 Find the concurrence of below

Solution

The density operator in this case is given below.

The matrix representation is

$$p = 1/2 \begin{matrix} 0 & 0 & 0 \\ 0 & 1 & -1 \\ 0 & 0 & 0 \end{matrix}$$

So, we have

$$\rho(Y \otimes Y)\rho^\dagger(Y \otimes Y) \otimes \begin{pmatrix} 0 & 0 & 0 & 0 \\ 0 & 1 & -1 & 0 \\ 0 & -1 & 1 & 0 \\ 0 & 0 & 0 & 0 \end{pmatrix} \begin{pmatrix} 0 & 0 & 0 & -1 \\ 0 & 0 & 1 & 0 \\ 0 & 1 & 0 & 0 \\ -1 & 0 & 0 & 0 \end{pmatrix} \begin{pmatrix} 0 & 0 & 0 & 0 \\ 0 & 1 & -1 & 0 \\ 0 & -1 & 1 & 0 \\ 0 & 0 & 0 & 0 \end{pmatrix} \begin{pmatrix} 0 & 0 & 0 & -1 \\ 0 & 0 & 1 & 0 \\ 0 & 1 & 0 & 0 \\ -1 & 0 & 0 & 0 \end{pmatrix}$$

$$= \frac{1}{4} \begin{pmatrix} 0 & 0 & 0 & 0 \\ 0 & 1 & -1 & 0 \\ 0 & -1 & 1 & 0 \\ 0 & 0 & 0 & 0 \end{pmatrix} \begin{pmatrix} 0 & 0 & 0 & -1 \\ 0 & 0 & 1 & 0 \\ 0 & 1 & 0 & 0 \\ -1 & 0 & 0 & 0 \end{pmatrix} \begin{pmatrix} 0 & 0 & 0 & 0 \\ 0 & -1 & 1 & 0 \\ 0 & 1 & -1 & 0 \\ 0 & 0 & 0 & 0 \end{pmatrix}$$

$$= \frac{1}{4} \begin{pmatrix} 0 & 0 & 0 & 0 \\ 0 & 1 & -1 & 0 \\ 0 & -1 & 1 & 0 \\ 0 & 0 & 0 & 0 \end{pmatrix}$$

The eigenvalues of this matrix are

$$\lambda_1 = 1, \lambda_2 = \lambda_3 = \lambda_4 = 0$$

Using (3.29), we find the concurrence to be
$$C(p) = \max \{0, \lambda_1 - \lambda_2 - \lambda_3 - \lambda_4 = \max \{0, 1\} = 1$$

Example 3.11   Find the concurrence of below

$$|\varphi\rangle = \frac{|00\rangle + |11\rangle}{\sqrt{2}}$$

Solution
The density operator in this case is given by

$$\rho(Y \otimes Y)\rho^\dagger(Y \otimes Y)$$

$$= \frac{1}{4} \begin{pmatrix} 1 & 0 & 0 & 1 \\ 0 & 0 & 0 & 0 \\ 0 & 0 & 0 & 0 \\ 1 & 0 & 0 & 1 \end{pmatrix} \begin{pmatrix} 0 & 0 & 0 & -1 \\ 0 & 0 & 1 & 0 \\ 0 & 1 & 0 & 0 \\ -1 & 0 & 0 & 0 \end{pmatrix} \begin{pmatrix} 1 & 0 & 0 & 1 \\ 0 & 0 & 0 & 0 \\ 0 & 0 & 0 & 0 \\ 1 & 0 & 0 & 1 \end{pmatrix} \begin{pmatrix} 0 & 0 & 0 & -1 \\ 0 & 0 & 1 & 0 \\ 0 & 1 & 0 & 0 \\ -1 & 0 & 0 & 0 \end{pmatrix}$$

$$= \frac{1}{4} \begin{pmatrix} 1 & 0 & 0 & 1 \\ 0 & 0 & 0 & 0 \\ 0 & 0 & 0 & 0 \\ 1 & 0 & 0 & 1 \end{pmatrix} \begin{pmatrix} 0 & 0 & 0 & -1 \\ 0 & 0 & 1 & 0 \\ 0 & 1 & 0 & 0 \\ -1 & 0 & 0 & 0 \end{pmatrix} \begin{pmatrix} -1 & 0 & 0 & -1 \\ 0 & 0 & 0 & 0 \\ 0 & 0 & 0 & 0 \\ -1 & 0 & 0 & -1 \end{pmatrix}$$

$$= \frac{1}{2} \begin{pmatrix} 1 & 0 & 0 & 1 \\ 0 & 0 & 0 & 0 \\ 0 & 0 & 0 & 0 \\ 1 & 0 & 0 & 1 \end{pmatrix}$$

Concurrence is 1 since the eigenvalues are 1, 0, 0, 0. The Shannon entropy will be explained in the following paragraphs.

$$h(p) = -p\log_2 p - (1-p)\log_2 (1-p) \tag{3.46}$$

Concurring opinion is used to describe the interconnectedness in development.

$$E(p) = h\left(\frac{1+\sqrt{1-C(p)2}}{2}\right) \tag{3.47}$$

In mathematics, the resources needed to construct an entangled state are described.

Example 3.12 Find the entanglement of formation for the Werner state

$$\rho = \frac{5}{6}(\emptyset+)\rho^{\dagger}(\emptyset) + \frac{1}{24} \Rightarrow l4 = \begin{pmatrix} \frac{11}{24} & 0 & 0 & \frac{5}{12} \\ 0 & \frac{1}{24} & 0 & 0 \\ 0 & 0 & \frac{1}{24} & 0 \\ \frac{5}{12} & 0 & 0 & \frac{11}{24} \end{pmatrix}$$

Solution
First, we have

$$\rho(Y \otimes Y)\rho^{\dagger}(Y \otimes Y) \Rightarrow \rho^2 = \begin{pmatrix} \frac{221}{576} & 0 & 0 & \frac{55}{144} \\ 0 & \frac{1}{576} & 0 & 0 \\ 0 & 0 & \frac{1}{576} & 0 \\ \frac{55}{144} & 0 & 0 & \frac{221}{576} \end{pmatrix}$$

The eigenvalues of this matrix are
$$\lambda_i = \frac{49}{64}, \frac{1}{576}, \frac{1}{576}, \frac{1}{576}$$
From (3.12) the concurrence is
$C(p) = 0.76$
From the entanglement of formation is

$$E(p) = -\frac{1 \pm \sqrt{1-C(p)^2}}{2a}\log_2\frac{1 \pm \sqrt{1-C(p)^2}}{2a} - \frac{1 \pm \sqrt{1-C(p)^2}}{2a}\log_2$$
$$\times \frac{1 \pm \sqrt{1-C(p)^2}}{2a} = 0.67$$

The entangled formation in Example 13.10, as well as the entangled formation in Example 13.11, are both 1, according to this proof.

3.9 Information Content and Entropy

Entropy is a helpful metric for quantifying the amount of data included in a signal. Suppose, for the sake of argument, that X is a completely random event. Prior to taking a measurement, entropy reveals how little we know about the random input. Variables another way of looking at it is that the entropy of X informs us how much information we can expect to learn about it from the evaluation. The probability of an outcome is expressed as an entropy value. Take the case when there are n possible outcomes and the probability of the jth outcome is $pj = 1$. To that end, we may determine the Shannon entropy H by

$$H = -\sum_{j=1}^{n} pj \log_2 Pj \tag{3.48}$$

A few different types of entropy functions, including the binary entropy function. The graphic demonstrates that entropy has a concave shape. In other terms,

$$\lambda H(p) + (1 - \lambda) H(q) \le H(\lambda p + (1 - \lambda)q) \tag{3.49}$$

The highest levels of entropy occur in conditions of maximum ignorance. In the case of discrete possibilities pj, the least amount of data is available when all of the possible outcomes of a study are of equal likelihood. This means that there is a probability assigned to each of the n possible outcomes.

$$pj = \frac{1}{n}$$

Binary entropy is one example of this. Is there a third option? To begin, let us assume that $x = 1/2$ is a mathematically probable outcome for both. Then, we have

$$-x \log x - (1 - x) \log(1 - x) = 1$$

Suppose, for the moment, that one result is much more probable than the other. As an example, if x is equal to 0, the likelihood of discovering an option is $1x = 0.8$. Because one possibility is more frequent than the other, we have more information about the state before the measurement in this case. Here's how it works:

$$-x \log x - (1 - x) \log(1 - x) = 72$$

It is possible to view the alternatives if $x = 0.05$, which means that there is a 95% likelihood.

$$-x \log x - (1 - x) \log(1 - x) = 0.29$$

For example, if there are two alternative possibilities and we are unsure of which one will occur, then we should choose the one that is more likely to occur.

$$H(X) = 1$$

The entropy in this situation is at its highest point. The rest of the time

$$H(X) < 1$$

The greater the entropy, the more uncertain you are about the result. Let us say X and Y are two independents randomly initialized. $P(x, y) = (x, y)/p(x, y)$ is the joint Shannon entropy of the two results.

$$H(X, Y) = -\sum_{x,y} p(x, y) \log(p(x, y)) \tag{3.50}$$

In general, the accompanying inconsistency, referred to as principal component analysis, is respected:

$$H(X, Y) \leq H(X) + H(Y) \tag{3.51}$$

If the distributions X and Y are independently, equality holds in (3.35) Given X and Y, the unconditional entropy is

$$H(X \mid Y) \leq H(X) - H(Y) \tag{3.52}$$

An analog of the Shannon entropy is needed to measure the entropy in a quantum state. Density operators, rather than conditional probability elements, are used in this case (3.32). Von Neumann entropy refers to the entropy of a superposition state whose density operator has a value of 0 and is given by

$$S(p) = -\mathrm{Tr}(p \log_2 p) \tag{3.53}$$

A state's relative Von Neumann entropy is

$$S(p \| \sigma) = \mathrm{Tr}\,(p \log p) - \mathrm{Tr}\,(p \log \sigma) \tag{3.54}$$

Note that $S(\rho \| \sigma) \geq 0$ with equality if and only if $\rho = \sigma$. Say that I is a density operator, and then assume that its principal components are given by the Von Neumann entropy may be expressed in terms of eigenvectors.

$$S(p) = -\sum_i \lambda_i \log_2 \lambda_i \tag{3.55}$$

Example 3.13   A qubit's most fully mixed state is

$$p = \begin{matrix} \dfrac{1}{2} & 0 \\ 0 & \dfrac{1}{2} \end{matrix}$$

What is the von Neumann entropy for this state?

Solution

The eigenvalues are

$$\lambda_1 \lambda_2 = \frac{1}{2}, \frac{1}{2}$$

Using we find the entropy to be

$$S(p) = -\sum_i \lambda_i \log_2 \lambda_i = -\frac{1}{2} \log_2 \left(\frac{1}{2}\right) - \frac{1}{2} \log_2 \left(\frac{1}{2}\right) = -\log_2 \left(\frac{1}{2}\right) = \log_2 2 = 1$$

In general, the totally mixed configuration of a quantum states in a Hilbert space of size n possesses entropy.

$$\log_2 n \tag{3.56}$$

Example 3.14   Find the entropy of the two states

$$p = \begin{matrix} \dfrac{3}{4} & 0 \\ 0 & \dfrac{1}{4} \end{matrix}, \quad \sigma = \begin{matrix} \dfrac{9}{10} & 0 \\ 0 & \dfrac{1}{10} \end{matrix}$$

Solution

In certain cases, the similarity may be determined by looking at the major components of the matrix. The eigenvalues of this matrix are all 0, which means that the entries are not equal. Key features of the matrices may also be utilized to characterize concurrency.

$$S(p) = -\frac{3}{4} \log_2 \left(\frac{3}{4}\right) - \frac{1}{4} \log_2 \left(\frac{1}{4}\right) = 0.81$$

For σ we find that

$$S(p) = -\frac{3}{4} \log_2 \left(\frac{3}{4}\right) - \frac{1}{4} \log_2 \left(\frac{1}{4}\right) = 0.47$$

We have a better understanding of the situation before a measurement is taken since it is significantly more likely that the result will be accurate $|0\rangle$.

Example 3.15   The state's entropy may be determined.

$$p = \begin{matrix} \dfrac{1}{2} & \dfrac{1}{4} \\ \dfrac{1}{4} & \dfrac{1}{2} \end{matrix}$$

Solution

These are the matrix's eigenvectors:

$$\lambda_{1,2} = \left\{ \frac{3}{4}, \frac{1}{4} \right\}$$

The question is whether this is a clean or a composite state. In Example 5.6, we discovered that this was the case.

$$\rho^2 = \begin{pmatrix} \frac{1}{2} & \frac{1}{4} \\ \frac{1}{4} & \frac{1}{2} \end{pmatrix} \begin{pmatrix} \frac{1}{2} & \frac{1}{4} \\ \frac{1}{4} & \frac{1}{2} \end{pmatrix} = \begin{pmatrix} \frac{5}{16} & \frac{1}{4} \\ \frac{1}{4} & \frac{5}{16} \end{pmatrix}$$

$$\Rightarrow \mathrm{Tr}(\rho^2) = \frac{5}{16} + \frac{5}{16} = \frac{10}{16} = \frac{5}{8}$$

As a result, we are in a state of flux. In spite of the obvious differences, the permeability is the same as in the preceding example:

$$S(p) = -\frac{3}{4} \log_2 \left(\frac{3}{4} \right) - \frac{1}{4} \log_2 \left(\frac{1}{4} \right) = 0.81$$

The most entropic state is a fully mixed one, whereas the least entropic state is a pure one.

Example 3.16   Find the state's entropy.

$$|\varphi\rangle = \frac{|0\rangle + |1\rangle}{\sqrt{2}}$$

Solution

The densities operator is the first step. It seems to us

$$\rho = |\psi\rangle\langle\psi| = \left(\frac{|0\rangle + |1\rangle}{\sqrt{2}} \right) \left(\frac{\langle 0| + \langle 1|}{\sqrt{2}} \right)$$

$$= \frac{1}{2} \left(|0\rangle\langle 0| + |0\rangle\langle 1| + |1\rangle\langle 0| + |1\rangle\langle 1| \right)$$

Thus, the matrix form of this manufacturing capacities is thus

$$p = \frac{1}{2} \begin{pmatrix} 1 & 1 \\ 1 & 1 \end{pmatrix}$$

These are the matrix's eigenvalues:

$$\lambda_{1,2} = \{1, 0\}$$

The fact that we can employ to compute entropy

$$\lim_{x \to 0} x \log x = 0$$

As a result, we merely have to think about =1 and discover that

$$S(p) = -\log_2 (1) = 0$$

There is no entropy in this state since it is a pure state. We have complete knowledge of the system's status prior to measuring; therefore, there is no room for guesswork.

The differences in communication govern the entropy of a superposition state in n dimensions:

$$\log_2 n \geq S(p) \geq 0 \tag{3.57}$$

Both extremes have been shown. The bottom limit in is the entirely mixed state, which has entropy provided by $\log_2 n$ and is defined by equally likely outcomes $p_i = 1/n$ (3.41). Next, we will illustrate how the von Neumann entropy remains constant even when the basis is changed.

Example 3.17 Let $\rho = \frac{3}{4}|+\rangle\langle+| + \frac{1}{4}|-\rangle\langle-|$. The entropy of the state must be shown to be invariant by a change in the base.

Solution
The matrix representation of this state is

$$p = \begin{matrix} \frac{3}{4} & 0 \\ 0 & \frac{1}{4} \end{matrix}$$

Note that this matrix is written in the $\{|\pm\rangle\}$ basis. The eigenvalues are $\lambda_{1,2} = \left\{\frac{3}{4}, \frac{1}{4}\right\}$ and we have already seen that the entropy in this case is

$$S(p) = -\frac{3}{4}\log_2\left(\frac{3}{4}\right) - \frac{1}{4}\log_2\left(\frac{1}{4}\right) = 0.81$$

What will happen if we represent the information in the supercomputing basis? If so, the matrices representations may be found in

$$p = \begin{matrix} \frac{1}{2} & \frac{1}{4} \\ \frac{1}{4} & \frac{1}{2} \end{matrix}$$

In Example 3.15, we saw this matrix. Once again, we see that the eigenvalues are identical.

$$S(p) = -\frac{3}{4}\log_2\left(\frac{3}{4}\right) - \frac{1}{4}\log_2\left(\frac{1}{4}\right) = 0.81$$

Consider now the states that are created by the tensor combinations of qubits. If a composites state can be broken down into its component parts, then a state like as $\rho \otimes \sigma$, entropy is additive in the sense that

$$S(p \oplus \sigma) = S(p) + s(\sigma) \tag{3.58}$$

Entropy, in general, is not additive. Reduction matrices of the composite structure are given by the following equations: Suggests there is a subadditivity inequality.

$$S(p) \leq S(PA) + S(PB) \tag{3.59}$$

Since ignorance reduces while evaluating the system as a whole, finding $S()$ less than the modified density matrices entropies shows that studying the system as a whole gives you the greatest knowledge about an entangled system. The reduced density matrix multiplication A and B provide Alice and Bob additional information about the structure of the network while just examining their sections of the system.

Example 3.18 Each of Alice and Bob has a member of an EPR pair in the Bells state that they share with the other:

Entropy as observed by Alice and Bob is a measure of the whole system's entropy.

Solution
We showed that the density operator for this state is

$$\rho = |\beta_{10}\rangle\langle\beta_{10}|$$

$$= \left(\frac{|0_A\rangle|0_B\rangle - |1_A\rangle|1_B\rangle}{\sqrt{2}} \right) \left(\frac{\langle 0_A|\langle 0_B| - \langle 1_A|\langle 1_B|}{\sqrt{2}} \right)$$

$$= \frac{|0_A\rangle|0_B\rangle\langle 0_A|\langle 0_B| - |0_A\rangle|0_B\rangle\langle 1_A|\langle 1_B| - |1_A\rangle|1_B\rangle\langle 0_A|\langle 0_B| + |1_A\rangle|1_B\rangle\langle 1_A|\langle 1_B|}{2}$$

As a result, the entropy is easily calculated to be $S(P) = -\log 1 = 0$. We calculate the partial trace of this density operator to get the states as seen by Alice and Bob separately.

$$P_B = \frac{1}{2} \begin{pmatrix} 1 & 0 \\ 0 & 1 \end{pmatrix}$$

This is the utterly mixed state with entropy given by

$$S_B(P_B) = \log_2\left(\frac{1}{2}\right) = 1$$

We find a similar result for Alice, and clearly (3.43) is satisfied.

References

1 Stanzl-Tschegg, S. (2014). Very high cycle fatigue measuring techniques‖. *International Journal of Fatigue* 60: 2–17.

2 Zhu, Y., Davis, S.W., Narayan, R. et al. (2012). The eye of the storm: light from the inner plunging region of black hole accretion discs‖. *Monthly Notices of the Royal Astronomical Society* 424 (4): 2504–2521.

3 Paul, H. (2004). *Introduction to Quantum Optics: From Light Quanta to Quantum Teleportation.* Cambridge University Press.

4 Guillemin, V. (2003). *The Story of Quantum Mechanics.* Courier Corporation.

5 Harrison, P. and Valavanis, A. (2016). *Quantum Wells, Wires, and Dots: Theoretical and Computational Physics of Semiconductor Nanostructures.* Wiley.

6 Pinski, P., Riplinger, C., Valeev, E.F., and Neese, F. (2015). Sparse maps—a systematic infrastructure for reduced-scaling electronic structure methods. I. An efficient and simple linear scaling local MP_2 method that uses an intermediate basis of pair natural orbitals. *The Journal of Chemical Physics* 143 (3): 034108.

7 Gilman, J. (2003). *Electronic Basis of the Strength of Materials‖.* Cambridge University Press.

8 Bollig, T. (2018). *Scientific Revolution in the Development of the Rutherford-Bohr Model of the Atom.* Springer.

9 English, N. (2016). *Space Telescopes: Capturing the Rays of the Electromagnetic Spectrum.* Springer.

10 De Broglie, L. (2012). *Heisenberg'S Uncertainties and the Probabilistic Interpretation of Wave Mechanics: With Critical Notes of the Author*, vol. 40. Springer Science & Business Media.

11 Capra, F. (2010). *The Tao of Physics: An Exploration of the Parallels Between Modern Physics and Eastern Mysticism.* Shambhala Publications.

12 Roca, C.P., Cuesta, J.A., and Sánchez, A. Evolutionary game theory: Temporal and spatial effects beyond replicator dynamics. *Physics of Life Reviews* 6 (4): 208–249.

13 McMahon, D. (2007). *Quantum Computing Explained, "IEEE Computer Society".* A John Wiley & Sons.

4

Foundations of Quantum Computing

In both classical processing and quantum entanglement, bits serve as fundamental measurement units. Quantum bits may be physically implemented in an array in the same ways that classical bits can be: in a wide number of ways. As with traditional computer science, we will not give much thought to the actual implementation of quantum bits.

4.1 Single-Qubit

4.1.1 Photon Polarization in Quantum Computing

There exists a simple experiment that can demonstrate the nonnutritive behavior of quantum systems, which is put to great use in quantum algorithms and protocols. Any photography supply store should have everything you need to do this experiment: a polaroid camera, a laser pointer, and three (polarization filters). The theories and mathematical models of theoretical physics that were used to explain this uncomplicated experiment [1] also give a clear explanation of the quantum bit, which is the primary component of quantum systems on which computational and mathematical computation is carried out.

Using this experiment, we can see how a quantum bit may be realized in the physical world, which reveals some of the fundamental aspects of quantum measurement. We strongly recommend that you do the investigation on your own time and collect the data on your own schedule.

- Give this simple experiment a shot: project a moving image onto a screen by making use of a laser beam. When polaroid A is positioned in between the screen and the source of light, there is a reduction in the amount of light that reaches the monitor. Take into account the fact that polaroid A has a horizontal polarization. Slide polaroid C in front of the projection screen and behind polaroid A.

Quantum Computing: A New Era of Computing, First Edition.
Kuldeep Singh Kaswan, Jagjit Singh Dhatterwal, Anupam Baliyan, and Shalli Rani.
© 2023 The Institute of Electrical and Electronics Engineers, Inc. Published 2023 by John Wiley & Sons, Inc.

Because the polarization of A is orthogonal to the plane of the film, polaroid C is invisible on the monitor (vertical).

It makes sense to put A and C adjacent to each other. Since no light has traveled through the first two polaroid layers, it is safe to conclude that no light will travel through the third. The screen is visible from at most B polarization angles.

If B's polarization is perpendicular to those of A and C, the effect will be strongest.

Since adding polaroid B increases the number of photons reaching the display, it is evident that the polaroids are not acting as simple sieves [2].

- The Quantum Role in the Explanation:

Waves may be the most appropriate conceptual framework within which to frame investigations that make use of concentrated rays of light. The experiment that is detailed here makes use of light that is so dim that there is just a single photon's worth of interaction between the polaroid and the light. Similar experiments have been conducted with more complex pieces of machinery. As a consequence of these single-photon investigations, the traditional nonlinear dynamics can no longer satisfactorily explain the outcomes that have been seen. This peculiar behavior may be seen in other realms outside the domain of light. The two components that make up the molecular mechanics description of the experiment are a photon polarization information address and a polaroid-photon application interface. In order to carry out this investigation, basic mathematical concepts, such as the idea of a qubit [3], are used extensively. The percentage difference of a photon is characterized as a unit vector in quantum physics, and this vector points in the appropriate direction. Consider it to be a vector that has had the letter v slapped on top of it to denote either transversal or longitudinally polarization. The conventional notation for a vector that expresses the physical phenomenon of a subatomic particle is seen in Figure 4.1.

$$1v' = a|-1^4 + b| \rightarrow 0$$

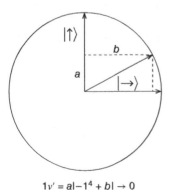

Figure 4.1 Measurement of state.

$1v' = a|-1^4 + b| \rightarrow 0$

This use of the letter *v* for a vector is consistent with other uses of the letter *v*. For any desired polarization, just add the two basis vectors together linearly to get a unit vector representing a 45°- polarization angle. Coefficients *a* and *b* in the orientations [4] represent the amplitudes.

When seen through the lens of quantum physics, the interaction that takes place between a photon and a polaroid looks somewhat like this. In a polaroid, polarization may be achieved most effectively along one particular axis. By quadrupling the concentration of the polarization along the photon's preferred axis, one may determine the likelihood that a photon will be able to pass through a polaroid and reach its destination. The probability of the polaroid capturing a photon is related to the cube of the amplitude of the light traveling in a direction that is perpendicular to the polaroid's preferred axis.

Now, the direction in which photons enter the camera, rather than the direction in which they exit, is used to determine the polarization of the photons. All linkages between qubits and measurement equipment are characterized by their probabilistic nature, as shown by this experiment, as well as the state change that follows [5].

As an illustration of what a quantum bit is, take into consideration the whole range of possibilities for the polarization of a single photon (or qubit). There is no limit to the amount of values that may be expressed in a qubit so long as just one unit vector is used. Even if the amplitudes (*a* and *b*) are not necessarily essential for the interpretation of the experiment, it is possible for them to have values that are complicated. Circular polarization may be thought of as the equivalent of the imaginary portions of a polarized photon.

The collection of all the different potential configurations of a physical system is referred to as that system's state space. Two-dimensional complex vector spaces, often known as qubits, are one way that quantum mechanical systems may be represented. (Every time a vector is multiplied by a quadratic function of length modulus one, this representation shows the same quantum state as a result.) There is a need for redundancy.

Effects such as photon dispersion, electron spin, and the atomic states of matter are examples of two-state quantum phenomena. It is not meant to imply that there are only two distinct states that are attainable within the context of this state space; rather, the term "two-state" is used to describe the possibility that any state that can be imagined can be represented by a straightforward linear combination of the two forms. A two-dimensional complex vector space may be thought of as a qubit if and only if it is possible to differentiate between two separate labeled representative equation states. According to the quantum cognitive theory of multimedia learning, existing nuclear levels and electron spin are equally effective as two-state systems. This holds true for both of these types of systems. The physical realizations of high-performance computing input devices, such as quantum mechanics, have not yet been defined, and it is still uncertain whether two-state systems are particularly appropriate for the development of such technologies [6].

4.2 Multi-qubit

Systems with more than one qubit provide us a glimpse of the potential advantages of using quantum states to encode data. In contrast to classical systems, when more particles are added, the quantum state space expands in a way that is exponential. When compared to classical encoding, the process of storing computing knowledge in the quantum states of a system consisting of *n* particles allows a great deal more flexibility. Chapter 5 of this book will investigate several ways in which these enormous state spaces might be used to speed up the calculating process.

The differing ways in which classical and quantum states combine contribute to their enormous size differences. Let us pretend you have a multi-part, macroscopic physical system. It is possible to provide a complete description of the state of this classical system by first detailing the states of its individual parts. Characterizing a complicated quantum system in terms of the states of its components gets increasingly challenging as the system's complexity increases. "Entangled" states are those that defy description. The entangled state is a crucial part of quantum computing [7].

Entangled states are a quirk of quantum mechanics with no counterpart in classical physics. Entangled states populate the vast quantum state spaces of a multi-qubit system. Since the behavior of entangled states cannot be simulated by conventional computers, the field of quantum computing had to be established by pioneers like Feynman and Manin.

The early parts of this chapter include mostly abstract information essential for developing the mathematical framework required to comprehend multi-qubit systems. Lots of examples will be provided to help illustrate the points spoken and the difference between the tensor product of most of the example imply on problem to solve. We define a collection of vector spaces, investigate the ramifications of this formalization, and then analyze the direct sum of two or more vector spaces. In this section, we launch into an analysis of how the unique quantum features of the entangled states come to be. We demonstrate this phenomenon in the setting of a second quantum key content delivery system [8].

4.2.1 Blocks of Quantum States

Since each member of an ensemble may be represented by a single vector in a two-dimensional space, it is possible to utilize $2n$-dimensional vector spaces to depict the possible states of *n* items. For classical state space integration, the direct sum is utilized. Each individual system's state space is substantially smaller than the aggregated state space when dealing with quantum coherence in this double vector representation. When we linearly combine the vector spaces of our quantum particles, we obtain a space with $2n$ dimensions. To begin comparing the sizes of produced spaces, we will first examine the comprehensive definitions of a direct sum and the tensor products.

4.2.2 Submission of Vector Space in Quantum Computing

To get the distance matrix with basis $,\ldots, m$, just take the direct sum $V\,W$ of two vector spaces, each of which has bases A, and you will have the desired result. This fundamental arrangement is wholly determined by chance. Because $V\,W$ has a dimension of $n + m$, it follows that for every element with n and m dimensions, there are $n + m$ zeros in $V\,W$.

$$\dim(V \oplus W) = \dim(V) + \dim(W)$$

Integrating the outcomes of operations performed on the two linked vector spaces gives rise to the definitions of the mathematical operations of addition and scalar multiplication. When spaces V and W are embedded, the result is a product referred to as the typical $V\,W$ kernel function.

$$(\omega_2) \oplus (w_2 l)(1\,v_2)J = \varsigma_2^v \big| 4 \vdash \langle w_2 \big| 4 \rangle$$

Since v and w are mirror images of one another when evaluated with the standard kernel function, they naturally embed in $v\,w$.

Only two points need to be considered in order to completely characterize the states of O_1, O_2, and O_3 using only their dimensions (x_i, y_i) and angular velocities (p_i, r_i). Therefore, the state of the environment may be described as a straightforward tally of all of its components, which are as follows:

$$\begin{pmatrix} x \\ R \end{pmatrix}^{-} \oplus \begin{pmatrix} x_2 \\ 312 \end{pmatrix} \oplus \begin{pmatrix} n_3 \\ l_3^s \end{pmatrix} = \begin{pmatrix} \sum_{s_{13}}^{n_1} x \end{pmatrix}$$

In general, the number of possible states for n such conventional objects is $2n$. In this way, the total number of items in the dynamical system grows exponentially.

4.2.3 Vector Spacing in Quantum Blocks

The nautical miles vector interior with the basis comprising of the nm elements of the form where is the convolutional product, an abstract binary operator that satisfies the following connections, can be obtained by combining different vector spaces V and W with bases $A = |1, |2,\ldots,|n$ and B, respectively. This results in the nm-dimensional embeddings.

$$(|v_1\rangle + |v_2\rangle) \otimes |w\rangle = |v_1\rangle \otimes |w\rangle + |v_2\rangle \otimes | w$$

Taking $k = \min(n,m)$, all elements of $V \otimes W$ have form

$$|v_1\rangle \otimes |w_1 \quad v_2\rangle \otimes |w_2 \qquad + | \quad + \cdots + |v_k\rangle \otimes |w_k$$

for some $v_i \in V$ and $w_i \in W$. Since the tensor product is defined by a set of relations, its representation is not special. More so, although it is true that $V\,W$'s constituent parts may be reduced to a set of

$$\alpha_1(|\alpha_1\rangle \otimes |\beta_1\rangle) + \alpha_2(|\alpha_2\rangle \otimes |\beta_1\rangle) + \cdots + \alpha_{nm}(|\alpha_n\rangle \otimes |\beta_m\rangle),$$

most elements of $V \otimes W$ cannot be written as $|v\rangle \otimes |w$, where $v \in V$ and $w \in W$. It is common to write $v\,w$ for $v\rangle \otimes |w|\,|\,|$.

Example 4.1 Let V and W both be two-dimensional vector spaces, and let A and B, their respective orthonormal bases, have the values $|1,|2$. We are able to define the components of V and W by making use of the notation $|v = a1|1 + a2|2$ and $|w = b1|1 + b2|2$, respectively. Then, if we make the assumption that V and W are both vector spaces that map to a qubit and make use of the conventional basis of $|0,|1$, then $V\,W$ has as its basis. When two single-qubit states are combined into a tensor, the result is $1|0+ 1|1\ 2|0+ 2|1$.

When working with vectors, the ordering of the base of the tensor computational grid is required when using the more popular matrix form. It is possible that we will decide to alter the way the dictionary is indexed.

The Fourth and Twelfth Example Calculating the tensor packing of the basis functions using a linear transformation is possible if one uses the dictionary sequences of the basis for the tensor mathematical model as their starting point. $|\,\dagger\,\dagger$ Because an inner product on $V\,W$ is produced when the inner products on V and W are multiplied together, we can say that $V\,W$ is an inner product space. Since the embeddings of and is given by, we can also say that $V\,W$ is an initial feature space. If and only if the bases on which the two unit vectors are defined are orthonormal, then the tensor product of the two unit vectors will also be a unit vector; in the case of W, the basis for $V\,W$ will also be orthonormal. Given that the size of the tensor product is determined by the ratio of the $\dim(V)\dim(W)$ values, the dimensions of the tensor product of n vector spaces in two dimensions are equal to $2n$.

Rarer than them all $|A$ tensor product of two W-vectors that is not the case (though they are all linear combinations of such elements). This discovery is very important to our overall understanding of quantum computing. We refer to these states as entangled since the linear combination of a vector in state V and a vector in state W does not constitute a valid computation for them. As we are going to show, it is pointless to speak to the state of a single qubit in an n-qubit system when discussing the majority of the quantum states, including all of the entangled ones [9].

Additionally serving as the cornerstone of probability theory is the tensor product structure. Direct sum structures are often confused with tensor product structures, despite the fact that tensor product structures are seldom brought up in this context. There is a possibility that this may lead to misunderstandings. Readers who have a solid grasp of the tensor product structure that underpins probability theory will have a much easier time comprehending the application of this idea in more everyday settings.

4.2.4 States of n-Qubit Technology

When the contents of two quantum mechanically, V and W, are each defined by unit vectors, then the many states of any combined quantum state may be represented by vectors in the dimensional space $V \otimes W$. Let V_i be the vector space for a single qubit, where I is an integer between 0 and n, and the basis is since the associated qubit is readily apparent from the position, the components are commonly removed from the conventional basis for the vector space $V_{n1} \, V_1 \, V_0$ for an n-qubit system, which consists of the 2^n vectors. The rule that the arrangement of kets signifies the multiplication of tensors allows for a simple expression of this assumption.

Tensor combination space for an n-qubit system is often used in quantum cryptography; hence, a shorter and clearer notation is desirable. To express this, we will use the notation $|b_{n1} \ldots b_0$. This terminology may be used to represent the underlying structure of an n-qubit system.

Due to the complexity of binary notation compared to mathematical language, we may refer to the binary representation of the state $|b_{n1} \ldots b_0$ as $|x$. This sequence expresses the typical basis for an n-qubit system.

The standard basis for a three-qubit system may be stated as $= |0, |1, |2, |3$, and the standard basis for a two-qubit system can be summarized as $= |0, |1, |2, |3$.

Since $|3$ might mean either a two-qubit state or a three-qubit state depending on the context, it is important to know how many qubits are being referred to in order to make sense of the terminology used here (see [10]).

To distinguish between individual qubits, signify different registers in quantum computers, or to denote that different people own qubits, we often resort to a less concise language. State may be represented as or, where the second number indicates which qubits are managed by Alice and which are managed by Bob if Alice controls the first two qubits and Bob controls the final three.

Example 4.2 The superpositions

$$\frac{1}{\sqrt{2}} \left| 0 > + \frac{1}{\sqrt{2}} \right| z' = \frac{1}{\sqrt{2}} 1000, + \frac{1}{\sqrt{z}} |111|$$

and

$$\frac{1}{2}(11, +12 > +14) + 177 = \frac{1}{2}\left\|1001 + 0^{10} + 1100 + 11\right\|$$

depict the states a system with three qubits may take.

To represent the basic functions of an n-qubit system in matrix form, the order of the coordinate axes must be established. Unless explicitly indicated differently, basis vectors with integer labels are assumed to be in a sequential sequence. This method has the potential to be used as a representation of the two-qubit state.

This method has the potential to be used as a representation of the two-qubit state will be represented by a matrix.

The standard foundation is the one we rely on the most, although we do utilize other bases on occasion. A two-qubit system's Bell basis is an example of this $\{|\Phi^+\rangle, |\Phi^-\rangle, |\Psi^+\rangle, |\Psi^-\rangle\}$, where

$$\begin{aligned}
|\Phi^+\rangle &= 1/\sqrt{2}(|00 + |11 \\
|\Phi^-\rangle &= 1/\sqrt{2}(|00 - |11 \\
|\Psi^+\rangle &= 1/\sqrt{2}(|01 + |10 \\
|\Psi^-\rangle &= 1/\sqrt{2}(|01 - |10,
\end{aligned}$$

(4.1)

The presence of this feature is essential for the implementation of quantum teleportation and other applications. If a state $|v$ is the linear combination of a set of orthonormal states, then it is a superposition with respect to these states, because $|v = a1|1+ +a_i|i$, where at least two of the ai are nonzero. When considering the usual basis, a superposition will be read as a lack of a fixed set of orthonormal states.

It is possible for a single unit vector in 2^n-dimensional state space to express all possible states of an n-qubit system. According to the properties of a tensor product [11], the same phase component in different qubits of a tensor product indicates the same quantum state in a multiple-qubit scenario.

Each qubit in a superposition may have its own term-specific phase component factored out into a single coefficient.

Example 4.3

$$\left(\frac{1}{2}|0\rangle + \frac{\sqrt{3}}{2}|1\rangle\right) \otimes \left(\frac{1}{\sqrt{2}}|0\rangle + \frac{i}{\sqrt{2}}|1\rangle\right)$$

$$= \frac{1}{2\sqrt{2}}|100 + \frac{i}{2\sqrt{2}}|01\rangle + \frac{\sqrt{3}}{2\sqrt{2}}|10\rangle + \frac{i\sqrt{3}}{2\sqrt{2}}|11\rangle$$

In the case of a single qubit, the identical occurrence in the physical world may be represented by vectors with the exception of a global phase difference. Any quantum state that is even somewhat imaginable may be recorded.

If starting ai is nonzero and nonnegative, then each quantum state must have a required property if it is to be consistent with the theory. Since this interpretation uniquely characterizes quantum properties, the quantum state space of an n-qubit system has problematic dimensions of 2^n 1. Complex projective space of dimension N 1 is the name given to the space in any challenging N-vector space that treats vectors that are different versions of each other as being equal. Since this is the case, the n-dimensional projective space of the n-qubit system is a complicated projective space with a dimension of $2'1'$.

Even if it is more practical to do calculations in vector space, one must be careful not to confuse the distance matrix with the quantum state space. This may be a dangerous mistake. Keep in mind that even though words that are superposed could have distinct relative phases, the global phase does not have any meaning that is based on physics and should be avoided at all costs. We are a group of writers working together. It is possible to draw the conclusion that $|v$ and $|w$ both represent the same quantum state as a result of the absence of any local change in the sequence between the two. Nevertheless, the following symbols indicate how various quantum states behave in a variety of settings. For example, $|11$ $|00$, the vectors $|1$ and $|0$ illustrate how distinct quantum states react in different circumstances.

Due to the linear nature of vector spaces, computations in quantum physics are best performed in these spaces as opposed to the parametric space. When we represent the outcomes of our computations as quantum states, however, we absolutely must forget to keep the equivalency in mind at all times.

The fact that states' laws are worded differently adds another layer of complexity. $|+=$ and $|-=$. Similar to the previous statement, $(|++|)$ also expresses the same vector but in a slightly different form.

If you want to make any headway in this book, you will need to be comfortable with the notation we just introduced and the features of tensor products. The reader is strongly encouraged to keep on at this stage to start becoming fluent.

4.2.5 States of Entangled

One complex number is all that is needed to characterize a tensor product that is made up of n separate states that each contains a single qubit. A set of arithmetic operations of dimensions 2^n 1 is required for a system that has n qubits, where n is the total number of qubits in the system. It is not possible for the current state of n independent single-qubit systems to accurately characterize the situation for the overwhelming majority of n-qubit states. Because it is not feasible to express these situations as the linear combination of any quantity of single-qubit states, the term "tensor product" will not be used. We refer to them as entangled states. Large numbers of quantum states are inherently intertwined [12].

Illustration 4.1 The Bell system links them all together (Eq. (3.1)). As an example, consider the Bell System, a quantum state machine whose behavior cannot be understood in terms of the states of its constituent qubits. Since there is no way to get the values a_1, a_2, b_1, b_2 such that, this state cannot be reduced to a lower one.

When $a_1 b_2 = 0$, $b_1 b_2 = 0$, and so on, $a_1 a_2 = 0$. A pair of EPR particles in the Bell state |+ is referred to as an EPR pair for reasons that will become evident later on.

Four states of entanglement

$$|\phi^+\rangle = \frac{1}{\sqrt{2}}(100 + 1, 1)$$

$$|\phi^+\rangle = \frac{1}{\sqrt{2}}(100 - 1, 1)$$

and

$$|\phi^+\rangle = \frac{1}{\sqrt{2}}(101 + 1, 0)$$

$$|\phi^+\rangle = \frac{1}{\sqrt{2}}(101 + 1, 0)$$

The states known as bell states are those that fulfill the conditions of Eq. (4.1). The study of quantum data processing relies heavily on the concept of "Bell states." Quantum entanglement and dense coding are two examples of such technologies. To put it another way, it exemplifies the highest possible level of dependency between the different states.

When the idea of entrainment is brought up, it is always from the perspective of an specific tensor product compression of state spaces. This is the case whenever the topic is brought up. To put it another way, if the quantum state of a system can be expressed as: $V = V_1 \, V_n$, then that state may be deemed to be recoverable or unentangled with respect to that decomposing.

When we refer to a state of n qubits as being entangled, we mean that it is so with regard to the tensor product biodegradation of the vector space V into the n two-dimensional vector interiors $V_{n1}, \ldots, V_0$ that conform to each qubit in the state. This is what we mean when we say that an n-qubit state is entangled. We can show that it is not entangled if we provide an alternative decomposition. V's tensor decomposition into a two-dimensional space must be either explicitly supplied or immediately apparent from the investigation's collection of qubits [13].

In particular, states that are entangled with respect to a single-qubit biodegradation may be unentangled with respect to another problem under consideration, so it is important to keep in mind that entanglement is not a property of all quantum states but rather depends on the government under consideration. Quantum states do not always exhibit entanglement. Particularly relevant to the field of quantum computing would be entanglement in the context of registers, subsystems made up of numerous qubits, and the fragmentation of individual qubits. An entangled state exists with respect to one decomposition but not the other.

Where $|v_i$ is included in V_i, we have $|=|$. Otherwise, this decomposition would cause $|$ to get entangled.

Illustration 4.2   The word "entanglement" may signify a variety of things. For the four-qubit state, we have psi=frac12($|00>+|11>+|33>$)=frac12($|0000>+|0101>+|1010>+|1111>$).

It is entangled because the tensor product of four independent qubit states does not explain it. If this claim is true, then entanglement must exist between the individual qubits that make up the whole. There is no additional main component analysis that links this state. Multiplying two states of two qubits together yields the following:

This indicates that separating the system into two compartments, one for the first two qubits and the other for the third and fourth, has no impact on the value of $|\psi$. Alternately, the reader may observe that $|$ is entangled when broken down into the two-qubit network consisting of the first and second qubits and the three and four qubits, respectively.

Even if the tensor deconstruction that is being examined has an effect on the concept of synchronicity, it is essential to bear in mind that the idea of interconnectedness does not make any reference to a base. This fact is very crucial. However, the tensor deconstruction that is being considered varies based on the base that is being used [14], and not the entanglement states on their own.

We were completely unaware of the implications that quantum superpositions were intended to have. As a follow-up to our prior discussion on superpositions, we are going to look at the scenario involving many qubits right now. The nontrivial studied to evaluate basis vectors is used to build the overwhelming majority of n-qubit states. Because of this, the concept of combination is always rooted in the fundamental basis, given that all states are either superpositions with regard to specific bases or they are not superpositions at all with reference to any individual basis. When there are more qubits involved, it is even more difficult to understand superpositions.

When compared to a single-qubit illustration, the multiple-qubit perturbations theory has a considerably more profound effect on one's understanding of the weirdness of quantum mechanics. According to this school of thought, there is no distinction between states since there is no such thing as a difference between states. $+i|$ they continue to react in the same way regardless of the surrounding conditions, but with slightly altered phases. In addition, the expression "being in the same location at the same time" may have many meanings depending on the context in which it is used.

While it is proven that |00 and |11 are in the same state, it is shown that |++ and | are in distinct states at the same time. This is despite the fact that both |++ and | are in the same state and thus behave infrequently in all situations. It is a common misconception that a quantum superposition is a collection of undetermined variables; however, this is not the case.

This interpretation is very reliant on the basis in which the states in issue are viewed, and as a direct consequence, it obscures part of the fundamental quantum character of these variables when they are examined in other bases. It is possible that thinking about quantum mechanics in terms of several states at the same time may be beneficial for the time being; nonetheless, this explanation should not be taken at face value. In this Chapter 4, you will get further knowledge on the inner workings of various phases.

Entangled particles may be utilized to facilitate the propagation of both classical mechanics information, as we will see, but they are also essential to the expansion of quantum state spaces in systems that include a large number of qubits. This will become clear in Section 4.2.6. The quantum algorithms described in Part 2 may also be able to take use of the potential for entanglement to speed up processing.

One of the most perplexing aspects of quantum physics and a potential source of power for quantum information processing is the question of how entangled states behave when subjected to measurement. In quantum computing, the concepts of entanglement and quantum measurement, which are trademarks of quantum physics, are put to use.

4.2.6 Classical Measuring of Multi-Qubit

When one qubit at a time is measured, the state of a quantum particle is converted into a form that is suitable for the apparatus that is doing the measurement. A similar conclusion holds true for measuring devices that include more than one qubit, but with a much larger number of observations and measurement techniques that can be performed. In the lines that follow, a mathematical structure is constructed in order to deal with the issue in its entirety.

For n-qubit systems, the $N = 2^n$-dimensional vector space is denoted by the letter V. Any machine that is capable of producing this system will also be capable of decomposing direct sums into symmetrical substrings.

There are several instances in which $V = S_1 \, S_k \, K > N$. The largest number of readings that are achievable for a particular situation based on the measurements taken by the instrument is k. Figure 4.1 will shift even while measuring the same system with the same equipment. Any device's direct sum decomposition may be thought of as a natural extension of the one-qubit case. It is necessary to have an orthonormal basis for the vector space V, denoted as $|v_1, |v_2$, if you want to do measurements on a single-qubit system. To define V, we write $V = V + S_1 + S_2$, where S_1 and S_2 are one-dimensional subspaces generated by the vectors |v_i (and include all multiples of the real number $A|v_i$). Any choice of basis functions from each of the sub-images produces an orthonormal basis [15], and there are two nontrivial decompositions for V: one in one dimension and the other in the other.

When an n-qubit system is in state | and it interacts with the direct sum decomposing $V = S_1 S_k Sk$, the state is transmogrified into one that is entirely encapsulated within one of the subcarriers, and the dimension is chosen with a probability that is equal to the square of the magnitude of the parts | in that subspace. Informal use is made of the unit vector in the set S_i as well as the real, nonnegative coefficient of the deconstruction, which is denoted by the symbol |i; nonetheless, the state | has a singular direct sum decomposition. |a_i|2 represents the likelihood of being in state |i, where is being measured. It is feasible to describe the interaction by making use of a direct sum deconstruction, which is applicable to all of the many kinds of measuring devices that are conceivable. This is a basic premise of quantum mechanics. The approach has resulted in a very promising model that predicts the results of experiments with a high degree of accuracy. While it is evident that it is not possible to show that every device acts in this manner, the procedure has resulted in this model.

In Section 4.3.1, an example of standard-based measurements of a single qubit is shown. Take into consideration the vector space V, which is exclusive to a system that consists of a single qubit. Every apparatus that measures a qubit in the standard basis has an innate capacity to do the direct sum decomposition, denoted by the equation $V = S_1 S_2$, where S_1 is created by |0 and S_2 is generated by. When measured by such a device, the possibility of a random state with the value |0 is equal to the amplitude of | in the subspace S_1, but the likelihood of |1 is equal to |b|. This means that the probability of |0 is equal to the amplitude of | in the subspace S_1.

Example 4.4 A measurement using a single qubit based on the Hadamard equation.

A device that is capable of measuring a single qubit using the Hadamard basis.

$$\{|+\rangle\} = \frac{1}{2^{1/2}}|0\rangle + |1\rangle$$

$$\{|+\rangle\} = \frac{1}{2^{1/2}}|0\rangle - |1\rangle$$

has a decomposed subspace connected with it written as $V = S + S$, where $S+$ is generated by |+ and S is generated by |. Given that |= $a|0+b|1$ is equivalent to |, the probability that | is measured as |+ is equal to |, while the probability that | is measured as | is equivalent to |.

The technique of entanglement-based cryptographic techniques is used to make measurements that are more exact for two-qubit states. Additionally, the standard arithmetic operations colloquialism that is used to describe the outcomes of quantum measurements is enlarged.

A technique for the distribution of quantum keys that makes use of entangled states was devised by Artur Ekert in the year 1991. The BB84 protocol and the Ekert 91 protocol are comparable to one another in a number of respects. According to the protocol that he has designed, Alice and Bob need to perform random measurements on their respective EPR pair halves before they can compare the bases that they have used over a classical channel in order to construct a shared key. This is required in order to ensure that the key is secure.

It is impossible for Eve to know and understand the key unless she interacts with a putative EPR pair while the protocol is being set up. This is due to the fact that Alice and Bob do not exchange their quantum states at any point during the protocol, and an unauthorized user, Eve, is unable to learn anything constructive from listening in on the deterministic exchange alone. It is much simpler to validate the safety of protocols when entangled states are used. Changes made to the viability proofs of other QKD protocols, such as BB84, have shown that these protocols, too, are reliable. In a manner similar to BB84, we will simply explain the protocol and will rely on the tools that will be developed in subsequent chapters to describe the several assaults Eve may conduct and to demonstrate that the protocol is safe. It is possible that Eve's most fundamental assaults do not do as much damage as they used to.

The first step in the procedure is to produce a number of qubit pairs that are entangled with one another.

Bob gets the second qubit in each pair, whereas Alice gets the first qubit in each pair. In the same way, as the BB84 protocol does it, they measure each qubit using either the standard basis (0, 1) or the Hadamard basis (+,). After collecting their measurements, they compare their bases and discard any data that does not line up with their assumptions.

As soon as Alice measures the first qubit in the progressing premise and obtains a result of |0, the state immediately transitions to |00. Bob is aware that if he pursues the endeavor in the conventional manner, he will end up with the outcome |0. Because in 00=| (|++|), he will obtain both a plus sign and a minus sign because he is basing his measurements on the Hadamard system. Because he considers the states |+| and | to be analogous to the traditional bit values 0 and 1, he only receives the same bit value as Alice when going to measure on the basis |+| and the conventional basis 50% of the time. This is because he interprets the states as being comparable to the bit values 0 and 1. The same thing takes place when Alice's qubit is in state |1 as described before. If Alice measures her qubit using the Hadamard basis and discovers that it is in the state |+, then the whole state is changed into the form |+|+. This is an alternate measurement option. As a consequence of this, Bob is able to be positive that he will always receive |+ when comparing measurements taken inside the Hadamard framework to those taken within the normal framework. If the original pairings were EPR pairs, then this technique will provide a random key that is shared by both parties since EPR couples always measure using the same basis. It is necessary for us to include additional phases into the protocol that we have just outlined so that Alice and Bob may validate the EPR pairings that they have created in order for this strategy to be safe. The particulars of these kinds of exams have not yet been specified in full. Bell's disparities serve as the foundation for Ekert's tests. New tests that are superior and more productive have been developed.

Alice and Bob do not have to worry about storing their shared keys for any period of time since they can produce new ones whenever they need them. In order to produce keys on requested in this manner in reality, Alice and Bob will need to have the capability to store their EPR pairs in a way that protects them from being compromised throughout the time that this process takes place. At this point, there is no foolproof method available that can maintain entanglement of states for any appreciable period of time.

4.3 Measuring of Multi-Qubit

When it comes to quantum information processing, the nonclassical feature of quantum measurements is absolutely necessary. This chapter provides a description of the nonclassical behavior of entangled states during measurement using the traditional method for measuring multiple-qubit devices. Example 4.9 such as the EPR paradox and Bell's theorem are used to back up this claim.

4.3.1 Mathematical Functions in Quantum Operations

Specifying linear transformations on quantum states is made easier using Dirac's bra/ket notation. Keep in mind that the vector notation ket | has a conjugate transpose of bra |, and that the vectors | and | have an inner product of |. The outer product of two vectors, denoted by |xy|, may be thought of as a vector. The following relations hold because multiplication of matrices may be done in an associative manner, and scalars commute with everything.

Imagine that a system consisting of a single qubit is accompanied by a vector space that is designated by the letter V. The matrix for the operator "0 0" in terms of the canonical basis, as determined by the scriptural order, is

$$|0\rangle\langle 0| = \begin{matrix} 1 \\ 0 \end{matrix} (1\ 0) = \begin{matrix} 1 & 0 \\ 0 & 0 \end{matrix}$$

The notation |0 1| suggests a link between |1 and |0, where |0 is the null vector, and |1 is the one that is transformed linearly to become |0.

Similarly that is why Dirac's notation may be used for any linear transformation in V's two dimensions:

That is why Dirac's notation may be used for any linear transformation in V's two dimensions:

$$\begin{matrix} a & b \\ c & d \end{matrix} = a|0\rangle\langle0| + b|0\rangle\langle1| + c|1\rangle\langle0| + d|1\rangle\langle1|$$

Example 4.5   The linear transformation that exchanges $|0$ and $|1$ is given by

$$X = |0\rangle\langle1| + |1\rangle\langle0|$$

We will also use notation

$$X : |0 \rightarrow\!|1 \; |1 \rightarrow\!|0$$

which specifies a linear transformation in terms of its effect on the basis vectors. The transfer can also be represented by using the matrix to explain everything in comparison to the accepted norm.

Example

To symbolize this modification in a matrix, we may swap basis vectors $|00$ and $|10$ while keeping all other vectors constant: $|10\ 00|+|00\ 10|+|11\ 11|+|01\ 01|$.

$$0\ 0\ 1\ 0$$
$$0\ 1\ 0\ 0$$
$$1\ 0\ 0\ 0$$

on the basis of the general norm.

For an n-qubit system, it is feasible to define an operator that inverts the basis vector $|j\rangle|i\rangle$ and makes all of the other standard fundamental elements equal to 0.

$$O = |i\rangle\langle j|$$

The O-matrix in the standard basis has a single nonzero element, 1, at position ij. The standard foundation allows us to write a generic operator O with entries a_{ij}.

$$O = \sum_i \sum_j aij\, |i><j|$$

In a similar vein, $i|O|j$ denotes the ijth entry of the matrix for O in the usual basis.

We use the notation to explicitly record the output of implementing operator O on a vector. $|\psi\ \sum_k b_k k = |$

$$0|\ \psi = 1 = \sum_i \sum_j aij\, |i><j| \sum_k bk\, |\ k = \sum_i \sum_j \sum_k aijbk\, |i><j||k$$
$$\cdot \sum_i \sum_j aij\, |i>$$

More generally, if $\{|\beta_i\}$ is a basis for an N-dimensional vector space V, then an operator $O: V \rightarrow V$ can be written as

$$\sum_{i=1}\sum_{j=1} b_{ij} \mid \beta_i\beta_j$$

assuming that this is the case. With respect to the ith basis, the O-matrix is written as $O_{ij} = b_{ij}$.

The reader may find the vector/matrix notation more familiar and convenient when it comes to doing calculations. Selecting and arranging a solid base is a need for success. In bra/ket notation, the basis and order do not matter. Like the outside product, it is more condensed and suggests the appropriate connections, making it easy to grasp after some practice.

4.3.2 Operator Measuring Qubits Projection

In this measurement, one qubit is projected onto a basis vector specific to the measuring device. The concept presented here might be implemented in measurements involving systems with several qubits. All vectors that are orthogonal to the variables that are included in S are likewise considered to be a part of the subspace S of V. Because $V = S\,S$, it is possible to describe any vector | as the product of two vectors in the subspaces S and S. This is possible because $V = S\,S$. The linear operator PS: $V\,S$ is the projection operator PS for each set S. This operator projects $|v\,S_1$ everywhere it is used. We make use of the notation since the majority of the instances we see in the actual world do not deal with data. The operator $|\,|$ is responsible for performing the projections into the subdomain that is covered by. It is common practice to abbreviate the title of those who operate projection equipment to "projectors." The following expression represents the formula $V = S_1$ for any direct sum decomposed of V: The framework of spacetime should be partitioned into orthogonal pieces. As a result, there is such a thing as k-related projecting operators. P_i equals V times S_1, where $P_i|v$ equals S_1 and V equals S_2. The breakdown of a measuring instrument is $V = S_1$ in this notation. When S_k is applied to a state, that state

$$|\Phi\rangle = \frac{P_i\varphi >}{P\varphi}$$

likely to the extent of $|P_i||2$.

Illustration 4.3 When applied to a one-qubit state, the projector $|0\,0|$ returns the subspace created by $|0$'s operation on $|$, where $|=a|0+b|1$ is the qubit's component. So, if $a = 0$, $b = 1$, and $c = 0$, then $(|0\,0|)|= a = 0$, $b = 1$, and $c = 0$.

This projector operates on two-qubit states, namely those with the notation |1|0 1| 0|. In this case, let PS = a00|00+a01|01+a10|10+a11|11.

Then

Let PS denote the operator for mapping a vector space V in n dimensions to a subspace s in s dimensions.

Illustration 4.4 In the case of a two-qubit system, let the subspace of the corresponding vector space, denoted by the symbols |= a00|00+a01|01+a11|11, be the state. For the (nonnormalized) vector 00|00+ 01|01, the projection operator is PS01|.

Let us suppose that there are two vector spaces, V and W, and that both of these vector spaces have an inner product. An operator's partial derivative operator is the operator that satisfies the initial feature connection that is shown below. This operator is also known as the manufacturer's conjugate transposition $O: V\,W$. The inner product of $O(v)$ and $w(Ow)$ has the same value as the inner product of $v(Ow)$, which is equivalent to the inner product of W (Ow).

The adjoint of operator O is also an operator. When V and W are used as bases in a consistent fashion, O may be created by taking all of the entries and transcribing the matrix that O uses. This exemplifies the conjugate transposition of |x, which was covered in more detail in Section 4.2. The reader may verify this by comparing the values $(A|x)$ and $(A|x)|A$. The inner combinations of $O|x|w$ in the bra/ket interpretation is connected to the embeddings of $O|x$ and |w.

When a projection operator is described, a number of problems emerge, including the following: It does not make a difference how many times a projection operator is used while P is present, indicating that this does not apply. That is to say, P and PP may be substituted for one another. Because the projection operator is a member of its own adjoints, the equation $P = P$ is always true. As a consequence of this, the paradigm enables a more precise comprehension of projection operations and the terminology used by Dirac in relation to single-qubit measurements.

The fourth observation A_n in-depth explanation of the formal foundations of measuring with a single qubit. Take into consideration the vector space V that is exclusive to a system that only contains one qubit. The direct sum decomposition for the variable V in the standard basis for measurement is where S is the subspace produced by | and is the subspace generated by |1. The projection operators $P: V\,S$ and $P: =|1\;21|$ are connected with one another. The measurable state, denoted by the notation |P || | ||, may be obtained by measuring the state denoted by the notation |= a|0+b|1. In light of the fact that $P = (|0\;0|)|=|0\;0|= a|0$, the result of a measurement is a probability that takes the form |a0 | |a1 |a2|. Because we now know, according to Section 2.5, that an overall phase factor is worthless from a physical perspective, we can conclude that the state specified by 2|0 has been reached with probability 2 $|a|$. This allows us to claim that an overall phase factor is pointless. In a similar vein, we are able to provide evidence that the state designated by $|1$ may be reached with a probability equal to $|b|$.

Before moving on to more interesting cases, the complete decomposition of the consistent schedule is applied to the measurement of a two-qubit state. This is done before moving on to more interesting examples.

Illustration 4.5 The process of breaking down a two-qubit state into its component pieces by using the whole standard basis. Let us say that each nonzero two-qubit state is denoted by the notation $|= a00|00+ a01|01$ 11, and let V be the vector space that corresponds to a two-qubit system. Consider the scenario of a measurement that uses the decomposition 00 01 10 11, where S_{ij} is the one-dimensional complex subspace that $|ij$ covers. The projection operators $|$, and $|$ are sometimes considered to be one and the same. After the reading is taken, the system will be in state P_{ij}, which is denoted by the notation $|P_{ijij}||$ with the probabilities [01 01] and $[P_{ijij}|||2]$. You may recall that if $|v = e|w$ for some, then $|v$ and $|w$ represent the same quantum state, and that $|$ indicates that $|v$ and $|w$ represent the same quantum state. You should also recall that $|$ signals that $|v$ and $|w$ represent the same quantum state. After the measurement is complete, the state will either be $|01$ with probability2 $|P00|=|a01|22$, $|10$ with probability2 $|P10|=|a10|$, or $|11$ with probability2 $|P11|=|a11|$.

In order for the reader to have a deeper comprehension of the subject matter, they may now rephrase the passage using this notation.

Instead of looking at the individual qubit values directly, it would be more fascinating to observe measurements that reflect the relationships between the qubit values. One such example is the testing of bit equivalency, in which two qubits are compared to one another without disclosing the values of each qubit individually. The field of quantum error correction is going to make extensive use of these results.

Example 4.6 Testing the bit-equality of a two-qubit state using the canonical basis. Let us give the vector space associated with a two-qubit system the name V for now. When it comes to a measurement, the direct sum decomposition looks like this: $V = S_1$. The subspaces S_1 (which are generated when the two bits are equal to one another) and S_2 (which are formed when the two bits are not equal to one another) are identified by the value S_2. Let us say we have two different projection operators, P_1 and P_2, and that they map onto different spaces, S_1 and S_2.

In the event that the first criterion is met, there is no way for us to determine if either of the numbers is 0 or 1. In the second scenario, on the other hand, we are unable to determine with absolute certainty which bits are ones and which are zeros. In this scenario, we are able to draw the conclusion that the two-bit values are distinct from one another. Since this is the case, the measurement itself determines whether or not the two bits may be compared to one another.

In the same way that single-qubit states may be represented as linear combinations in terms of the subspace deconstruction of measuring instruments, most states can be written in this way as well. In the earlier example, monitoring may lead to a state in which all bit values are equal, or it may lead to a state in which all bit values are not equal. Both of these outcomes are possible (often still a superposition of bit values that vary).

During the process of constructing the quantum measurement formalism, we offer an example in which the subspaces are formed by non-subsets of the standard component parts [15].

Useful Section 4.2.6 When compared to the Bell basis decomposition, the size of a two-qubit state is shown to be less. In order to recall the four Bell states |= (|01+|10) discussed in Section 4.3.2, we are going to take advantage of the direct sum decomposition into the subspaces produced by the Bell states. The reader is able to compute the outcomes and their probability for the other three traditional basis elements as well as a typical two-qubit state by measuring the state |00 with respect to this decomposition, which yields |+withprobability1 | withprobability1/2. This method applies to both the other three traditional basis elements and the typical two-qubit state.

In this next phase, the development of a universal framework for the explanation of quantum measurement will go to the next stage.

It is not essential to write down the breakdown of the subspaces for each measurement since a generating set is directly determined by the subspaces that are linked with a measurement. The unique orthogonal subspace decomposition that is produced by the Hermitian operators' eigenspace decomposition cannot be produced by any other method. There is a Hermitian operator whose eigenspace decomposition is equivalent to this decomposition for every such decomposition. This decomposition may be applied to any such decomposition. Due to the nature of this connection, Hermitian operators may be used to provide an explanation for measurements. In the first step of this process, we will go over some background knowledge on Hermitian operators and eigenspaces.

In this situation, it makes the most sense to use a linear operator such as $O: V V$. There is an eigenvalue and an eigenvector of O for any nonzero vector V, and if v and w are both eigenvectors of $+w$, then the region created by these eigenvectors is referred to as the eigenspace of O. If V is 0, then there is no eigenvalue or principal component of O. Only the values that are on the diagonal of a matrix are regarded to be eigenvalues when an operator is being represented by a diagonal matrix.

If and only if $O: V V$ is equivalent to $O = O$, then O is said to be Hermitian. Eigenspaces of operations with Hermitian operators are distinguished by a number of unique qualities. Let us suppose for the sake of argument that the eigenvalue of the Hermitian operator O is the letter x. Because this is the case, each eigenvalue of a Hermitian operator is a real number.

The linearization and the fulfillment of the orthogonality criterion by the eigenspaces of a Hermitian operator are necessary for the relationship that exists between Hermitian operators and transverse subspace decompositions. $S\lambda_1 \oplus S\lambda_2 \oplus \cdots \oplus S\lambda_k = V$. Since $O|x= 0|x$ and $O|x= 1|x$ imply that $(0\ 1)|x= 0$, which in turn implies that $0 = 1$, every operator with two distinct eigenvalues has disjoint eigenspaces. This is due to the fact that for any unit vector $|x$, $O|x= 0|x$ and $O|x= 1|x$ imply that $(0\ 1)|x= 0$. Different eigenvalues of a Hermitian operator are required to have eigenvectors that are orthogonal to one another. Consider the situation in which both $|v$isa and $|w$ are eigenvectors, and both of them have the equal sign (=). Since and are unique eigenvalues, we have $v|w = 0$. Because of this, if I equals j, Si and Sj are considered to be orthogonal. Offers a more tangible demonstration of this notion by demonstrating that the whole vector space is comprised the operator that is being used is a Hermitian operator OV, then the value V is identical to the direct sum of all of the eigenspaces. In the case when V represents the eigenspace of O with eigenvalue 1, and S_1 represents the eigenspace of O with eigenvalue 0, then $V = S_1\ S_k$. The direct sum decomposition is the eigenspace decomposed of V when the operator O being considered is a Hermitian operator. Any Hermitian operator, O: $V\ V$, may be used to create a subspace decomposition of the variable V in this form. Further, any desired direct sum decomposition of a vector space V into subspaces $S_1, \ldots, S_k$ can be realized by using the eigenspace breakdown of a Hermitian operator O, where V is the vector space, Pi are the smartwatches onto the subspaces Si, and k is any collection of distinct actual beliefs. This can be done for any desired straightforward sum biodegradation of a vector space V. In lieu of explicitly expressing the subspace deconstruction that is correlated with the measurements, we could find it more convenient to make use of a Hermitian operator whose eigenspace is the measurement itself.

It is permissible to make use of the Hermitian operator provided that it has a direct sum decomposition and is utilized to define the measurements. It is strongly suggested that the I be labeled with either the names of the relevant subspaces or, as a substitute, the names of the characteristics that were measured. These labels are used in quantum physics to designate a common attribute among the eigenstates in the corresponding eigenspace. Some examples of this shared characteristic include energy. Eigenvalues are more than adequate replacements for descriptive labels at this point in time.

In theoretical physics and the processing of subatomic particles, it is standard practice to make use of a Hermitian operator in order to describe a measurement. Hermitian operators on states, on the other hand, cannot be utilized to replicate quantum measurements in any way. The projectors denoted by the letters Pj that are connected to a Hermitian operator O, and not O by itself, are the ones that carry out the action on a state. It is possible for us to determine, on the basis of the probabilities $pj = |Pj|$, which projector is accountable for the current state. The following is an illustration of the output produced by the Hermitian operator Z:

$$\begin{matrix} 1 & 0 \\ 0 & -1 \end{matrix} \cdot \begin{matrix} a \\ b \end{matrix} = \begin{matrix} a & 1 \\ 1 & b \end{matrix}$$

If you multiply two integers with a Hermitian operator, you probably will not get a clear result.

$$\begin{matrix} 0 & 0 \\ 0 & 1 \end{matrix} \; |0\rangle = \begin{matrix} 0 & 0 \\ 0 & 1 \end{matrix} \; \begin{matrix} 1 & 0 \\ 0 & 0 \end{matrix} = \begin{matrix} 0 \\ 0 \end{matrix}$$

Since the symmetric operator just provides a convenient shorthand for stating the subspace reduction involved in the measurement, it is of little practical value.

4.3.3 The Measurement Postulate

Example 4.7 A formalization based on Hermitian operators that makes it possible to measure a single qubit while maintaining the canonical reference frame. Using the characterization that is provided in Example 4.4, let us create a Hermitian operator that specifies the assessment of a single-qubit system in the standard basis. This dimension corresponds to a split of the subspace into the constituents I and I1. The projection devices associated with the 0I and PI values are connected to this dimension. Consider two distinct real numbers assigned with constant to show the particular dimension. it is easy to measure specific assessment.

After that, the operator the Hermitian operator is responsible for specifying the measurement of a single-qubit state on a standard basis both are free-floating parameters in this equation.

The Hermitian operator is responsible for specifying the measurement of a single-qubit state in the standard basis. Both are free-floating parameters in this equation. When expressing single-qubit measurements in the normal basis, we will use either I or as our notation of choice in the typical situation.

In Section 4.3.2, an example of measuring one qubit using the Hermitian operator framework on the Hadamard basis is shown for readers' reference. The end goal is to construct a Hermitian operator that will transfer the measurement of a single qubit to the Hadamard basis represented by the notation I+,I. Subspaces $S+$ and S are taken into consideration; $S+$ is produced by I+, and S is produced by I; related projectors PI1 1I and $P =$I I= (1) may be defined in any way that we wish, as long as they are distinct from one another. When we combine 1 and 1, we get 1.

When we combine 1 and 1, we get 1 is a Hermitian operator with a Hadamard basis that is used for measuring one qubit.

Example 4.8 The sequence 00, 01, 10, and 11 is the matrix representation of the Hermitian operator I with regard to the standard basis. Utilizing the traditional basis vectors 00, 01, 10, and 11 is all that is required in order to effortlessly decompose A's eigenspace into subspaces. Operator A is only one of numerous 1-dimensional operators that are utilized to give measurements for the whole traditional basis deconstruction process. In addition to it, there is the Hermitian operator I.

Example 4.9 The Hermitian operator

$$B = 100^2 x\infty, +101 > (0, +\pi\{[lox, o' + 111)\}''') = \begin{pmatrix} i0 & 8 & 0 \\ g & :\frac{1}{0} & \prod_{0}^{0} \frac{8}{i'} \end{pmatrix}$$

In this norm, |00, |01 generates a subspace decomposing $V = S0 + S_1$, and B determines the screening uptake of the first qubit in a two-qubit system.

Example 4.10 *The Hermitian operator*
As an illustration, C provides a description of the measures for bit equivalency that are shown in Example 4.6. C provides specifications for measurements in relation to the subspace formed by $V = S_2 S_3$.

Given the subspace deconstruction, there is an overcomplete eigenbasis for the variable V that corresponds to the symmetric operator O. Eigenbasis may differentiate up to one complex factor for O when there are n separate eigenvectors, as is the case with the generalized form. When the number of eigenvalues is more than N, it is possible that more than one dimension will be related to some of O's eigenvalues. A basis function basis may be chosen at random for each eigenspace S_i. This can be done with any basis function basis. When considering any of these eigenbases, the matrix for the symmetric operator O will always be diagonal.

Any Hermitian operator O that has principal components of j may be represented as, where Pj is the projections for the j-eigenspaces of O. This expression can be used to describe any Hermitian operator O. This formula may be used to calculate the Hermitian operator O for any Hermitian operator. Every projector has a Hermitian structure, and the eigenvalues that it contains are either one or zero. The 1-eigenspace is what represents the image of the operator. The corresponding projector is in charge of mapping the vectors in V into the corresponding vectors in S. This mapping takes place for an m-dimensional subspace S of V that is contained inside the basis. If we assume that PS and PT are projectors for perpendicular subspaces S and T, respectively, then the projector for the direct sum of S and T is PS + PT. If P is a projector into subspace S, then the dimension of S is equal to the sum of the elements on the diagonal of any matrix that symbolizes P. If P is not a projector onto subspace S, then the dimension of S is equal to 1.

The symbol Tr is used to represent this total (P). This line of reasoning may be used to any basis, since the trace does not depend on any basis in particular. Box 4.1 outlines all of the trace's features, including this one as well as the others.

The following is how the tensor product AB acts on the components v and w of the tensor business develops $V\,W$ when linear operators A and B are applied to vector spaces V and W, respectively: $(AB)(v\,w) = A_v\,B_w$.

As a consequence of this interpretation, the statement "$(-A-B)(-C-D)$" is equivalent to "$AC-BD$."

Notation O_0 and notation O_1 are used to refer to Hermitian operators that operate on spaces V_0 and V_1, respectively. If this is the case, then the Hermitian operator on the space $V_0\,V_1$ is represented as $O_0\,O_1$. In addition, if O_i contains eigenvalues ij coupled with corresponding eigenspaces S_{ij}, then $O_0\,O_1$ also possesses principal components. The eigenspace that corresponds to an amplitude that is the only one of its type is indicated by the tensor product of S_{0j} and S_{1k} when the eigenvalue in question is the only one of its kind. In most situations, it is not necessary for the eigenvalues to be distinguished from one another. An eigen value with the eigenspace S equal to $(S_{0j1}\,S_{1k1})\,(S_{0jm}\,S_{1km}\mathrm{km})$ has the property that it is the product of the eigen values of both O_0 and O_1 in a variety of different ways if it has the property that it has the eigenspace S equal to $(S_{0j1}\,S_{1k1})$ $(S_{0jm}\,S_{1km})$.

There is no way to characterize a tensor combination that consists of two Hermitian operators, O_1 and O_2, both of which are operating on V_0 and V_1; this is because most operators operate on V_0 and V_1. These kinds of decompositions are only possible if S_0 and S_1 in the subspace deconstruction connected to O_1 and O_2 can be represented in terms of S_0 and S_1 in the subspace main component analysis linked to O_2. It is not true for the vast majority of Hermitian operators; nonetheless, it is true for all of the observables that we have discussed up to this point in the discussion. For instance, the symbol I may be used to define the full measurement in the standard basis, but it does so by using a different non-singular operator than the one that was used in Example 4.8. This is because the symbol specifies the whole measurement in the standard basis. The operator who is being questioned is the operator that was used in that particular scenario denotes measurement of the first qubit in the standard basis as mentioned in Example 4.9; similarly, $Z\,I$, where I, also signifies measurement of the first qubit in the standard basis. Likewise, this measurement describes how the second qubit should be measured using the standard basis. Example 4.10 utilizes both the Hermitian operator and the metric in order to determine whether or not two bits are comparable to one another. The goal of this example is to determine whether or not two bits are equivalent to one another. We shall present an example here since it is not feasible to characterize the measurements of two qubits as the product of the measurements of two single qubits.

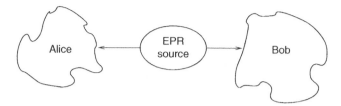

Figure 4.2 Structure of Bell theorem.

Please refer to the illustration provided in Section 4.3.6. The results of observations carried out with a single qubit do not always constitute tensor combinations of tensor products in each and every instance. The illustration in Figure 4.2 depicts an example of a state that is made up of two qubits. A matrix-based representation of the variable M, which may be seen.

$$\begin{pmatrix} 0^0 & 0 & 0 \\ 0^0 & 0 & 0 \\ 0^0 & 0 & 0 \\ 0^0 & 0 & 1 \end{pmatrix}$$

checks to verify whether both bits have a value of 1, which would indicate that the check was successful. One of the two possible subspaces that may be covered by a measurement result from the operator M is either S_0 or S_1, whereas the other possible subspace, 01,10, can only be covered by a measurement result from S_1.

It is not the same as monitoring both qubits in a progressing premise and then doing the classical operation in order to take measurements. That is a different process entirely. This is a totally different kind of procedure. The state does not alter when measured with M; nevertheless, when both qubits are measured, it is feasible to obtain the states |01 or |10, respectively. When monitored with M, the state does not change.

For example, one interpretation of $Q_1 Q_2$ maintains that it integrates single-qubit measurements for each and every symmetric operator that is supposed to function on two-qubit systems. This view is supported by the argument that $Q_1 Q_2$ is a generalization of Q_1 and Q_2.

Hermitian operators, designated by the symbols Q_1 and Q_2, respectively, are present in qubit systems that each consist of a single qubit. To do a measurement on a single qubit inside a system that contains two qubits, any Hermitian operator of the type QI or IQ may be used. This particular kind of Hermitian operator is regarded as being the more broad option.

$$I \otimes \cdots \otimes I \otimes Q \otimes I \otimes \cdots \otimes I$$

The measurement of a single qubit is referred to as such when it is performed within the framework of an n-qubit system. A measurement of a subsystem V is a Hermitian operator of the type AI when it is applied to a system $V W$. This is because A refers to a Hermitian operator that is applied to V.

It is proof that one may conduct arbitrary quantum experiments by using just the basic standard measurement operators and quantum state transformations. As a result of this, if we begin with a subspace decomposition in which all of the subspaces are derived by conventional basis vectors and transforming is possible, then we have the potential to receive all of the conceivable subspace wavelet decompositions of the state space. This is because all of the subspaces are generated by the standard basis vectors. In order to have a comprehensive understanding of entangled states and the quantum executive function, it is vital to have an understanding of the influence that quantum measurements have on a range of different bases. It is essential to underline these quantum key distribution techniques' capacity to detect in several bases in order to have a comprehensive understanding of the capabilities offered by these approaches. In the next section, we will discuss Bell's theorem, which will help further clarify the nonclassical properties of entangled states. This will contribute to the overall goal of this discussion.

An indirect sum reinterpretation into k 2^n subspaces associated with the measurement tool and a tensor combination demolition of buildings into n discrete qubits are the two or more independent components that are required for the categorization of an n-qubit system. Both of these features are associated with the measurement tool. Both of these deconstructions happen at separate locations inside the vector space V. When it comes to the components that make up each of them, they could not be more different from one another. To provide more clarity, a tensor component V_i of $V = V_1$ Vn does not belong to V as a subspace even if it is part of V. In a manner analogous to this, the subspaces that are related to measurement do not correlate to the subsystems that make up the overall system, such as particular qubits.

It was said that a single qubit could only retrieve one conventional piece of information at a time. This assertion may now be generalized, as well as made more particular by the addition of additional details. Because each observable on an n-qubit system may have one of at most 2^n unique potential eigenvalues, the maximum number of distinct outcomes that can result from a measurement is thus limited to 2^n. Only a certain number of classical bits may be revealed at any one moment by a single measurement that is performed on an n-qubit system. In most cases, taking a measurement will cause the state of a system to change. As a result, subsequent measurements will yield information that is more relevant to the system's present condition as opposed to the state it was in before the measurement was taken. The current state of the observational is written to an eigenvector if it has 2^n unique eigenvalues, and subsequent observations will not be able to derive any further knowledge from the preserved state of the observational.

4.3.4   EPR Paradox and Bell's Theorem

In 1935, Albert Einstein, Boris Podolsky, and Nathan Rosen collaborated on a research titled "Can basic physical representation of material reality be regarded complete?" (Can fundamental physical representation of material reality be declared complete?) The thought experiment in the study made reference to one of the more complicated tests that David Bohm had conducted. Within the state, the demonstration makes use of two photons. Despite the fact that such states were not mentioned in their publication, Einstein and Podolsky's names have been given to two EPR pairs. These pairs are named in their honor.

Alice will get the first particle, and Bob will be responsible for receiving the second particle. There is no limit to the distance that separates Alice and Bob. It is only feasible for one person to perform a measurement on the particles that they have received for themselves. When measuring the system, Alice can only make use of observables that are of the type $O\,I$, but Bob may make use of observables that are of the form $I\,O$.

This quantification has the effect of presenting the state of the quantum particle onto that area of the province that is interoperable with Alice's results obtained, as we saw when we investigated the Ekert91 quantum content delivery proper procedure in Section 3.4. This monitoring has the effect of superimposing the state of the quantum states onto that part of the state that is compatible with the results of Alice's measuring device. When Alice measures her particle using the simple single basis and observes the state |0, the effect of this measuring device is to visualize the state of the quantum computer onto that region of the state that is similar to the findings of Alice's measuring device. This part of the state is referred to as the "zero state." After that point, the status of the united entity will be denoted by the number 00. The value that is sent to the observer by Bob's particle will always be represented by the symbol |0. To put it another way, it would seem that the measurement that Alice made was the cause of the status change that was seen in Bob's particle. The number 1 will be measured by Bob as well, exactly as Alice did before. If Bob were to initially measure his qubit, then Alice would see the same result that Bob would if she were to perform the same thing. If Alice and Bob measured using the works finding the relative chronological of the events even if they took the measurements at different times. As a direct consequence of this, there is an equal potential for deciding that both qubits have the value |0. This is because of the way that direct results are determined.

Depending on the distance that separates the particles and the time at which the observations are made, it is possible that it will seem as if an interaction between the particles is taking place at a pace that is faster than the speed of light. To be sure there is no confusion, we have said in the past that a measurement done by Alice seems to alter the condition that Bob's particle is in. Because one observer can see Alice measure before Bob, the EPR scenario might be set up such that one observer sees Alice measure before Bob. This is because one observer can see Alice measure before Bob. Because of special relativity, this is an incorrect assumption. According to Einstein's theory of relativity, science must be able to satisfactorily explain the results obtained by both sets of observers.

It is possible to provide a reasonable explanation of the outcomes of the experiment by instructing Bob to measure first and then Alice to measure second, despite the fact that the causal terminology we employed is incompatible with the field observations made by both observers. Alice and Bob's EPR pair cannot converse more rapidly than the speed of light because of a symmetry between the two particles, even if there is a relationship between them. What we do know is that both Alice and Bob will display correlated random behavior.

Despite seeming to be in line with general relativity, the observations remain puzzling. If Alice and Bob measured a large number of EPR pairs, they would get an unusual mix of correlated and probabilistic results; each sequence of measurements would seem to be entirely random, but when they compared their results, they would see that they both observed the same random sequence from their two different particulates. A pair of magical coins thrown together will always land with the same side up. The behavior of an entangled pair is identical to that of any other randomly generated pair. These results are also explicable within the framework of a classical theory that postulates particles have a hidden internal state that determines the measured data and that this embedding layer is identical in colloidal bodies engendered at the same time by the EPR generator, but varies haphazardly over time as the pairs are produced. While this may be one possible explanation, it is not the only one. According to the conventional perspective, since we do not know how to access these hidden states, it seems as if we always end up with random results instead of deterministic ones. Supporters of these theories have long hoped that technological developments in the field of physics may allow us to learn more about this mysterious phenomenon. In this class, hypotheses with "local hidden variables" are included. The local portion is predicated on the idea that each particle's hidden variables are entirely under its control and unaffected by anything outside the particle itself; in particular, the hidden variables do not depend on the location of any other particles or the condition of any measuring devices. The most crucial part of this assumption is this.

We utilize experimental data to simulate quantum physics, yet there are discrepancies across these data sets. Can these discrepancies be explained by a theory of local hidden variables? To distinguish quantum mechanics from other local hidden-variable theories, no one had any clue how to do so until John Stewart Bell's discovery in 1964. It is possible to distinguish quantum mechanics from other local hidden-variable theories. Several similar tests have been conducted since then, and each has led to findings that are in line with those predicted by

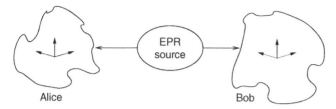

Figure 4.3 Setup of Bell theorem.

quantum mechanics. To put it simply, the natural world cannot be explained by a single hidden-variables-only model at the local level.

4.3.5 Layout of Bell's Theorem

Imagine an EPR source that produces pairs of photons with polarizations that are in an entangled state (|+|), where the notations | and | refer to the polarization of the photon, respectively. According to our hypothesis, the two photons go in different directions, each in the direction of a polaroid (polarization filter). These polaroids have three distinct angular settings available to choose from. In the first exceptional circumstance that we will examine, the polaroids in Figure 4.3 may be aligned to be vertical, $+60°$ off vertical, or $-60°$ off vertical.

4.3.6 Statistical Predicates of Quantum Mechanics

Take into consideration as a single qubit, an observation that has a 1-eigenspace that was formed by $\cos|0+\sin|1$ and an a_1-eigenspace that was generated by $|v=\cos |0+c\cos|1$. Quantum mechanics makes the prediction that a state will have an eigenvalue of 1 based on the probability that will be measured with O_1-O_2. As a consequence of this, the cosine of one plus two is proportional to the probability that the state will ultimately end up in the sub-eigenspace produced by rather than the 1-eigenspace generated by. The purpose of Exercise 4.1 is to demonstrate that this is in fact the case. The discussion here focuses on nonclassical repercussions.

Each polaroid camera has three distinct exposure settings—60, vertical, and $+60$—that map to three distinct quantities: P (the photon passes through the polaroid), M (the photon absorbs), and n (the photon is not absorbed) (the photon passes through the polaroid). For instance, we may compute the probability that two photons, each of which has an observed $O =1$, $O =2$, $O =1$ eigenvalue, would produce the same outcome when recorded by polaroid cameras at angles 1 and 2. When both polaroid's are positioned at the same angle, it is quite likely that the measurements of both photons will provide the same findings. This is because $\cos^2 0 = 1$. Either both photons will be stopped at the barrier, or both will be allowed to travel through. When both parameters were measured at +60 and vertically aligned in a polaroid camera, as indicated, the equation for $\cos^2 60$ was obtained as 1/4. Because it is difficult to get correct measurements until both polaroid's are at the same angle, this indicates that the two parameters are only accurate one-quarter of the time under all of these situations.

One-third of the EPR pairings are aligned properly, which results in one-third of the EPR pairings being aligned wrongly overall; on average, two-thirds of EPR pairings are aligned incorrectly.

As a direct consequence of this, the two measures will agree fifty percent of the time and disagree fifty percent of the time. In an investigation of this kind, there are the several outcomes that are possible to observe.

4.3.7 Predictions of Bell's Theorem

In this part, we see why no locally concealed theory can provide this probability under the conditions under which it is being studied. Assume that the result of the polaroid measurements is affected by the secret state of each photon, independent of which of the three potential combinations it is in. We do not know what they are since there are only 23 possible binary configurations in which they react to observations performed with polaroids in any of the three possible configurations. These eight potential solutions are denoted by the numbers from h_0 to h_7, and their names are derived from those numbers.

	$\uparrow$		
h_0	P	P	P
h_1	P	P	A
h_2	P	A	P
h_3	P	A	A
h_4	A	P	P
h_5	A	P	A
h_6	A	A	P
h_7	A	A	A

Hidden states, regardless of how they seem, are identical to h_i in terms of the results of measurement, and we may think of h_i as comparable to hidden states. Both methods provide the same findings when used to detect EPR photons using polaroids that are oriented in the same direction and positioned at the same angle l.

If a local hidden-variable theory is to explain observational evidence, then there must be a set of hidden states called hi that are equal for the entangled pair. The photon on the left may be in any of the three polaroid positions, but the others must all follow suit.

In this case, we will look at the nine possible orientations for the two polaroids, and measurements for photon pairs in each of the hidden states are expected to be in accordance with hi. There is a 100% agreement between the h_0 and h_7 hidden state observations ("PPP," "PPP," and "AAA," respectively). Only five of the nine potential orientations of the hidden state h_1 are in accordance with the data, whereas the other configurations do not make sense. H_1 agrees with the position in 5 out of 9 situations and disagrees with it in 4 out of 9 circumstances. In all likelihood, the degree of agreement between the two measurements will be at least 5/9 of the total possible points, regardless of the stochastic processes used by the EPR source to produce photons with extracted features. The results from the research and the use of a local hidden-variable theory are incompatible.

4.3.8 Bell's Inequality

The idea that was presented before may be elaborated on in a sophisticated manner by using Bell's inequality. EPR pairs are emitted by a photon source in the direction of two polaroids, with three possible configurations for each pair. We have the option of arranging these polaroids in any combination of three distinct orientations because of their versatility.

By repeatedly measuring the polaroids at different settings, we can determine the frequency with which our chosen two polaroids provide identical results. If the first polaroid is tilted at an angle x and the second at an angle y, then either (i) both photons communicate with both polaroids in the same way (either both pass through everything and both are severely damaged), or (ii) both photons communicate with both polaroids when the first polaroid is tilted at an angle x and the second is tilted at an angle y. The end effect is the same in either case: both photons must be allowed to pass, or neither.

Adjusting both polariscopes to the same position ensures that photons are always measured in the same manner. Assume that x is a constant and P_{xx} always equals 1. It will be proved that Bell's contradiction holds for every local hidden-variable hypothesis as well as for any arbitrary succession of setting configurations for each of the polaroids.

First, it must be shown that the discrepancy is true for some equivalence class of concealed states, after which the proof may be given. Inequality is valid for any arrangement of these basis functions, which may be deduced from the previous result. A photon's local embedding layer, designated by the letter h, is what ultimately decides the result of a polaroid measurement, according to any explanation of local random states. It is possible to arrange things in three different ways. All conceivable hidden states that result in the required outcomes may be grouped together into a single intermediate node, which we shall refer to as h from now on. It follows that the two interlaced photons must belong to the same intermediate node, since polaroids are always evaluated at the same angle under an EPR situation. To rephrase, if the right-hand photon makes use of PAP in order to react to the polaroid locations a, b, and c, then the left-hand photon must do the same. When the two components agree on conditions containing a hidden variable and zero, the outcome is 1, and otherwise it is 0. At least one of the three polaroid settings, a, b, and c, may deliver the same result when a photon with a certain hidden state h is measured. Simple deduction will lead you to this conclusion. The main consequence of state always hidden photons.

We will refer to this number as "ω_h," which stands for the probability that the source produces photons of type h. The next step is to add up all the probabilities that have been established. $P_{ab} + P_{ac} + P_{bc}$ is a weighted sum, with weights ω_h, of the results for photons of each hidden class h.

$$R_b + P_{ac}t_b^P c = \sum_h \omega_h \left(R_b^h t_{acsc}^{P^h + P^s} \right)$$

Since $P_{abh} + P_{ach} + P_{bch}$ 1 for any h, we may assume that $P_{ab} + P_{ac} + P_{bc}$ 1. This follows because the weighted average of all numbers larger than 1 is greater than 1.

Since this inequality holds for every local hidden-variable theory, it meets the requirement that the theory is amenable to experimentation.

Using Exercise 4.6 as a guide, we may deduce that the likelihood of receiving two different answers that are the same is proportional to the square cosine angles of each other, in accordance with quantum theory. The inequality is modified to read as follows: $\cos^2 + \cos^2 + \cos^2(+)$ 1 if we assume that the angle between points a and b and the angle between points b and c are and, respectively.

According to quantum theory, given a value equal to 60, each term is equivalent to one-fourth of the whole. Because Bell's inequality is violated by these probabilities, we may draw the conclusion that no other local, deterministic theory is capable of making the same predictions as quantum mechanics. It is possible that the quantum theory and the observation that nature violates Bell-like inequalities will be validated as a result of these tests.

According to Bell's theorem, it is not even remotely imaginable to make use of a local hidden-variable theory in order to describe entangled states and their measurement. When discussing entangled states, there is no need to discuss local hidden states or the links between causes and effects, since none of these topics are relevant. Entanglement will be a topic of conversation as long as either of these two schools of thought is represented in published works of intellectual inquiry.

4.4   States of Quantum Metamorphosis

Information encoding and measurement in quantum states are explored in the book's last two chapters, which highlight their unique quantum properties. In this context, concepts like entangled states and the exponential state space were discussed. In this section, the foundations of quantum computing are laid forth. Quantum computations are conducted by the continuous adaptation of quantum systems. In order to fully comprehend quantum computing, we must first have a strong understanding of the types of modifications that are permitted by nature and those that are not. In this section, we apply modifications to closed quantum phenomena with the goal of remapping the system's state space to the original storage space. Measuring is not the same thing as development in this setting. As part of a larger quantum system, a quantum subsystem undergoes modifications that we shall discuss in this article.

As a prelude to discussing systems with many qubits, this chapter provides a short overview of the types of transformations that may be applied to generic quantum systems. This chapter provides a comprehensive analysis of the unitarity criterion and the no-cloning condition as they apply to changes in quantum states. For example, the no-cloning constraint is crucial to both the restrictions and the advantages of encoding information in quantum states, and so it is essential to the security of quantum cryptographic methods. This is due to the fact that quantum systems are unable to duplicate themselves due to the no-cloning limitation. Another crucial piece of evidence is that there are a maximum of n classical bits of information that can be extracted from an n-qubit system.

After looking at the problems associated with transformation for general quantum systems, Section 4.4.1 of the chapter narrows its attention to n-qubit systems and defines the fundamental building elements of a conventional circuit model for quantum computing. This notion is used to explain quantum algorithms in Part II of this article. To represent every quantum transition on an N-qubit quantum system, one or two-qubit subsystems may be employed as a representational unit. It may be possible to employ these basic gates to carry out some quantum state transitions in a more straightforward manner than others. The effectiveness of a quantum transition may be evaluated using gates with either one or two qubits. It investigates the transformations of a single qubit and of a pair of qubits, as well as how to combine these two types of transformations, and it presents a visual language for encoding sequences of transformations. It illustrates how these fundamental gates might be utilized to overcome two communication challenges, namely dense coding and the teleportation of quantum states. According to the findings of this study, every quantum transformation may be accomplished as a sequence of transformations involving one qubit and two qubits, respectively. It investigates a group of gates that may be used universally to approximate any quantum transformations. At this point in the chapter, we have reached the point where we can define the standard circuit model for quantum computing.

4.4.1 Solitary Steps Metamorphosis

A quantum transformation shall be understood here as a one-way mapping from the state space of the quantum system to the state space of the system itself. Since there are only a finite number of really plausible possibilities, every single measurement applied to a specific scenario can only produce a probabilistic conclusion. This chapter examines subsystems of larger subatomic particles, such as those found in open quantum systems, to learn more about the effects of modifications made to the larger systems on the smaller systems. In this chapter, we will focus only on the changes that occur inside closed quantum systems.

It is impossible for nature to randomly change the characteristics of a quantum system. For these changes to be natural, they must adhere to the tenets of quantum measurements and quantum superposition. For a state that is already a combination of other states to become a superposition of their images, the transformation must be linear in the feature space that is associated with state space. To be more precise, this implies that for every U-type quantum transition,

This occurs on every superposition described by the equation $|= a1|1++ak|k|$, since the existence of orthogonal subspaces implies that unit-length vectors lead to other unit-length vectors. Given these features, it is equivalent to measuring the transformed basis directly rather than doing the measurements on the result. The probability of achieving outcome $U|$ is the same whether U is applied first, then the decomposition iS_i is measured, or vice versa. There is an equal likelihood of achieving outcome $U|$ if U is used to $|$ first, then the decomposition iS_i is measured. Specifically, $u|u=uu=uu$ if U preserves the inner product, and $u|u=uu=uu$ if U preserves the inner product of their pictures.

We may use the following elementary mathematical reasoning to show this. The condition holds for each and every person if and only if $UU = I$. If the adjoint U of a linear transformation is equal to its inverse, then the transformation is said to be unitary. This is true for any conceivable quantum process. In addition, this criterion is all that is needed; the set of unitary operators on the complex vector space related to the state space of a quantum system is identical to the set of allowed changes to the system. Since a quantum system's state space is a complex vector space, this makes sense. It is possible to utilize unitary operators to map orthonormal bases onto one another to generate new orthonormal bases since they retain the inner product. The translation from one orthonormal basis to another is an example of a unidirectional transformation matrix.

The complex vector space associated with the quantum state space rotates with every state change. Matrix representations of unitary transformations may be considered orthonormal if the collection of columns in the matrix is orthogonal to the transformation in issue. Because of this, and only because of this, orthonormality may be achieved. In other words, U is also unitary if and only if its rows are orthonormal. Two unitary translations, U_1 and U_2, may be combined to produce a third unitary transformation, U. In the case when U_1 and U_2 are both unitary translations of X_1 and X_2, then the tensor product $U_1 U_2$ must likewise be a unitary transition of the space $X_1 X_1$. Conversely, there may be cases when unitary operators are combined in a nonstandard fashion.

If the operator meets the unitarity criteria, then it is consistent with quantum mechanics and does not break any of its fundamental rules. Not all unitary operators have approximate efficient implementations. As we continue our exploration of quantum algorithms in Chapter 5, we will pay special attention to questions about the efficiency of different quantum transformations.

The unitary condition must be met since all transitions between quantum states are reversible. Before the advent of quantum information processing, scientists Charles Bennett, Edward Fredkin, and Tommaso Toffoli found a way to make all classical calculations reversible with a negligible hit to efficiency. If you are looking for an alternative explanation, know that quantum algorithms are not constrained in any way by the reversibility restriction.

Standard models of quantum computers use circuits in which quantum transformations do all the work, and observations are simply used to "read out" the results. The dynamics of size, rather than the transitions between quantum states, may provide an alternate method for computing in quantum physics. In this part, we will discuss an alternative model of quantum computing that is equally as effective as the standard model. All computation in this model is achieved by direct measurement.

"Quantum transformation" and "quantum operator" relate to the activities of unitary operators on the state space and not to measurement processes per se. The postulate of measurements provides an indirect, statistical method for understanding how measures function rather than the direct action of the Hermitian operator on the represented state space. This does not depict the Hermitian operator's direct influence on the state space.

4.4.2 Irrational Metamorphosis: The No-Cloning Principle

Due to the necessary prerequisite, remember that unknown quantum states cannot be duplicated or cloned. The linearity of the unitary transformation really hints to the solution on its own. All quantum states are equal in |a|a| for the unitary transformations, a phenomenon known as cloning in the context of U. Let us call the two mutually exclusive quantum states |a| and |b|. Clone technology is proof of this theory.

One of the benefits of quantum mechanics is that it can be used to design and analyze systems of any complexity using just the most basic building blocks. One or two qubits may be used to implement every quantum state transition that is possible on an n-qubit system. Changing the quantum state of some number of bits (qubits) at a time is what a quantum gate does. There are many different ways that mathematical operations may be grouped together, and the terms "quantum circuit" and "quantum gate array" are also used to represent these varied approaches.

Gates are mathematical abstractions used in quantum entanglement processing literature to describe quantum algorithms. Quantum gates, unlike their classical counterparts, do not have to correspond to physical objects. The words and images on the gates should not be taken at face value. While physical gates may be used in solid state or optical implementations, in nuclear magnetic resonance (NMR) and ion trap system (ITS) implementations, the qubits are immobile and the gates are magnetic field or laser pulse transformations. Specifically, the qubits are employed as data storage in these systems. In such setups, a physical register containing qubits serves as the operating medium for gates to carry out their tasks.

From a practical standpoint, the standard explanation of computing based on the idea of one- and two-qubit gates is insufficient. Since we do not know which gates can be performed physically and safely, we cannot provide a full explanation of our calculations in terms of these gates. Furthermore, a computer program that can cope with arbitrary quantum transformations would need a highly specialized collection of gates, each of which must be able to perform the whole range of potential unitary transformations. Unfortunately, there is no finite set of generators since the number of quantum transformations is infinite. Despite this, it is possible that representations near to those of all unitary transformations may be obtained using limited sets of gates. However, it is unknown which of these clusters will be the most workable from a logistical standpoint. In order to evaluate the efficacy of a quantum algorithm, researchers need a consistent set of gates to work with. All gates with a qubit size of one and one with a qubit size of two are part of the set that we use.

A great number of algorithms are represented visually, and their descriptions and analyses are performed by using a sequence of quantum state transformations that are carried out on various amalgamations of qubits. For the purpose of depicting basic modifications and linking them together to build more complex circuits, boxes with appropriate labels are employed. An example of a graphical portrayal is shown here in Figure 4.4. A qubit is denoted by the representation of a vertical line. The flow of processing operates from left to right, beginning with the transformations on the left and progressing to the right. Boxes with the names U_0, U_1, and U_3 are used to indicate transformations involving a single qubit, while box U_2 is used to represent transformations involving two qubits. To say that an operator U has been applied to qubit I is equivalent to saying that the operator has been performed on all of the other qubits in the system. In an n-qubit quantum state, this is what it implies to apply operator U to a single qubit.

Figure 4.4 An example of a graphical representation of a quantum gate array containing three qubits. The flow of data via the circuit is from left to right.

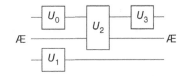

In the following paragraphs, we are going to talk about a few different kinds of quantum gates that are often used.

4.4.3 The Pauli Transformations

The Pauli deformations are the ones that are employed the vast majority of the time for single-qubit translations.

A superposition of 0 and 1 regarded as classical bits may be interpreted as a state of the system that is compatible with the schedule, and a superposition of 0 and 1 can be considered as a quantum state of 0 and 1. In visual notation, these gates are shown in the form of boxes.

In visual notation, these gates are shown in the form of boxes appropriately labeled.

Writers in the research literature seldom argue with one another about the application of Pauli transformation to their particular research. The main point of debate is whether or not $i([0\ 1][1\ 01])$ should be regarded as the Pauli transformation instead of $Y = [0\ 1][1\ 0]$, which is what we do. The Hermitian character of the operator iY makes it applicable in a wide range of settings, including discussions of measurement. Alternately, one might use the x, y, and z notation. The Pauli operators used to describe the translation of a single qubit are denoted by the letters I, X, Y, and Z throughout this whole book. Each operator will be represented by one of those letters. Pauli operators, written as "$x = X$," "$y = iY$," and "$z = Z$," are used in Chapter 10 to characterize quantum states.

4.4.4 The Hadamard Metamorphosis

The Hadamard modernization is another significant single-qubit translation.

4.4.5 Multi-Qubit Metamorphosis from Single-Qubit

It is possible to construct multiqubit transformations by making use of the tensor product of single-qubit transformations. These operations are pointless in terms of multiple-qubit transformations since they are effectively the same as carrying out single-qubit transformations on each qubit one at a time, in some arbitrary order. This renders them uninteresting. For illustration's sake, the combination of $U I$ and $I V$ may result in $U V$.

Modifications to the system that include several qubits and have the potential to affect its entanglement are more fascinating. There is no way that the entanglement that exists between two or more components can be impacted by modifications that only affect one of those subsystems. This is because there is no way that this entanglement can be affected. To be more specific, suppose that I is a two-qubit state and that U and V are unitary transformations of this state that involve just a single qubit. In this scenario, $(U V)$I only becomes entangled if also becomes entangled. In the next section, we will investigate a well-known kind of controlled trial gate to discover how different kinds of transformations influence entanglement.

4.4.6 The Controlled-NOT and Other Singly Controlled Gates

If the first bit is 0, then the second bit is not changed; however, if the first bit is 1, then the second bit is changed. When the first bit is set to zero, the state of the second bit is not affected. There is an example of the CNOT translation that may be seen here.

It makes it very simple to deduce its impact on the components of the standard basis: CNOT :I00

$\rightarrow$I 00

I 01 $\rightarrow$I 01

I10 $\rightarrow$ I11 I11 $\rightarrow$ I10

The symbol stands for the matrix representation of CNOT, and it is expressed in the standard basis.

CNOT is an inverse that is identical to itself in every way. Another thing that the CNOT gate cannot do is to construct a tensor product of two single-qubit transformations.

CNOT gates are crucial to quantum computing because of their capacity to modify the link between two qubits. For instance, entangled qubits have a different state from the state of two qubits:

It may convert an entangled state into one in which it is absent since it is the antithesis of itself. The controlled-not gate is so often used that a graphical notation for it has been created.

It is not hard to deduce that this denotes a negative value for the target bit, and that the line joining them shows how the value of the control bit determines whether or not the negation is legitimate. When the control bit is set to 0 instead of 1, the target bit is inverted, as seen by the usage of a solid circle by certain writers.

Gates that conduct a single-qubit alteration Q on the second qubit when the first qubit is set to |1 and do not do anything when the first qubit is set to |0 are the last two gates that enhance the CNOT gate's capabilities. Here, a graphical representation of these gate controls is provided for your perusal.

Since the shift at hand is not an absolute phase shift but rather a subjective shift, the single-qubit transformation that was done during the controlled shift is no longer strictly useless. It seems that the time connections between the constituent parts of a composite may be significantly altered by this. Create quantum circuits using visual symbolism, for instance. Several methods exist for achieving this goal, one of which is shown here:

In other words, this swap circuit takes

|00 → |00

|01 → |10

|10 → |01

|11⟩ ↦ |11⟩,

and $|\psi⟩|\varphi⟩ → |\varphi⟩|\psi⟩$ for all single-qubit states $|\psi⟩$ and $|\varphi⟩$.

There are three things that you need to keep in mind. The use of a basis and the actual modification are the two components that make up this initial part.

In the second part of this article, we will investigate the relationship between the idea of control and its basis. When dealing with quantum circuits, approaching the graphical depiction in a cautious manner is recommended.

To begin, it is necessary to have a firm grasp of the difference between the quantum state space (also called the "projective space") and the "complex vector space," which is related to the quantum state space in a number of ways. Always keep this in mind while seeking to grasp the common explanations for the transition between quantum states. Only the effect a unitary transformation has on its base may properly characterize it in a complex vector space. Differentiation: It is not feasible to prove the unitary transformation by pinpointing where all the basic states are moved. For instance, the controlled switching frequency adopts the four quantum qualities represented by |00, |01, |10, and |11i as its own; |10 and e |10 represent the same quantum state, as do |11 and e |11i. However, as we have seen before, this change does not equal a metamorphosis of identity since it requires so much effort and time. Notations like |00 |00 |01 |01i |10 ei|10 |11 e|11 might be useful for avoiding mistakes, so keep that in mind.

Unitary transformations on the complex vector space are expressed in terms of the vector space itself, rather than the states that correspond to the variables under consideration. Due to the fact that _1 and |1 are two separate vectors that correspond to the same state, asserting that _0 and _1 are the same vectors is not the same as saying that _0 and _1 are the same vectors. Unitary operations on the complicated dimensional space associated with the state's pace generate the quantum transformations of the pace.

Second, the foundation on which the concept of control rests is crucial. You cannot accept the ideas of "control bit" and "target bit" at face value when applied to the classical gate. The CNOT operator acts exactly like a conventional gate when used with classical bits. Still, this does not prove that the control bit is never altered in any manner. Using a controlled gate with input qubits that are not typical basic components may result in unexpected behavior. Consider the Hadamard basis as an example and specifically the CNOT gate that it entails. {|+,|−}: CNOT: |++ → |++ |+− → |−− |−+ → |−+ |−− → |+− .

According to the Hadamard basis, when one qubit's state is affected by another qubit's state, the states of the two qubits are mutually exclusive. This shifts the paradigm such that the control bits are the ones being targeted. But what has shifted is how we interpret the transformation; the underlying mechanism remains same. The fact that most bases lack both a control bit and a target bit compounds this problem. There are a few issues with this. It has been shown, for instance, that the controlled-not changes.

Once the controlled-not operations have been carried out on the qubits, it is very difficult to separate them.

Since the two circuits under discussion are equivalent, we may exploit this knowledge to our advantage in developing quantum error correction methods.

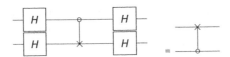

Thirdly, take great care to avoid electrocution while studying circuit diagrams. If the user does not take the time to properly grasp a visual depiction of entangled circuits, the results might be deceptive. It is not easy to tell what the transformations will do to a qubit by looking at the line in the diagram that represents it, even if the qubits being fed into it are all in their usual ground states. Examine the component of the circuit that is responsible for the output when the input value is zero. It would seem at first that the state of the first qubit is unaffected by the Hadamard translation since the Hadamard translation is its own inverse. However, this is not the case. To summarize, the controlled-not gate does not preserve the original state of the first qubit. To observe how the impact of this circuit is exerted on the input state, it is required to do an explicit computation. |00 to 1/2(|00+|10+|01|11).

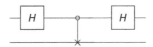

4.4.7 Opaque Coding

For a number of years, oddities in quantum mechanics, such as EPR pairings and entanglement in general, were written off as only being theoretical problems. Entanglement has been considered a purely theoretical idea for a significant amount of time; nevertheless, recent advances in quantum information processing have made it possible to successfully use the concept. Dense coding and teleportation are two applications that illustrate how useful EPR pairings and a few fundamental quantum gates can be when used in conjunction with one another.

In dense coding, one quantum bit is used with a shared EPR pair to encrypt and transmit two classical bits. Once EPR pairings are set up in advance, a single qubit of data may be used to transmit two bits of information. Given that a qubit can only hold the information corresponding to a single conventional bit, this result comes as a bit of a surprise. In contrast to dense coding, which employs many more bits, teleportation conveys the state of a single qubit using just two regular bits. There are two aspects of teleportation that are quite astounding. Although it is impossible to copy an object exactly in quantum physics, it is possible to copy its quantum state. Every feasible qubit state may be sent using just two classical bits, and this number is not constrained in any way.

Quantum entanglement is crucial for applications in both dense coding and transportation. To maintain uniformity, both processes begin with the same setup. They cannot wait to share their thoughts and opinions with one another. An EPR pair consists of two subatomic particles, one of which is shared by the two people. In physics, these particles are referred to as EPR pairs.

$$|\psi_0\rangle = \frac{1}{\sqrt{2}}(|00\rangle + |11\rangle)$$

Think about the following case: The first particle is delivered to Alice, while the second is given to Bob.

$$|\psi_0\rangle = \frac{1}{\sqrt{2}}(|0_A\rangle \mid 0_B + \mid 1A \mid 1B)$$

When Alice gives Bob her particle, or when Bob receives Alice's particle from Alice, Bob can only make alterations to Alice's particle. Since Alice and Bob may only do transformations that involve a single qubit until a particle is exchanged,

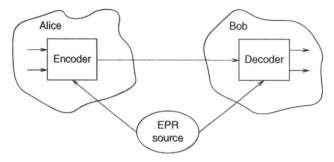

Figure 4.5 Structure of dense coding.

the only sort of transformation that they can perform on the EPR pair is of the kind $I\,Q$, where Q refers to the translation of a single qubit. Let $I(K)$ represent the square matrix with dimensions of $2k \times 2k$ when $K = 2k$. When both systems have n qubits, Alice can only do transformations of the form $U\,I(M)$, and Bob's only capable of transforming in the $N\,U$ configuration. according to Figure 4.5. This is the case when both systems have the same number of qubits.

4.4.8 Basic Bits in Opaque Coding

Alice just has to send one of the digits 0 through 3 across the wire, encoded as the state based on classical bits. If the qubit that Alice is controlling in the entanglement pair I0 has had this amount, then she implements one of the Pauli modifications I, X, Y, or Z to it. You may see the whole set of results in the table that follows.

Value Conversion
A whole new territory has come into existence.
From there, Alice will send Bob her qubit.

The first qubit of the entangled pair undergoes the Hadamard substitution H, which Bob uses to decipher the encrypted message.

After that, Bob may measure the two qubits in line with the consistent schedule and recover the two-bit binary approximation of the quantity Alice wanted to convey.

4.4.9 Quantum Message Teleportation

For quantum entanglement to be successful, the quantum state of a particle must be sent in such a manner that it can be exactly reassembled by a receiver using just classical bits. According to the no-cloning principle of subatomic particles, a quantum state cannot be copied, and as a result, the quantum superposition of the

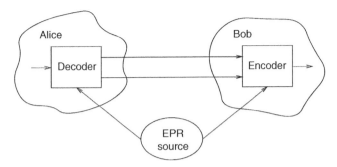

Figure 4.6 Structure quantum teleportation.

initial particle cannot be maintained. Figure 4.6 illustrates the concept of quantum teleportation, which gets its name from the fact that to produce the destination state, the source state must be destroyed.

Alice although wonderland can now see her qubit, she has no way of knowing its state at any given time. She intends to tell Bob how she really feels using the more traditional means at her disposal. Alice and Bob, like the configuration for dense programming, each have one of two qubits that are intertwined.

$$|\psi_0\rangle = \frac{1}{\sqrt{2}}(|00\rangle + |11\rangle)$$

The three-qubit quantum state is the initial condition of the system.

Alice continues to manage the first two qubits, while Bob handles the third.

The half of the entangled pair that belongs to Alice uses an algorithm quite similar to Bob's in order to decode the state of the qubit. Alice begins her treatment of her illness with CNOT I and then transitions to $H I I$.

Alice has only to examine the first two qubits and randomly choose a number between zero and eleven to determine which of the four standard basis states she will ultimately end up in. Through this, she can predict the location she will eventually call home. The quantum state of Bob's qubit is expected to be $a|0+b|1$, $a|1+b|0$, $a|0b|1$, or $a|1b|0$, depending on the outcome of her experiment. It is also possible that the answer is $a|1b|0$. Alice's measurement result is sent to Bob in the form of two binary bits.

After these adjustments, Bob's qubit will know more about the initial state than it did before. Using just her own powers, Alice can no longer reset her qubit to its original state. Only one of Alice or Bob may revert to their original quantum state at any one time, in accordance with the no-cloning principle. They are both affected by this.

Bob It is immediately obvious to Bob, upon receiving the two classical bits from Alice, how the state of one qubit in an entangled pair relates to the state of the other qubit in the pair. The original qubit that became entangled with Alice's | can be decoded, allowing reconstruction. With this, there is hope that I can be restored. Once Alice's bits have been decoded, Bob may use the table below to determine which decoding operator to apply to his own qubit based on the value of the bits.

State	Bits received	Decoding
$a|0\rangle + b|1\rangle$	00	I
$a|1\rangle + b|0\rangle$	01	X
$a|0\rangle - b|1\rangle$	10	Z
$a|1\rangle - b|0\rangle$	11	Y

$a|0\rangle + b|1\rangle$ is the quantum state in which Bob's qubit will be after decoding.

These two processes are in some ways opposites of one another since they both encode and decode in reverse; therefore, they are in some sense inseparable.

4.4.10 Designing and Constructing Quantum Circuits

After a series of primary adjustments have been made, it may be possible to make adjustments at the unitary level. The CNOT gate, which operates on two qubits, is included in the basic set with four other types of single-qubit gates. All possible n-qubit unitary transformations may be performed using the following four kinds of procedures. Control over many qubits may be achieved by generalizing single-qubit manipulations. The products of the three basic single-qubit operators are the building blocks of all single-qubit transformations. It takes the changes you make and generates a unique unitary metamorphosis.

This chapter does not concentrate on the efficiencies of such representations; rather, its primary purpose is to demonstrate that any quantum transformation may be carried out by using fundamental gates. Because of their low level of productivity, the use of simple gates to carry out the majority of quantum transformations is impracticable. Chapter 5 of the book will focus on determining which quantum changes are able to occur continually and how to use that information to solve computing issues.

4.4.11 Single Qubit Manipulating Quantum State

Phase shifts ($K()$), rotations ($R()$), and phase rotations ($T()$) are the three forms of single-qubit procedures that may be written as a combination of the three (). Rotations $R()$, phase rotations $T()$, and phase shifts $K()$ are all examples of angular motions (). Adjusting the tempo using It is common practice to replace the constant K with the scalar component $ei()$. For this reason, we include $K()$ here since this component constitutes a relative phase shift that has physical significance, while being analogous to the identity modernization of a single-qubit system when implemented to a multiple-qubit irrevocable metamorphosis. This is the case even if applying the identity update to a single-qubit system has similarities to applying the unconditional transformation to a system with multiple qubits. On the Bloch sphere, the y- and z-axes are rotated by a factor of 2 through the transformations $R()$ and $T()$.

The unitary translation of a single qubit (represented by the letter Q) may be expressed as a chain of three linear transformations: $Q = K()T()R()T$. Due to the global phase shift introduced by the function $K()$, the space encompassing all possible transformations of a single qubit has only three physical dimensions. The unitarity criteria is easily shown to be met after the adjustments are considered. QQ It is known from the symbol $= I$ that $|u00|2 +|u01|2 = 1$, $u00u10 + u01u11 = 0$, and $|u11|2 +|u10|2 = 1$. It does not take much mental gymnastics to figure out that $|u00|=|u11|$ and $|u01|=|u10|$. Since the sine and cosine of an angle may be used to express the magnitudes of the coefficients u_{ij}, we can express Q as what is more, the stages are not completely separate: Since $u10u00 + u11u01 = 0$, $10 = 00 = 11 = 01$.

4.4.12 Controlling Single-Qubit Metamorphosis

Changing the phase depending on certain conditions. Any circuit that operates just on the first qubit without making any changes that act directly on the second qubit, might be used to build $K()$. As opposed to affecting just one qubit, a phase shift modifies the whole quantum state. It is sufficient to perform operations on the qubit that was used initially. Specifically, $x\rangle \otimes a\, y\, a\, x\rangle \otimes |y|| = |$.

Implementing Q is slightly more involved. For $Q' = T(\alpha)R(\beta)T(\gamma)$, define the following transformations:

It is asserted here that Q may be characterized as It is not hard to understand that this circuit is responsible for the change described here.

A realization of an arbitrary one-qubit transformation that is controlled by a single qubit is possible for us to do in this manner.

4.4.13 Controlling Multi Single-Qubit Metamorphosis

The pictorial notation for regulated procedures introduced in Sections 4.2.4 and 4.4.2 is applicable to situations when there is more than one control bit in play. In this case when qubit start 1 to k are all, but let assume $k + 1$ qubit apply on variable Q and it should be the initial value of qubit is 0. The following diagram illustrates the controlled–controlled-not gate (also known as the Toffoli gate), which inverts the third bit of a three-bit number if and only if the first two bits are 1.

The notational subscript 2 denotes two control bits. Specifically, the CNOT gate is represented by the notation both.

By repeatedly iterating the construction of the k qubits may control an infinite number of changes to a single qubit. To construct a three-qubit gate with two inputs, first replace Q_0, Q_1, and Q_2 with their single-qubit managed counterparts.

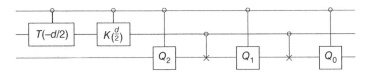

It is possible to perform arbitrary single-qubit changes under ink-qubit control by a process of repeated construction. To begin, a single qubit-regulated form of Q_0-Q_1 and Q_2-Q_3 from the prior design should be used in its place.

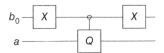

By momentarily negating the control qubits that are relevant for any length k bit-string s, the controlled gate that applies Q to qubit 0 may be realized when the other k qubits are in the pattern s. In this way, the controlled gate may be realized. After being annotated with bit strings, the k-qubit standard basis vector may be expressed using the notation $|s$. When all k qubits are in the base state $|s$, this design is accomplished using a gate that is controlled by $(k+1)$ qubits. The gate has no effect on qubit 0 when the k qubits are in any other base state. When the other qubits are in a different base state than I, the $(k+1)$ qubit-controlled gates change I according to Q, but do nothing else. It is not possible to apply the transformation Q to the system since the other qubits are in a different base state. Subspaces of dimension two are transformed by Q in this way; they are constructed from the orthonormal basis vectors, which vary from one another by a single bit. The orthogonal subspace is also preserved in this translation.

Any desired unitary transformation may be proven to be explicitly implemented with the help of such gates. This is exemplified by the following: As an example, consider the following: For instance, the build employs two separate transformations, each of which is associated with the same pair of qubits. The first applies Q to the ith qubit using the standard basis "0,|1" while the other k qubits are in state "s"; the second applies Q to the ith qubit using the inverse order of the basis. Qubit I undergoes the XQX transformation, while the other qubits stay in state $|s$. We utilize a specific notation in our writings.

Depending on the value of x_i, any of these modifications is represented by the $(k + 1)$-bit string x, which is constructed so that $xk...x_{k+1}x_{k+1}x_{k+1}...x_0 = s_{k+1}...s_0$. Here, Q is used to effect change in a single qubit, represented by the index x_i. When the x_i value of an expression is 1, it may be rewritten in one of two ways. The operation of inverting the ith bit of a bit-string is denoted by the symbol x, and it is defined as $x = x\ 2i = x$ will function with $Q = XQX$ as the input if Q is a one-qubit transformation. In mathematics, a revolution is defined as the two-dimensional complex subspace bounded by the standard basis vectors $|x_2$ and $|x_3$.

Illustration 4.6 The traditional CNOT in a two-qubit system is denoted by the symbol $|$, where b_1 is the control bit and b_0 is the target. The CNOT transformation is also reflected in the notation since X is invariant by the ordering of the basis for qubit b_0. In this case, $X = XXX$ is the exact notation used. This syntax enacts a controlled-not transformation, with the key distinction being that X is executed only when b_1 equals 0. The notation describes the standard CNOT with b_0 as the control bit and b_1 as the target bit.

In this section, we saw how to create multiple-qubit gates by combining many different basic gates, the complexity of which grows exponentially with the number of qubits. It demonstrates the feasibility of doing any operation using many qubits. One extra qubit is used in this design, which employs a growing number of fundamental gates.

4.4.14 Simple Metamorphosis

In this section, we use the 2^n-dimensional vector space of the state space of an n-qubit system to build an arbitrary unitary transformation. Rotating the 2^n-dimensional complicated vector space underlying the n-qubit quantum state space produces a unitary translation; hence, any rotation may be generated by rotating a series of 2-dimensional subspaces. This is due to the fact that a unitary transformation always results in another unitary transformation.

For the sake of argument, let us say N equals 2^n. In this step, we use a nonstandard ordering for "xx" to construct all matrices in the standard basis; nonetheless, there is only a single bit of variation between each consecutive element in the basis. Gray codes are made up of a series of binary digits. Every shade of gray between the two extremes is acceptable. It is crucial to keep in mind that the pattern for all of the other bits in the $|x_i+1$ is the same as in the $|x_1+1$, and that the only variation is on the bit designated ji. In Section 4.4.15, we explain how every arbitrary unitary operator may be represented as a chain of one-qubit operators rotating in a two-dimensional subspace spanned by consecutive basis elements. For this to work, the space being rotated must be covered by a sequence of basis elements.

Check out these many kinds of changes: where $I(m)$ is the identity matrix for m and VN_m is a $(N\,m)(N\,m)$-unitary matrix with $0\,m\,N_2$. We aim to show that for any $(N\,N)$-matrix Um_1, where m may take on the maximum value of 0 and N is the total number of qubits, there exist operators C_m, which are the products of multiple-controlled single-qubit operators, and an U_m, which now has a larger identification component $I(m)$, such that $U_{m1} = C_m U_m$. $U = U_0 = C_1\,CN_2 UN_2$ is an expression for the unitary operator that takes this into account.

The operation that occurs when $x = xN_2$ and, using the gray code condition, $j = JN_2$ is the bit that differentiates the last two basis vectors $|xN_2$ and $|xN_1$, respectively, is the form that the transformation UN_2 takes. In mathematics, the UN_2 transformation is represented by the symbol UN_2. After we show how to build C_m using multiply controlled single-qubit operators, we will have shown that every unitary operator can be stated in terms of these operators and hence can be performed with only CNOT, $K()$, $R()$, and $T()$. Once we demonstrate how to build C_m with multiply regulated single-qubit operators, this will be the case.

U_{m1} has a nontrivial effect on the first basis vector denoted by the symbol $|x_m$. Notation: $|v_{mket} = U_{m-1}\,|\,X_{mket} = a_m\,|\,X_{mket} + \cdots + a_N |x_N$.

Due to the fact that U_{m1} may be multiplied by a global phase, we can safely assume that a_N is a real number. If we can find a unitary metamorphosis W_m that maps $|v_m$ to $|x_m$ and does not change any of the first parts and elements of the basis, then $W_m U_{m1}$ will have the required shape. To that end, we will make C_m equal to W_m and set U_m equal to $W_m U_{m1}$. It is necessary to recast the coefficients of the last two components of $|v_m$ before defining W_m, as shown below.

Makes the amplitude that was previously part of $|x_N$ part of $|x_{N1}$. All other basis vectors are unaffected since the regulated part of the operators only affects those with bits in pattern B_{N1}. To get the operator and hence the missing portion of W_m, we must apply the method to all feasible sets of coordinates. The final ensures that it is a positive real by adding 1, since the image of $|v_m$ must be a unit vector. The reason is as follows:

While this approach does give an implementation for each unitary operator U in terms of straightforward modifications, the required gate count rises exponentially with the number of qubits. Since more efficient implementations are needed for actual calculations, their usefulness is restricted. Consequently, its applicability is limited. Finding efficient unitary operators that can be implemented in terms of simple gates is the most difficult part of the procedure. This practice, which has the same name as the methodology, is known as quantum evolutionary computation.

4.4.15 Unique Setup Gates

It is also possible to use single-qubit translations or controlled-not gates to achieve any unitary transformation. For convenience's sake, we have found that a smaller set of gates is better to deal with. Although unitary transformations cannot be performed by combining any finite collection of gates, it is easy to prove that any finite set of gates may be used to generate an approximation of any unitary conversion with arbitrary accuracy. Not only are these approximations feasible, but they can be accomplished by using no more than $p(d)$ gates from the finite set of gates to achieve the requisite degree of precision $2d$. What is more, it is not impossible to do this. Although we will not be presenting the efficiency result reached by the Solovay–Kitaev theorem, we will show that all unitary modifications may be approximatively estimated with a small number of gates.

Since single-qubit and CNOT gates are capable of executing any unitary transformation, it is sufficient to find a small set of gates that approximate all single-qubit transformations. This is due to the fact that both single-qubit and CNOT gates only contain a single qubit. The set has the Phase gate, the Hadamard gate H, and the CNOT gate. Despite the obvious problems with the name, it has unfortunately persisted in usage. This phase becomes a relative phase with physical significance when employed as part of a gated control system. When taken by themselves, however, the phases are meaningless since they occur only inside a global phase.

Alteration to the traffic pattern A rotation R is considered rational if and only if the equation $R_m = I$ holds for all positive integers m. Without this form of m, R will degenerate into an irrational rotation. Some reasonable rotations of the Bloch sphere should, in theory, be able to mimic single-qubit transformations. Do not you think it is about time we did something a little bit out of the ordinary? In the demonstration, these gates are used to build an irrational rotation. Because the rotating group of a sphere is different from that of a Euclidean plane, it is conceivable to build such a structure. The sum of rational rotations is also always rational on a Euclidean plane but not on a spherical surface. Explanation of the relevance of the rotation groups of the sphere and the Euclidean plane.

In the exercises, you will dig further into the following explanation, which relies on spherical geometry. The z-axis of the Bloch sphere rotates by a factor of $P_i/4$ due to the gate's influence. The x-axis has been rotated by a factor of four ($/4$). Here is a chance to work on your spherical geometry skills.

With the hope of demonstrating the absurdity of such a switch. To an arbitrary accuracy of $2d$, every rotation W along the same axis may be approximated by a power of V because V is irrational. The statement still holds even if V is not a rational number. For every single-qubit operation W, there is a plethora of angle combinations that may be employed to complete the transformation, and this holds true all the way up to the global phase.

$$W = K(\delta)T(\alpha)R(\beta)T(\gamma)$$

where $T()$ rotates about z at an angular location and $R()$ rotates about y at an angular position. A single qubit may undergo translation in either direction by combining rotations along any two axes.

Since the HVH transformation has a separate axis from the V transformation, we use it for all single-qubit operators. Several sets that are close to being finite worldwide may be found with some effort.

4.4.16 The Standard Circuit Model

All calculations may be described in terms of a circuit made up of basic gates, with measurements occurring in a predetermined order. Directly from a universal set of simple gates or indirectly from a rough set of quantum gates, we choose our simple gates. Traditional versions of quantum computing circuitry make use of the CNOT gate and all other single-qubit transformations as part of the gate set. As part of the measurement set, these models make use of single-qubit measurements in the canonical basis. A single qubit and CNOT gate form the foundation of each calculation, and subsequent measurements on individual qubits in the standard basis (also known as the "standard model") fill out the picture. Although it would be simpler to work with an unlimited set of all the possible transformations of a single qubit, it would be more useful to have a finite collection of gates. Furthermore, studies by Solovay and Kitaev show that processing capacity is not noticeably improved by using an infinite set. Registers are subsets of the entire number of n qubits used in a calculation and are often partitioned for the purpose of conceptual simplicity.

Currently, you may choose from a variety of different quantum computer models. Insights into the inner workings of quantum computing can be gained from any model, and all models have contributed to the advancement of the field in some way, whether through the creation of new algorithms, novel approaches to resilient quantum processing or innovative approaches to building quantum computers. Our attention here will be directed on the most important models.

Searching for quantum calculations that are equivalent to classical ones is made much easier by the conventional circuit model. In the next paragraph, we will hone in on this issue as we go into further depth. Finding quantum analogs for classical circuits is a far easier undertaking than creating a reversible classical circuit from scratch. It is feasible to perform any conceivable quantum transformation using just the fundamental gates of the traditional circuit model. However, the extent of its effectiveness is seldom discussed. Quantum computations have been proven to be just as efficient as classical ones. The fundamental goal of this study is to build quantum algorithms, which entails discovering quantum transformations that can be effectively implemented using the basic gates of the conventional circuit model, and exploring the potential applications of doing so.

References

1 Clerk, A.A., Devoret, M.H., Girvin, S.M. et al. (2010). *Reviews of Modern Physics* 82 (1155), arXiv:0810.4729.

2 Shor, P. W. (2000). Introduction to Quantum Algorithms, pp. 1–17. https://doi .org/10.48550/arXiv.quant-ph/0005003.

3 DiVincenzo, D.P. and Shor, P.W. (1996). *Physical Review Letters* 77: 3260.

4 Steane, A.M. (2003). *Physical Review A* 68: 42322.

5 Neill, C., Roushan, P., Kechedzhi, K., Boixo, S., Isakov, S. V., Smelyanskiy, V., Barends, R., Burkett, B., Chen, Y., Chen, Z., Chiaro, B., Dunsworth, A., Fowler, A., Foxen, B., Graff, R., Jeffrey, E., Kelly, J., Lucero, E., Megrant, A., Mutus, J., Neeley, M., Quintana, C., Sank, D., Vainsencher, A., Wenner, J., White, T. C., Neven, H., and Martinis, J. M. (2017), arXiv:1709.06678.

6 Axline, C., Reagor, M., Heeres, R. et al. (2016). *Applied Physics Letters* 109: 042601.

7 Jiang, L., Taylor, J.M., Sørensen, A.S., and Lukin, M.D. (2007). *Physical Review A* 76: 062323.

8 Nickerson, N.H., Fitzsimons, J.F., and Benjamin, S.C. (2014). *Physical Review X* 4: 041041.

9 Monroe, C., Raussendorf, R., Ruthven, A. et al. (2014). *Physical Review A* 89: 1, arXiv:1208.0391.

10 Blumoff, J.Z. (2017). Multiqubit experiments in 3D circuit quantum electrodynamics, Ph.D. thesis, Yale University.

11 Feynman, R.P. (1982). *International Journal of Theoretical Physics* 21: 467.

12 Deutsch, D. (1985). *Proceedings of the Royal Society of London. Series A: Mathematical and Physical Sciences* 400 (97).

13 Shor, P. (1994). *Proceedings 35th Annual Symposium on Foundations of Computer Science*, 124–134. IEEE Computer Society Press.

14 Grover, L.K. (1997). *Physical Review Letters* 79: 4709.

15 Kassal, I., Whitfield, J.D., Perdomo-Ortiz, A. et al. (2011). *Annual Review of Physical Chemistry* 62: 185.

5

Computational Algorithm Design in Quantum Systems

5.1 Introduction

Unlimited precisions are assumed. Quantum physics permits statistical connections among states to be controlled in parallel, which is used in the experiment [1].

In principle, a quantum computer may enable algorithmic methods that are theoretically more optimal than those that can be achieved using a conventional computer. While the theory of quantum mechanics is true, there are substantial problems with implementing that theory in technology [2]. To use quantum parallelism, it is essential to scale quantum resources (in terms of the number of gates) in a feasible and theoretically sound way. The scalability of the number of mathematical operations required to perform specific quantum algorithms may perfectly balance the apparent quantum concurrency, such that the net result is comparable to classical parallelism [3].

5.2 Quantum Algorithm

Most presentations on quantum computing concentrate initially discussion of quantum mechanics and the foundations of aims at enhancing may be utilized to accomplish calculations that cannot meet the technical on a conventional computer, which is why they are sometimes referred to as "physics-centric." Even though this presentation mirrors the historical development of quantum computing, it obscures the abstract computation paradigm indicated by subatomic particles with regards to the finer points of subatomic particles as they apply to actual systems, which are unnecessary. Boolean algebra and programming language may be explained using analogies to the electrons that make up semiconductor devices [4].

Quantum Computing: A New Era of Computing, First Edition.
Kuldeep Singh Kaswan, Jagjit Singh Dhatterwal, Anupam Baliyan, and Shalli Rani.
© 2023 The Institute of Electrical and Electronics Engineers, Inc. Published 2023 by John Wiley & Sons, Inc.

This chapter aims to present computer technology as a mathematical formulation devoid of any physical links. Only the usage of notation and language acquired from quantum physics may be considered moderation. Most of the physics-oriented quantum computing literature would be rendered unreadable if concepts like measurement and read operation were replaced with more traditional computer science ones [5].

We'll go through eight quantum computational paradigm characteristics in the following paragraphs. They do not create formal assumptions upon which the quantum concept is trained, which may be formalized. Still, they each capture one distinctive element that distinguishes quantum virtualization technologies from conventional ones.

5.3 Rule 1 Superposition

A definition of what information means in the material universe is the first attribute of the new computing paradigm based on quantum physics. As a new reportable segment, the qubit is a development of the conventional bit [6].

There are two possible scalar bit values: 0 or 1. Unambiguous, distinctive, and unpredictable are the characteristics of a bit. Regarding computing, qubits are far more general since they reflect the chance that the qubit's value will be either 0 or 1 [7]. A pair of complicated integers (a, b) determine the state of a qubit. As a result, a qubit may exist in one of three states: zero, one, or a combination of the two, known as "entangled particles." According to (a and b), the superposition's 0 and 1 weights are ascertained:

$$\text{qubit} = (a, b) = a \cdot 0\,\text{bit} + b \cdot 1\,\text{bit} \tag{5.1}$$

The quantum bit's (qubit) opposite state maybe both 0 and 1. The state of a qubit is a square matrix of the 0 and 1 conditions, where the strengths are specified by the quantities a and b. There is no entanglement in a bit. Hence it may be considered a particular instance of a qubit. If a bit is in state 0, then a qubit $(1, 0)$ symbolizes that bit, whereas a bit in state 1 is represented by the qubit $(0, 1)$ [8].

Quantum states are often expressed using Bracket, a notation invented by scientist Paul Dirac. In this variant on standard vector notation, the inner combination $|0$ is called a parenthesis, where $|1$ is a row vector (pronounced "bra psi") and $|\Psi$ is a characteristics equation scale parameter (pronounced "ket psi") (which is the origin of the root terms bra and ket). A single qubit's state may be expressed as follows in this number system:

$$|\Psi\rangle = a\,|0\rangle + b\,|1\rangle$$

or

$$|\Psi\rangle = a^* |0\rangle + b^* |1\rangle$$

Note that |0 is not a zero vector; instead, the zero is labeling a unit-basis variable that is perpendicular to |1 [9]. To put it another way, the states of a qubit may be represented by any pair of basis function vectors in a complex two-dimensional space. Our most typical form, known as a computation foundation, has these elements:

$$|0\rangle = (1,0)$$

$$1\rangle = (0,1)$$

And

$$|0\rangle = \begin{pmatrix} 1 \\ 0 \end{pmatrix}$$

$$|1\rangle = \begin{pmatrix} 0 \\ 1 \end{pmatrix}$$

Because $|0\rangle$ and $|1\rangle$ are orthogonal unit vectors:

$$\langle 0|0 \rangle = \langle 1|1 \rangle = 1 \tag{5.2}$$

$$\langle 0|1 \rangle = \langle 1|0 \rangle = 0 \tag{5.3}$$

Remember that the logical bits |0 and |1 are conventionally represented as |0 and |1 (0 and 1, respectively). A qubit may therefore be seen as a highly involved linear aggregation of classical bits [10].

Instead, it is possible to think of *a* qubit as a vector in a typical bit space that is more conceptual and has more sophisticated architecture. To put it another way, the previously demonstrated states for one qubit, $a|0 + b|1$, might be written as follows in vector notation [11].

$$\vec{v} = a\vec{i} + b\vec{j} \tag{5.4}$$

$$\vec{v} = a\vec{t} + b\vec{j}$$

with

$$\vec{i} \cdot \vec{i} = \vec{j} \cdot \vec{j} = 1$$
$$\vec{i} \cdot \vec{j} = \vec{j} \cdot \vec{i} = 0$$

$$\vec{i} \cdot \vec{i} = \vec{j} \cdot \vec{j} = 1 \tag{5.5}$$

$$\vec{i} \cdot \vec{j} = \vec{j} \cdot \vec{i} = 0 \tag{5.6}$$

These include, but are not limited to, vectors that are parallel to |0 and |1. It cannot be denied that the two pictures are very similar. Improvements of Bra–Ket notation over standard vector representation become more obvious when working with several qubits. Each qubit is capable of being in one of two states, but the linear combination of n qubits symbolizes 2^n. In the 2-qubit state, linear relationships of four fundamental states are symbolized by two bit-digits:

$$|q^{(2)} = \alpha\,|00\rangle + \beta\,|01\rangle + \gamma\,|10\rangle + \delta\,|11\rangle \tag{5.7}$$

In abstract space, this translates to a four-dimensional vector of basis functions and two-bit states. Just as in our previous example, all four superposition parameters are complicated integers.

Because two one-qubit states may be combined to form a two-qubit state, this term refers to this fact:

$$\left|q^{(2)}\right\rangle = a\,|0\rangle + b\,|1\rangle \oplus c\,|0\rangle + d\,|1\rangle \tag{5.8}$$

$$= ac\,|0\rangle \oplus |0\rangle + ad\,|0\rangle \oplus |1\rangle + bc\,|1\rangle \oplus |0\rangle + bd\,|1\rangle \oplus |1\rangle \tag{5.9}$$

In order to accommodate these two-qubit situations, we may now define an expanded computation foundation as follows:

$$|00\rangle = |0\rangle \oplus |0\rangle \tag{5.10}$$

$$|01\rangle = |0\rangle \oplus |1\rangle \tag{5.11}$$

$$|10\rangle = |1\rangle \oplus |0\rangle \tag{5.12}$$

$$|11\rangle = |1\rangle \oplus |1\rangle \tag{5.13}$$

And then

$$|q^{(2)} = ac\,|00\rangle + ad\,|01\rangle + bc\,|10\rangle + |11\rangle \tag{5.14}$$

In theory, there exist two-qubit circumstances that cannot be written as the tensor product of two qubits. Examples include

$$|q^{(2)} = \frac{1}{\sqrt{2}}\,|00\rangle + |11\rangle! = \left|q_a^{(1)}\right\rangle \oplus \left|q_b^{(1)}\right\rangle \tag{5.15}$$

We call these quantum coherence superpositions those that cannot be expressed as the linear combination of more fundamental states.

However, the same method might be used to build the foundations for qubits of any size. For the most part, the following can be said about the condition of an n-qubit quantum accumulator:

$$|\Psi\rangle = \sum_{i=0}^{2^n-1} \alpha_i\,|i\rangle \tag{5.16}$$

Wave function of 2^n states of n-bit binary numbers, where each I represents a distinct n-bit complementary sequence [12] is thus a part of the computational foundation for a system that utilizes n-qubits, and its elements are encoded as a binary enumeration, where,

$$|\Psi\rangle = \alpha_0 |00...00\rangle + \alpha_1 |00...01\rangle + ... + \alpha_{N-1} |11...11\rangle \tag{5.17}$$

where $N = 2^n$, a rule we will stick to throughout the whole document.

The basis functions associated with the proposed n-qubits may be defined as follows:

$$\langle 00...0| = (1, 0, 0, ..., 0)$$

$$\langle 00...1| = (0, 1, 0, ..., 0)$$

$$\langle 11...0| = (0, 0, 0, ..., 1)$$

In the linear function of a set, the weights I are supposed to have a Euclidean norm of one:

$$\langle \Psi | \Psi \rangle = \sum_{i=0}^{2^n-1} \alpha_i \alpha_i^*$$
$$= \sum_{i=0}^{2^n-1} |\alpha_i|^2$$
$$= 1$$

This decision will become more apparent when we explore the second feature of the quantum computing paradigm.

While discussing Property #1, it is vital to note that the computation foundation is not solely responsible for operating quantum states in the quantum computation paradigm. We might, for example, employ the alternate basis that arises from rotating the computational base in the case of two-qubits. This foundation consists of the following:

$$|+\rangle = \frac{|0\rangle + 01\rangle}{\sqrt{2}}$$
$$|-\rangle = \frac{|0\rangle - 01\rangle}{\sqrt{2}}$$

Any other orthonormal foundation is just as feasible as this one. The quantum programmer must make the choice on which basis to utilize, since various bases give a decentralized organizational structure for the algorithm in certain cases [13]. If the foundations are employed consistently, it is completely OK to use any of them.

5.4 Rule 2 Quantum Entanglement

Computing in the quantum realm is based on a probability paradigm. Read operations will cause the superposition of 2^n states in a quantum register to "collapse" to one classical state when applied to an n-qubit quantum recorder.

In other words, measuring a two-qubit state yields a two-bit answer. Weights in the linear function of a set influence the probability with which it will collapse to a given state; this state is specified by the weights [14]. Think of a two-qubit register R being read, or being measured, as follows:

$$|R\rangle = \alpha|0\ 0\rangle + \beta|0\ 1\rangle + \gamma|1\ 0\rangle + \delta|1\ 1\rangle \tag{5.18}$$

Assuming a probability of $||2$, one may expect to see the classical bit state2 00 and so on.

The probability of obtaining the state I in a measuring of an n-qubit state provided Eq. (5.18) by the following equations:

$$P_i = |\langle i|R\rangle|^2 \tag{5.19}$$

where is an n-bit binary vector in the computational basis.

To ensure that all potential outcomes are equally likely, we wish to apply on Eq. (5.19) the following equation:

$$P_{\text{total}} = \sum_i P_i = 1 \tag{5.20}$$

That means, in the earlier illustration:

$$|\alpha|^2 + |\beta|^2 + |\gamma|^2 + |\delta|^2 = 1 \tag{5.21}$$

Because of this, we need to make sure that all quantum registers are normalized to one.

All future observations will be able to acquire the same condition if the first observation is performed. In case the state 10 is read, the aforementioned aggregation has collapsed, such that it contains the values and all other components are 0. Because of this, for now, R is equivalent to a conventional register in state 10:

$$|R\rangle \rightarrow |1\ 0\rangle \tag{5.22}$$

The content of a classical register is changed when an operation is done to it. For example, in the quantum register R, a classical action that changes the state to 11 may be understood as setting equal to 1 and setting to zero after a measurement provides the state 01 Right now, we can get the state 11 with probability 1 by taking measurements of the register [15].

Permutations of the constituents of each state vector in the combination may be seen as classical operations in general because they can be represented as permutations of the components in each state vector. After a combinatorial modification, the weights' normalizing is kept as intended. As an example, using Eq. (5.21) considers the following:

$$\alpha \,|00\rangle + \beta \,|01\rangle + \gamma \,|10\rangle + \delta \,|11\rangle \quad \to \quad \alpha \,|00\rangle + \beta \,|01\rangle + \gamma \,|10\rangle + \delta \,|11\rangle \tag{5.23}$$

with

$$|\alpha|^2 + |\beta|^2 + |\gamma|^2 + |\delta|^2 = |\alpha|^2 + |\beta|^2 + |\gamma|^2 + |\delta|^2 = 1 \tag{5.24}$$

Among the QC framework, every unitary translation is included in the potential operations. Consider the following properties of a unitary modernization:

$$U - 1 = U\dagger \tag{5.25}$$

and therefore:

$$U\dagger U = I \tag{5.26}$$

where U is the Fourier transform transpose matrices of U, and I is the array of numbers. As a result, a vector v is transformed as follows using Eq. (5.25):

$$v \to w = Uv \tag{5.27}$$

will maintain v's original intensity because (with Eq. (5.26))

$$|w|2 = w\dagger w = v\dagger U\dagger Uv = v\dagger v = |v|2 \tag{5.28}$$

A unitary transformation in the quantum setting keeps the Euclidean norm of the domain at unity. If you're interested in:

$$U \begin{pmatrix} \alpha \\ \beta \\ \gamma \\ \delta \end{pmatrix} \to \begin{pmatrix} \alpha' \\ \beta' \\ \delta' \\ \gamma' \end{pmatrix} \tag{5.29}$$

As a result, the probability of each condition is affected as follows using Eq. (5.23):

$$\alpha|0\,0\rangle + \beta|0\,1\rangle + \gamma|1\,0\rangle + \delta|1\,1\rangle \to \alpha'|0\,0\rangle + \beta'|0\,1\rangle + \gamma'|1\,0\rangle + \delta'|1\,1\rangle \tag{5.30}$$

with

$$|\alpha|^2 + |\beta|^2 + |\gamma|^2 + |\delta|^2\rangle = |\alpha'|^2 + |\beta'|^2 + |\gamma'|^2 + |\delta'|^2 = 1 \tag{5.31}$$

A well-defined probabilistic computing model should include this as an anticipated characteristic. According to this paradigm, if quantum computing if computation is a probabilistic one, then the possibilities should always sum to 1. That holds true even if the states are changed in some way. That's why QC only allows unitary operations and not measurement [16].

Since using a $2^n \times 2^n$ matrix would result in quantum circuits with exponential size and/or processing periods, it is not possible to employ such a matrix for classical or quantum operations. Computational activities approximating highly structured unitary matrix are important for the success of quantum algorithms because they may be expressed implicitly with low complexity (e.g. using a limited number of logic gates, proportionate to the number n). Since computing is abstracted by mathematical concepts in a 2^n-dimensional space, its potential speedups in QC may be studied in their whole rather than just in individual operations.

In this section, we will dive further into how certain modifications might pave the way for the creation of novel quantum cryptography that are more advanced than the best conventional counterparts. These optimization algorithms stand out because they are guaranteed to provide a correct result a certain percentage of the time. The approach has to be executed several times to ensure that a solution is found with a likelihood of occurrence as close to one as feasible [17].

5.5 Rule 3 Quantum Metrology

In the quantum optimization problem, measurements (read: operations) are destructive.

A classical state may be obtained by reading the content of a quantum register, as has already been stated. So, all forms in a superposition with the observed state are wiped out. Furthermore, once a superposition is broken down by measurement, it is impossible to regain the lost states. As a result, measurements are a dangerous force that cannot be reversed.

No matter how many states an n-bit quantum register can store, Rule 3 says that only one of those states, assessed with the complete n-bit logical information, can be an actual n-bit state.

Multi-qubit registers may be used to evaluate the simple qubit state. Complicating the transcript, on the other hand, will determine its condition after the measurements. What if we had two qubits, each in its non-entangled state?

$$|q_{ab}\rangle = (\alpha |0_a\rangle + \beta |1_a\rangle) \oplus (\gamma |0_b\rangle + \delta |1_b\rangle) \tag{5.32}$$

With a chance of $|\alpha|2$ of finding the qubit in the state 0 and collapsing the register to:

$$|q_{ab}\rangle = \alpha |0_a\rangle \oplus (\gamma |0_b\rangle + \delta |1_b\rangle) \tag{5.33}$$

Likewise, if we discover an in-state 1, the chance is $|\beta$. The measurements of qubit a have no effect on the state of qubit b in either circumstance. Consequently, the observation of qubit b is entirely unaffected by any later measurements on a.

Assume, however, that we have access to a two-qubit particle physics storage that is in an entangled state, as shown by:

$$|Q\rangle_{ab} = \frac{1}{\sqrt{2}} \left(|0_a 0_b\rangle + |1_a 1_b\rangle \right) \tag{5.34}$$

With a 50% chance of finding an in-state 0, the application form will deteriorate to:

$$|Q\rangle_{ab} = |0_a 0_b\rangle \tag{5.35}$$

and any future measurement of b will confirm that it is in the value 0 without a doubt. Furthermore, if we previously measured the state of one, we may be confident that the form of the other will be in the same place. Measurement of b is dependent on an earlier measure of a. Therefore, when using entangled states, the measurements of a qubit will have an impact on the state of other qubits.

The possibility of verifying the contents of a quantum register during a quantum algorithm is also eliminated by Rule 3 of the Diffie–Hellman code. In other words, there is no method to get and utilize partial products or do other standard algorithmic operations. It is not permitted under the quantum model to use print expressions for debugging purposes.

This irreversible degree of uncertainty is a problem that must be overcome if appropriate and efficient quantum algorithms are to be designed. However, quantum computing's strength is derived from its capacity to manipulate the superposition to enhance the likelihood of detecting a desired solution state. As a result, accessing the contents of the quantum register must be the last step in the optimization technique.

5.6 Rule 4 Quantum Gates

The parallel computing space that can be accessed by quantum computers is several orders of magnitude greater than the space accessible by conventional registers [18].

Keeping this in mind, a single bit can only hold a single memory location, either 0 or 1. To put it another way, although a single qubit can have either 0 or 1 at any one time, it may concurrently hold both states at any given time.

An n-bit register can generally index $N = 2^n$ states, but it can only store and modify the index of one state. When it comes to quantum registers, on the other hand, the weights of all N states may be simultaneously altered.

In particular, $N \log(N)$ bits are required for the classical storing of indices to N distinct states. For example, a 24-bit address may hold eight 3-bit identifiers. To store N indices, $\text{Log}(N)$ qubits are required, on the other hand. There are more than 224,000,000,000 unique addresses that might be stored in one 24-qubit quantum register. You may also use 3 qubits to hold 8 different 3-bit talks [19].

An array of size N may be searched using quantum superposition to acquire the index of each requested element in less than N consecutive steps, as will be shown in this chapter. To put it another way, the superposition of indices in a quantum algorithm allows it to analyze N items of an array simultaneously and genuinely.

One of the most significant benefits of the quantum model is encapsulated in Rule 4. However, as we previously said, we can only retrieve the address indicated by a string of n-bits from an n-qubit register holding a superposition of 2^n unique addresses. However, we cannot access most of this computing space in the quantum model until we have made a standard measure. Quantum algorithms have the issue of using the vast combinatorial space available before a balance is achieved.

5.7 Rule 5 Fault-Tolerant Quantum Gates

All actions on qubits, except observations, must be bidirectional.

To keep the superposition stable, only procedures that may be reversed are allowed to be performed to a quantum memory.

This is due to the general rule that only unitary modifications may maintain a superstring theory.

It is possible to reverse a unitary matrix U to get the initial state of the system since $U-1 = U^\dagger$. In other words, there is a corresponding inverse procedure:

$$|\psi\rangle \to U|\psi\rangle = |\psi'\rangle \tag{5.36}$$

$$|\psi'\rangle \to U^{-1}|\psi'\rangle = |\psi\rangle \tag{5.37}$$

Unitary operations sustain superposition because every permanent action results in a loss of information and hence causes the quantum states to collapse. Conversion efficiency may be seen as the explanation for this. As stated in Rule 2, the quantum computing paradigm is random, and hence Rule 5 follows. The real possibility can only be conserved by unitary operations, as explained above.

Let's look at the Control-Not (CNOT) operations, one of the most fundamental quantum operators. The CNOT operator requires two bits: a controlling bit and a destination bit. If the managing bit is 0, nothing happens. If the specific to a particular is 1, however, the state of the targeted bit is inverted. As a result, the following is the truth table for the CNOT operating condition:

a	b	a′	b′
0	0	0	0
0	1	0	1
1	0	1	1
1	1	1	0

An instruction's target bit is determined by the control bit (a). For each pair of outputs, we know the inputs without a doubt (a,b). As a rule, bijective binary functions mapping 1 to 1 are used to express reversible operations.

If you want to use the CNOT in the quantum realm, you can do it easily. A quantum operator based on the CNOT truth table might be built, utilizing the combinatorial basis of two-qubit states, to achieve this purpose. What happens to two-qubit quantum registrations when a CNOT is present?

$$|R\rangle = \alpha\,|0\ 0\rangle + \beta|0\ 1\rangle + \gamma|1\ 0\rangle + \delta\,|1\ 1\rangle \tag{5.38}$$

$$\text{CNOT}|R\rangle = \alpha\,|0\ 0\rangle + \beta|0\ 1\rangle + \gamma|1\ 0\rangle + \delta\,|1\ 1\rangle \tag{5.39}$$

Evaluate how the CNOT gate affects every condition of the quantum system that matches the values discovered in the set of equations in the truth table implementation. There is another way to express CNOT:

$$\text{CNOT}|R = \begin{pmatrix} 1 & 0 & 0 & 0 \\ 0 & 1 & 0 & 0 \\ 0 & 0 & 0 & 1 \\ 0 & 0 & 1 & 0 \end{pmatrix} \tag{5.40}$$

and therefore

$$\text{CNOT}|R \geq \begin{pmatrix} 1 & 0 & 0 & 0 \\ 0 & 1 & 0 & 0 \\ 0 & 0 & 0 & 1 \\ 0 & 0 & 1 & 0 \end{pmatrix} \begin{pmatrix} \alpha \\ \beta \\ \gamma \\ \delta \end{pmatrix} = \begin{pmatrix} \alpha \\ \beta \\ \gamma \\ \delta \end{pmatrix} \tag{5.41}$$

which are equivalent.

Figure 5.1 depicts the graphical representation depiction of the CNOT gate. The following are the two possible inputs:

$$|\psi\rangle_a = \alpha|0\rangle + \beta\,|1\rangle \tag{5.42}$$

$$|\psi\rangle_b = \gamma|0\rangle + \delta\,|1\rangle \tag{5.43}$$

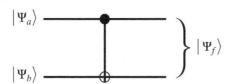

Figure 5.1 Structure of CNOT gate.

and this may be done by the input state's tensor product

$$|\psi\rangle_i = |\psi\rangle_a \oplus |\psi\rangle_b \tag{5.44}$$

$$\alpha|0\rangle + \beta|1\rangle \oplus \gamma|0\rangle + \delta|1\rangle \tag{5.45}$$

$$\alpha\gamma|0\ 0\rangle + \alpha\beta|0\ 1\rangle + \beta\gamma|1\ 0\rangle + \beta\delta|1\ 1\rangle \tag{5.46}$$

and the final state is given by:

$$|\psi_f = \alpha\gamma|0\ 0\rangle + \alpha\delta|0\ 1\rangle + \beta\gamma|1\ 1\rangle + \beta\delta|1\ 0\rangle \tag{5.47}$$

Another way of putting this rule into practice would be to say that any knowledge that is lost during the process of changing the quantum weirdness is a measurement. However, bidirectional gates may emulate traditional logic circuits and gates that cannot be reversed. Take a look at the truth table of exclusive-or, often known as arithmetic operations:

a	b	$a + b$
0	0	0
0	1	1
1	0	1
1	1	0

We can easily observe that binary addition is nonreversible because the values of a and b cannot be uniquely determined from the result $a + b$. However, the operation can be made reversible by augmenting it with an extra variable c:

a	b	c	a	b	$a + b + c$
0	0	0	0	0	0
1	0	0	1	0	1
0	1	0	0	1	1
1	1	0	1	1	0
0	0	1	0	0	1
1	0	1	1	0	0
0	1	1	0	1	0
1	1	1	1	1	1

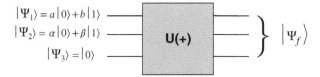

$|\Psi_1\rangle = a|0\rangle + b|1\rangle$
$|\Psi_2\rangle = \alpha|0\rangle + \beta|1\rangle$
$|\Psi_3\rangle = |0\rangle$

U(+)

$\left.\right\} |\Psi_f\rangle$

Figure 5.2 Reversible implementation of the binary addition on quantum states.

Clearly, this is a reversible operation because given a set of output numbers $(a, b, a + b + c)$, we can always determine the value of the output (a, b, c). Furthermore, by choosing $c = 0$ we get the same functionality as the binary addition of a and b.

Since knowing the value of c enables us to recover the values of a and b, it is feasible to create a quantum unitary operator, $U(+)$, that may be employed in place of arithmetic and logical.

It is now possible to build a convertible quantum gate that performs binary addition on two qubits. Figure 5.2 depicts a diagrammatic depiction of the quantum circuit used to construct this gate.

Following are the steps necessary to do numerical simulations of a quantum circuit like this. We draw a vertical line before starting each procedure. Our system's current condition is written on each vertical line in the diagram.

One operator is used in the quantum circuit for arithmetic operations. Circuit analysis is limited to two curved stripes, one before and the other after the operator, representing the system's two beginning and end states.

The tensor product of the three input states is what we have for the starting state:

$$|\psi_i\rangle = |\psi_1\rangle \oplus |\psi_2\rangle \oplus |\psi_3\rangle$$
$$= (a|0\rangle + b|1\rangle) \oplus (\alpha|0\rangle + \beta|1\rangle) \oplus |0\rangle$$
$$= (a\alpha|000\rangle + (a\beta|010\rangle + b\alpha|100\rangle + b\beta|110\rangle$$

The manufacturer's conceptual table works upon every element of the combination to evaluate its effect:

$$|a, b, c\rangle \rightarrow U(+)|a, b, c\rangle = |a, b, a + b + c\rangle \tag{5.48}$$

So, for instance,

$$|01\ 0\rangle \rightarrow U(+)|01\ 0\rangle = |01\ 1\rangle \tag{5.49}$$

As a result, the terminal condition is defined as:

$$|\psi_f\rangle = U(+)|\psi_i\rangle$$
$$= (a\alpha|00\ 0\rangle + (a\beta|01\ 0\rangle + b\alpha|10\ 0\rangle + b\beta|11\ 0\rangle$$

When using the $U(+)$ quantum operator, one executes binary addition, but any modifications or enhancements are implemented at the level of the bits themselves that demonstrate the quantum mechanical states. That is to say, the end outcome is different than:

$$|\psi_f\rangle! = |\psi_1\rangle + |\psi_2\rangle + |\psi_3\rangle \tag{5.50}$$

Such a procedure would be illegal.

It should also be noted that the binary addition of two one-bit components yielded all four possible results in a single calculation. As Rule 6 of the quantum computing paradigm, we'll look at this crucial aspect of quantum computing technology.

A similar approach may be used to supplement any classical logic circuit and provide reversible replacements at the expense of a few more gates. Furthermore, it is possible to demonstrate that switching a circuit from nonreversible to reversible may work with just a constant delay.

Except for observations, all algorithmic procedures must be repeatable and characterized by unitary operators, according to Rule 5.

5.8 Quantum Concurrency

An inherent concurrency may be found in the quantum computing concept.

All states in aggregation may be transformed concurrently using a unitary transformation U, as previously mentioned. For instance, a given U may be implemented to a given X. $|R\rangle$,

$$|R\rangle = a|0\ 0\rangle + b|0\ 1\rangle + c|1\ 0\rangle + d|1\ 1\rangle \tag{5.51}$$

As

$$U|R\rangle = aU|0\ 0\rangle + bU|0\ 1\rangle + cU|1\ 0\rangle + dU|1\ 1\rangle \tag{5.52}$$

and a single computing step performs all four state modifications.

Rule 6 is one of the main benefits of the quantum computing paradigm. For example, we may do a single calculation to determine the value of a binary function for all N potential input variables. When f is a Boolean functional, it is true that

$$f : \{0, 1\}^n \rightarrow \{0, 1\} \tag{5.53}$$

the bidirectional quantum operator U, which accomplishes the events that happened, is also considered.

$$U|x\rangle|0\rangle = |x\rangle f(x)\rangle \tag{5.54}$$

For each qubit, the n-qubit operational base is encoded in the binary integer that corresponds to it. If we begin with a balanced superposition state to which the operator U is applied, the following result is obtained.

$$\frac{1}{\sqrt{N}} \sum_{x=0}^{N-1} |x\rangle|0\rangle \xrightarrow{U} \frac{1}{\sqrt{N}} \sum_{x=0}^{N-1} |x\rangle f(x)\rangle \tag{5.55}$$

All the values of f have been calculated sequentially. N assessments of f are obviously beyond the traditional difficulty of the task. In this case, the superiority of QC over CC is evident.

However, if the registers are accessed after the f data are processed, the following is the outcome:

$$|x_i\rangle\, |f\,(x_i)\rangle \tag{5.56}$$

with a probability of $1/N$, the aggregation of all function values is annihilated.

The procedure described here might, of course, be used in a series of assessments and measures. However, it would take $O(N\,\log(N))$ repeats to get all N values. This is an inferior strategy since it can only be completed traditionally in a certain amount of time. In other words, this is only an example of getting your mind in the right frame of mind. Later on, we'll go into further depth on how this trait may be used in the real world.

It is possible to think of a quantum algorithm as a specific case of a parallel architecture known as MIMD. Since, the qubit is a vector of bits (multiple data), several unitary operations may be applied parallel to it (multiple instructions).

Designing quantum algorithms involves using a superposition of states' inherent concurrency.

5.9 Rule 7 Quantum Interference

It is impossible to replicate quantum entanglement. In other words, the entanglement in one quantum register cannot be "copied" into the next quantum register.

A 2-qubit quantum register in any configuration is equivalent to the following:

$$|R\rangle = a|0\,0\rangle + b|0\,1\rangle + c|1\,0\rangle + d|1\,1\rangle \tag{5.57}$$

In the hypothetical Xerox machine, U cannot be used on a two-qubit quantum storage Q if and only if.

$$|R\rangle\,|Q\rangle \to U\,|R\rangle\,|Q\rangle = |R\rangle\,|R\rangle \tag{5.58}$$

Quantum states may exist in any imaginable combination. Two random, normalizing quantum states and an assumed unitary translation that precisely duplicates quantum states indicate this right away:

$$|\psi\rangle \oplus |s\rangle \xrightarrow{U} \mathrm{U}\,(|\psi\rangle \oplus |s\rangle\,|\psi\rangle\,|\psi\rangle \tag{5.59}$$

$$|\phi\rangle \oplus |s\rangle \xrightarrow{U} \mathrm{U}\,(|\phi\rangle \oplus |s\rangle\,|\phi\rangle\,|\phi\rangle \tag{5.60}$$

There are two calculations, each with a left-hand side term, a right-hand side term, and an interior combination.

$$\langle\phi \,\|\, \psi\rangle = \langle\phi \,\|\, \psi\rangle^2 \tag{5.61}$$

which implies either

$$|\psi\rangle = |\phi\rangle \tag{5.62}$$

To ensure the preceding, states must be equivalent (the inner product equals unity) or orthogonal (opposed to each other) (the inner product is zero). According to our hypothesis of a copy modification U, it does not hold in general. The quantum no-cloning hypothesis is the name given to this conclusion.

This no-cloning theorem is important because it stops us from making carbon copies of quantum fluctuations. Consider the possibility of a workaround for this issue by relaxing the demand for exact copies and instead requesting approximate copies. The universal quantum copying machine (UQCM), a transformation capable of making approximate copies of any quantum state, has been constructed in previous studies. UQCM can be the best method use case: copying a single qubit into another single qubit b.

$$|0\rangle_a \,|\,|0\rangle_b \,|\,|Q\rangle_x \;\to\; \frac{\sqrt{2}}{\sqrt{3}}|0\;0\rangle\,|\uparrow\rangle + \frac{\sqrt{1}}{\sqrt{3}}\,|+\rangle\,|\downarrow\rangle \tag{5.63}$$

$$|1\rangle_a \,|\,|0\rangle_b \,|\,|Q\rangle_x \;\to\; \frac{\sqrt{2}}{\sqrt{3}}\,|1\;1\rangle\,|\uparrow\rangle + \frac{\sqrt{1}}{\sqrt{3}}\,|+\rangle\,|\uparrow\rangle \tag{5.64}$$

where

$$|+\rangle = \frac{1}{\sqrt{2}}\,(|0\rangle + 0\;1\rangle) \tag{5.65}$$

The script machine's quantum states after the copying are while $|\uparrow$ and $|\downarrow$. What was its quantum state before it was copied? This is an approximate cloning approach at best, since the translated output will also include states that are different from the input. Additionally, a 2/3 fidelity description may be made for the UQCM transformation. Two-thirds of the time, readings for a and b will be the same if we measure the output [20].

In addition, if the qubit is in the general superposition defined by,

$$|\psi\rangle = \alpha\,|0\rangle + \beta\,|1\rangle \tag{5.66}$$

Then, willing to employ a UQCM causes:

$$|\psi\rangle_a|0\rangle_b\,|Q\rangle_x \to \alpha\left(\sqrt{\frac{2}{3}}|0\;0\rangle\,|\uparrow + \sqrt{\frac{1}{3}}\,|+\rangle\,|\downarrow\right) + \beta\left(\sqrt{\frac{2}{3}}|1\;1\rangle\,|\downarrow + \sqrt{\frac{1}{3}}\,|+\rangle\,|\uparrow\right) \tag{5.67}$$

Examining this equation shows a complex relationship between how many copies are generated and the status of each duplicating machine. No way to divide this physical phenomenon into its tensor combination of the three states, unfortunately.

For N-dimensional governments, this approximation copying conversion may be expanded to cases in which there are K originals and M clones that arise. The following characteristic may be used to assess the output's accurateness:

$$n = \frac{K}{M} \frac{M+N}{K+N} \tag{5.68}$$

For a constant K, the cloning computer's fidelity drops significantly as M and N increase in size. Due to the nature of our applications, we are limited to a small number of qubits ($N = 2^n$) and a single intelligent ($K = 1$). As a result, low-quality copies are often produced when UQCM is used. Since it has so many flaws, there are very few places where UQCM may be used.

In terms of computational flexibility, the inability to duplicate arbitrary quantum states is restrictive. Most nontrivial classical algorithms require a mixture of components to store outcome variables, namely copying.

As a result of the above analysis, it is permissible to replicate classical states. Keep in mind that classical learning may be retrieved using superpositions of single forms in the computation foundation. Our ability to make perfect replicas of these states is unlimited.

If we have an atomic and molecular register to an unprecedented extent, we have no method of determining its value. This is a critical part of the process of Rule 7. It's true, if we have got:

$$|R\rangle = \alpha|0\ 0\rangle + \beta|0\ 1\rangle + \gamma|1\ 0\rangle + \delta|1\ 1\rangle \tag{5.69}$$

As long as we do not know the values of the other parameters, we will get 00 with the possibility $|\alpha|^2$, and so on. To ascertain these characteristics, if we did not have the no-cloning limitation, we could simply generate many copies and measure each one. As a result of using statistical techniques, we were able to make educated guesses about the size of these variables. However, in the quantum world, this is not feasible.

Avoiding such actions is necessary due to the fact that a quantum algorithm cannot duplicate quantum states. It is also possible to avoid cloning by setting up numerous identical quantum registers and carrying out the identical actions on each one until many duplicates of the same state are created. This, however, may be an ineffective, unworkable, and costly solution for the majority of the issues at hand.

5.10 Rule 8 Quantum Parallelism

The "0" location is always required in quantum cryptography.

The "0" location is always the starting point for every quantum algorithm. In order to avoid the unintended effect of not being able to tell whether a register is in an unknown state, this limitation was put in place.

The quantum register may enter an arbitrary physical phenomenon when the multicore processor is initially started; making it hard to discern exactly what is going on. Thus, when the quantum register is booted, it must be in a pre-determined state. There must be architecture in place that assures that the starting state of a quantum computer cannot be tampered.

When building a quantum computer, it's common to utilize this state by analogy to the "ground state" of the fundamental quantum system. If the physical phenomena used to create the register is allowed to settle to its ground state, the "0" state may be obtained in practice. However, in theory, you may give whatever meaning you choose to the numbers 0 and 1. For practical reasons, the initial state of the quantum computer must have field strength of zero in the quantum register.

Accordingly, the starting point for every quantum algorithm is always "0" in the quantum register. In contrast, it is possible to generate any initial state by a unitary transformation. For instance, in a single-qubit register, a Hadamard transformation is used to create a uniform superposition of the two values. This is the matrix representation of the Hadamard gate definition:

$$H = \frac{1}{\sqrt{2}} \begin{pmatrix} 1 & 1 \\ 1 & -1 \end{pmatrix} \tag{5.70}$$

which has the following effects on the one-qubit $|0\rangle$ state:

$$H\,|0\rangle = \frac{1}{\sqrt{2}} \begin{pmatrix} 1 & 1 \\ 1 & -1 \end{pmatrix} \begin{pmatrix} 1 \\ 0 \end{pmatrix} \tag{5.71}$$

$$\frac{1}{\sqrt{2}} \begin{pmatrix} 1 \\ 0 \end{pmatrix} \tag{5.72}$$

$$\frac{1}{\sqrt{2}}\,|0\rangle + |1\rangle \tag{5.73}$$

When the requisite uniform combination of one-qubit states may be found, we can implement one. Those that register more than one-qubit will have their basis functions gated for each qubit as a linear combination. For instance, consider a two-qubit register:

$$H^{\oplus 2}|0\,0\rangle = H^{(1)} \oplus H^{(2)}\,|0\,0\rangle \tag{5.74}$$

$$H^{(1)}\,|0\rangle \oplus H^{(2)}\,|0\rangle \tag{5.75}$$

$$\frac{1}{\sqrt{2}}(|0\rangle + |1\rangle) \oplus \frac{1}{\sqrt{2}}(|0\rangle + |1\rangle) \tag{5.76}$$

$$\frac{1}{2}(|0\,0\rangle + |0\,1\rangle + (|1\,0\rangle + |1\,1\rangle)) \tag{5.77}$$

In this case, all four states of the two-qubit register are combined into a single state. In general, the recursive formula may be used to generate the matrix form of the Integro-differential gate for n-qubit registers:

$$H^{\oplus n} = \begin{matrix} H^{\oplus n-1} & H^{\oplus n-1} \\ H^{\oplus n-1} & -H^{\oplus n-1} \end{matrix} \tag{5.78}$$

Initial states other than uniform combination may be created; however, the initiation procedure may entail a significant computing burden. What if we want to initialize an n-qubit register with a state that by 2^n important contributory factors? For example, a 2^n-by-2^n unitary matrix U is what we need to find to achieve our goal. This is what I mean:

$$|\emptyset_{init}\rangle = U |0\rangle \tag{5.79}$$

We must first solve a system of 2^n equations with 2^n variables to get all the components of the linear transformation U. And it may take as many as $O(2^n)$ computations to solve such a system of equations.

So although a quantum register may potentially be started in any state, this operation may take a long time. Quantum register activation is thus a critical step that must be considered when analyzing the computational burden of quantum cryptography. The transformation matrix may, of course, be kept and utilized several times if a task demands the same beginning state.

5.11 Summary

1. The following is a short summary of the features of quantum computing:
2. The qubit is a unique nonvolatile memory unit that is distinct from the conventional bit.
3. Third, unless the gravitation on one of the states is similar to unity, the results of a measurement of a superposition of states are inherently unpredictable (i.e. all other weights are zero).
4. Measuring always has an element of destruction built into it (read operations). Quantum entanglement, even though it can index 2^n states, cannot be unmeasured and restored to its original state.
5. The indices of 2^n and n-bit states may be saved in parallel in an n-qubit quantum register, whereas only the index of one n-bit state can be saved in an n-bit conventional register.
6. Only if the translating of quantum states is reproducible can we prevent the collapsing of a superposition. Nearly all classical logic gates can be affordably replaced with functionally indistinguishable reversible gates.
7. The intrinsic parallelism in QC allows for some operations to be carried out more efficiently than is possible with the best possible classical alternatives.

8. Since quantum strangeness cannot be copied, the no-cloning theorem severely limits the class of techniques that may effectively exploit dynamic parallel processing.

References

1 Gisin, N., Ribordy, G., Tittel, W., and Zbinden, H. (2002). *Reviews of Modern Physics* 74: 145.

2 DiVincenzo, D.P. (2000). *Fortschritte der Physik* 48: 771.

3 Heeres, R.W., Vlastakis, B., Holland, E. et al. (2015). *Physical Review Letters* 115: 137002.

4 Hsu, J. (2018). CES 2018: Intel's 49-Qubit Chip Shoots for Quantum Supremacy.

5 Bremner, M.J., Montanaro, A., and Shepherd, D.J. (2016). *Quantum* 1: 8, arXiv:1610.01808.

6 Courtland, R. (2017). Intel Now Packs 100 million Transistors in Each Square Millimeter.

7 Pfaff, W., Axline, C.J., Burkhart, L.D. et al. (2017). *Nature Physics* 13: 882.

8 Rønnow, T.F., Wang, Z., Job, J. et al. (2014). *Science* 345: 420.

9 Briggs, B. (2016). Things to Come: Could the cloud and quantum computing help feed the world?.

10 Heathman, A. (2017). Microsoft quantum computer: the things quantum computing could solve.

11 Jordan, S. (2018). Quantum Algorithm Zoo.

12 Lanyon, B.P., Whitfield, J.D., Gillett, G.G. et al. (2010). *Nature Chemistry* 2: 106.

13 Perdomo-Ortiz, A., Dickson, N., Drew-Brook, M. et al. (2012). *Scientific Reports* 2: 571.

14 Georgescu, I., Ashhab, S., and Nori, F. (2014). *Reviews of Modern Physics* 86: 153.

15 Abrams, D.S. and Lloyd, S. (1999). *Physical Review Letters* 83: 5162.

16 Mermin, N.D. (2007). *Quantum Computer Science an Introduction*. Cambridge University Press.

17 Gottesman, D., Kitaev, A., and Preskill, J. (2001). *Physical Review A* 64: 12310, arXiv:0510107[quant-ph].

18 Vlastakis, B., Kirchmair, G., Leghtas, Z. et al. (2013). *Science* 342: 607.

19 Leghtas, Z., Kirchmair, G., Vlastakis, B. et al. (2013). *Physical Review Letters* 111: 120501.

20 Lu, D., Xu, B., Xu, N. et al. (2012). *Physical Chemistry Chemical Physics* 14: 9411.

6

Optimization of an Amplification Algorithm

6.1 Introduction

There is a lot of intuitive appeal to the concept that human judgments and decisions might exhibit behavior consistent with quantum physics, and this idea forms the foundation of a relatively new area of study that can be referred to as "quantum cognition." Several writers have investigated this concept, for example [1] for making choices and [2] and [3] for making assessments of people. However, the possibilities of the quantum formalism have not been thoroughly explored, especially in regards to quantum parallelism and an identification of quantum algorithms in terms of human activities, even though the quantum-like framework presented there appears to sufficiently reflect experimental findings.

This chapter proposes to describe the obtained measurements regarding motivated reasoning with these algorithms. The quantum amplitude amplification algorithm [4] is a recent sweeping generalization of Grover's algorithm [5], while the particle physics sound pressure estimation algorithm and the quantum trying to count algorithm are implementations of the amplitude instrumentation followed by a quantum Fourier transform. In this work, I show that these algorithms may simulate crucial experimental findings from social neuroscience that apply to motivated reasoning. The amplitude amplification algorithm in particular allows for a mathematical identification of the ease with which one recounts items or conceptual frameworks, and the high-frequency rough guesstimate algorithms allow for the emergence of a formal device that is connected between such ease and determinations of statistical likelihood. As such, I will refrain from providing extensive explanations of whether or not it is physically possible for the human brain to execute quantum algorithms; instead, I will focus on the issue of computational complexity and the possibility of defining mathematically the ease of memory from a purely formal perspective. For searching large, unsorted databases, the Grover's method is a significant quantum technique that uses parallelism to provide far higher search speeds than can be

Quantum Computing: A New Era of Computing, First Edition.
Kuldeep Singh Kaswan, Jagjit Singh Dhatterwal, Anupam Baliyan, and Shalli Rani.
© 2023 The Institute of Electrical and Electronics Engineers, Inc. Published 2023 by John Wiley & Sons, Inc.

achieved with traditional, sequential approaches (quadratic speedup). Franco's [6] attempt to apply of this method (more particularly, a generalization [7]) to describe the effect of emotions on memory recall is groundbreaking in the field of cognitive psychology. Methods based on quantum concurrency and the amplitude amplification approach provide the same quadratic speedup.

As a form of motivated reasoning, the "availability bias" causes people to inaccurately estimate the frequency or likelihood of occurrences depending on how easily they can recall or see instances of such events. The purpose of this essay is to explain the availability bias in a quantum setting. The availability bias, first described by researchers Amos Tversky and Daniel Kahneman (2002 Nobel Prize in Economics), is the foundation for a wide variety of additional biases and cultural influences at the individual and societal levels. To demonstrate the availability bias, I will employ a well-known experiment by Tversky and Kahneman [8]. Participants were asked to choose whether they thought the letter R would appear more often in the first location or the third location. Most respondents thought the first option was more plausible. In English, however, the letter R appears more often in the third place of words than in the first. According to Tversky and Kahneman, this is because the availability heuristic influences how individuals estimate the quantity of words; specifically, the first letter of a word serves as a stronger signal for remembering occurrences of that term than the third letter. In the second case, it is clear that a large number of theoretical calculations are involved in the judgments individuals make about the words. In actuality, there are around 500,000 words in the English language, and the work stated above theoretically requires calculations over such a collection. With this in mind, the quantum-like perspective becomes more compelling since the suggested quantum algorithms exhibit a quadratic speed increase and are therefore more efficient than any standard algorithm [9].

6.2 The Effect of Availability Bias

Individuals are susceptible to availability bias, a kind of cognitive bias, when they make estimates about the frequency or quantity of certain classes of things based on how readily they can remember or visualize them. When defining the availability bias, it is critical to operationalize the convenience with which systems are connected. Different definitions, in particular, have seen widespread use in accessibility trials, serving as an experimental metric for how simple a memory task is as follows:

- First, there is "availability by number," which measures the ratio of excellent to poor products produced in a certain amount of time.
- The time ratio between the consumed retrieval times for the same number of good items and destructive items is known as availability-by-speed. Two sets

of participants are often used in availability experiments: those who are tasked with remembering information and those who are asked to make probabilistic or numerical judgments regarding the availability of objects. Thus, the availability studies confirm a positive link between the subjects' quantitative assessments and the participants' level of availability by quantity or availability by speed as a metric for how simple or complex a memory exercise. The following two types of experiments will be the subject of my talk.

- Probability judgments: in Combs and Slovic [10], for example, subjects were asked to estimate the likelihood of plane accidents, and availability effects may be at work because the topics found it easy to recall the relevant information (as in the example from the first or third place of English nouns mentioned in the introductory paragraph (quite events are rare, even if the vast majority of the population overestimates their probability).

- Numerical assessments: an easy recall experiment is given in which participants are played back a list of male and female celebrities' names. Some participants were asked to determine if the list comprised more males or females, while others were asked to try to remember the names from memory. For example, there were 19 well-known people of one sex and 20 lesser-known people of the other sex on the list. The number of names associated with the more prominent group is positively correlated with the number of names expected to be in that group, as shown by the results of the experiment.

6.2.1 Optimization of an Amplification Algorithm

This issue may be addressed by the amplitude amplification method, a generalization of Grover's technique. Find the t good items such that $[0, 1]$ $[N\ t]$ for any collection of N items and a boolean function f: $[0, 1, ..., N-1]$ $[0, 1]$ that separates the set into t good items (those for which f is equal to 1) and $N\ t$ bad things (those for which f is equal to 0). This kind of method may obviously be used to simulate neuroscientific retrieval issues. By applying the experiment by Tversky and Kahneman [8] to words with the letter R in the first or third location, the English vocabulary may be divided into two groups, representing good things (words with R in the first position) and bad items (words without R in the first position) (words with R in the third position). While the mathematical details of the technique will be discussed in Section 6.2.2, I will summarize them here with as little formality as possible. Insights are provided that are similar to those briefly mentioned in Franco [6]. The quantum amplification algorithm consists of the same three parts as Grover's:

- The starting point, where the points in an N-dimensional vector space are described by the elements of a basis, the amplitude amplification method differs from Grover's algorithm in that the items included inside the origin point may have various weights; specifically, the measurement is the probability to measure a good build in the first state. According to Grover's approach, $a = t/N$. Initially, the objects' mental weights are assigned a random value, which may be thought of as the starting state. If an is greater than t/N, then the good things are more important at the outset than the bad ones. If the subjects have no prior knowledge of good/bad objects, then their guessing state will be a uniform distribution across all items ($a = t/N$).

- The amplification engine is a recursive procedure that emphasizes positive factors by testing the Boolean function f in parallel across all variables. Because of these interference effects, high-quality things become even more prized. In contrast to Grover's technique, the success of the procedure is determined by the number of repetitions, which is proportional to $1/a$ and is affected by the guessing state. If $a = t/N$ and the number of steps is proportional to pN/t, then the procedure is the same as Grover's method. In contrast to the conventional approach, which takes N/t steps to finish, Grover's algorithm only needs pN/t steps to do the same thing. This is because the initial guessing state gives more weight to the good items than the poor ones, which speeds up the processing of information, and the amplitude amplification technique offers an extra speedup since the number of needed steps is proportional to $1/a\, pN/t$.

When applicable to cognitive activities, such an amplifier may be thought of in terms of unconscious motives; it allows for simultaneous evaluation of the boolean function across all the items, but needs a number of repetitions equal to $1/a$ to amplify the chance of affirmative items. As a result, they can apply $f(x)$ to any and all x. (thus deciding if each item is good or bad). The algorithm suggests that, compared to a sequential method, making such a choice simultaneously and unconsciously yields better results. The third step is to assess the final state. The guess state is nearly completely replaced by great states after the algorithm is tweaked. When this last action produces the desired result, the recall process is over. The methodical act of remembering is represented in my explanation by this actuality. With the help of the amplitude amplification algorithm, we can give a concise mathematical definition of attribute-based encryption in terms of its availability by speed: the amount of time required to find a good item is commensurate with $1/a$, where an is the beginning of the assumed measurement; a high value of a results in a short amount of time to obtain a good item. The parameter a indicates how well mental images of the retrieved items may be formed before actual recovery. Similarly, our model assumes that the accessibility is proportionate to an, where an is the greatest number of valuable items that subjects can remember in a particular time period. A study of where the letter R appears in English words found that it is faster to form the word when R appears as the first letter rather than the third. Since this is a guess, I will assume that there are N items in the prediction state (the most common English terms) and that the words closer to the beginning of the inference have more significance than the words closer to the end.

6.2.2 Specifications of the Mathematical Amplification Algorithm

In quantum formalism, considering N sets of good and bad things corresponds to considering N sets of Hilbert spaces, where each vector represents one of the N objects. That is, by introducing a suitable subspace (spanned by the) into H, the function f creates a partition of the vectors as $|si = 0i|x|$ is the superposition of negative vectors (if $ix+ = 0)|1i$. Thus, any superposition $f(x) = 1)|1$ i and a is the superposition of good vectors (bad subspace $f|(sxi) = 1).=($Pspanned by the vectors $x(x)|xi$ may be written $f(x) = 1)|xi$ for which and | Good vector maintain subspace.

The stages of the algorithm are as follows.

In the initial state, have ready the vector $A|0i = |0i + |1i$, where A is a measurement-free quantum method and $a = h1|1i$ is the probability of taking a valid measurement. We get a If A is the quantum Fourier transform FN: $|xi$, then xi is a homogenous accumulation of vector states with magnitude $N1/2$, and $a = t/N$ (as in traditional Grover's method).

Amplifier $(Q = AS_0A_1S_f)$, where S_0 and S_f are recrystallization operators (S_0 inverts the waveform if and only if the condition is the zero state $|0i$, and S_f inverts the dynamic range of the knowledge that helps).

Get a search result, and then take a measurement of the final state in the underlying computational framework.

If the value of x is a multiple of $-4\arcsin(a)$, then the measurement is accurate to within max $(a, 1\,a)$. When N is large and an is small, the required number of iterations to converge on the optimal solution is $1/a$. The optimal number of iterations, which corresponds to the speedup of Grover's approach, is given by (pN/t) if A is the quantum Fourier transforms. If $a > = t/N$, then pN/t fewer iterations are needed.

6.3 Quantum Amplitude Estimation and Quantum Counting

Knowledge of quantum information retrieval and amplitude amplification is required for quantum amplitude estimation and counting. Let us say that instead of focusing on finding a solution, we are only interested in how many options there are. In an N-element search, it is important to know how many of those elements include solutions for $f(x) = 1$. That's the counting problem that arises whenever the letter f is used. In addition, we will check out the less complex problem of trying to guess the value of t.

Our described numbering method for determining amplitude in n-qubit circuits is one such example. For solutions of $f(x) = 1$, A is the corresponding subspace.

6.4 An Algorithm for Quantitatively Determining Amplitude

Quantum amplitude estimation is a technique for approximating the strength of a quantum state by periodic amplification. The chance of identifying a good item (according to the partitioning established by function f) may be predicted with great precision when the opinion state about the N items is used as the starting point for guessing. I will now describe the algorithm's essential features with as little formalism as possible, leaving it for the following part, which will cover the algorithm's mathematical intricacies. There are three parts to this approach, and they are as follows: we will start with Stage 1, which consists of the first guessing state we discussed before. Second, "parallel amplifications" use many instances of the amplification engine, each with its own set of iterations. Every level of the amplification engine applies $f(x)$ to the items simultaneously.

Analyzing amplification processes at different iteration counts enables one to estimate a within a few standard deviations, after several evaluations of f proportional to $1/a$, since the efficiency of each amplification engine is a function of this parameter.

This technique is extremely helpful for studying mental operations since it allows researchers to construct tasks in which participants generate subjective probabilities relating to occurrences. There is a formal connection between a quantum-like approach to expressing choices and a quantum-like approach to defining subjective probability since both are the consequence of simple measurements on quantum states. The experiment mentioned in the introduction may be explained using the suggested method; it examines the likelihood of the letter R appearing in the first or third position of English words; and it is related to availability bias. To find English words that include R in the first or third position, we need to use two different word partitioning and amplification techniques with parameters a and a'. We assume that subjects' minds contain N words (the guess state) and that words having R in the first place are more important than those containing R in the third place by a factor of a and a', respectively. According to our model, the predicted likelihood of remembering words with R is near to a, and the ease with which one may do so is proportional to the availability-by-number.

The estimated likelihood of discovering a word containing the letter R in the first place is higher if more words containing the letter R can be thought of than words containing the letter R in the third position. The same formalism may be used to explain the experiments in [10], where participants overestimated the likelihood of airplane accidents due to the vividness of such memories in memories.

Similar to the amplitude amplification technique, the estimated probability that was generated may be regarded as the result of a series of intuitive amplification operations (with evaluations of function f) and a final analysis and measure.

6.4.1   Mathematical Description of Amplitude Estimation Algorithm

Est Amp(A, f, M) is an amplitude estimating technique that can predict the value of $|1i$ (excellent states superposition) in terms of $A|0i$. The amplitude amplification algorithm is the foundation of this method. Most notably:

First, initiation condition: set up the MMN-dimensional vector FM$|0iA|0i$, where M and N are the respective dimensions of the first and second registers. For those who may have forgotten, FM is the quantum version of the Fourier transform.

Second, to do parallel amplifications, where $Q = AS_0A\ S_f$ is the regular amplitude amplification engine, we use the operator1 M(Q), defined as $|ji|yi\ |jiQj|yi$ with $0\ j\ M$. This means that the guess state $A|0i$ is amplified by a range of magnitudes, from 0 to M, in a parallel fashion through the operator M(Q).

Third, compute the wave function's period by applying a measurement to the first register and reading off the resulting integer value y. As a result, a reasonable approximation for the amplitude is $a = \sin2(y/M)$; the precision of this estimate is described in Theorem 12 of [4]. By setting $M = 1/a$, we may derive a probability estimate within a few sigmas of the true value.

6.5   Counting Quantum Particles: An Algorithm

The quantum counting technique estimates the number of elements in a set X of N items for which a logical transfer function is true by calculating $t = |x\ X|f(x) = 1|$, where f is a Boolean function defined on X. In other words, the approach allows for an approximate calculation of the total number of valid items (those for which $f(x) = 1$). In the best classical method, we put f to the test on a subset of X data; this requires N evaluations, which a lot is given that a precise estimate of t requires much more data. Quantum counting, on the other hand, can obtain accurate approximations of this number in a very small number of steps – approximately N (quadratic speedup).

An extension of the amplitude estimation process is the quantum-counting algorithm. If the guessing state gives equal importance to each item, then the estimated probability of excellent things is very close to t/N; by multiplying this estimate by N, we may get a rough estimate of how many items are good. A basic version of the quantum counting process is proposed below, and its mathematical underpinnings are laid forth in the following section: the probability that is important for first-rate items is $a = 6\, t/N$ if the guessing state assigns unequal weights to the items. We have an overstatement of the number of items, due to the estimating state in the amplification process, if, for instance, $a > t/N$, which means that the expected number of items is near to $aN > t$.

This oversimplification is used to explain the memory test described in [11], in which participants were played a taped list of famous numbers and symbols, including those of both sexes, with a request to recall as many as they could. Some participants were asked to determine if the list comprised more males or females, while others were asked to try to remember the names from memory. For example, there were 19 well-known people of one gender and 20 lesser-known people of the other gender on the list. The number of names associated with the more prominent group is positively correlated with the number of names expected to be in that group, as shown by the results of the experiment. Recalling the names of a group is correlated with an increase in the estimated size of that group because of the same parameter being engaged in both processes (aN).

6.5.1 Mathematical Description of Quantum Counting Algorithm

For a Boolean function f over a discrete set X with N elements, the amplitude estimate is $t = N$ Est Amp, and the quantum counting technique Count (FN, f, M) is a special example of this estimate (FN, f, M). Substituting a generic operator A for the Fourier transform FN in the quantum counting technique Count (A, f, M) leads to an inaccurate estimate of t, the number of valid items. If an is more than t/N, the modern counting method predicts $t > t$, and otherwise predicts $t = t$.

6.5.2 Related Algorithms and Techniques

Amplitude amplification has been demonstrated to be a fundamental computer operation that can be used in a variety of contexts. When used more subtly, it may solve problems like element distinctness more quickly than conventional approaches. Given a black box implementation of the function f, we are to discover whether $f(x) = f(y)$ holds for arbitrary values of x and y.

It is possible to attain the quadratic speedup of the quantum search method in continuous time variations as well. Our proposed paradigm for quantum circuits has several striking similarities to continuous-time computing models, which may or may not be practically feasible to apply in practice. Possible use of alternative models to help in the development of novel quantum algorithms.

The adiabatic theorem gave rise to the adiabatic algorithm paradigm, which is based on the idea of continuous-time processing. The user may, for instance, infer the existence of an adiabatic search method that, when used, yields the same quadratic speedup as amplitude augmentation. A wider definition of adiabatic computing may be found in the polynomial time equivalent of the quantum circuit model.

Wide varieties of techniques exist for generating quantum walks, which are analogous to random walks but based on quantum mechanics. Quantum walks are an intriguing paradigm for developing novel numerical methods. It's possible, for instance, to determine the best quantum algorithm for characterizing individual elements by using a quantum walk approach.

References

1 Busemeyer, J.R., Matthew, M., and Wang, Z. (2006). An information processing explanation of disjunction effects. In: *The 28th Annual Conference of the Cognitive Science Society and the 5th International Conference of Cognitive Science* (ed. R. Sun and N. Miyake), 131–135. Mahwah, NJ: Erlbaum.

2 Franco, R. (2007). Quantum mechanics, Bayes' theorem and the conjunction fallacy, arXiv:quant-ph/0703222v2.

3 Franco, R. and Busemeyer, J.R. (2008). A quantum probability explanation for the inverse fallacy. *Psychonomic Review & Bulletin* 4: 1–49.

4 Brassard, G., Hoyer, P., Mosca, M., Tapp, A. (2000). Quantum amplitude amplification and estimation. Vol. 6, 1–32, http://arxiv.org/abs/quant-ph/0005055.

5 Grover, L. (1997). Quantum mechanics helps in searching for a needle in a haystack. *Physical Review Letters* 79: 325.

6 Franco, R. (2008). Grover's algorithm and human memory. Vol 6, 1–10, http://xxx.lanl.gov/pdf/0804.3294.

7 Long, G.L. (2001). Grover algorithm with zero theoretical failure rate. *Physical Review A* 64: 022307.

8 Tversky, A. and Kahneman, D. (1973). Availability: a heuristic for judging frequency and probability. *Cognitive Psychology* 5: 207232.

9 Fox, C.R. (2006). The availability heuristic in classroom: how soliciting more criticism can boost your course ratings. *Judgement and Decision Making* 1: 8690.

10 Combs, B. and Slovic, P. (1979). Newspaper coverage of causes of death. *Journalism Quarterly* 56: 837–843.

11 Manin, Y.I. (1999), Why quantum computing?. Vol. 8, 1–21, https://arxiv.org/abs/quant-ph/9903008v1.

7

Error-Correction Code in Quantum Noise

7.1   Introduction

Techniques for addressing a wide range of interactions that confound quantum calculations are essential if viable computer programs are to be constructed. No one had any idea how to remediate for errors in quantum communication, despite the widespread praise for Shor's work, and he was initially dismissed as a cognitive-psychological curiosity. At the time, estimates reported that environmental interactions were far too strong to run Shor's factoring automated system on a number of fundamental interests. A direct application of classical procedures to the quantum scenario is not conceivable due to the difficulty of replicating an unknown quantum state, and it was far from evident what else to do in this situation. Many experts were led to assume that robust quantum processing was theoretically unattainable by results such as the no-cloning theorem. It turns out, however, that classical approaches are the cornerstone of advanced quantum error correction. One of the most advanced aspects of quantum computing is quantum error correction. The discovery of quantum error correction, as well as Shor's methods, made quantum information processing a prominent area in and of itself [1].

Error-correcting codes are the primary method of transmitting data in the classical world. Because of this, quantum systems may be challenging to isolate adequately from the surrounding environment while still allowing calculations to take place. The effects of contact with the atmosphere are expected to be so widespread in any quantum system utilized to do quantum learning and memory that quantum error correction will always be needed [2].

Quantum Computing: A New Era of Computing, First Edition.
Kuldeep Singh Kaswan, Jagjit Singh Dhatterwal, Anupam Baliyan, and Shalli Rani.
© 2023 The Institute of Electrical and Electronics Engineers, Inc. Published 2023 by John Wiley & Sons, Inc.

7.2 Basic Forms of Error-Correcting Code in Quantum Technologies

Error-correction code (ECC) for error detection and correction: codes use redundant linking of the messaging word sin to a broader set of words in the error-correcting code. Using quantum simple regression codes, the vector space storing message states (called words) is embedding into a subdomain of a broader, higher-dimensional space, the code storage. When developing an algorithm for use with n-qubits, it is necessary to encode the n-qubits within an m-qubit system, which is a much larger system. Errors are found and fixed by computations into ancilla qubits and measurements of the ancilla qubits. Depending on the measurement's outcome, error-correcting modifications are performed. Encoding and measuring must be deliberately constructed to offer information just on the mistake that happened and not on the encoded state of the computations to maintain superpositions [3].

Our first code, which corrects just bit-flip mistakes, is followed by a code that corrects only single-qubit phase errors, and then a final code that corrects all single-qubit faults. This gives us a broad notion of how fundamental error correction works.

7.2.1 Single Bit-Flip Errors in Quantum Computing

To one of the qubits of a quantum system, X is applied due to a bit-flip error. To condense the traditional [3,1] repeating code, we will use the following code, which is a quantum equivalent. To determine if any of the three single bit-flip mistakes are present and to correct them, this algorithm uses the formulas shown in the following table. It finds and tries to correct all three of the single bit-flip faults using the formulas shown in the table [4].

Each bit is encoded in three bits using the [3,1] repeating code.

$$\rightarrow 000$$

$$\rightarrow 111$$

Decoding is done by majority rules

$$\left.\begin{array}{c} 000 \\ 001 \\ 010 \\ 100 \end{array}\right\} \mapsto 0$$

$$\left.\begin{array}{l} 011 \\ 101 \\ 110 \\ 111 \end{array}\right\} \mapsto 1$$

By combining the first bit with each of the subsequent bits, you may establish if an error has occurred and then apply majority rules. For formal purposes, the $b_2\, b_1$ and $b_2\, b_0$ computations are stored in two extra bits termed ancilla. The syndrome computations are the name given to this process. Table 7.1 shows the error detection and correction modifications based on the values for the b_2, b_1, and $b_2\, b_0$ forms of the $b_2 b$ syndrome. If both $b_2\, b_1$ and $b_2\, b_0$ equal 0, then nothing should be done, according to the first line of the table. According to the second line, there is a two-thirds majority. No matter what happened previously, this procedure results in a codeword. However, if more than one error has occurred it will correct to the wrong word. For example, if the original string was 000 and two bit-flip errors occur, one on the first qubit and one on the third, the resulting string, 101, will be "corrected" to 111 under this procedure. Only one bit-flip mistake may be corrected by the [3,1] repetition code. It is possible to rectify more mistakes using more powerful codes like [n,1] codes that repeat a message over and again until the correct message is found [5].

It is possible to reduce the impact of individual mistakes by using conventional and quantum lossy compression, both of which use many qubits to spread the material to be safeguarded. The [3,1] repetition code Table 7.2 uses the bit strings 000 and 111 to signify 0 and 1, respectively. In the quantum model, let C_{BF} be the subdomain represented by [000, 111]. When applied to the states of |000 and |111, this quantum code denotes |0 and |1, respectively. The C_{BF} encoding for single-qubit data is defined by the linearity of the code and these relationships.

Table 7.1 Classical [3,1] repetition coding syndrome and associated error-correcting modifications.

$b_2 \oplus b_1$	$b_2 \oplus b_0$	Error-correcting transformation
0	0	identity
0	1	flip b_0
1	0	flip b_1
1	1	flip b_2

states into the C_{BF} region of the three-qubit state space:

Table 7.2 Error correction.

Bit shifted	Syndrome	Error correction
none	$|00$	$Z_2 = Z \otimes I \otimes I$
0	$|11$	$Z_1 = I \otimes Z \otimes I$
1	$|10$	$Z_0 = I \otimes I \otimes Z$
2	$|01$	None

$a|0 + b|1 = a|000 + b|111$, therefore $a|000 + b|111$ is $a|0 + b|1 \ |0''$ and other states are encoded using the notation $|0''$ in a quantum code. For this code, $|0$ Equals $|000$ and $|1 = |111$.

For example, the two-dimensional vector universe of a $|000 + b|111$ may be regarded as a qubit in and of itself. An eight-dimensional code environment is formed by combining the three computational qubits, which are known as logical qubits. It is impossible to have a legitimate state on a qubit if it is in a value like $|101$, which is not a logical qubit value. We use the term "codewords" to denote the possible states of logical qubits. A logical qubit can no longer have a plausible computational architecture that is not a codeword if a single bit is flipped incorrectly, as in $a|000 + b|111$. In the event of a bit flip on the first qubit, the resulting state, $a|100 + b|011$, is not a codeword since it does not conform to the CBF. Finding and fixing off-codeword errors is the main job of an error-checking method [6].

The first and second qubits are computed into one ancilla, while the first and third are computed into another to identify an error. In a more official tone,

$$U_{BF} : |x_2, x_1, x_0, 0, 0\rangle \rightarrow |x_2, x_1, x_0, x_2 \oplus x_1, x_2 \oplus x_0\rangle$$

$$U_{BF} : |x_2, x_1, x_0, 0, 0\rangle \rightarrow |x_2, x_1, x_0, x_2 \oplus x_1, x_2 \oplus x_0$$

To put it another way, when it comes to extracting symptoms, U_{BF} is known as a disorder extracting operation.

The error phenomenology for the ancilla qubits is then assessed on a reasonable basis.

Repeatedly employing the condition is the same as [3,1] code three times. Because the code must not contaminate correct states in addition to resolving any single bit-flip fault, we will treat $I\,I\,I$ as an "error" that we may fix for the sake of simplicity. We may pick the proper transformation to rectify the inaccuracy based on the evidence we get from monitoring the ancilla [7]. Correcting this mistake involves doing the exact same fundamental shift as creating the original error,

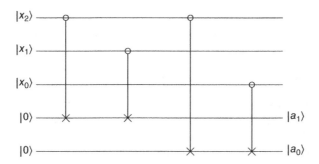

which is $X = X_1$. The ancilla's measurements are shown in the following table, which provides the high-performance data:

Bit flipped	Syndrome	Error correction
none	l00	$X_2 = I \otimes I \otimes X$
0	l11	$X_1 = I \otimes X \otimes I$
1	l10	$X_0 = X \otimes I \otimes I$
2	l01	None

It is not astonishing that this approach fixes Its near similarity to the traditional [3,1] code makes it robust against even a single bit-flip error on the encoded conventional basis variables $|0 = |000$ and $|1 = |111$. It also attempts to fix the occasional single bit-flip error that occurs during the aggregation of codewords.

Example 7.1 Fixing a faulty superposition caused by a bit flip. Essentially, it is a superposition $|\psi = a|0 + b|1$ is encoded as

$$|\tilde{\psi}\rangle = a|\tilde{0}\rangle + b|\tilde{1}\rangle = a|000\rangle + b|111\rangle.$$

Suppose $|\tilde{\psi}$ is subject to the single bit-flip error $X_2 = X \otimes I \otimes I$, resulting in

$$X_2|\tilde{\psi}\rangle = a|100\rangle + b|011\rangle$$

Applying the syndrome extraction operator U_{BF} to $X_2|\tilde{\psi}\rangle \otimes |00$ results in the state

$$U_{BF}((X_2|\tilde{\psi}\rangle) \otimes |00\rangle) = a|100\rangle|11\rangle + b|011\rangle |11$$
$$= (a|100\rangle + b|011\rangle) |11$$

As a result of evaluating the two auxiliary qubits, we get $|11$, and the current state is $(a|100 + b|011)\otimes|11$.

The problem might be fixed using the |11 syndrome's inversion error operator X_2 to the first three qubits. The underlying encrypted state may be reconstructed by doing so.

$$|\psi\rangle = a|\tilde{0}\rangle + b|\tilde{1}\rangle = a|000\rangle + b|111\rangle)$$

One way to think about why this methodology does not permanently alter the quantum state is because the ancilla monitoring is performed by our syndrome harvesting. Only the extraction faults are revealed by the operator, not the machine learning qubit states themselves. Whether the secret code is |0, |1, or a mixture of the two, the output of the psychosis extracting operator is always the phenomenon 00, regardless of the codeword. If error $X_2 = X I I$ happens, the syndrome will be in state |11 regardless of whether the computational qubits are in state |100, |011, or any mix of the two. As a result, knowing what went wrong requires monitoring the ancilla qubits, but this does not offer the status of the computation qubits. Even if the starting state is a|000 + b|111, monitoring the ancilla qubits provides knowledge about the mistake without disrupting the calculation [8].

Quantum mistakes may be combined in a linear fashion, unlike in the classical situation. Possible combinations of bit-flip mistakes may also be corrected using the same method.

Example 7.2 Fixing a sequence of bit-flip mistakes made in linear fashion [14]. Let us say an error occurs while encoding state |0 as |0 = |000. $E = \alpha X \otimes I \otimes I + \beta I \otimes X \otimes I$, errors X_2 and X_1 are both caused by a single bit flip, and when added together, they create error X_3. $E|\tilde{0} = \alpha|100 + \beta|010$.

Applying the syndrome extraction operator U_{BF} to $(E|\tilde{0}) \otimes |00$ results in the state

$$U_{BF}((E|\tilde{0})) \otimes |00\rangle) = \alpha|100\rangle|11\rangle + \beta|010\rangle|10\rangle.$$

A value of |11 or |10 may be obtained by measuring the two auxiliary qubits in this condition. It is now |100 if the measurement results in the former. All but one summand of the error is eliminated by the measurement, which is nearly amazing. The remaining error may be eliminated by using the inverse error operator $X_2 = X_1$, which is mapped onto the dysfunction |11 that was measured. The original encoded state |0 = |000 may be reconstructed by doing so. Instead of measuring |10, we would use X_1 to return the initial state |0 = |000 by applying X_1.

This algorithm can correct linear combinations of single bit-flip mistakes, but it cannot correct multiple bit-flip errors. Many bit-flip errors are unique from linear combinations of single bit-flip mistakes in that a single component in the superposition reflecting a computational state might include multiple faults that the syndrome would misread.

If a single-bit mistake is detected, the [3,1] code corrects the problem. Although it is based on the [3,1] code, the quantum code CBF does not rectify all faults involving a single qubit. Unlike in the classical situation, there may be an infinite number of individual qubits in the quantum situation, and mistakes may occur. Phase problems are not even detected or corrected by the CBF code.

Example 7.3 A phase mismatch that went undetected. Let us assume the $|+$ quantum state (represented by the symbols)

$$|\tilde{+}\rangle = \frac{1}{\sqrt{2}}(|000\rangle + |111\rangle)$$

is subjected to a phase error $E = Z \otimes I \otimes I$. The state $|\tilde{+}$ becomes the error state

$$E|\tilde{+}\rangle = \frac{1}{\sqrt{2}}(|000\rangle - |111\rangle))$$

U_{BF} syndrome extraction operator used for $E|\tilde{+}\rangle \mid 00$ results in $E|\tilde{+}\rangle \mid 00$, hence neither the error nor its correction is identified.

Single-qubit phase-flip mistakes are simple to fix, whereas single-qubit bit-flip faults are not. As an example, look at the code that follows. Single-qubit mistakes must be corrected by a cleverer code. It turns out that a code that corrects all single-qubit faults may be produced by using a combination of codes that, when used together, can fix bit-flip and phase-flip errors.

7.2.2 Single-Qubit Coding in Quantum Computing

Consider the three single-qubit phase-flip errors Z_2, Z_1, and Z_0 of a three-qubit system, where

$$\{Z_2 = Z \otimes I \otimes I, Z_1 = I \otimes Z \otimes I, Z_0 = I \otimes I \otimes Z\}$$

$$\{|+\rangle, |-\rangle\}$$

$$\text{code } C_{BF}$$

No matter how you look at it in the conventional basis, phase-flip mistakes are bit-flip mistakes in the Hadamard base. A code C_{PF} that fixes phase-flip errors will be created if the bit flip in Figure 7.1 can be optimized. After translating the C_{BF} code's logical qubits using the Walsh–Hadamard formula $W(3) = H H H$, we get the CPF code's conceptual qubits of $|0\rangle = |+++\rangle$ and $|1\rangle = |.$

Phase-flipping fault Z_2 changes $|+++\rangle$ to $|++\rangle$ and $|+\rangle$. The syndrome-extracting operator U_{PF} for C_{PF} may be derived from U_{BF} by switching from the conventional basis to the Hadamard basis. The U_{BF} code, derived from C_{BF}, pinpoints the issue caused by phase transitions in the Hadamard basis. After the error has been detected by measuring the auxiliary qubits in the variety of grounds, it may be

Thus $U_{PF} = WU_{BF}W$, with implementation

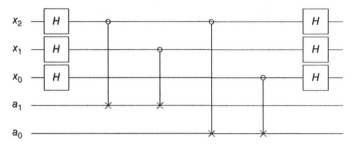

Figure 7.1 Structure of CPF.

corrected by applying the bit-flip operator that corresponds to the requirement for coding C_{BF} and then reverting back to the original basis using W. Since $HX = ZH$, we know that the error may be fixed by first implementing W and then making the appropriate adjustment for error correction, as seen in the figure.

Because the error at each single stage is a linear combination of Z and I up to a negligible global phase component, the CPF code tries to correct all single-qubit relative phase faults, not just Z.

$$\begin{pmatrix} 1 & 0 \\ 0 & e^{i\phi} \end{pmatrix} = e^{i\frac{\phi}{2}}\left(\cos\frac{\phi}{2}I - i\sin\frac{\phi}{2}Z\right)$$

Bit-flip mistakes, not to mention more generalized single-qubit issues, cannot be fixed using the CPF method.

7.2.3 Error-Correcting Code in Quantum Technology

All X_i and Z_i mistakes may be corrected by C, which is shown in the following states quantize error correction code (QEC). In doing so, it proves that every chain of fixable flaws can be fixed. Pauli errors I, X, Y, and Z provide the groundwork for single-qubit errors. A single-qubit code can fix any problem on a single qubit, including X_i and Z_i errors.

C_{BF} and C_{PF} are a logical starting point when trying to create such a code. The nine-qubit code is created by first transmitting a qubit with C_{PF} and then transmitting each subsequent qubit with C_{BF}.

The standard encoding operator used with this code sends well-known as Shor's nine-qubit code. These places are often referred to as

$$|0 \rightarrow |\bar{0}\rangle = \frac{1}{\sqrt{8}}(|000\rangle + |111\rangle)^{\otimes 3}$$

$$|1 \rightarrow |.\bar{1}\rangle = \frac{1}{\sqrt{8}}(|000\rangle - |111\rangle)^{\otimes 3} \tag{7.1}$$

To compensate for probable X mistakes, utilize U_{BF} on each block of three qubits independently. As of this moment, all three qubits of each block are equal in their bit values; nonetheless, it is possible that their relative phases are incorrect. Instead of using three qubits, a variation of U_{PF} using nine is employed to compensate for phase faults.

The collection of codewords is what is referred to as a code in both classical and quantum contexts.

If an alternative mapping can be used to repair the same problems, the original strings or states are of little consequence. In addition, the encrypting map is not always implemented. Instead of starting with qubits in the form of the mapping, we begin with an abstraction of the type $a|0 + b|1$ and then encode it. To put it another way, we create a system's logical qubits in this manner and then use these logical qubits to build gates and interpret measurements. Rather than calculating directly on n single qubits as in Shor's code, each qubit is encoded in 9 qubits, giving a grand total of $9n$ qubits. There are n logical qubits in a quantum computer; each of them consists of nine qubits. We do not compute on the whole $29n$-dimensional space, but rather on a subspace of $2n$ dimensions that contains the logical qubits. To correct faults, states must be restored to this $2n$-dimensional subdomain; a universal set of gates is needed for this feature space but not for the whole $29n$-dimensional space [9].

It will be discussed in detail in the next sections how to use less than nine qubits to rectify all the faults that occur in multiple-qubit codes. We must first establish more scientific methodology for thinking about and characterizing codes before we can debate these patterns.

7.3 Framework for Quantum Error-Correcting Codes

Linear, but not generally unitary, effects may result from interactions with the environment or from errors in the computing system. It is possible to fix a unitary inaccuracy because unitary transformations are invertible. Because of this, even if we can identify the specific fault that happened and how to fix it, there may be no clear way to do so when dealing with generic issues. Such problems may seem impossible to fix without access to and control over the environment in which the system interacts. Unitary quantum transformations applied to the computer system alone cannot remedy these flaws, it is true. However, nonunitary mistakes may be addressed by monitoring, involving extra qubits in the system, or introducing chaos into the system.

When a system experiences a nonunitary change due to decoherence, it loses knowledge about its initial state. This might result in a total loss of knowledge about the atmosphere's qubits, save for what can be derived from the computing system's qubits, for example. There would be no way to know the qubit's state if it were totally statistically independent of the states of the other qubits. To preserve information held in quantum fluctuations, it is common practice to place the quantum states of interest inside a broader quantum system whose states are strongly linked. This correlation must be fundamental; these variables must be understood as complex states to adjust for generic quantum flaws [10].

One of the most challenging aspects of developing error-correcting quantum codes is to determine how best to embed an n-qubit system with many logical qubits so that measurements can correct for the most prevalent types of mistakes. A one-to-one correspondence between the k-dimensional vector space of the *em* algorithm and the n-dimensional vector space of the larger system is often used to represent this embedding. We are simply looking at linear codes at this point. Quantum codes have been developed to withstand a wide range of mistakes. Errors on t or less qubits are the most common kind of error to be considered. These types of mistakes are our primary focus after the presentation of a comprehensive framework for quantum error correction. There is a great deal of potential in developing physical quantum computers so that error-correcting codes and other types of error prevention may be designed to defend against the faults that are most common.

Classical block codes and linear quantum codes have a lot in common. We begin by reviewing similar principles from classical coding before moving on to quantum error correction. Because of this, the subsections in this section alternate between brief explanations of classical error correction and longer explanations of quantum error correction [11].

Classical error-correcting codes should be studied in full by anybody unfamiliar with error-correcting codes to obtain a sense of the broad tactics applied in error correcting. Group theory is used extensively in both conventional and quantum error correction. It provides boxes with short summaries of groups, subgroups, and Abelian groups. This chapter has a few more boxes. There are certain portions in a group theory book that need to be studied by those who are new to group theory. After this chapter, there is a reference section that includes recommended readings [1].

For linear quantum error-correcting codes, this section outlines a nonconstructive framework that specifies requirements for every code in the category. This framework does not care whether or how a code is implemented effectively. Whether or not the code is beneficial depends on how this problem is handled [12].

7.3.1 Traditional Based on Error-Correcting Codes

Ancient n-k block coding. C is a subset of the space occupied by strings of length k bits, where n is an integer between 1 and 2^n. The set of n-bit strings is a group under bitwise addition modulo 2. When the subset C of size $2k$ is included, the code is referred to as a $[n,k]$ linear block code. It is crucial to choose a certain $Zn2$ encoding function, where $Zn2$ approximates the original between $Zk2$ (the message space) and C (the code space). In general, there are several encoding functions for every code C. While this lack of an encoding function may appear weird, it is the only way the code is specified. For this reason, the same set of faults may be repaired regardless of the encryption algorithm that is used.

Ciphertexts that are longer than mk are encoded using c to encode each and every one of the m blocks that are k in length. Therefore, they are referred to as "block codes." One way to describe c's decoding functionality is to look at it as a multiplication of the n-by-k numbers G, where G is the matrix that is multiplied by the message word and returns the secret code that corresponds to that communication word. An autonomous binary word set may be found in each of G's k columns.

Example 7.4   Using the $[3,1]$ code for iteration. As a subset of all 3-bit codes, the $[3,1]$ repetition code is specified to be $C = 000, 111$ strings.

Under binary arithmetic subtraction modulo 2, this subset is a subgroup of $Z32$.

If you are using an encoder, you will see the following:

$0 \rightarrow 000$

$1 \rightarrow 111$

Example 7.5   Hamming's code of digits $[7,4]$. To represent the 7 elements of Z_2 that are encoded as 4-bit strings in C, we need to use 7-bit strings. The subgroup of Z_2 formed by the numbers "1110100,1101010,1011001,1111111" has the code C. After some thought, the logic behind this structure becomes obvious. The output of a single C encoding function is

$1000 \rightarrow 1110100$

$0100 \rightarrow 1101010$

$0010 \rightarrow 1011001$

$0001 \rightarrow 1111111$

Encoding is completely defined by these connections and linearity. For this encoding, the generating matrix G is

$$G' = \begin{pmatrix} 1 & 1 & 1 & 0 & 1 & 0 & 0 \\ 1 & 1 & 0 & 1 & 0 & 1 & 0 \\ 1 & 0 & 1 & 1 & 0 & 0 & 1 \\ 1 & 1 & 1 & 1 & 1 & 1 & 1 \end{pmatrix}^T$$

When using an alternate encoding algorithm,

$$1000 \rightarrow 1000111$$
$$0100 \rightarrow 0100110$$
$$0010 \rightarrow 0010101$$
$$0001 \rightarrow 0001011$$

with generator matrix G

$$G = \begin{pmatrix} 1 & 0 & 0 & 0 \\ 0 & 1 & 0 & 0 \\ 0 & 0 & 1 & 0 \\ 0 & 0 & 0 & 1 \\ 1 & 1 & 1 & 0 \\ 1 & 1 & 0 & 1 \\ 1 & 0 & 1 & 1 \end{pmatrix}$$

7.3.2 Quantum Error Decode Mechanisms

This section demonstrates a quantum block code size of $[n,k]$. The state space of an n-qubit system is represented by the vector space V, and a subspace C of C has dimension 2^k. A pair of quotation marks is required when contrasting quantum and classical coding. The k-qubit message space W is a subspace of the set V with the traditional basis consisting of all strings with the first nk element set to 0. For encoding C, any unitary transformation UC: V from W to C might suffice. So, when we design an encoding operator, we are more likely to specify simply how UC works on W and not on the rest of the V states. As in the classical situation, elements are referred to as communication words, while elements C are referred to as codewords. Bit strings in W and coded messages in C are not to be interpreted literally; rather, they represent state quantum mechanics with k and n qubits, respectively.

Since the code is determined by the subspace C and not the encoding function, the same set of faults may be repaired using different decoding mechanisms. Given an encrypting mechanism and any state defined by, the image w of $|w$ is an n-qubit state called the logical k-qubit state comparable to [13].

Example 7.6 The bit-flip code revisited. The code C is the subspace spanned by $\{|000\rangle, |111\rangle\}$. The standard encoding operator is UC: $|0 \to |000$

$$| \to |111$$

So $|\tilde{0} = |000$ and $|\tilde{1} = |111$
Strictly speaking, we should write

$$\text{UC} : |000 \to |000$$

$$|001 \to |111$$

To make things simpler to understand, we will omit the initial prefix string of zeroes when defining encoding algorithms in this manner. This is because we do not worry about how the decoding acts on states even outside.

Example 7.7 Analyzing Shor's rule again. Specifically, Shor's code is a [9,1] code, where C is the two-dimensional domain bounded by

$$\frac{1}{\sqrt{8}}(|000\rangle + |111\rangle)^{\otimes 3}$$

and

$$\frac{1}{\sqrt{8}}(|000\rangle - |111\rangle)^{\otimes 3}$$

The standard encoding operator used with this code sends

$$|0 \to |\tilde{0}\rangle = \frac{1}{\sqrt{8}}(|000\rangle + |111\rangle)^{\otimes 3}$$
$$|1 \to |\tilde{1}\rangle = \frac{1}{\sqrt{8}}(|000\rangle - |111\rangle)^{\otimes 3}$$

It is also possible to encode a function that maps $|0\rangle$ and $|1\rangle$ in the subspace C to two orthogonal axes.

The encoding and decoding routines do not need to be implemented in practice. A computational task begins by creating a legitimate starting state, and at the conclusion, we derive the final conceptual state by interpreting the classical intelligence gathered via measurements as well as the majority performing computations on encoded data directly.

7.3.3 Correction Sets in Quantum Coding Error

To simplify, consider an n-bit string that performs bitwise addition to decode a language. A classical error may be interpreted as inverting some of the code bits. Almost all C code can fix errors, but not all. Confusion is caused by many mistakes.

It is necessary that E has at least one error leading to w for it to be correctable, as the errors $e_1, e_2 > E$ and C and $c_1, c_2 > C$ are always equivalent to one another.

This condition is called the disjointness condition for classical error correction. Usually E is taken to be a group under bitwise addition modulo 2, so E contains the identity element, the non-error 00...0. The disjointness condition for $e_1 = 00...0$ means that a correctable error cannot take a codeword to a different codeword. For any code C, there are many possible sets of correctable errors. Some correctable sets of errors are better than others from a practical point of view.

Example 7.8   The [3,1] repetition code has repairable error sets. Variations in the [3,1] repetition code C may be fixed if they fall under the set $E = [000,001,010,100]$. Errors in C may likewise be reduced to the set $E = 000,011,101,110$. C cannot be shown to have a correctable set in the union of E and E.

7.3.4 Quantum Errors Detection

Errors caused by bit flips are a small, discrete group used for conventional fault detection. When considering quantum error detection and correction, neither the modulated signal signals nor the likely faults can be thought of as a random subset. Thus, it is more challenging to create student error sets for a quantum code C than for a classical code. It is a relief that this is the case since it is a lot less complicated than we initially thought.

Let BC represent a (orthonormal) basis for C: $= |c_1,...,|c_k$. In unitary physics, the affine transformation set $E = E_1, E_2,...,EL$ E_i: Code C is said to have a correctable set of mistakes, $V \to V$, if and only if there is a matrix M with entries m_{ij} such that.

$$\left\langle c_a \mid E_i^\dagger E_j \mid c_b \right\rangle = m_{ij}\delta_{ab} \tag{7.2}$$

for all $|c_a\rangle$, $|c_b\rangle \in C$ and $E_i, E_j \in \mathcal{E}$.

The description and reasoning behind it will be further discussed in the subsequent sentences. For a code C, there are about as many alternative sets of remediable faults as there are in the classical situation. The maximum repairable set does not exist; however; certain sets are more beneficial from a practical standpoint than others. In order to execute error correction, a single collection of repairable mistakes is selected, and the error correction techniques are constructed around that set. If a method is available for code C, it may correct any superposition or mixing of mistakes in the original morphology set E. General errors, such as those outlined in Section 10.4, which may be characterized as probabilistic mixes of the transformation matrix, can be corrected using this characteristic. Unitary mistakes E may be repaired using the inverse transform E, which means that the errors of a correctable set can be readily fixed. The correctable error set condition is explained in detail in following two paragraphs (Eq. (7.2)).

Like the classical case, Error E has two structural changes that lead two different codewords to the same state. In light of this mistaken chain, rescue is impossible. If E has two separate errors, then two errors must cause subatomic particles that are orthogonal to one another. We need to make sure the two systems are orthogonal because we need to take measurements to determine which mistake is more likely to have transpired. This condition guarantees that, because the initial mnemonic devices are separate, the images of two different codewords under errors in E are distinguishable. All of the terms of this agreement have been documented in writing.

$$c \left| E_i^\dagger E_j \mid c' \right\rangle = 0 \tag{7.3}$$

for all $E_i, E_j \in E$, and all $|c, c'\rangle \in C|$ such that $cc'| = 0$.

Equation (7.2), the disjointness criterion for conventional error correction, has an orthogonality equivalent.

To prevent quantum computing from being destroyed by error correction, an additional requirement must be met. Error observations must not reveal the logical state to preserve superpositions, rendering quantum computing pointless. As a result, we need

$$c_a \left| E_i^\dagger E_j \mid c_a \right\rangle = \langle c_b | E_i^\dagger E_j | c_b \tag{7.4}$$

for all $|c_a\rangle, |c_b\rangle \in C$ and $E_i, E_j \in \mathcal{E}$. According to this condition, there must be a value m_{ij} between any two indices i and j such that

$$c_a E_i^\dagger E_j c_a \quad m_{ij} \| =$$

Putting conditions 7.2 and 7.3 together results in the original Eq. (7.4):

$$c_a \left| E_i^\dagger E_j \right| c_a \rangle m_{ij} \delta_{ab} \tag{7.5}$$

for all $|c_a, c_b\rangle \in C$ and $E_i, E_j \in \mathcal{E}|$, where a significant part of the meaning of this formula is that m_{ij} is independent of a and b. Condition 7.2 holds if $c_a \left| E_i^\dagger E_j \right| c_b \rangle = 0$ (7.5) for all $|c_a, c_b\rangle \in C$ and $E_i, E_j \in \mathcal{E}|$ such that $i \neq j$, but this condition is stronger than necessary.

If two separate errors E_1 and E_2 result in the same state, then applying (or equally well) fixes the error, regardless of which error happened. In general, condition 7.5 holds for quantum codes. But this is not always the case. Degenerate error set codes are those that do not satisfy this criterion. In E. Shor's degenerated code, a mistake in the first qubit's frequency components has the same effect as an error in the second qubit's phase difference. Inherent complexities are increased by the existence of degenerate code. Unlike their classical counterparts, morally bankrupt computational codes have no analogues in the field of quantum mechanics.

All E_i errors have a size of 2^k because of the unitarity of the E_i. A set E of corrective maintenance faults for a hence has code can have a maximum size of $2nnk$. k if the complete design code has $2nk$ orthogonal similarity measure of dimension 2^k. For those who are depraved.

Example 7.9 An update on the bit-flip algorithm. Errors that have accumulated $E = \{E_{ij}\}$ with

$E_{00} = I \otimes I \otimes I, E_{01} = X \otimes I \otimes I, E_{10} = I \otimes X \otimes I, E_{11} = I \otimes I \otimes X$ is a correctable error set for the bit-flip code.

The set of errors $\mathcal{E}' = \left\{ E'_{ij} \right\}$ with

$E'_{00} = I \otimes I \otimes I, E'_{01} = I \otimes X \otimes X, E'_{10} = X \otimes I \otimes X, E'_{11} = X \otimes X \otimes I$

There is a novel kind of fixable error in the bit-flip code. In this case, it fixes errors in two-qubit flips but not in one-bit flips. Since digital signal flip faults are more prevalent than several bit-flip errors, a repairable problem collection has little practical importance. The bit-flip error may be more prone to occur in pairs in specific mechanical arrangements.

7.3.5 Basic Knowledge Representation of Error-Correcting Code

We will assume C is a traditional $[n,k]$ block code, with a collection of correctable errors called E. Errors are encoded as codewords. We would like to change the letter w to the letter c. Consideration of code C's cosets aids in the discovery of e and c.

This section demonstrates that each coset has a typical mistake. Suppose that H is a set of all the cosets of when an error occurs, the code word C is transformed into a component of some C coset. Because of the disjointness criterion, coset e_1 c_1 and coset e_2 c_2 are distinct from each other. For this to be evident, consider the case when e_1 and e_2 are both in the same coset. Then, e_1 c_1 $c_3 = e_2$ c_2 would exist if c_3 C.

There are two different correctable faults that may lead two codewords to the same word; however; it is not disjoint since c_1 c_3 are in C criterion, and knowing which coset ec falls within informs us what kind of mistake has happened. Let us be more specific about this.

All cosets form a group, H, since it is Abelian. It measures $2nk$. H is isomorphic to Z because every one of its components has order 2, making it Abelian and nontrivial. Let us transform it into an isomorphism. In this scenario, the map (w (w C)) directs all of the elements in C to the zero element in Z. The condition that the two variables w and w belong to the same coset is necessary for the element $h(w)$ describes each coset. This coset is related to a single instance of the mistake e E, as stated in the preceding paragraph. When the coset is characterized by $h(w)$, so is this mistake. That is why it is dubbed the "error syndrome" or "syndrome" for short.

An $(nk)n$ matrix P may be used to realize h in more detail. Learn how to count rows in a matrices by counting the linearly independent components pi that are equal to zero modulo 2 in any one of the ranges $c - C$.

$$P = \begin{pmatrix} p_1^T \\ \vdots \\ p_{n-k}^T \end{pmatrix}$$

If you have a particular many matrices P are possible given a given code C (just as there are many potential isomorphisms). Pw, the syndrome, characterizes the w-containing coset C when seen as a binary column vector. The first P in each column is multiplied by the inner composition (mod 2) of w for each of these n-values. The Ps in code C is a binary sequence, and the pis in the rows are parity checks. If $P(ei) = P$, then the parity check matrix P can tell the difference between the two classes of errors that can be fixed (ej). If G is a codeword generating matrix and P is an arbitrary $(nk)n$ matrix, then PG is a zero-sum product and P is a parity check matrix for C. The C-code represents not only the image of Z under G, but also the kernel of P, the set of $Zn2$ elements transferred to 000 under P.

Hamming is one of the simplest classical codes, and it serves as a foundation for many quantum codes. There exists a Hamming code C_n for every positive integer $n = 2$. Each nonzero n-bit string is represented in a column of a Hamming code convolutional code. C_n is a $[2n - 1] - [2n - 1]$ Hamming code since its generator matrix is $(2n\ 1)[2n\ n1]$, which is the result of the parity check matrix of the Hamming code. Single bit flip errors are fixed across the board in Buttering programs.

Example 7.10 Code C_2 of the Hamming distance. Hamming code C_2, the code with parity check matrix, is equivalent to the [3,1] repetition code.

$$P = \begin{pmatrix} 0 & 1 & 1 \\ 1 & 0 & 1 \end{pmatrix}$$

For the same code, an alternative complex valued matrix is

$$P' = \begin{pmatrix} 1 & 1 & 0 \\ 1 & 0 & 1 \end{pmatrix}$$

The shape of the matrix P is $(A|I)$. Is a code generating matrix, as determined by $\left(\frac{I}{A} \right)$ Exercise 7.2. The resulting generator matrix, derived from P, is

$$G = \begin{pmatrix} 1 \\ 1 \\ 1 \end{pmatrix}.$$

Since $0 = 000$ and $1 = 111$, the code C_2 is referred to as a repetition code.

Here is a case in point from Section 7.2: code C_3 of the Hamming distance metric. Hamming code C_3 is a [7,4] code. The quantum Steane code is defined in terms of C_3.

The [7,4] Hamming code's parity check matrix is

$$P' = \begin{pmatrix} 0 & 0 & 0 & 1 & 1 & 1 & 1 \\ 0 & 1 & 1 & 0 & 0 & 1 & 1 \\ 1 & 0 & 1 & 0 & 1 & 0 & 1 \end{pmatrix};$$

The seven nonzero 3-bit strings that make up its columns are all there. The search for a generating matrix is our next objective. P is orthogonal to itself because each row includes an even number of 1s. These components are also orthogonal to each other; thus, we may consider row P transposed onto the first three numbers of G. One more orthogonal and linearly independent vector must be discovered. The arrowhead

$$(1 \ 1 \ 1 \ 1 \ 1 \ 1 \ 1)^T$$

fulfills both of the criteria. So, generating matrices for the [7,4] Time-frequency code may be found here.

$$G' = \begin{pmatrix} 0 & 0 & 0 & 1 & 1 & 1 & 1 \\ 0 & 1 & 1 & 0 & 0 & 1 & 1 \\ 1 & 0 & 1 & 0 & 1 & 0 & 1 \\ 1 & 1 & 1 & 1 & 1 & 1 & 1 \end{pmatrix}^T$$

It is also possible to use a more user-friendly use a complex-valued matrix to generate a [7,4] Hamming code $(A|I)$,

$$P = \begin{pmatrix} 1 & 1 & 1 & 0 & 1 & 0 & 0 \\ 1 & 1 & 0 & 1 & 0 & 1 & 0 \\ 1 & 0 & 1 & 1 & 0 & 0 & 1 \end{pmatrix}$$

As seen in Exercise 7.2, this version of the parity check matrix corresponds to a random number generator in which: $\left(\frac{I}{A} \right)$,

$$G = \begin{pmatrix} 1 & 0 & 0 & 0 \\ 0 & 1 & 0 & 0 \\ 0 & 0 & 1 & 0 \\ 0 & 0 & 0 & 1 \\ 1 & 1 & 1 & 0 \\ 1 & 1 & 0 & 1 \\ 1 & 0 & 1 & 1 \end{pmatrix}.$$

7.3.6 Quantum Codes as a Tool for Error Detection and Correction

In this part, we detail an approach for fixing bugs in quantum codes with a fully completed design. Code quantum $n(k)$ for n bits Suppose C is nondegenerate on a set $[[n,k]]$ of correctable errors. Therefore, if you have a codeword in C and an error in E, the only way to retrieve $|w$ is by using $Es|v$, your options are the only two possible values for Es and $|v$. Since there are M subspaces in EsC, we may find the state $|w$ in one of them and repair the mistake by applying E to it. We must first measure the state $|w$ to arrive at this conclusion. Only one qubit may be measured at a time in the typical quantum computing paradigm. Ancilla qubits and standard basis observations may be used for any other examination, although only a limited quantity of information can be effectively carried out in this manner. This section serves as an overview. Throughout the rest of this chapter and the next one, we will discuss development concerns for individual codes.

To find out where the state $|w$ is in the error subspace, a measurement must be performed. Suppose that W_i equals $E_i C$.

$$W = \bigoplus_{i=0}^{M-1} W_i$$

All mnemonic devices and all stages that depict codewords in a recognizable, fixable format The subdomain of the functional space V transverse to W, where E_i E have orthogonal vectors, may be empty. Due to notational constraints, we define WM to be equal to W. $|w$ does not belong in WM since it is defined there as an error E_i applied to a codeword. Because W_i is orthogonal, we can find an observable O that has the same eigen subspaces.

Allowing U_P to operate on $n + m$ qubits and P_i to be the projectors into the subspace results in the following:

$$U_p : |w\rangle|0\rangle \mapsto \sum_{j=0}^{M-1} b_j|w_j\rangle|j\rangle \tag{7.6}$$

where $|$ is expressed as $b_j|w_j = P_j|w$ in terms of its constituents. To get the error syndrome, the subspace index j, you need to take the measurements of auxiliary qubits of type m in the conventional framework. The use of M as an index is forbidden in WM. After measurements, the state of the first n qubits is in the subspace $W_j = E_j C$, therefore applying the operator E_j fixes the error. Operator U_p is known as a situation-separating operator because it serves a purpose similar to that of the syndrome in conventional error correction. Standard error correction employs a unitary operator called U_p to carry out the parity check matrix P. Due to the flexibility of the labels for the subspaces, many different unitary operators may be employed to extract syndromes from a specified code C and error set E.

One may get a binary observable with two $2n1$ eigen subspaces by isolating a single auxiliary qubit (l), one in which the lth bit of the encoding scheme of its index I is 0 and the other in which the lth bit of the encoding scheme of its index I is 1. This is in line with a well-characterized qubit l operating in isolation to produce a binary that has been validated experimentally. The syndrome extraction operator may be seen as a collection of m explanatory variables.

Example 7.11 The bit-flip algorithm yet again. Consider the bit-flip code C and the set of correctable errors $E = \{E_{ij}\}$ with

$$E_{00} = I \otimes I \otimes I, E_{01} = X \otimes I \otimes I, E_{10} = I \otimes X \otimes I, E_{11} = I \otimes I \otimes X$$

More simply, $E_{00} = I, E_{01} = X_2, E_{10} = X_1$, and $E_{11} = X_0$, where X_i is the operator X applied to the ith qubit. The orthogonal subspaces corresponding to this error set are $W_{00} = E_{00}C$, $W_{01} = E_{01}C$, $W_{10} = E_{10}C$ and $W_{11} = E_{11}C$ with bases $B_{00} = \{|000\rangle, |111\rangle\}$, $B_{01} = \{|100\rangle, |011\rangle\}$, $B_{10} = \{|010\rangle, |101\rangle\}$ and $B_{11} = \{|001\rangle, |110\rangle\}$, respectively. The operator

$$U_p : |x_2, x_1, x_0, 0, 0\rangle \rightarrow |x_2, x_1, x_0, b_1 = x_1 \oplus x_0, b_0 = x_0 \oplus x_0\rangle$$

operates on C with error set E to retrieve syndromes. For example, in the consistent schedule, monitoring the first For example, the eigen-spaces W_{00} and W_{01} are distinguished from one another by the bit (b_1 in the consistent schedule). Measuring b_0 is analogous to detecting W_{00}, W_{10}, and W_{01}, W_{11} in that it may be used to discriminate between deviations that lie in the W_{00}, W_{10}, and W_{01}, W_{11} range. By taking b_1 and b_0 as I and j, we may project the state into $W_{ij} = E_{ij}C$, where it may be possible to apply E_{ij} to the situation at hand. Auxiliary measurements (B_1) and (B_0) both provide 0, thus we use transformations (X_2) to arrive at the same result.

The observational ZIZ (resp. IZZ) may be used to directly measure b_0 (resp. b_1) without the usage of bits. The standard parity check matrix may be compared to this one.

$$P = \begin{pmatrix} 1 & 0 & 1 \\ 0 & 1 & 1 \end{pmatrix}$$

for the [3,1] code with the array

$$\begin{array}{ccc} Z & I & Z \\ I & Z & Z' \end{array}$$

columns in which each factor is listed for both observables. For example, if the word is a codeword, then the parity check matrix multiplied by the word equals zero. When a non-codeword is combined with the binary sequence, at least one row will not be zero. It is possible for a non-codeword to be present in both the +1 and 1-eigenspaces for at least one of the observables in the quantum scenario. Section 7.4's stabilizer codes make use of this link.

In order to better understand an alternative to the syndrome assessment, let us look at this one first. Using ancilla qubits to rectify general faults in quantum video processing is one of quantum computing's most beautiful and startling features. Unitary errors may be generated by calculating information into ancilla qubits and then measuring them. We may use the inverse unitary operator to fix the remaining unitary error when the measurement is complete. Alternative and comparable methods include correcting errors by performing a supervised transaction from the ancilla qubits to the calculation itself, rather than monitoring the ancilla after they've already been computed. The ancilla may be used as the control bits in an affect the duration rather than evaluating after U_P has been applied to the computer system and its peripherals.

$$V_P = \sum_s E_s^\dagger \otimes |s\rangle\langle s|$$

As a result, mistakes may be fixed without resorting to measurements.

Example 7.12 Code using bit-flip algorithm C_{BF} corrections are performed via regulated methods. If universal bit flipping (U_{BF}) is employed instead of measurement, then an ancilla-to-computational VP procedure may be performed, with each of the three error-correcting transformations being carried out as the ancilla qubits transition between states.

$$V_P = I \otimes |00\rangle\langle 00| + X_2 \otimes |01\rangle\langle 01| + X_1 \otimes |10\rangle\langle 10| + X_0 \otimes |11\rangle\langle 11|$$

This regulated action is enabled by the circuit

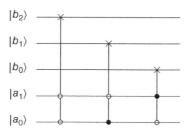

Suppose an error $E = \alpha X_2 + \beta X_1$ has occurred. Applying this circuit to the state

$$U_{BF}(E|\tilde{0}\rangle \otimes |00\rangle) = \alpha|100\rangle|11\rangle + \beta|010\rangle \,|\, 10$$

results in $\alpha|000|11 + \beta|000|10 = |000(\alpha|11 + \beta|10)$.

The two auxiliary qubits are not measured during quantum error correction, but rather converted to |00 and reused in a later round of error correction.

Example 7.13 *Conditional Formatting*

A second look at the phase-flip algorithm. You may remember that the bit-flip code is the counterpart of the frequency and phase code introduced in Example 7.1.2 through the transformations $W = H\,H\,H$. An error correction algorithm for the relative phase code may be derived by applying W to all states and substituting WTW for all transformations T utilized. Since $X = HZH$, the observables corresponding to the syndrome operator U' $X \otimes I \otimes X$ $I \otimes X \otimes X$ P are and, which have a corresponding array which is related to the classical parity check matrix

$$P = \begin{pmatrix} 1 & 0 & 1 \\ 0 & 1 & 1 \end{pmatrix}$$

In this case, errors can be corrected without measurement using

$$V'_P = I \otimes |00\rangle\langle00| + Z_2 \otimes |01\rangle\langle01| + Z_1 \otimes |10\rangle\langle10| + Z_0 \otimes |11\rangle\langle11|$$

7.3.7 Quantum Error Correction Across Multiple Blocks

While Section 7.2.1 describes classical $[n,k]$ block codes that $\dfrac{[[n,k]]}{\text{blocks of } k}$ encode length mk bit thread as mn binary strings by codifying each of the m blocks of k bits, also describes a quantum code (C) that codifies length mk bit strings as mn machine learning bit sequence by codifying each of the m logical bits in C. a superposition of logic like as

$$|\psi\rangle = \sum_i \sum_j \alpha_{ij}(|w_i\rangle \otimes |w_j\rangle)$$

is encoded as

$$|\tilde{\psi}\rangle = \sum_i \sum_j \alpha_{ij}(|c_i\rangle \otimes |c_j\rangle)$$

C's internal encoding function is represented by $|c_i\rangle = U_C|w_i\rangle$. Such superpositions need the use of quantum block codes that can remedy mistakes. The encoding state must also be able to remedy mistakes of the type $E_i 1$ *Eim* if C can correct errors of the form *Ei1 Eim* when applied blockwise. Throughout the rest of this section, quantum error detection is shown in the two-block situation.

Suppose the encoded state $|\tilde{\psi}\rangle = \sum_i \sum_j \alpha_{ij}(|c_i\rangle \otimes |c_j\rangle)$ were subject to error $E_a \otimes E_b$, where E_a and E_b are both correctable errors for code C. Applying the syndrome extraction operator U_P for C to each block separately, measuring the ancilla for each block, and applying the appropriate correcting operators will restore the state $|\tilde{\psi}$:

$$U_P \otimes U_P((E_a \otimes E_b |\tilde{\psi}\rangle) \otimes |0\rangle |0\rangle) = \sum_{ij} \alpha_{ij} (U_P(E_a |c_i\rangle |0\rangle) \otimes (U_P (E_b |c_j\rangle |0\rangle))$$

$$= \sum_{ij} \alpha_{ij} (E_a |c_i\rangle |a\rangle \otimes E_b |c_j\rangle |b\rangle)$$

where we have reordered the qubits for clarity. Measurement of the two ancilla yields $|a\rangle$ and $|b\rangle$ respectively, with the computation qubits in state $|\phi\rangle = \sum_{ij} \alpha_{ij}(E_a |c_i\rangle \otimes E_b |c_j\rangle)$. The syndrome $|a|b$ indicates that the error can be corrected by applying $E_a^\dagger \otimes E_b^\dagger$. Applying $E_a^\dagger \otimes E_b^\dagger$ does indeed correct the error:

$$E_a^\dagger \otimes E_b^\dagger |\phi\rangle = \sum_i \sum_j \alpha_{ij}(|c_i\rangle \otimes |c_j\rangle) = |\tilde{\psi}\rangle$$

7.3.8 Computing on Encoded Quantum States

After the states have been encoded, we must still be able to compute on them for error-correcting codes to serve as a tool for quantum computing. Embedding function for $[[n,k]]$ quantum code $C:V\ W:C:C:C:C:C$ You will need to discover an equivalent if you wish to conduct general computation on encrypted states, you need a unitary operator U operating on the encoded states, one that sends $UC(|w)$ for each $|$ to a corresponding unitary operator U $(U|w)$. Multiple V-functioning unitary operators share this property quality since we do not worry about how U acts outside C. There are several methods to implement a given unitary operator U in terms of fundamental gates. There may be more economical ways to implement one of the multiple logical analogs $U: W: V$ than the other and some representations are more resilient than others for a particular $U: W: W$.

The encoding operator may be used to create one of these operators. Let UC serve as the unitary coding function for transmitting $|$ 0 to. A valid codeword is sent to $|$. through the UC transformation. On the code space, the operator $U = UC(U\ I)UC$ has the desirable impact; on encoded states, U is the logical counterpart of U. The state is unencoded when UC is applied, thus any errors made at this time are visible. In general, this approach generates a U with weak durability attributes.

7.3.9 Using Linear Transformation of Correctable Codes

Probabilistic mixes of linear transformations A_i may be used to describe general errors E, and these linear error transformations A_i are not always unitary:

$$E : \rho \mapsto \sum_{i=1}^{K} A_i \rho A_i^\dagger$$

It is shown in this section that the code in question can correct mistakes that include elements from a set E of correctable errors and have nonzero complex linear combinations. The term "set of correctable faults" usually refers to all potential linear connections of flaws that the code is able to correct through a unitary translation. Measurement is used to map a conditional probability of mistakes onto one of the correctable errors in order to implement unitary error transformation. Additionally, it is analyzed to determine the source of any remaining experimental error. As is customary, there are many distinct maximum sets of correctable defects for each given code, and certain of these maximal sets constitute distinct subspaces.

Assume that the error is a probabilistic sum of errors, a correlation between two errors E_i from the set of solvable errors, such that in a more general setting, we show that the error E is not uniform if it takes a codeword |c| with the density operator |c|.

$\rho = |c\rangle\langle c|$, to a mixed state $\rho' = E_\rho E^\dagger$, we can correct the error. The mixed state ρ can be written $\rho' = \sum |\alpha_i|^2 E_i |c\rangle\langle c| E_i^\dagger$.

Since the $E_i|c$ is mutually orthogonal and contains a single trace and a hybrid character. Since this is the case, is a probability distribution over the orthogonal pure states. $E_i|c$. Think on what can be seen $O = \sum_i \lambda_i P_i$, where I is a unique identifier and P_i is a projector into the subspace $E_i C$. Measuring with O, according to the definitions, yields a condition with probability |i|2. As a result of the measurement, we now know the pure state $E_i|c$, which subspace of $E_i C$ the state occupies may be determined from the measured signal I when E_i is used to fix a problem, it becomes better.

7.3.10 Model of Classical Independent Error

Detecting non-codewords, finding the most probable mistake, and then implementing a transition to fix that error are the three components of a generic error correction technique in both quantum and conventional cases. An error model is necessary for identifying the most probable source of a problem. In classical computing, a common family of error models is the independent error model, in which each bit has a probability of flipping the p 1/2. To flip a single bit incorrectly, there is a chance of $p(1p)^{n-1}$, to flip two bits incorrectly, there is a probability of $p2(1p)^{n-2}$, and the likelihood of no error at all is $(1p)^n$.

This paradigm is used to direct the process of fixing errors. Under this method, there is no one kind of error that is more likely than any other, thus if a codeword is received, we must conclude that it was not a mistake. Suppose we would want to make w a non-codeword again. Let c be the closest element of C to w in an independent error model, and let $e = cw$ be the most likely mistake that could have occurred if c is unique. Since W is a member of the coset C in which $k > C$, we may consider w to be another element of C. If c is the element in C that is most closely related to w, then C experiences the same thing. If e is the most likely slip-up, then w is also probably wrong.

Each of a coset's subsets is a compact set that is no more than C units away from C along any Euclidean path. Following definition c, the coset member with the lowest Hamming weight is the most likely to be incorrect.

The syndrome calculation's lightest member e is used to make the necessary adjustments to the coset. If the actual error was somewhat different, we "corrected" the erroneous phrase, because there is currently no other way to handle the situation. We do not do anything if we obtain a codeword. Faults that cause words to be converted into code cannot always be corrected by error detection and repair codes. Therefore, it is unclear how to address the problem if there are several closest components to w in C. The independent error model often makes use of E_t, the set of all words of Hamming weight t or less, where t is as large as possible without increasing ambiguity or, similarly, breaching the disjointness criterion for a collection of correctable errors.

The lowest Hamming distance between any two codewords is the code's distance. Words with a length of k bits must be encoded as pairs of nk and k bits in order to be represented in a [nk,d] code. The set of words that are no more distant from c than the distance measure t is what we will call et(c), where v is the distance between c and the word. Included in et(c) are all the words v that result from subtracting an error of weight t from the given c. If every pair of codewords is disjoint, then every weight t error in the code may be fixed by mapping words in the set et(c) to the codeword c. The sets et(c) are disjoint only when $d = 2t + 1$. This means that errors with a magnitude less than or equal to [n,k,d]! may be fixed. If two codewords could translate to the same error word under two different t-bit errors, then the disjointness criteria would not apply, and hence the largest possible t for a distance d code C must meet 2t + 1 d.

7.3.11 Independent Quantum Inaccuracies Models

Errors that may be corrected in a quantum code C might have different effects depending on the code's practicality. Reducing the interfacial tension sets are preferable based on which mistakes have the greatest likelihood of occurring. There are more quantum error models to pick from since there is a wider range of quantum mistakes. The traditional autonomous given below, we provide an error model motivated by the local and Markov assumptions that errors on different qubits occur independently and that a specific qubit is impacted by an error with probability p.

Only sets of correctable errors with unitary error transformations are utilized since inverted transformations can correct only unitary errors. In particular, identifying a set of fixable errors using the generalized Pauli group G_n is a common practice. Each member of the generalization Pauli group G_n is the product of two Pauli variables contributing; hence, there are n-fold tensor products of Pauli group elements. All G_n may be represented as an international brand using the thanks to technological advances of the Pauli group.

$$\mu(Xa_1 \otimes \cdots \otimes Xa_n)(Zb_1 \otimes \cdots \otimes Zb_n)$$

showing that every mistake can be written as a combination of mathematical operations where a_1 and b_1 are binary variables

$$\frac{A_i}{\sqrt{\text{tr}\left(A_i \rho A_i^\dagger\right)}}$$

An n-qubit system's associated vector space, as modeled by linear equations, is based on the generalized Pauli group G_n. The found in connective where $E_j\, G_n$ may be used to describe a generic error E on an n-qubit classical register. Generalized Pauli operators are able to express any of the following that arise in an operator sum decomposition in terms of homogeneous operators. Errors, which may be rectified by a specific technique, are all fixed by the same procedure.

One qubit is transformed into another, while the rest remain unchanged: X_i.

$$\underbrace{I \otimes \cdots \otimes I}_{i} \otimes X \otimes \underbrace{I \otimes \cdots \otimes I}_{n-i-1}$$

Y_i and Z_i have a similar connotation. The amount A Pauli miscalculation's significance is proportional to the number of nonidentity variables used in the tensor product formulation. The error weight is only defined for Pauli errors.

The generic Pauli group may include useful properties. There is a high probability that stabilizer algorithms will make extensive use of the fact that Pauli components g_1 and g_2 commute (either as an anticommute or as an example of a transportation) if this is the case. As an added bonus, the correctable set E for a code C may be expanded to include the Yi errors for all I if it already contains the X_i and Z_i single-qubit bit flip and phase-flip defects for all I. If errors X_i and Z_i can be fixed, then for any integer I, the following four formulas all evaluate to zero under the non-orthogonality criteria of E and C.

It is sufficient to prove that for any I and j and for all orthonormal y values, the Y_i are acceptable repairable faults.

$$|c1 = |c_2\rangle \in C$$

$$c_1 \left| X_j^\dagger Y_i \right| c_2 = 0$$

$$c_1 \left| Z_j^\dagger Y_i \right| c_2 = 0$$

$c_1 |IY_i|c_2 = 0$, and for all $j = i$

$$c_1 \left| Y_j^\dagger Y_i \right| c_2 \rangle = 0$$

Multiplication in the Pauli group leads directly to these equality results. Reasons why include, but are not limited to:

$$X_i^\dagger Y_i = -X_i^\dagger X_i Z_i = -IZ_i$$

$$c_1 X_i^\dagger Y_i c_2 \parallel = -c_1 \mid IZ_i \mid c_2 = 0$$

So, any method that attempts to fix X and Z errors will also fix Y errors.

The set of Pauli people with weight t or less satisfies the corrective maintenance error set condition up to a maximum weight, denoted by t.

It is impossible for any nondegenerate $[[n,k]]$-quantum code to repair mistakes with more than the weight of t. A nonde generated code's correctable set may include up to 2^{nk} entries, as seen. The weight's total number of components t is $3^t \binom{n}{t}$. Thus, for any nondegenerate piece of code to be error-free below a certain threshold, called t, it must conform to a quantum Hamming constraint.

$$\sum_{i=0}^{t} 3^i \binom{n}{i} \leq 2^{n-k}$$

When the quantum Hamming constraint is equalized, we have a perfect code since it is nondegenerate. It discusses the classic Hamming bound. Degenerate codes are exempt from the quantum Hamming constraint. This Hamming bound is satisfied by every classical code. Quantum degenerate codes aggravate the quantum landscape by making the quantum Hamming constraint inapplicable to all codes.

Perfect codes are not always the best codes to employ in practice, just as they were not always the best in classical cases. Code multiplication and the quantum Hamming bound provide a measure of the limits of both encoding (the ratio of the encoded state to the input message state) and error correction (the number of single qubit errors the code can fix). Another factor that is quite significant in practice is the efficiency with which errors may be uncovered. Several codes approach the quantum Hamming limit but lack efficient error detection systems, as assessed by the number of gates needed for syndrome extraction and the number of qubits that must be monitored. Effective error detection strategies need substantial structure, and this is true in both the qualitative and conventional settings. Quantum-based error correction techniques that properly balance the need for more space for data storage with the need for security are still a topic of active study. Stabilizer codes, which make up the vast majority of quantum error-correcting codes, provide this environment. CSS codes (Calderbank-Shor-Steane), which belong to the larger category of stabilizer codes, have an advantage over other stabilizer codes since they may be built from pairs of classical codes that are coupled in a novel way.

7.4 Coding Standards for CSS

Bit-flip errors can be fixed by encoding a single qubit into three, and phase-flip errors can be fixed by encoding the logical qubits again. As indicated, bit-flip errors are feasible when $X_i = HZ_iH$. Phase-flip errors Z_i are directly related to bit-flip errors in the standard basis ($Z_i = 0$, $Z_i = 1$), which are phase-flip errors in the Hadamard basis ($Z_i = +$, $Z_i = -$), and vice versa. Calderbank, Shor, and Steane demonstrated that by exploiting this relationship, it is possible to produce classical coding from any two conventional codes satisfying a certain duality relation. This collection of rules, named after the creators of the system (CSS) as the name implies, is termed CSS codes. By using a single encoding to correct all phases and bit flip errors, we can reduce the number of qubits needed to repair t qubit defects. Steane's [[7,1]] CSS code only needs seven qubits to correct all single qubits, whereas Shor's code needs nine.

7.4.1 Multiple Classical Identifiers

Assuming the transposition of a convolutional codes is the generate matrix of another conventional code. If the inner product of the two sets of terms (here, vectors) is zero, then the assertion that V and W are orthogonal holds. Assume that we have two codes, C and C, and that each code has two matrices, G, P and GT, P, for generating and checking parity, respectively. In other words, because G is orthogonal to P and the codewords of C are orthogonal to one other, we may say that the codewords of C are orthogonal to each other.

Example 7.14 It can be shown that the [7,4] Hamming code has a mirror code in the [7,3] code C with two – dimensional array.

$$G^\perp = P^T = \begin{pmatrix} 1 & 1 & 1 & 0 & 1 & 0 & 0 \\ 1 & 1 & 0 & 1 & 0 & 1 & 0 \\ 1 & 0 & 1 & 1 & 0 & 0 & 1 \end{pmatrix}^T$$

and parity check matrix

$$P^\perp = G^T = \begin{pmatrix} 1 & 1 & 1 & 0 & 1 & 0 & 0 \\ 1 & 1 & 0 & 1 & 0 & 1 & 0 \\ 1 & 0 & 1 & 1 & 0 & 0 & 1 \\ 1 & 1 & 1 & 1 & 1 & 1 & 1 \end{pmatrix}$$

Since the rows of P are a subset of those of $P^{\perp}$, it follows that C contains its own dual: $C\perp \subset C$. The eight codewords of $C\perp$ are the linear combinations of the columns of $G\perp$:

$$C \perp = \{0000000, 1110100, 1101010, 0011110, 1011001, 0101101, 0110011, 1000111\}$$

The sixteen codewords of C are those of $C\perp$ plus those obtained by adding 1111111 to all of the codewords of $C\perp$.

For any $[n,k]$ classical code C,

$$\sum_{c\in C^{\perp}}(-1)^{c\cdot x} = \begin{cases} 2^k & \text{if } x \in C \\ 0 & \text{otherwise} \end{cases} \tag{7.7}$$

It is possible to establish this identification by linking it to the identity

$$\sum_{y=0}^{N-1}(-1)^{y\cdot x} = \begin{cases} 0 & \text{for } x \neq 0 \\ N = 2^n & \text{for } x = 0 \end{cases}$$

The resultant vector of the two$T$ n-bit strings x and Gy is equivalent to the weighted sum of the two k-bit strings Gx and y, as shown in Equation 7.1, because $x\,Gy = G^T\,x\,y$.

$$\sum_{c\in C}(-1)^{c\cdot x} = \sum_{y=0}^{2^k-1}(-1)^{Gy\cdot x}$$

$$= \sum_{y=0}^{2^k-1}(-1)^{y\cdot G^T x}$$

$$= \begin{cases} 2^k & \text{if } G^T x = 0 \\ 0 & \text{otherwise} \end{cases}$$

Identity 7.7 follows, since $G^T x = P\perp x = 0$ precisely when $x \in C\perp$.

7.4.2 Traditional CSS Codes Satisfying a Duality Consequence

It facilitates coordination of dual C codewords on the Hadamard basis and permits the construction of states that are superpositions of abbreviated from a classical C code on the consistent schedule. To further demonstrate their existence in the states $|h_i$ where the I is smaller than C, we generate states $|g$ that have amplitude only in the states $|h_i$, which are Hadamard basis components.

$$|h_i = W|i = H \otimes \cdots \otimes H \,|\, i$$

This section demonstrates how the properties may remedy phase-flip and bit-flip issues after it has been constructed.

Let C_1 and $C_2^{\perp}$ be $[n, k_1]$ and $[n, k_2]$ classical codes, respectively, and suppose both codes 1 2 correct t errors. Furthermore, suppose $C_2^{\perp} \subset C_1$. There are $2k - k$ distinct cosets of $C_2^{\perp}$ in C_1; every $c \in C_1$ defines a coset $c \oplus C_2^{\perp} = \{c \oplus c' \mid c' \in C_2^{\perp}\}$ and $c \oplus C_2^{\perp} = d \oplus C_2^{\perp}$ if and only if $c \oplus d \in C_2^{\perp}$. The set of cosets forms a group, the quotient group $G = C_1/C_2^{\perp}$. Since $C_1 \equiv \mathbf{Z}_2^{k_1}$ and $C_2^{\perp} \equiv \mathbf{Z}_2^{k_2}$, the quotient group $G \equiv \mathbf{Z}_2^{k_1-k_2}$. For each element $g \in G$, define a quantum state

$$|\psi_g\rangle = \frac{1}{\sqrt{2^{k_2}}} \sum_{c \in C_2^{\perp}} |c_g \oplus c\rangle$$

where C_g is any member of the coset designated by g, and C_1 is the empty set. A $[[n, k_1\ k_2]]$ quantum code C, also known as the CSS code, is defined as the subspace of dimension $2k_1 k_2$ covered by the $|g$ for all g G. (C_1, C_2).

This paragraph demonstrates that $|g$ has amplitude exclusively in the C_2 codewords when examined in the Hadamard basis. Hadamard basis components of $|g$ are written as $hi|g|hi = i|W|gW|i$.

Because of this, proving that $W|g$ is a superposition of codewords $|$ is sufficient; remember from Section 7.3.4 that

$$W|y\rangle = \frac{1}{\sqrt{N}} \sum_{x=0}^{N-1} (-1)^{y \cdot x} |x\rangle$$

So

$$W|\psi_g\rangle = \frac{1}{\sqrt{2^{k_2}}} \sum_{c \in C_2^{\perp}} \frac{1}{\sqrt{2^n}} \sum_{x=0}^{N-1} (-1)^{(c_g \oplus c) \cdot x} \mid x$$

$$= \frac{1}{\sqrt{2^{n+k_2}}} \sum_{x=0}^{N-1} (-1)^{x \cdot c_g} \sum_{c \in C_2^{\perp}} (-1)^{x \cdot c} \mid x$$

$$= \frac{1}{\sqrt{2^{n+k_2}}} \sum_{x \in (C_2^{\perp})^{\perp}} (-1)^{x \cdot c_g} \left(2^{k_2}\right) \mid x$$

$$= \frac{1}{\sqrt{2^{n-k_2}}} \sum_{x \in C_2} (-1)^{x \cdot c_g} |x\rangle,$$

where line 3 follows from line 2 by identity 7.7.

This brings us to the topic at hand: fixing the errors. Since each $|g$ in C_1 is a string of codewords, a quantum implementation of the C_1 syndrome may be used to fix all t bit-flip errors. The parity check matrix (P_1) checks whether the sum (mod2) of each bit is even or odd. Each column of the parity-checking matrix The controller with value a_1 in $Z\ n_1 b_1 = \ldots$ indicates that introspection performs the same check on quantum states Z whenever the parity check yields a 1 and an I whenever the parity check yields a 0 in b Z. For each unitary transformation Q on a single qubit, let Qb denote the tensor product $Qbn_1\ Qb_1\ Qb_0$. If b is bigger than P, then b is a row in P.

For the sake of materializing these explanatory variables in terms of single-qubit measurements, each row $b\ P_1$ corresponds to an element of a quantum circuit on $n+1$ qubits, the n computing qubits plus an ancillary qubit. If there is a 1 in the ith position of the row, then there is a C_{not} between the ith qubit and the accessory.

First, we need to make sure that phase-flip errors are really bit-flip faults under W so that we can demonstrate how the algorithm handles phase mistakes. Phase-flip faults are indicated by a string of bits called an e. This instance of $|g$ gets renamed to $|g$.

$$\frac{1}{\sqrt{2^{k_2}}}\sum_{c\in C_2^\perp}(-1)^{e\cdot(c_g\oplus c)}\ |\ c_g\oplus c$$

which, after applying W, becomes

$$\frac{1}{\sqrt{2^{n+k_2}}}\sum_{c\in C_2^\perp}(-1)^{e\cdot(c_g\oplus c)}\sum_{x=0}^{N-1}(-1)^{x\cdot(c_g\oplus c)}\ |\ x=\frac{1}{\sqrt{2^{n+k_2}}}\sum_{x=0}^{N-1}(-1)^{(e\oplus x)\cdot c_g}\sum_{c\in C_2^T}(-1)^{(e\oplus x)\cdot c}\ |\ x$$

$$=\frac{1}{\sqrt{2^{n-k_2}}}\sum_{x\oplus e\in C_2}(-1)^{(e\oplus x)\cdot c_g}\ |\ x$$

$$=\frac{1}{\sqrt{2^{n-k_2}}}\sum_{y\in C_2}(-1)^{y\cdot c_g}\ |\ y\oplus e\rangle$$

There is a bit-flip mistake in this state that corresponds to the string e, as opposed to $W|g$.

When faults occur in the phase-to-bit conversion, the original error is lost. A quantum analog of the syndrome for C_2 might be used to correct phase errors when W is applied to $|g$. If the ith element of the parity matrix P_2 is a 1, then the corresponding row in the quantum circuit must have a component with a C_{not} operation linking qubit I and the ancilla qubit.

This design, on the other hand, establishes a direct connection between the parity-checking matrix and the determination of quantum syndromes. Each of the two extra circuits has the same effect on the $||0$ conditions if $||0$ is a single-qubit state.

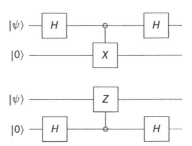

You may expect the same result from ancilla measurements in any of these cases. Instead of applying the Walsh–Hadamard transformations on the computational qubits and then C_{not} from the supervised classification qubits to the ancilla, it is preferable to use a Hadamard gate to regulate phase flips on the computationally qubits. By manipulating the bit flips of the operational qubits using a Hadamard transformation, we can fix errors caused by bit discrepancies.

An extension of CSS codes known as stabilizer codes may explain why the right computational states are unaffected by the syndrome computations. As a result, the CSS code has two nonzero-terminals, one for the Z and one for the I, each of which is free of bit-flip mistakes. The CSS code also contains two nonzero-terminals, one for each of the X and I, both of which are free of phase-flip errors. A more logical approach would have been to start with the C_1 and C_2 code explanatory variables, rather than superimposing classical codewords, and then work our way up.

Section 7.4 on stabilizer codes will use this approach.

7.4.3 Code of Steane

Code C is derived from the Hamming [7,4] code. This code appears twice in our book: the first in Chapter 12 as an illustration of a fault-tolerant technique, and the second in Section 7.4, as an example of a stabilizer code.

Refer back to Example 7.14 to refresh your memory:

$$C^\perp = \{0000000, 1110100, 1101010, 0011110, 1011001, 0101101, 0110011, 1000111\}$$

And C includes 16 encoded communications, such as those formed by adding 1111111 to all of the abbreviations of C. Since C includes its own dual, the conditions of the CSS construction are met by the equations $C_1 = C$ and $C_2 = C$. After assembling the CSS,

$$|0 \rightarrow |\tilde{0}\rangle = \frac{1}{\sqrt{8}} \sum_{c \in C^\perp} |c$$

$$= \frac{1}{\sqrt{8}} (|0000000\rangle + |1110100\rangle + |1101010\rangle + |0011110$$

$$+ |1011001 + |0101101 + |0110011 + |1000111)$$

and

$$|1 \rightarrow |\tilde{1}\rangle = \frac{1}{\sqrt{8}} \sum_{c \in C, c \notin C^\perp} c|$$

$$= \frac{1}{\sqrt{8}} (|1111111\rangle + |0001011\rangle + |0010101\rangle$$

$$+ |1100001 + |0100110 + |1010010 + |1001100 + |0111000)$$

Figure 7.2 An U_P circuit for syndrome extraction in the Steane programming language.

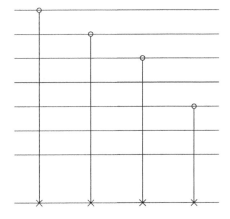

For the Steane code, the U_P asyndrome extracting operators is based on a [7,4] Buttering code parity check matrices P.

$$P = \begin{pmatrix} 1 & 1 & 1 & 0 & 1 & 0 & 0 \\ 1 & 1 & 0 & 1 & 0 & 1 & 0 \\ 1 & 0 & 1 & 1 & 0 & 0 & 1 \end{pmatrix}$$

A circuit diagram for S_1 is illustrated in Figure 7.2. The six Steane explanatory variables are as follows:

$$S_1 = Z \otimes Z \otimes Z \otimes I \otimes Z \otimes I \otimes I$$
$$S_2 = Z \otimes Z \otimes I \otimes Z \otimes I \otimes Z \otimes I$$
$$S_3 = Z \otimes I \otimes Z \otimes Z \otimes I \otimes I \otimes Z$$
$$S_4 = X \otimes X \otimes X \otimes I \otimes X \otimes I \otimes I$$
$$S_5 = X \otimes X \otimes I \otimes X \otimes I \otimes X \otimes I$$
$$S_6 = X \otimes I \otimes X \otimes X \otimes I \otimes I \otimes X \tag{7.8}$$

We will look forward to the future of calculating on encrypted states by studying the evolution of stabilizers codes, the class of codes that encompasses CSS codes.

7.5 Codes for Stabilizers

In Section 7.4 of this document describes how to design a CSS code stabilizer. An important first step in building this structure is realizing how easy it is to describe collection of operators that maintains stability of a $2k$-dimensional subspace embedded in a 2^n-dimensional space.

Example 7.15 The six observables S_1, S_2, S_3, S_4, S_5, and S_6 of Eq. (7.8) serve to stabilize the Steane code, and the two Steane code states, $|0$ and $|1$, are +1-eigenvectors of all six.

7.5.1 The Use of Binary Indicators in Quantum Correction of Errors

An operator serves to stabilize the underlying vector space W. S: $|w = |w$ for every $|$. Or to put it another way, the 1-eigenstate of S stabilizes W.

Subspace WV consists of all the operators that stabilize W. A collection of binary observables on V with only positive and negative values is known as S. This is the biggest subspace C that is stabilized by all of the observables in S_iSS. As a quantum error correcting code, C might be desirable in certain circumstances and unappealing in other cases. Examples include the zero vectors for various sets of observables. By learning how to deduce an error set for C from the observables that define C, our next goal is to figure out for which sets we obtain interesting code.

T is an anticommutator of S, therefore $ST = TS$ if S stabilizes $|v$. As a result, Since $ST|v = TS|v = T|v$, $T|v$ is a 1-eigenvector of S. If $T|v$ is a codeword of the stabilized code C, then for some $|$. $T|v$ is not a code word, as confirmed by S measurements. A set E of unitary errors satisfying the criterion given by equation is a convenient way to describe this fact. Suppose that $S_1,...,S_r$ specify code C as the code to be executed. All pairs E_i and E_j are unique elements, therefore either C is stabilized, or there is at least one S_1 that anti commutes with E_iE_j. E is a series of mistakes that can be corrected by C, as shown in the next paragraph.

The value of a and b in foralli Eq. (7.2) shows the quantum error assumption denoted by E. It is degenerate with respect to E if the transformations is stable for some I and j. A nondegenerate code C is one in which all $I = j$ anticommute with at least one Sl.

7.5.2 Using Pauli Indicators to Fix Errors in Quantum Techniques

According to Section 7.4, a generic method for building codes C and E from a collection of operators meeting particular relations may be established. The commuting relations of the generalization Pauli group makes finding sets of generalized Pauli operators that fulfill these connections extremely simple. To put it another way, every member of the generalized Pauli group Gn containing at least one even number of Y terms, as well as any number of X and Z terms, is Hermitian.

Next, we will assume that S is a non-empty Abelian subgroup of Gn that does not include I. All the constituents of Gn are square to either I or I, making it a specialized Pauli group. Due to the fact that subgroup S does not include subgroup I, all S elements square to I, implying that their eigenvalues must all be 1. Isomorphism between the Abelian group S and for some k is a precondition for its existence. Let S_1, S_r serve as S's generators. Reasonably stable subspace: C.

It follows that Since all nonidentity items S of Gn have trace 0, and only $+1$ and 1 are the real numbers, the $+1$ eigenspace of S must have half the dimensions of V. To compensate for V's full size of 2^{n+1}, subspace C_1 must have a dimension of 2^{n-1}. Given that the operator is a projector onto the $+1$-eigenspace of S_i, then $C_1 = P_1 V$ for every I. S_2's $+1$-eigenspace contains precisely half of C_1, since C_1 has trace zero. Thus, the dimension of C_2 is $2n2$. $DimC = 2nr$ is the result of induction since $C = Cr$. To determine C directly, for each element S S, the set of elements $SS|S$ $S = S$ since S is a group has the effect of stabilizing any n-qubit state, where I is a single bit.

It is possible to identify mistakes that either stabilize or anticommute with at least one S element by using the E-Gn set of errors. In a nutshell, here, the subgroup Gn with elements that commute with each other is known as $Z(S)$. E E $|cb = ab$ in Section 7.4.1 if it stabilizes C and anticommutes with a S_1, then zero in all other cases except for those where $(i) = (j)$ and $(a) = (b)$. All faults in the code C may be corrected by a collection of defects in the code E that fulfill all E_i, E_j and/or $Z(S)$ when there are more qubits than this, all errors E_i and E_j satisfy this formula.

The smallest weight in $Z(S)S$ is determined by the stabilizer code's distance d. The notation $[n,k,d]$ describes the distance between n-qubit codeword representations of k-qubit message words. Double brackets are used to denote the difference between quantum and classical coding. It is possible for a $[[n,k,d]]$-quantum code to fix all errors with a weight of t or less if d is less than 2^{t+1}.

7.5.3 Using Error-Correcting Stabilizer Algorithms

Allowing for the stabilization of S by S_1, S_r independent generator sets, let C be the stabilizer code. No matter how many other S_j have been measured previously, the likelihood that a state is seen and interpreted as being in the 1-eigenspace of S_i is the same regardless of the number of S_j. Subspace "Ve" of V is divided into 2^r subspaces, each with a dimension of 2^{nr}. If Ve is in the $S_i + 1$- or $S_i - 1$-eigenspace, the ith bit of the signatures says such. The length of the string specifies how many bits are in the signatures.

$$V_e = \bigcap_i (-1)^{e_i}\text{-eigenspace of } S_i$$

Each S_i either commutes or anticommutes with any mistake E Gn that may exist. First, we looked at the fact that any $|v$ stabilizing by for all commuting states $E|v$, S_i is in the $+1$-eigenspace of S_i, while for all noncommuting states $E|v$, S_i is in the 1-eigenspace of S_i. Dimensionally, EC and Ve are equivalent in 2^{nr} for some e. If E_iC and E_jC are anticommutes with S or transverse to each other, then there exists a subset of features that is orthogonal to both of them. If $E_jC == E_jE$, then $E_jC == E_jE$. Observables, it is essential that in the first case S_i distinguish between E_iC and E_jC. Whether an error E_i or a mistake E_j occurred is irrelevant to the

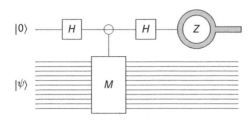

Figure 7.3 Measurement of the ancilla qubit.

evaluation since correcting either one returns the system to its original state its natural position. In E, each E_i is linked to a certain E_i.

Operators M that are Hermitian and unitary may be measured indirectly. If the ancilla qubit is measured in the usual way, the resulting state on the quantum register has the same probability as if it had been measured directly with M, using a unique email address. After the S_i has been measured, applying E_i to any of the E_i with a signature of e would return the system to its initial condition regardless of which error $E_j E$ occurred.

Let us pretend n qubits are subjected to an n-bit unitary Hermitian operator M. Indirect measurements may be performed with the use of an additional ancilla qubit and the Hermitian operator shown by the gray circle in Figure 7.3. Here, operator Z is used to determine the size of the auxiliary qubit in the canonical reference frame. The next paragraphs elaborate on how this circuit realizes M's objective evaluation.

Since M is both unitary and Hermitian, no more eigenvalues can be derived from it. In other words, when expressing I in terms of M Eigenstates, the 1-eigenvector of M and the normalizing factor, c I, cancel out in the resulting 1-eigenvector. The circuit takes use of this. To illustrate, $1 (M I) = P I$ if and only if M is a 1-eigenspace, and $1 (M I) = P+$ if and only if P is the projection onto P. It is possible that $PP++ I$ $IP++ I$ and $P+I$ $IP++ I$ $IP+$ are generated from an M-based direct measurement I.

According to this section, Figure 7.2's circuit also produces these two states with a same probability. The situation is as follows prior to the measuring device:

$$\frac{1}{\sqrt{2}}(|+\rangle|\psi_{+|-}M|\psi\rangle) = \frac{1}{2}((|0\rangle + |1\rangle)|\psi\rangle + (|0\rangle - |1\rangle)M|\psi\rangle)$$

$$= \frac{1}{2}(|0\rangle(|\psi\rangle + M|\psi\rangle) + |1\rangle(|\psi\rangle - M|\psi\rangle))$$

$$= \frac{1}{2}\left(\frac{1}{c}|0\rangle(c(|\psi\rangle + M|\psi\rangle)) + \frac{1}{c'}|1\rangle(c'(|\psi\rangle - M|\psi\rangle))\right)$$

When the ancilla qubit is measured using Z, the result is always 0. $p_+ = \langle\psi|P^+ | \psi$ and results in the n-qubit state $c(|\psi + M|\psi)$. The result of the measurement is also 1, with equal probability $p- = \psi|P - |\psi$ resulting in $c'(\psi \quad M \psi)| - |$ as the n-qubit register's current state. Another argument is that $M = P + -P-$ and $I = P + +P -$,

$$c(|\psi\rangle + M|\psi\rangle) = c((P^+ + P^-)|\psi\rangle + (P^+ - P^-)|\psi\rangle) = cP^+|\psi\rangle$$

An accurate determination by M has the same impact on the n computation qubits as the circuit shown in Figure 7.2. We require m such circuits and m ancilla qubits to monitor each S_i for 1 I m. The string e is formed when these qubits are measured.

7.5.4 Stabilizer State Encoding Computation

The operators U that are logically comparable to those in the Pauli group are readily produced, and they may be found in a number of other places as well. Errors may also be handled effectively with stabilizer codes. To design an encoding, we first explore potential logical operations, rather than describing an encoding function and then trying to find logical operators that work with it. In this work, we develop encoding functions using Pauli amplifiers with a single logical qubit, denoted $Z_1',...',Z_k'$.

Common basis elements for k-qubit systems may be classified as either $+1$- or 1-eigenvectors of the various modes $Z_1,...,Z_k$. This is because eigenstates of a given state may be used to describe the state itself. Example: the stabilizing operators' cluster zones are defined. The above-mentioned algorithm C brings any standard basis vector $|b_1...b_k$ to the singular state that is a $(1)b_i$-eigenstate of ZI for all I. The five-qubit code is discussed in further detail below, along with a working example.

Example 7.16 The set of observables

$$S_0 = X \otimes Z \otimes Z \otimes X \otimes I$$
$$S_1 = Z \otimes Z \otimes X \otimes I \otimes X$$
$$S_2 = Z \otimes X \otimes I \otimes X \otimes Z$$
$$S_3 = X \otimes I \otimes X \otimes Z \otimes Z$$

establishes a [[55,1]] code. Each of the four observables 5 4 1 separates the two-dimensional code space into two eigen spaces, resulting in a space of $2/2 = 2$ code word dimensions when they are independent. If this code satisfies the quantum Hamming condition, it will be the most efficient possible.

Consider the following: (S). $A|v$ is a $+1$-eigenstate of all the S_i since $S_iA|v = AS_i|v = A|v$, which is the case for any I. It is nontrivial to operate on C when A is in $Z(S)S$, but this is not the case for every instance of A in $Z(S)$. A_1 and A_2 act identically on C if $A_1 = A_2Sa$ for some Sa S. S/Z acts on C in different ways for each of its members. Understanding the structure of the centralizer Z will help us better understand how they interact with C (S). Gn's symplectic interpretation sheds light on Z's structural details (S). For each Gn element there is a $2n$-bit $(a|b)$ string associated.

The phase relevant information is lost in the homomorphism h, which is a four-to-one performance of the construction. Since S does not include iI or iI, and hence h is a homomorphism, it is one-to-one on S. No component S_1, Sr of Gn may be represented as a product of any other component until and until the matching bit strings $(a|b)$ are linearly independent.

When $(a|b)$ equals the total of the bitwise matrix multiplication of the two elements, we say that the two elements are exclusively commutable. For those curious, "Symplicit inner product" is defined as mod2.

Example 7.17 When these four variables are combined, they provide a 16-element stabilizer group denoted by S:

$$S_i S_i = I = I \otimes I \otimes I \otimes I \otimes I \qquad S_0 = X \otimes Z \otimes Z \otimes X \otimes I$$
$$S_1 = Z \otimes Z \otimes X \otimes I \otimes X \qquad S_2 = Z \otimes X \otimes I \otimes X \otimes Z$$
$$S_3 = X \otimes I \otimes X \otimes Z \otimes Z \qquad S_0 S_1 = -Y \otimes I \otimes Y \otimes X \otimes X$$
$$S_0 S_2 = -Y \otimes Y \otimes Z \otimes I \otimes Z \qquad S_0 S_3 = -I \otimes Z \otimes Y \otimes Y \otimes Z$$
$$S_1 S_2 = -I \otimes Y \otimes X \otimes X \otimes Y \qquad S_1 S_3 = -Y \otimes Z \otimes I \otimes Z \otimes Y$$
$$S_2 S_3 = -Y \otimes X \otimes X \otimes Y \otimes I \qquad S_0 S_1 S_2 = -X \otimes X \otimes Y \otimes I \otimes Y$$
$$S_0 S_1 S_3 = -Z \otimes I \otimes Z \otimes Y \otimes Y \qquad S_0 S_2 S_3 = -Z \otimes Y \otimes Y \otimes Z \otimes I$$
$$S_1 S_2 S_3 = -X \otimes Y \otimes I \otimes Y \otimes X \qquad S_0 S_1 S_2 S_3 = I \otimes X \otimes Z \otimes Z \otimes X$$

The following Table 7.3 describes the code's error diagnosis based on the explanatory variables. The observable S_i measurements result after a single mistake on a codeword is shown in the appropriate column for qubit 0 through 4 single-errors X, Y, and Z. S_i measurements on that qubit provide either positive or negative results, denoted by plus and minus signs $(+/-)$. To accurately pinpoint a mistake, we used four different metrics. All four observables are counted in the final row, resulting in a distinctive decimal value.

Table 7.3 Error code diagnosis.

	bit 0			bit 1			bit 2			bit 3			bit 4		
	X	Z	Y	X	Z	Y	X	Z	Y	X	Z	Y	X	Z	Y
S_0	+	−	−	−	+	−	−	+	−	+	−	−	+	+	+
S_1	−	+	−	−	+	−	+	−	−	+	+	+	+	−	−
S_2	−	+	−	+	−	−	+	+	+	+	−	−	−	+	−
S_3	+	−	−	+	+	+	+	−	−	−	+	−	−	+	−
	6	9	15	3	4	7	1	10	11	8	5	13	12	2	14

Consider the set S to consist of many different generating sets, $S_1,\ldots,S_r$. Generate the $r2n$ binary matrix.

$$
M = \begin{pmatrix} (a \mid b)_1 \\ (a \mid b)_2 \\ \vdots \\ (a \mid b)r \end{pmatrix}
$$

with the columns $(a \mid b)i = h(S_i)$. Because the rows of M are independent, M has rank r, which is why the S_i are. $(a \mid b)$ is transformed into a symplectic inner product of $(a \mid b)i$ by the matrix M on the $2n$-bit string $(a \mid b)$, which may be thought of as a column vector. $2nr$ dimensions make up the kernel of M. All the stabilizer's constituents communicate with the kernel's components, which are all components of Gn. These values are irrelevant for the rest of the discussion because the string $(a \mid b)$ that corresponds to each element in $Z(S)$ is unique; thus, $Z(S)$ contains elements. The stabilizer subgroup for a $[[n,k]]$ stabilizer code is $2nk$. There are $22nr = 2n + k$ elements in Z for a $[[n,k]]$ code (S).

Any element of $Z(S)$ that is independently of $S_1 \ldots S_r$ may be taken as Z_1. Add the 2^n-bit string equivalent to the (rn) binary matrix M_1 as an extra row. A complete rank of $r + 1$ is found in the matrix M_1. This is a collection of binary strings, regarded as column vectors that are in the kernel of M_1 and have a size of 22^{n+1} $(r + 1)$. So, every bit string in C_1 that is represented by $Z(S)$ may serve as Z_2. To create operators $Z_1,\ldots,Z_k$ that communicate with each other and with every element of S, we may repeat this operation k times in the other direction. S will be used as the M_k kernel.

Let us take a look at conventional basis vectors that are unencoded. K-qubit state $|00\ldots0\rangle$ is the only $Z_1 \ldots Z_{k+1}$-eigenstate. It may be expressed more generally: The sole feasible state that is an a-eigenstate of Z_i for any and all I is given by the standard basis vector $|b_1 \ldots b_k$. Any k-bit string $b_1 \ldots b_k$ possesses a distinctive property that is a (1)bi -eigenstate of Z_i for all I; the explanation why there is a unique advantage is comparable to the argument that showed C's dimension. Encoding U_C is described for the code C that takes conventional basis components to components of C that have comparable eigenstate connections with logical versions Z of the Z_i. The following is the encoding for the Ak-qubit state:

$$
U_C : \sum_{x=0}^{2^k-1} a_x |x\rangle \rightarrow \sum_{x=0}^{2^k-1} a_x \mid \tilde{x} \tag{7.9}
$$

where $|\tilde{x}\rangle$ is the unique element of C that is in the $(-1)x_i$ –eigen space of $\tilde{Zi}$ for all $0 \le i \le k$.

The $(r + k) \times 2n = n \times 2n$ matrix Mk has full rank; therefore for any i, there is a bit string $(a \mid b)$ that, when viewed as a column vector $\left(\dfrac{b}{a}\right)$, yields the n-bit string e_i

which has a 1 in the ith place and 0 elsewhere: in particular, there is a $2n$-bit string $(a|b)$ that satisfies

$$M_k \left(\frac{b}{a} \right) = e_1$$

Let $\tilde{X}_1$ be the element of $Z(S)$ with bit string $(a|b)$ that yields e_1 when multiplied by M_k. Construct M_{k+1} by adding as a row to M_k the bit string corresponding to $\tilde{X}_1$. Let $\tilde{X}_2$ be such that its bit string $(a|b)$ satisfies

$$M_{k+1} \left(\frac{b}{a} \right) = e_2$$

We can continue in this way until we obtain $\tilde{X}_1, \ldots, \tilde{X}_k$. By construction, $\tilde{X}_i$ anticommutes with $\tilde{Z}_i$, and commutes with all of S, all $\tilde{X}_j$, and all the $\tilde{Z}_j$ for $j \neq i$.

Example 7.18 For the [[5,1]] code of Example 7.17, the binary matrix corresponding to the independent generating set $\{S_i\}$ is

The bit string $(a|b) = (11111|00000)$ is independent of the rows $m \in M$ and satisfies $M_b = 0$, so we may take

$$\tilde{Z} = Z \otimes Z \otimes Z \otimes Z \otimes Z$$

and, since $(b|a)$ is orthogonal to $(a|b)$ and all rows of M, we may take

$$\tilde{X} = X \otimes X \otimes X \otimes X \otimes X$$

Let $|\tilde{e}_i\rangle$ be the unique state in C that is a -1-eigenstate of $\tilde{Z}_i$ but a $+1$-eigenstate for all the $\tilde{Z}_j$ with $j \neq i$. For $j \neq i$,

$$\tilde{Z}_j \tilde{X}_i \mid \tilde{e}_i \rangle = \tilde{X}_i \tilde{Z}_j \mid \tilde{e}_i \rangle = \tilde{X}_i \mid \tilde{e}_i \rangle$$

so $\tilde{X}_i \mid \tilde{e}_i \rangle = $ is $a + 1$-eigenstate of $\tilde{Z}_j$ for $j \neq i$. For $\tilde{Z}_i$,

$$\tilde{Z}_i \tilde{X}_i \mid \tilde{e}_i \rangle = -\tilde{X}_i \tilde{Z}_i \mid \tilde{e}_i \rangle = -\tilde{X}_i \mid \tilde{e}_i \rangle$$

so $\tilde{X}_i \mid \tilde{e}_i \rangle$ is in the $+1$-eigenstate of $\tilde{Z}i$ as well. This calculation suggests that $\tilde{X}i$ is the logical analog of X_i for C with encoding U_C. A full proof is straightforward.

Example 7.19 For the [[5,1]] code of Example 7.16, the $+1$-eigenspace of $\tilde{Z}$ is spanned by the standard basis states with an even number of 1s. Thus, we may take $|\tilde{0}$ to be

$$= \frac{1}{4} (|00000\rangle + |10010\rangle + |00101\rangle + |01010 + |10100\rangle - |10111\rangle - |11000\rangle$$
$$-|00110 - |01111\rangle - |10001\rangle - |11110\rangle - |11101\rangle - |00011\rangle$$
$$-|01100\rangle - |11011\rangle + |01001\rangle)$$

to be a superposition of all basis vectors with an odd number of ones.

For a stabilizers code C, the development of logical counterparts of other single-qubit gates and multiple-qubit gates is more difficult. For the Steane code, it gives structures for a universal approximation set of logical gates that may be used in any programming language.

7.6 A Stabilizer Role for CSS Codes

It is reasonable to assume that t faults can be corrected by the classical code C_1 and $[n,k_1]$ by the code C_2. Moreover, imagine that. In order to create a $[[n,k_1 \; k_2]]$ CSS code, these codes must meet a requirement. The stabilizer perspective is described as an alternative to the CSS code architecture described.

We will call this matrix P_1 (respectively P_2) (resp. C_2). Construct an observable $X_b = Xb_1 \; Xb_n$ for each row of P_1 as a bit string $b = b_1...b_n$. There are $n - 1$ independent variables since each row of P_1 is linearly independent. $Z_b = Zb_1 - Zb_n$ for each row of P_2 is likewise constructed. Nk_2 observational variables, as well as $2nk_1$ observational variables (X and Z), are all independently observable. S is a stabilizer code if and only if the group S formed by these observables is Abelian.

The CSS requirement implies that S is Abelian, as shown in this paragraph. All of $Xa|a \; P_1$ commutes. Similar to this, all of $Z_b|P_2$'s elements are on the move. Group components X and Z only commute if and only if a b is even, as they are anti-commuting. As a result, for all rows a and b of P_1 and P_2, the components of S commute. 0 mod 2 guarantees this equivalence. The generating matrix P_0 is $C_2 \; C_1$. Because $1 + 2 = 0$, we may conclude that. Consequently, S is Abelian, and C is an abelian stabilizer code in S.

Section 7.3.2's CSS(C_1,C_2) code is stabilized by S. It is known that a subset of the dimension $2n(2nk_1 \; k_2)$ equals $k_1 + k_2$, and this subset is stabilized by S, since S contains $n + n$ independent generators. CSS(C_1,C_2) is the stabilizer code for S because it has dimensions $k_1 + k_2 \; n$.

Example 7.20 The Steane code revisited. The parity check matrix

$$P = \begin{pmatrix} 1 & 1 & 1 & 0 & 1 & 0 & 0 \\ 1 & 1 & 0 & 1 & 0 & 1 & 0 \\ 1 & 0 & 1 & 1 & 0 & 0 & 1 \end{pmatrix}$$

defines the [7,4] Hamming code. The Steane code takes the [7,4] Hamming code as both C_1 and C_2. To obtain stabilizers for the Steane code, define an operator in G7 for each row in the parity check matrix that has a Z in every place a 1 occurs and an I for every 0:

$Z \otimes Z \otimes Z \otimes I \otimes Z \otimes I \otimes I Z \otimes Z \otimes I \otimes Z \otimes I$

$\otimes Z \otimes I$

$Z \otimes I \otimes Z \otimes Z \otimes I \otimes I \otimes Z.$

For each row in the parity check matrix, also define an operator that has an X wherever a 1 occurs:

$$X \otimes X \otimes X \otimes I \otimes X \otimes I \otimes I X \otimes X \otimes I \otimes X \otimes I$$

$$\otimes X \otimes I$$

$$X \otimes I \otimes X \otimes X \otimes I \otimes I \otimes X$$

These six observables stabilize exactly the Steane code C, so the Steane code is a [[7,1]] stabilizer code.

References

1 Monroe, C., Meekhof, D.M., King, B.E., and Wineland, D.J. (1996). *Science* 272: 1131.

2 Signoles, A., Facon, A., Grosso, D. et al. (2014). *Nature Physics* 10: 715.

3 McConnell, R., Zhang, H., Hu, J. et al. (2015). *Nature* 519: 439. arXiv:1508.03056.

4 Ourjoumtsev, A., Tualle-Brouri, R., Laurat, J., and Grangier, P. (2006). *Science* 312: 83.

5 Neergaard-Nielsen, J.S., Nielsen, B.M., Hettich, C. et al. (2006). *Physical Review Letters* 97: 83604. arXiv:0602198 [quant-ph].

6 Deléglise, S., Dotsenko, I., Sayrin, C. et al. (2008). *Nature* 455: 510.

7 Hofheinz, M., Wang, H., Ansmann, M. et al. (2009). *Nature* 459: 546.

8 Kirchmair, G., Vlastakis, B., Leghtas, Z. et al. (2013). *Nature* 495: 205.

9 Bretheau, L., Campagne-Ibarcq, P., Flurin, E. et al. (2015). *Science* 348: 776.

10 Reagor, M., Pfaff, W., Axline, C. et al. (2016). *Physical Review B* 94: 014506.

11 Ofek, N., Petrenko, A., Heeres, R. et al. (2016). *Nature* 536: 441.

12 Girvin, S.M., Devoret, M.H., and Schoelkopf, R.J. (2009). *Physica Scripta* T137: 014012.

13 Blumoff, J., Chou, K., Shen, C. et al. (2016). *Physical Review X* 6: 031041.

14 McMahon, D. (2008). *Quantum Computing Explained, IEEE Computer Society*. Wiley-Interscience.

8

Tolerance for Inaccurate Information in Quantum Computing

8.1 Introduction

The robustness of quantum processing can only be achieved via the use of quantum error correction (EC). The term "robust computation" refers to the ability to do calculations of any length with any level of precision. In quantum EC, approaches were examined on the false premise that they were carried out flawlessly. Gates used as part of computation may also transmit faults that cannot be corrected by the error- correcting code, even if the environment interacts exclusively in ways that the code can manage. Quantum EC must be used in conjunction with fault-tolerant methods to provide resilient quantum computing [1].

Here, we describe an approach to quantum processing that is both error correcting and fault tolerant. Quantum computing in the traditional equivalent circuit and other paradigms of communication both include other ways to achieve resilient quantum computation.

An error model threshold theorem finishes the chapter. According to threshold theorems, quantum computers may do arbitrary lengthy calculations with arbitrary high precision as long as the error rate is below a certain threshold. Fault-tolerant quantum computing is shown in this chapter by using a basic error conceptual framework. The technique is to replace a circuit with a more resilient expanded circuit; if the failure probability of the original circuit was $O(p)$, then the expanded circuit has only probability $O(p2)$. Concatenation may be used to create an arbitrarily low probability of failure by concatenating bigger and more resilient circuits. This process, known as concatenation coding, can be repeated until the required degree of precision is obtained. Concatenated coding has the advantage of using just polynomial resources to achieve rapid results with a low failure probability [2].

The area of fault-tolerant quantum computing is as well developed as quantum EC. Theorems and techniques for a wide range of error models and codes have

Quantum Computing: A New Era of Computing, First Edition.
Kuldeep Singh Kaswan, Jagjit Singh Dhatterwal, Anupam Baliyan, and Shalli Rani.
© 2023 The Institute of Electrical and Electronics Engineers, Inc. Published 2023 by John Wiley & Sons, Inc.

been devised and proven. Researchers are still working on fault-tolerant quantum, computing and like quantum EC, it will continue to progress as more quantum entanglement processing technologies are produced, more realistic error models are learned, and more advanced quantum computer topologies are established [3].

8.2 Initiating Stable Quantum Computing

To keep things simple, we will simply be looking at [[k,1]]. Even if more qubits and more operations are involved, the chance of a faulty calculation is lowered if a particular [[k,1]] quantum error-correcting code is used in a fault-tolerant manner to encode any circuit made of those universal gates. How to construct logical procedures on the processing qubits, syndrome extraction operators, assessments, state preparation, and correct decision manipulations in such a way that the resulting computations is more robust than the original one? (*p2*) We must first consider when and how to simulate faults in quantum EC procedures before moving on to fault-tolerant approaches in more depth [4].

Consider a quantum circuit called Q0, which is designed to ensure the robustness of a certain computation. We divide up the passage of time such that no more than one gate may affect any one qubit at a time (Figure 8.1). There are other ways to divide the time period in this circuit: instead of applying the single-qubit gate to the first qubit in the first time interval, the first time interval might have been divided in half and the two-qubit operation conducted in the second. Q0 is partitioned into two sections, one for the logical gates and the other for the syndrome measurement and EC transformations. Each time interval extends into two parts, one for the implementation of the logical gates, and the other for EC and the measurement of the syndrome (Figure 8.2). Both of these procedures may require ancill a qubits [5].

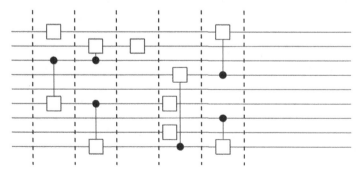

Figure 8.1 Computation of single bit.

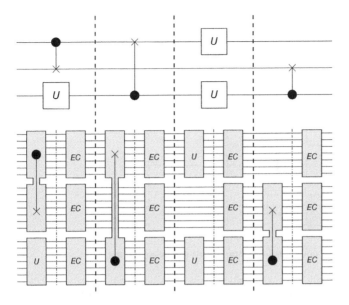

Figure 8.2 Structure of quantum code.

This simplified figure illustrates the high-level design of an extended circuit for a ([[7,1]]) quantum code and includes details such as the subdivided time intervals. The augmented circuit switches back and forth between logical operations and EC.

An ancillary qubit may be needed. To ensure that no qubit is affected by more than one gate at a time, the enlarged circuit is divided into smaller periods. There was a time when we could have used mistake correction less often. After every logical operation, we have opted to use it. It's possible to choose from a wide range of options. How the logic gates are constructed and how syndromes and error-correcting transformations are implemented are crucial in determining if the expanded circuit Q1 is more robust than the initial circuit Q0.

We utilize a model in which mistakes only occur at the beginning of periods to describe fault-tolerant algorithms. According to our model of flawed single-qubit gates, a single-qubit error is followed by a flawless gate. Faulty C_{not} gates are also represented as excellent C_{not} gates consisting of two single-qubit errors [6]. The combination of quantum EC applied locally to each sequence and our robust fault tolerance algorithms enable C_{not} translations across qubits in different components, so we may disregard correlations between these mistakes. Only at the beginning of a time are errors due to the exploration of the environment. We will start with the local and Markov error models for our first discussion. There are no past interactions between any of these qubits and their surroundings

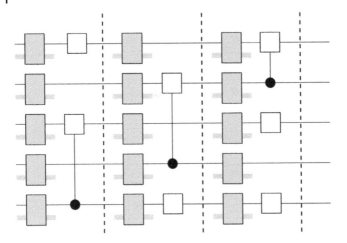

Figure 8.3 Structure of environmental interactions shows each qubit.

at the beginning of each time interval, and each time interval is entirely uncorrelated with the preceding ones in Figure 8.3. A broader error model is used in the threshold theorem presented in [7].

8.3 Computational Error Tolerance Using Steane's Code

Medical professionals take an oath to "first, not harm." The error rate of a quantum processor increases when more qubits and gates are used for EC, as described in the previous chapter. The examination of quantum error detection and correction made the erroneous assumption that all steps in correcting errors were executed without a hitch. In a minute, we'll see that if you follow the instructions for doing quantum EC from the preceding section to the letter, you're more likely to make problems than you are to fix them. No fault tolerance can be achieved using these techniques. Fortunately, these technologies can be adjusted so they don't create more issues than they solve. To demonstrate fault-tolerant quantum EC, we show how to make the Steane seven-qubit code robust with correction approaches. Fault-tolerant approaches include safeguards to prevent a single fault from spreading to numerous qubits, as Steane's algorithm cannot rectify multiple errors. As an alternative, a group of parts that only fail when there are two or more mistakes will be used to replace any failed parts that were initially part of the ensemble. This will result in a costume that only fails when there are two or more problems [8].

8.3.1 The Complexity of Syndrome-Based Computation

Calculating syndrome has the potential to be harmful to the computing state. Our Steane code parity check circuit, illustrated in Figure 8.4 (the first of six), is an example.

In Steane's seven-qubit code, this is one of the six pathological computational circuits. The first four encoded states and the first ancilla qubit are impacted. If one of the qubits is off by one bit, Steane's method can fix it. We want to make sure that if there is a mistake in the process of selecting the error, it will not make things worse for the consumer. The objective is to prevent the widespread corruption of encoded qubits due to a single mistake in the quantum error-correcting procedure. Errors caused by bit flips on auxiliary qubits may result in the "correction" of an error that does not exist. Even though it's irritating, a single-qubit mistake in the coding qubits introduced by the "correction" is not life-threatening. As long as no other errors arise, the next round of EC will fix the problem. To avoid propagating errors, the ancilla qubit must be reset to $|0\rangle$ before it may be utilized again. Later rounds of mistake correction may miss some of the more serious flaws in the coding qubits, rendering them unfixable. To determine if you're thinking about quantum circuits in the proper quantum or classical manner, take a moment to see if you can detect the issue [9].

Quantum code syndrome extraction operators often use controllable gates. Computing from the computational qubits to the ancilla qubits sounds like it would be a safe operation on the appearance. Please be aware of the following: Concepts of from and to are ground-dependent; in the Hadamard ground, the control and target qubits of C_{not} are swapped, phase flips become bit flips, and simultaneously. Consider the case of a *ZH* mistake occurring before the syndrome computation has begun, after the qubits in the state $|+\rangle$ have been utilized for encoding. All four ancilla qubits ($b1$, $b2$, $b3$, and $b5$) are flipped to the I state as a

Figure 8.4 Structure processing units.

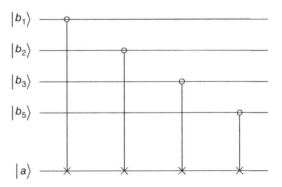

result of the error because it puts the ancill0061 qubit in the state I, making it the control bit for each C_{not}. If there's only one flaw, it may lead to several problems in the error-correcting qubits [10].

8.3.2 Error Removal and Correction in Fault-Tolerant Systems

According to the example an ancilla qubit should be coupled to no more than one basic programming qubit for fault-tolerant error detection and correction in Figure 8.5. We need to use a circuit like this to construct Steane's code in a fault-tolerant manner.

Although it is possible to get programmed qubits' quantum states, another related measurement is likely to have a detrimental effect on the state of the encoded qubits if the ancilla qubits are measured. A single-qubit mistake on qubit $B5$ in the encoded form would be an example. However, the superposition of qubits $b5$ has been ruined. Thus, the correcting operation will "restore" this qubit to a state of either $|0\rangle$ or $|1\rangle$ instead of correcting it to the proper state [11].

The idea is to place the ancilla qubits in a condition where it is difficult to learn anything about the current computational state. If you measure all four ancilla qubits, just one piece of information must be gained – the matching syndrome operator's value – from the non-fault-tolerant circuit's four qubits. When a single-qubit bit-flip mistake occurs on any one of the system's four qubits, an appropriately constructed initial start-up state $|0\rangle$ for the ancilla transforms into a second state $|e\rangle$, yielding only one bit of information. Consider

$$|\varphi_0\rangle = \frac{1}{2\sqrt{2}} \sum_{d_H(x)\text{ even}} |x\rangle$$

strings with equal Hamming weight are included in the total.

$$|\varphi_e\rangle = \frac{1}{2\sqrt{2}} \sum_{d_H(x)\text{ odd}} |x\rangle$$

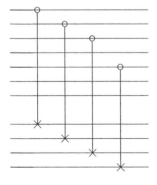

Figure 8.5 Structure of fault-tolerant error detection and correction.

The ancilla stays in state $|0\rangle$ even if the encoded qubits include mistakes that would have resulted in the original syndrome state $|0\rangle$. The ancilla ends up in state $|e\rangle$ in the event of faults that would have resulted in $|1\rangle$. In the no-error situation, a random even-weighted string is generated, but in the error case, an arbitrary odd-weighted string is generated. Only one piece of information may be gleaned from this measurement.

To get a fault-tolerant implementation of the Steane code syndrome measurement, one more issue must be resolved. The state $|0\rangle$ must be prepared before the solution can be applied. Our preparation of $|0\rangle$ must be fault-tolerant. We must ensure that this is the case. If a prepared state deviates too far from $|0\rangle$, we will not utilize it. Our primary goal is to ensure that any faults in the preparation of many coding qubits are not caused by a single mistake. For cats, the Walsh–Hadamard transformation yields $|0\rangle$. Using the circuit shown in Figure 8.6, the cat state is built in a non-fault-tolerant manner. By anticipating potential failure modes, this design may be made more robust [12].

A failure in one cat state qubit should not lead to a loss in another, and so on, in any of the coding qubits. Errors in the basic design of the ancilla state are not an issue. The worst that can happen is if the phenomenology is erroneous, in which case the "repair" matching for this condition will only affect one qubit. It is essential to avoid making any mistakes that might lead to many phase faults since this could contaminate the coding qubits. To prevent the spread of bit-flip errors, the first part of the circuit must be thoroughly tested before applying the final Hadamard transformations. No matter which qubits are affected, a bit-flip mistake may be propagated across this circuit. As an example, if the first and fourth qubits were flipped, they would have negative values, but in an error-free situation, they would be equal. Using a check for equality between these variables, if the check fails, we may reject the current state and start over from scratch.

This test is shown in Figure 8.7 as part of the cat state ancilla preparation.

In order to determine whether qubits 1 and 4 have the same value, the Z measurement is performed. If this evaluation is unsuccessful, the state is discarded, and the state preparation process is restarted.

Figure 8.6 Non-fault-tolerant construction of a cat state.

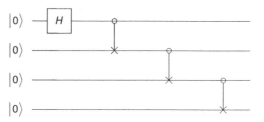

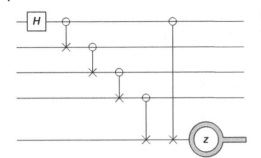

Figure 8.7 Fault-tolerant cat state ancilla preparation.

8.3.3 Steane's Code Fault-Tolerant Gates

A system as a means for performing unrestricted quantum calculations on the logical qubits of the Steane code, we need a set of fault-tolerant logical gates that can approximate any unitary operator on the logical qubits. Because a single flaw might affect several qubits, even the simplest implementations of logical single-qubit gates may not be fault-tolerant. Even if it's not ideal, a logical single-qubit operation may be conducted in the simplest way possible by decoding the logical qubit, executing a real single-qubit operation on the resulting qubit, and then reencoding. If a mistake is made in decoding even one qubit, that error will be repeated when re-encoding all seven qubits. For logic gates with many logical qubits, fault-tolerant methods must also prevent a single error in one block from propagating to multiple faults in another [13].

Fault-tolerant implementations are provided for several gates in the Steane code, such as X, H, and C_{not}. Other gates, such as the Toffoli gate and the /8-gate, are more challenging to find fault-tolerant implementation for since the only known responsibility to fix implementation need more qubits. To implement logical X in a fault-tolerant manner, it is helpful to keep in mind that the logical qubit $|0\rangle$ is the equal-weighted superposition of all elements of C, and that $|1\rangle$ is the equal-weighted combination of all components of C. Keep in mind that the non-C elements are formed when $1\,111\,111$ is added to the C elements. When applied to each qubit in the seven-qubit block, the logical X gate flips them from $|0\rangle$ to $|1\rangle''$ and $|1\rangle''$ to $|0\rangle''$. In Figure 8.8, the C_{not} operators are applied across the qubits of the two blocks, allowing the logical to be achieved by adding any component of C to any component of C as illustrated. If there is an error in one of these implementations, it will not propagate to other blocks. In these cases, gates are only deployed across pairs of connected qubits in the blocks, a transversal strategy that fails under most conditions.

Finding a fault-tolerant implementation when the transversal technique fails might be quite difficult. Fault-tolerant processes can only be built using a certain kind of code. Codes for which fault-tolerant implementations of particular logical

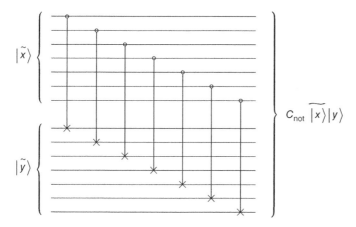

Figure 8.8 Fault-tolerant C_{not}.

gates are not known exist. It's impossible to transversely perform most single-qubit operations even using the Steane code [14].

A fault-tolerant implementation can be achieved by applying each qubit individually. However, this is not always possible. By way of illustration, not only does applying to each qubit not lead to anything, but it is also impossible to implement in any cross-sectional method. There is no known transversal implementation. Only ancilla qubit implementations are known to be fault tolerant.

According to Figure 8.9, since there are only three qubits across the three blocks, a logical Toffoli gate T cannot be constructed using Toffoli gates. In the same way that the gate can only use nontransversal T implementation, the Steane code can only use nontransversal T design and implementation.

For the Steane code to be used for fault-tolerant computation, we must show that a sequence of fault-tolerant gates may indefinitely closely mimic all logical unitary operators. We give robust arithmetic and logic such as the Hadamard gate H, phase gate, controlled-not gate C_{not}, and the previously described globally approximation gates. They have been covered extensively before. The logical Hadamard gate H may be implemented transversally by executing H on each of the qubits in the block. Locating a fault-tolerant architecture is more complicated.

Since not all modifications have built-in fault-tolerance mechanisms, several distinct fault-tolerant techniques include using an ancillary state. The trick is to measure everything. One possible use of these methods is a fault-tolerant /8-gate integration. It is possible to implement this using the state |/4 = +|. The circuit shown in Figure 8.10 may carry out the operation P under any input state |. Since we are familiar with fault-tolerant representations, it is not required to prepare the encoded form in this circuit in a way that makes it resilient to errors. The first stage in creating a fault-tolerant environment is conducting a foolproof assessment.

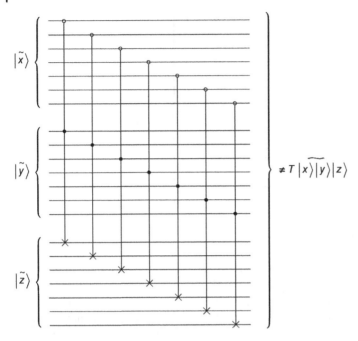

Figure 8.9 There is no transitive Toffoli gate T that can be constructed using this method.

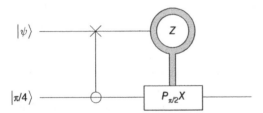

Figure 8.10 Circuit operation.

The designing of circuit of quantum work as on fault-tolerant versions. The result of the measurement using Z determines whether or not $P/2\,X$ is used.

8.3.4 Measurement with Fault Tolerance

Indirect measurements may be made with the help of the following circuit if M is Hermitian and unitary: this architecture is not fault-tolerant since a flaw in the ancilla qubit might potentially affect all n qubits. To make this design fault-tolerant, as shown in Figure 8.11, we employed measurements of the fault-tolerant phenomenon in a cat condition. The exact requirements for fault-tolerant EC in electromagnetism must be met for an n-qubit Cat state

Figure 8.11 Measurement of fault-tolerant measurement.

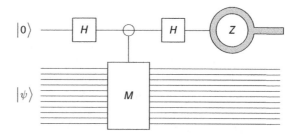

to be utilized in fault-tolerant creation. If they are not met, the state must be verified and destroyed. If M is well governed by the cat state, it may be used as a clear indicator that can tolerate failure. If M can be implemented in terms of transverse operators, then it is straightforward to construct a controllable variant by manipulating the corresponding cat state qubit to ensure that all single-qubit operators are run, or none. The state | 4's fault-tolerant preprocessing is a good illustration of where this structure may be used.

8.3.5 Readying the State for Fault Tolerance

By finding an inexpensive measurement operator M that is both likely to be implemented and fault-tolerant, a state | fault-tolerant may be created. In every fault-tolerantly constructed state that is not perpendicular to |a, the chance of |a being generated is positive. It is possible to employ a fault-tolerant gate to change an incorrectly acquired eigenstate into a desirable one if these measurements yield an inaccurate result. The procedure may be maintained until the destination is reached.

Starting with a basic insight about operators, we can get an inexpensive and fault-tolerant implementation for the state. The eigenvectors of PXP1 also have eigenvalues 1 and 1, consistent with the fact that X has eigenvectors | + and | with eigenvalues 1 and 1. The fact that $\pi/4$ is an eigenstate of may not appear relevant at first glance because we are really attempting to build $P/4$. The commutation connection, however, suggests that

$$M = P_{\pi/4} X P_{\pi/4}^{-1} = e^{-i\frac{\pi}{4}} P_{\pi/4} P_{\pi/4} X = e^{-i\frac{\pi}{4}} P_{\pi/2} X$$

We're also familiar with the fault-tolerant implementation of $P/2$ and X. To accomplish the indication of the amount, it is not necessary to design completely controlled implementations of these gates but rather ones that are adequately controlled by the cat state utilized to considerably execute the measuring system. In Measurement function, it is a considerably simpler undertaking an indirect measurement by M with a logical analog may be obtained by first performing seven controlled $P/2X$ gates between each pair of associated cat states and ancilla qubits, followed by one controlled phase gate. This completes the $P/2X$ implementation. Afterwards, the cat-state structure is dismantled and the remaining qubit is measured in a regular way. It is possible to achieve the desired condition when the measurement result is 0. Applying Z results in a state that is the intended state if the measurement yields a value of 1.

Let's take a look at each step of this circuit to determine whether it can measure M. C_{not} operations and the Hadamard transformation produce state.

Cat's qubits control the following eight gates, which execute M on the state's qubits, resulting in the state.

$$\frac{1}{\sqrt{2}}(|0\rangle^{\otimes 7}|\widetilde{\psi}\rangle + |1\rangle^{\otimes 7}\widetilde{M}|\widetilde{\psi}\rangle))$$

The six C_{not} result in the state

$$\frac{1}{\sqrt{2}}(|0\rangle^{\otimes 7}|\widetilde{\psi}\rangle + |1\rangle|0\rangle^{\otimes 6}\widetilde{M}|\widetilde{\psi}\rangle))$$

applies $\widetilde{M}$ controlled by the cat state, then the cat-state construction is undone and the first qubit of the cat state register is measured. Either $|\pi/{\sim}4$ or $P\pi2\,|-$ is obtained. In the latter case, a $\widetilde{Z}$ operator could be applied to obtain $|\pi/{\sim}4$.

The ultimate Hadamard transformation yields a condition known as

$$\frac{1}{2}(|+\rangle|0\rangle^{\otimes 6}\,|\,\widetilde{\psi}+|-|\,0\otimes 6\widetilde{M}\,|\,\widetilde{\psi})$$

which is equal to

$$\frac{1}{2\sqrt{2}}(|0\rangle|0\rangle^{\otimes 6}(|\widetilde{\psi}\rangle + \widetilde{M}|\widetilde{\psi}\rangle) + |1\rangle|0\rangle^{\otimes 6}(|\widetilde{\psi}\rangle - \widetilde{M}|\widetilde{\psi}\rangle)))$$

When the first qubit is evaluated in the consistent schedule, one of the eigenvalues of M is acquired.

8.4 The Strength of Quantum Computation

Code that repeatedly replaces circuits with bigger and more resilient ones is concatenation. Concatenation levels are also analyzed to illustrate the increasing potential for exponential precision growth when more resources (qubits and gates) are made available.

8.4.1 Combinatorial Coding

Q0 will be considered a time-separated circuit for the sake of this discussion. A success rate of 1 or more is desired. We need $Qi+1$ to use Steane's code to encode its qubits, Qi to have its gate logic replaced by fault-tolerant logical analogues, and Qi to do EC after each of its mode of existence logical equivalents. The circuit Qi is derived from the initial $Q0$ by a series of concatenated encoding operations. Concatenation happens on two different levels here. Mistakes on blocks equivalent to the final logical qubits occur less often than errors on blocks of seven qubits, and both types of blocks need EC. This hierarchical EC allows for exponentially high resilience to be achieved with just quadratically many resources, qubits, and gates.

As shown in the above paragraph, an exponentially small amount of resources is sufficient to achieve a polynomially large level of accuracy. To put it in terms of an error-correcting code, we may think of it as an ensemble of components that only fail when there are two or more errors, rather than just one, replacing the parts that fail when there is a single mistake in the qubit. If a component fails at a given moment with probability p, then the ensemble fails with probability $cp2$. A machine $M0$ has N parts, and each of those parts will break with a certain probability (p) at some point during the T intervals that the machine will be in operation. How likely it is that M will be implemented without a hitch is denoted by NT. While individual components still fail with probability p, the ensemble of K components fails to complete the intended operation with probability just $cp2$ for some constant less than or equal to 1. Machine's essential parts may now be replaced by ensembles of K individual parts. Machine M_i succeeds with a probability of $(c2i1p2i)NT$ in the long run if and only if, after I tries, it fails to carry out the planned operation with probability at most $c2i1p2i$. The accuracy improves twice as rapidly as the number of components Ki in the hierarchical ensemble corresponds to a single component in machine $M0$, which grows only exponentially in I. For the ensemble to attain a failure rate of less than $(1/2)r$, we only need to encode $O(\log_2 r)$ times. For any $i > \log_2 \left(\frac{\log_2 c - r}{\log_2(cp)} \right)$, the failure rate is less that $(1/2)r$ because

$$i > \log_2 \left(\frac{\log_2 c - r}{\log_2(cp)} \right)$$

implies that

$$2^i > \frac{r - \log_2 c}{-\log_2(cp)}$$

The denominator $-\log_2(cp)$ is positive, since $cp < 1$, so schematic diagram with circuits $Q0$, $Q1$, and $Q2$ showing two levels of concatenated coding.

Schematic diagram with circuits $Q0$, $Q1$, and $Q2$ showing two levels of concatenated coding. The number of qubits is only suggestive: for the Steane code, the circuit $Q2$ would use forty-nine qubits for each qubit of $Q0$.

$-2i \log_2(cp) > r - \log_2 c$, which implies

$$-r > 2^i\log_2(cp) - \log_2 c = \log_2 \left(\frac{(cp)^{2^i}}{c} \right)$$

Thus,

$$2^{-r} > \frac{(cp)^{2^i}}{c_i}$$

where $(1/2)^r$ is the failure rate we computed for an ensemble in machine Mi that replaces a single part in the original machine $M0$.

8.4.2 A Threshold Theorem

Threshold theorems are given, and their significance is described in the first paragraph of this section. After a brief conclusion, we go on to a set of more general threshold arguments and numerical approximations for the aforementioned thresholds.

For each $[n, 1, 2t + 1]$ quantum error checked, a theorem on the threshold pT guarantees the following properties. When working with C, we use a number of qubits and time steps proportional to a polylogarithm of C, where C is the total number of possible locations.

An error-correcting code has a full set of fault-tolerant procedures if it includes fault-tolerant operations for a comprehensive set of universal logical gates, error detection steps, state preparations, and measurement. If a circuit C is divided into discrete time intervals, then each qubit may undergo just a single preparation, gate, or measurement at any one moment. C-locations include things like gates, checklists, gauges, and forecasts (for the identity transformation storing the qubit for the next step). In a fault-tolerant protocol, each step is replaced by an error-correcting procedure that relies on a robust error-correcting code and a variety of other fault-tolerant processes. The circuit C in the threshold theorem is built by repeatedly using the fault-tolerant protocol and exchanging the gates, preparations, and measurements from the previous round. The number of iterations required to achieve a certain level of accuracy.

The probability of an error at each point in a set decreases exponentially with increasing set size, as shown by local stochastic error models. To put it another way, for each subset S of locations in a circuit C, the maximum chance of a fault happening at any given site is $1, p_i$, where p_i is the fixed probability of a fault occurring at place L_i. If the sum of the error probabilities at all possible locations, p_i, is less than p, then the error rate is less than p. Assuming the error was intentional will help you prepare for the possibility that your opponent specifically targeted these spots in order to throw off your calculations. Defects in a stochastic system are distributed arbitrarily.

The $L1$-distance is used to determine how different two probability distributions are when the probabilities of each of the N possibilities in P are equal to p_i and q_i.

$$\varepsilon = \|P - Q\|_1 = \sum_{i=1}^{N} |p_i - q_i|$$

Let's pretend the ideal circuit is built to perfection and the resulting state is quantified in a consistent way. In this case, we will assume that the measurement results follow a normal distribution, denoted by P. In the presence of local unpredictable noise at a rate p, implementing C and then observing the logical qubits yields a probability density function denoted by Q. Before taking any measurements, the output state of C may be modeled using ideal and noisy scenarios using density operators and. The statistics distance between the distributed ability and the standard basis is equivalent to the trace distance between Hermitian operators. Hermitian operators' trace distance (or trace metric) is computed using the trace norm $\|A\|$. Tr of A may be summed up as follows: $\|A\|Tr = tr|A|$, where $|A| = \sqrt{A\dagger A}$ is the positive square root of the operator $A\dagger A$. Let ρ and ρ be two density operators. The trace metric $d_{Tr}(\rho, \rho')$ on density operators is defined to be

$$\varepsilon = d_{Tr}(\rho, \rho') = \|\rho - \rho'\|_{Tr} = \mathbf{tr}|\rho - \rho'|$$

Threshold theorems have also been derived from other error models, including more extensive models. For error modeling, there exists threshold information and knowledge in which each basic gate is substituted with an interactive one that is near the real gate but still interacts with the user. Every elementary gate has a corresponding model, such as $U\,I$ for an action on the computing system and $I\,U$ for an action on the external world. In which the system and surroundings of the computer are subject to a unitary operator V, and V must fall inside the interval T of the unitary operator U models each immaculate gate's noisy equivalent.

$\|V - U \otimes I\|Tr < \eta T$ for a certain cutoff value T. Despite its simplicity, this noise model is quite versatile. Even the local stochastic error model is subsumed.

Several codes, fault-tolerant processes, and error models have yielded estimates of threshold levels such as pT or T. In the beginning, the thresholds were in the range of, but they have now been raised to. To get to the value of implementing trials, we will have to make more advancements. More realistic noise models, sophisticated error codes, and fault-tolerant approaches and analyses will all help to raise these numbers.

References

1 Dennis, E., Kitaev, A., Landahl, A., and Preskill, J. (2002). *Journal of Mathematical Physics* 43: 4452.
2 Fowler, A.G., Mariantoni, M., Martinis, J.M., and Cleland, A.N. (2012). *Physical Review A* 86: 032324.
3 Kitaev, A. (2003). *Annals of Physics* 303: 2.
4 Lekitsch, B., Weidt, S., Fowler, A.G. et al. (2017). *Science Advances* 3: e1601540.
5 Walter Ogburn, R. and Preskill, J. (1999). *Quantum Computing and Quantum Communications* (ed. C.P. Williams), 341–356. Berlin, Heidelberg: Springer Berlin Heidelberg.

6 Zhang, H., Liu, C.-X., Gazibegovic, S. et al. (2018). *Nature* 6: 1–30. https://doi .org/10.1038/nature26142.

7 Nickerson, N.H., Li, Y., and Benjamin, S.C. (2013). *Nature Communications* 4: 1756.

8 Wallraff, A., Schuster, D.I., Blais, A. et al. (2004). *Nature* 431: 162.

9 Schuster, D.I. (2007). Circuit quantum electrodynamics. PhD thesis. Yale University.

10 Paik, H., Schuster, D.I., Bishop, L.S. et al. (2011). *Physical Review Letters* 107: 240501.

11 Reagor, M. (2015). Superconducting cavities for circuit quantum electro- dynamics. PhD thesis. Yale University.

12 Tinkham, M. (2004). *Introduction to Superconductivity: Second Edition*, 2e. Dover Publications.

13 Houck, A.A., Koch, J., Devoret, M.H. et al. (2009). *Quantum Information Process* 8: 105.

14 Nakamura, Y., Terai, H., Inomata, K. et al. (2011). *Applied Physics Letters* 99: 212502.

9

Cryptography in Quantum Computing

9.1 Introduction of RSA Encryption

This form of strong encryption may be used to encrypt or scramble a message using a key distributed between two parties. The communication may be decrypted or recovered later using the key. A mathematical procedure is used to produce cryptographic keys that are difficult but not impossible to break. As an alternative, quantum cryptography (QKD) relies on the rules of physics to generate a key for distribution. Despite the fact that quantum cryptography is not completely secure, it has a number of benefits over other approaches [1].

First, let's have a look at a toy example of how communications may be encrypted before we go into quantum encryption. Let's say that Alice and Bob desire to send each other a secret message. If you are looking for an easy approach to jumbling up the message, all you need is to produce an encryption key called k. Each character in the message may be given a value of k, which will result in an unintelligible muddle. Let's pretend that we are utilizing a binary code to represent the alphabet's capital letters. Because $26 + 25 = 32$, the alphabet must be encoded in binary using at least five bits. If we start with the first four letters of A, B, C, and D as 0, 1, 2, and 3, the letters may be encoded as follows:

A → 0000

B → 0001

C → 0010

D → 0011

An eavesdropper (often referred to as Eve) may easily record our chat if we just sent our message through a public communications channel (such as a mobile phone). So, how can Alice and Bob keep the message secure? To make the communication more secure, we may simply add a key k to each character before sending it. After that, the message is encrypted and transferred across the public

Quantum Computing: A New Era of Computing, First Edition.
Kuldeep Singh Kaswan, Jagjit Singh Dhatterwal, Anupam Baliyan, and Shalli Rani.
© 2023 The Institute of Electrical and Electronics Engineers, Inc. Published 2023 by John Wiley & Sons, Inc.

network. In order to decode or retrieve the original message, Bob subtracts k from it. A private chat between Alice and Bob may be shared with Eve if she does not know k [2]. This means that Alice encodes the message, which is called m, with the key k by producing the sent string t in the following manner:

$$t = m + k$$

To be more precise, let $k = 3 = 0011$. This is added to each character in a message that we are working on. As a result, the strings above are transformed into

$\rightarrow 0000 \rightarrow 0011$

$\rightarrow 0001 \rightarrow 0100$

$\rightarrow 0010 \rightarrow 0101$

$\rightarrow 0011 \rightarrow 0110$

For our encoding system, this means AD, BE, CF, and DG. Using the key, Alice can encrypt the word BAD and send E D G to Bob. Public channels are used to send this data. A nonsensical jumble of letters and numbers appears as Eve attempts to touch the line. Bob, on the other hand, is aware that the critical $m = t\ k$ may be used to decode the signal. Someone may discover k by chatting with Alice or looking through Bob's hard disk if we use the same key every time. It is possible to reduce the danger by switching the key regularly, such as every time we send an email. A one-time pad approach is what we are employing when we often swap out the key [3].

9.2 Concept of RSA Encryption

Obviously, in the actual world, such a rudimentary system would never be used. Rivest, Shamir, Adleman (RSA), a standard encryption technology, is one of the many protections required to protect our data. The RSA algorithm uses two keys, one public and one private, to encrypt data. There are two things you need to decode a message: the private key and multiple integers that are difficult to factor. To get around the mechanism, you'd have to factor in the numbers. Starting with two prime numbers known as p and q, we begin our analysis. There are only two ways to divide a prime integer p: by itself and by one. 2, 3, 5, 7, 11, and 19 are examples of tiny primes. Because 9 is divisible by 9, 3, and 1, it is not a prime number. There are only two ways to divide the number 13: 13 and 1. There exist highly huge prime integers $p > 10100$ that make factoring impossible in RSA encryption. For huge prime numbers, it turns out that considering their products would take billions of years to complete in theory, regardless of how fast or powerful a computer we create. So, it should be noted that this has not been proven, and thus it is conceivable that someday a mathematically efficient program may break down big prime numbers on a classical computer. A quantum computer can factor numeric values with ease; hence, additional cryptographic techniques (quantum cryptography) must be utilized to protect communications [4].

An RSA scheme that is basic enough can be tested. We begin by taking the product of two huge prime numbers, p and q, and writing it down as

$$n : n = pq \tag{9.1}$$

Finally, a composition that some numbers of philosophers have dubbed the "totient" is computed.

$$\varphi(n) = (p - 1)(q - 1) \tag{9.2}$$

We now need to make sure that the only component in e and (n) that is equal is 1. Together, n and e provide the basis for the public key. It has already been noted that

$$1 \bmod \varphi(n)$$

The novel's private key contains only two characters, d and n. Recognize that because we currently know e, folks could decode the information if we knew d. To clarify for the uninitiated and unfamiliar, here's a brief primer on how mods work. The leftover we obtain when we divide two numbers by two is known as the compressive strength. 7 divided by 5 yields 1 with a residue of 2, for example [5]:

$$7 \bmod 5 = 2 \text{ is the answer}$$

As a result, we may complete a division using the mod function. A secret message known as "m" is encoded as follows:

$$c = me \bmod n \tag{9.3}$$

The secret key d is in the hands of the intended recipient. The communication may be decrypted by them, since

$$cd = med \bmod n$$

Due to the fact that $n = pq$, $med = m \bmod p$ $med = m \bmod q$ (9.4)

According to pure mathematics, we may conclude that this is the case.

$$cd = m \bmod n \tag{9.5}$$

Example 9.1 Using a tiny number as an example, we can understand how the system works in theory. A message $m = 6$ with $p = 3$ and $q = 11$ is encrypted and decoded using the aforesaid RSA technique.

Solution

We begin by constructing the product

$$n = pq = (3)(11) = 33$$

The solution is the next step

$$\varphi = (3 - 1)(11 - 1)$$
$$= (2)(10)$$
$$= 20$$

Let $e > 1$ such that e and $\varphi = 20$ have no common factors except 1. The smallest number that satisfies this criterion is $e = 3$. To find d, we use (9.3) and find the smallest x such that.

$$de = 1 + x\varphi$$

For $m = 6$, the secret message is sent.

$$c = me \bmod n$$
$$= 63 \bmod 33$$
$$= 18$$

It is best to calculate mod equations using MATLAB. To Bob, who possesses the private key $d = 7$, Alice sends this message. Using the encryption program

$$m = cd \bmod n$$
$$= 187 \bmod 33$$
$$= 6$$

In today's world, the RSA encryption technique may be used for various purposes. Since $n = pq$ can be calculated, Shor's approach shows that a functional classical computer can quickly break an RSA encryption system. In terms of encryption, is there a better method? Quantum mechanics, it turns out, has a number of applications.

9.3 Quantum Cipher Fundamentals

Quantum cryptography uses quantum physics to produce a secret key rather than relying on standard numerical techniques. Quantum cryptography, or QKD, is the name given to this process. Between Alice and Bob, two communication channels are utilized to accomplish QKD. Included in this category is a standard public route, such as the Internet, a mobile phone, or even your house phone. Communications over this line are secure. In addition, a quantum communications channel is employed to disseminate the quantum key as a second component of the QKD jigsaw. Individual photons with distinct polarization states are used in practice. Measurement upsets a quantum state, a fundamental concept of quantum theory. A measure must be taken to decode the information in a quantum state containing a key. In other words, if Eve connects to the line, she will have to take measures that will cause Alice and Bob to become aware of her existence [6].

The BB84 protocol is our first foray into the realm of cryptographic algorithms. The method was supposedly named after its inventors, Bennett and Brassard. These three tenets form the backbone of BB84 QKD:

According to the no-cloning theorem, it is theoretically impossible to make an exact clone of a superposition state. Since Eve cannot intercept a quantum communication channel, replicate the quantum states required to produce the key, and then send it to Bob, the key cannot be delivered to Bob. The breakdown of the state is caused by measurement. To construct a bit string in QKD, a variety of bases will be needed. To avoid state collapse, we must perform measurements on just one of the two bases provided. Disruption to the system is caused by obtaining information about its current condition. It is impossible to go back and change the results of a measurement.

If the system is in a state that conforms to points 2 and 3, then you should take note of those things.

$$|+\rangle = \frac{|0\rangle + |1\rangle}{\sqrt{2}}$$

With a computationally measuring device, we discard the system's original state. Let's pretend we get a measurement of 0. The state is now different from what it was initially in the | basis:

$$|0\rangle = \frac{|+\rangle + |-\rangle}{\sqrt{2}}$$

There is only a 50% chance of finding |+ if we measure in the |± basis—the state has been irreversibly alter.

To generate our key in the BB84 protocol, we rely on both the computational and the | basis. To recap, these two pillars are linked by means of

$$|+\rangle = \frac{|0\rangle + |1\rangle}{\sqrt{2}}, \quad |-\rangle = \frac{|0\rangle - |1\rangle}{\sqrt{2}} \tag{9.6}$$

Alice starts by generating a random string of 2^n qubits to use as the key. One of the four provinces is used to construct each qubit:

$$|0\rangle, |1\rangle, |+\rangle, |-\rangle$$

Table 9.1 Conversation between two objects.

Alice bits	0	1	0	0	0	1	0	1
Alice basis	$\{|0\rangle, |1\rangle\}$	$\{|0\rangle, |1\rangle\}$	$|\pm\rangle$	$\{|0\rangle, |1\rangle\}$	$\{|0\rangle, |1\rangle\}$	$|\pm\rangle$	$|\pm\rangle$	$|\pm\rangle$
Bob basis	$\{|0\rangle, |1\rangle\}$	$\{|0\rangle, |1\rangle\}$	$|\pm\rangle$	$|\pm\rangle$	$|\pm\rangle$	$\{|0\rangle, |1\rangle\}$	$|\pm\rangle$	$|\pm\rangle$
Match	Yes	Yes	Yes	No	No	No	Yes	Yes
Keep	Yes	Yes	Yes	No	No	No	Yes	Yes

and may be used to represent logical 0 in each case. After then, the qubits are physically sent to Bob. In order to obtain accurate readings, Bob chooses a basis or a | basis for each qubit as he measures it.

There are two possible qualities for each piece of the string, and Alice will select one of them at random. Standard probability theory demonstrates that about n bits will be made in the basis and n bits will be generated in the | basis. When comparing their notes, the only thing Alice and Bob talk about is the reasoning behind each decision they made. By switching to a new basis, Alice and Bob may safely dispose of the qubit. When bits from Alice and Bob's keys are discarded, the resulting key is referred to as the "sifted key."

Example 9.2 *An 8-bit string is created by Alice*

$$|0\rangle|1\rangle|+\rangle|0\rangle|0\rangle|-\rangle|+\rangle|-\rangle$$

In the following sequence, Bob involves measuring the bases $\{|0\rangle, |1\rangle\}\{|0\rangle, |1\rangle\}$ $\{|\pm\rangle|\pm\rangle\}|\pm\rangle|0\rangle, |1\rangle|\pm\rangle|\pm\rangle$, and explain informational strings of bits that Alice and Bob keep track of.

Solution
In Table 9.1 shows Bits 1 through 8 are discarded while counting backward to determine whether Alice and Bob utilized used the same or different foundations.

The final bit string is created by keeping the bits in locations 1, 2, 3, 7, and 8 and throwing out the bits in positions 4, 5, and 6. The filter key is $s = 01001$.

When Alice and Bob have finished creating the filtered key, they must verify it again to ensure it is error-free. It is possible for an eavesdropper to infiltrate a communication channel and induce mistakes, such as bit flip and phase flip errors, to occur [7]. Eve may be listening in if the mistake rate is too high. Alice and Bob examine the prediction error and destroy the key if it exceeds an agreed-upon level. For the sake of argument, let's pretend Eve had measured bit 8 in Example 9.2. The computation and the | bases have a 50% probability of being picked by her to make her measurement. She may have chosen a computational framework. Then

$$|-\rangle = \frac{|0\rangle - |1\rangle}{\sqrt{2}}$$

When Eve performs her measurement, the qubit will be in the state. Consider it to be. Alternatively, this might be worded as follows:

$$|0\rangle = \frac{|+\rangle + |-\rangle}{\sqrt{2}}$$

Even if Alice sets the qubit in the | state, Bob has only a 50% probability of seeing the right answer when he does his measurement. Eve's existence may be inferred if a high number of qubits are included in our string. Using the bit string 01001 as an example, Alice knows she made it. The bit string 01000, on the other hand, is in Bob's possession. Errors may also be caused by noise on the quantum channel. Those qubits can be repaired via quantum error correction.

9.4 The Controlled-Not Invasion as an Illustration

Suppose that Alice is in this situation.

$$|+_A\rangle = \frac{|0_A\rangle + |1_A\rangle}{\sqrt{2}}$$

This condition cannot be replicated in any manner by Eve. There is a possibility that Eve sought to create a state that both Alice and Eve could measure in the same way. From this starting point, Eve can establish a product state.

$$|+_A\rangle \otimes |0_E\rangle = \frac{|0_A\rangle|0_E\rangle + |1_A\rangle|0_E\rangle}{\sqrt{2}}$$

Look at what happens if Eve uses Alice's quantum computer as the signaling bit, with Eve's qubit serving as the control destination to apply a controllable NOT gate to the state. As a result, the state

$$\frac{|0_A\rangle|0_E\rangle + |1_A\rangle|0_E\rangle}{\sqrt{2}} \xrightarrow{\text{CN}} \frac{|0_A\rangle|0_E\rangle + |1_A\rangle|1_E\rangle}{\sqrt{2}}$$

For Eve, we need to know that Alice's measurement is zero. Eve will have one if Alice gets one. How does the | basis affect the results? Then there's

$$\frac{|0_A\rangle|0_E\rangle + |1_A\rangle|1_E\rangle}{\sqrt{2}} = \frac{1}{\sqrt{2}}\left[\left(\frac{|+_A\rangle + |-_A\rangle}{\sqrt{2}}\right)\left(\frac{|+_E\rangle + |-_E\rangle}{\sqrt{2}}\right)\right.$$
$$\left. + \left(\frac{|+_A\rangle - |-_A\rangle}{\sqrt{2}}\right)\left(\frac{|+_E\rangle - |-_E\rangle}{\sqrt{2}}\right)\right]$$
$$= \frac{1}{\sqrt{2}}\left(\frac{1}{2}\right)\left[|+_A\rangle|+_E\rangle + |+_A\rangle|-_E\rangle + |-_A\rangle|+_E\rangle + |-_A\rangle|-_E\rangle\right.$$
$$\left. + |+_A\rangle|+_E\rangle - |+_A\rangle|-_E\rangle - |-_A\rangle|+_E\rangle + |-_A\rangle|-_E\rangle\right]$$
$$= \frac{1}{\sqrt{2}}(|+_A\rangle|+_E\rangle + |-_A\rangle|-_E\rangle)$$

Alice and Eve's relationship has remained consistent! Both Alice's and Eve's qubits have the same quantity. Instead, imagine if Alice

$$|-_A\rangle = \frac{|0_A\rangle - |1_A\rangle}{\sqrt{2}}$$

Whether the association is still valid is the question. If we follow the same steps, we will wind up in the same situation.

$$|\psi\rangle = \frac{|+_A\rangle|-_E\rangle + |-_A\rangle|+_E\rangle}{\sqrt{2}}$$

Alice and Eve's measurement findings are, as we can see, opposed. Eve, on the other hand, does not know in advance what Alice's condition was; therefore, her measurements are worthless. In general, Eve cannot use a controlled-NOT gate to build a product state and discover what Alice possesses.

9.5 Cryptography B92 Protocol

The BB84 protocol has been simplified using an updated version of the QKD protocol. There are no orthogonal bases this time around. We use the mathematical fundamental for one of the foundations, which we call " the basis," as is customary. Here's the bare-bones rundown of what must happen:

Bob involves measuring the qubits using a random advanced computer foundation, or basis. Bob is a stickler for only taking measurements using the metric system [8].

In step two, Bob builds a key using the measured bit locations.

Bob broadcasts the locations of bytes, while Alice receives them over a public channel.

In the parallel computing model, Bob will get what Alice builds if he measures it. Assuming his length measurement begins at ground zero, he will be granted.

If Alice constructs a and Bob measurements it in the supercomputing basis, then Bob gets it. He receives | if he calculates on a | basis. Assume Alice generates the 8-bit string shown below:

$$|0\rangle|0\rangle|0'\rangle|0\rangle|0'\rangle|0'\rangle|0\rangle|0'\rangle$$

If Bob measures using

$$|0\rangle|0'\rangle|0'\rangle|0\rangle|0\rangle|0\rangle|0'\rangle|0'\rangle$$

The result is

$$|0\rangle|1'\rangle|0'\rangle|0\rangle|1\rangle|1\rangle|1'\rangle|0'\rangle$$

Regarding the key, Bob says he will be holding on to spots 2, 5, 6, and 7. Comparing this with BB84, it is easy to see the changes. Alice creates a key in BB84.

Whenever Bob gets results obtained, the key is produced. Alice utilizes just two states to construct the key instead of the four states that were previously utilized.

9.6 The E91 Protocol (Ekert)

Ekert's quantum entanglement-based cryptography is the last approach we will look at. Bell states are created by delivering send Bob the other half of the Einstein–Podolsky–Rosen (EPR) pair and Alice the first. Assume that the EPR pair's state equals

$$|\beta_{00}\rangle = \frac{|00\rangle + |10\rangle}{\sqrt{2}}$$

Then, we can be confident that Alice and Bob's measurements will be correlated. When it comes to the status of affairs, on the other hand, this is not the case.

$$|\beta_{01}\rangle = \frac{|01\rangle + |10\rangle}{\sqrt{2}}$$

Therefore, the measurements performed by Alice and Bob will be utterly discordant. The qubits of Alice and Bob are measured on a random basis. A normal channel is utilized for communicating, and the bit locations they use are determined from that. To make the key, they will need these pieces.

If an unauthorized individual is present, Alice and Bob will be able to tell because their findings will be perfectly correlated or perfectly anticorrelated. Potentially, regular errors might be fixed using quantum error-correcting techniques.

Every single case using QKD employs privacy amplification to provide a more secure key. Instead of trying to quantify them, as Eve could have done, these qubits are being wasted. To construct the refined key, all Eve has to do is eliminate the six bits she is aware of, leaving a key length of 14 bits [9].

References

1 Chang, J.B., Vissers, M.R., Córcoles, A.D. et al. (2013). Improved superconducting qubit coherence using titanium nitride. *Applied Physics Letters* 103: 12602.

2 Diamanti, E., Lo, H.-K., Qi, B., and Yuan, Z. (2016). Practical challenges in quantum key distribution. *npj Quantum Information* 2: 16025.

3 Ursin, R., Tiefenbacher, F., Schmitt-Manderbach, T. et al. (2007). Free-space distribution of entanglement and single photons over 144 km. *Nature Physics* 3: 481.

4 Nielsen, M.A. and Chuang, I.L. (2010). *Quantum Computation and Quantum Information*. Cambridge: Cambridge University Press.

5 Jiang, L., Taylor, J.M., Nemoto, K. et al. (2009). Quantum repeater with encoding. *Physical Review A* 79: 032325.

6 Kimble, H.J. (2008). The quantum internet. *Nature* 453: 1023, arXiv:0806.4195.

7 Dür, W., Lamprecht, R., and Heusler, S. (2017). Towards a quantum internet. *European Journal of Physics* 38: 043001.

8 Ritter, S., Nölleke, C., Hahn, C. et al. (2012). An elementary quantum network of single atoms in optical cavities. *Nature* 484: 195, arXiv:1202.5955.

9 Bernien, H., Hensen, B., Pfaff, W. et al. (2013). Heralded entanglement between solid-state qubits separated by three metres. *Nature* 497: 86.

10

Constructing Clusters for Quantum Computing

10.1 Introduction

In the cluster-state quantum computing concept, the processing is done without requiring quantum gates. On the other hand, this measurement-based model may be used to replicate the dynamics of quantum mechanics. The cluster state model may simulate or perform quantum computing since quantum gates are built using unitary operators [1].

Cluster states are multiqubit states that undergo a sequence of measurements to be processed. The outcome of each experiment is used to choose the basis for the next experiment, creating a feedback loop in quantum computing. Two phases may be used to summarize cluster state quantum computing

To begin with, the qubits must be put into a specific condition. Start with, for example, the states beyond which controlled phase gates are applied [2].

On some bases, calculate the qubits. Repeated measurement creates a feedback loop by determining the foundation for the next size based on past findings.

One computationally controllable stage of operation is the controlled-Z gate, which uses a linear transformation.

$$CZ = \begin{pmatrix} 1 & 0 & 0 & 0 \\ 0 & 1 & 0 & 0 \\ 0 & 0 & 1 & 0 \\ 0 & 0 & 0 & -1 \end{pmatrix} \tag{10.1}$$

Using a controlled phase gate causes the states to get entangled.

10.1.1 State of Clusters

Graphs, a collection of connected components, are used to represent cluster states. The vertices represent programmable phase gates, while each vertex is a qubit. Figure 10.1 depicts one such instance.

Quantum Computing: A New Era of Computing, First Edition.
Kuldeep Singh Kaswan, Jagjit Singh Dhatterwal, Anupam Baliyan, and Shalli Rani.
© 2023 The Institute of Electrical and Electronics Engineers, Inc. Published 2023 by John Wiley & Sons, Inc.

Figure 10.1 Cluster structure.

After setting up each qubit in the |+ state, we may begin performing cluster state quantum computing. Following that, qubits in the graphs are governed by phase gates [3].

10.2 The Preparation of Cluster States

Cluster state preparations begin with the creation of a product stage in Figure 10.1

$$|+\rangle_C = |+\rangle^{\otimes n} \tag{10.2}$$

The two vectors in the network recognize two qubits, and the line linking them represents the single regulated capital investment project done to them in figure. Then, the first product state is produced (Figure 10.2).

$$|+\rangle_C = |+\rangle \otimes |+\rangle \tag{10.3}$$

We must use a controllable phase gate to proceed to the next step. We may, for example, use a "controlled-Z" gate offered by

$$S = \frac{1}{2}(I \otimes I + Z \otimes I + I \otimes Z - Z \otimes Z) \tag{10.4}$$

to obtain

$$S|+\rangle \otimes |+\rangle = \frac{1}{2}(I \otimes I + Z \otimes I + I \otimes Z - Z \otimes Z)|+\rangle \otimes |+\rangle$$

$$= \frac{1}{2}\left[\left(\frac{|0\rangle + |1\rangle}{\sqrt{2}}\right)\left(\frac{|0\rangle + |1\rangle}{\sqrt{2}}\right)\right.$$

$$+ (Z \otimes I)\left(\frac{|0\rangle + |1\rangle}{\sqrt{2}}\right)\left(\frac{|0\rangle + |1\rangle}{\sqrt{2}}\right)$$

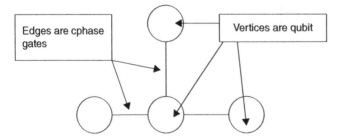

Figure 10.2 A graph represents cluster state quantum computation.

$$+ I \otimes Z \left(\frac{|0\rangle + |1\rangle}{\sqrt{2}} \right) \left(\frac{|0\rangle + |1\rangle}{\sqrt{2}} \right)$$

$$- Z \otimes Z \left(\frac{|0\rangle + |1\rangle}{\sqrt{2}} \right) \left(\frac{|0\rangle + |1\rangle}{\sqrt{2}} \right) \Big]$$

$$= \frac{1}{2} [|00\rangle + |01\rangle + |10\rangle - |11\rangle]$$

Example 10.1 Consider three qubits arranged in a triangle. What states result in creating the graphs?

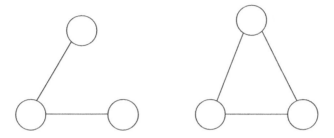

Solution

It is called qubit 1 for the top qubit and qubit 2 for the bottom qubits on the left and right, respectively. It is the result of the starting state.

$$|+\rangle \otimes |+\rangle \otimes |+\rangle = \left(\frac{|0\rangle + |1\rangle}{\sqrt{2}} \right) \left(\frac{|0\rangle + |1\rangle}{\sqrt{2}} \right) \left(\frac{|0\rangle + |1\rangle}{\sqrt{2}} \right)$$

$$= \frac{1}{8} (|000\rangle + |001\rangle + |010\rangle + |011\rangle$$

$$+ |100\rangle + |101\rangle + |110\rangle + |111\rangle) \tag{10.5}$$

Let's have a look at how the constrained gate works. In this example, the first qubit is the controlling qubit, while the second is the manipulated qubit. If the value of the primary qubit is zero, the subsequent qubit is not affected in any way. The second qubit goes via a Z gate if the first qubit is 1 [4]. Remember,

$$Z|0\rangle = |0\rangle, \quad Z|1\rangle = -|1\rangle \tag{10.6}$$

Qubits 1 and 2 must first be put via the dominated gate before moving on to qubits 2 and 3. We get (10.5) by qubits 1 and 2 are subjected to the CZ gate.

$$|\psi'\rangle = \frac{1}{\sqrt{8}} (|000\rangle + |001\rangle + |010\rangle + |011\rangle + |100\rangle + |101\rangle - |110\rangle - |111\rangle)$$

$$\tag{10.7}$$

Each term's control is the term's first qubit. We do very little to the destination in the first four terms since the control is set to 0. This is a 1 in the final four terms, but the target is a 1 for the last two terms. As a result, it's a 0 in the target.

CZ gates are applied to qubits 2 and 3 now. In other words, the second qubit is in charge, whereas the third qubit is the intended recipient. We can come up with

$$|\psi_\Lambda\rangle = \frac{1}{\sqrt{8}} (|000\rangle + |001\rangle + |010\rangle - |011\rangle + |100\rangle + |101\rangle - |110\rangle + |111\rangle)$$

(10.8)

Lambda state: The graph looks like a (tilted) lambda. Therefore, we've named it that.

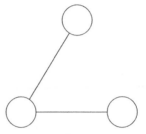

To produce the second graph, we must connect qubits 1 and 3. The *CZ* gate is used for these two qubits in the current state to accomplish this (10.8). We will be done with this when it is done.

$$|\psi_\Delta\rangle = \frac{1}{\sqrt{8}}(|000\rangle + |001\rangle + |010\rangle - |011\rangle + |100\rangle - |101\rangle - |110\rangle - |111\rangle)$$

(10.9)

To bring the subsequent qubit into this state when the original qubit was 1, we employed a *Z* gate. This is how the graph looks at this point.

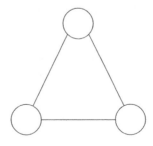

10.3   Nearest Neighbor Matrix

A numerical solution is a matrix-based representation of a graph. The graph's vertices are used to name the columns and rows of the underlying matrix. Matrix elements are either one or zero, depending on whether or not an edge connects the points symbolized by a specific row or column entry [5]. For instance, have a look at

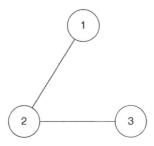

We've made things easier for you by giving each vertex its own label. The adjacency matrix will be 33 if there are three vertices. Between 1 and 2, as well as 2 and 3, there are several edges. To summarize, we may say that there will be 1's in the following mixture components: (3, 2). The remainder of the matrices will be set to zero, resulting in

$$A = \begin{pmatrix} 0 & 1 & 0 \\ 1 & 0 & 1 \\ 0 & 1 & 0 \end{pmatrix}$$

In the last example, we looked at a situation where

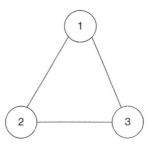

Now that coordinates 1 and 3 are linked, the (1, 3) and (3, 1) matrix entries must each have 1s added to them. Adjacency matrices are so defined.

$$A = \begin{pmatrix} 0 & 1 & 1 \\ 1 & 0 & 1 \\ 1 & 1 & 0 \end{pmatrix}$$

10.4 Stabilizer States

Stabilizing a state requires an operator, $A |\psi\rangle$ if

$$A|\psi\rangle = |\psi\rangle \tag{10.10}$$

In other words, a stabilizer is a simple operation that has an eigenvalue of 1. This shows that the identification of operators is a stabilizing factor, as it is the only one on the list [6].

$$I|\psi\rangle = |\psi\rangle$$

Now consider the state.

$$|+\rangle = \frac{|0\rangle + |1\rangle}{\sqrt{2}}$$

Notice that

$$X|+\rangle = \frac{X|0\rangle + X|1\rangle}{\sqrt{2}} = \frac{|1\rangle + |0\rangle}{\sqrt{2}} = \frac{|0\rangle + |1\rangle}{\sqrt{2}} = |+\rangle$$

Therefore, X and I are the $|+$ state's stabilizers. It is usual to write X, I as a symbol for this concept. The stabilizer for this one-qubit state has two operators. For n qubits in a state, $2n$ commutes operations are used to maintain the state [7].

Take the Bell state, for example.

$$|\beta_{00}\rangle = \frac{|00\rangle + |11\rangle}{\sqrt{2}}$$

Notice that

$$(X \otimes X)|\beta_{00}\rangle = \frac{(X|0\rangle)(X|0\rangle) + (X|1\rangle)(X|1\rangle)}{\sqrt{2}} = \frac{|11\rangle + |00\rangle}{\sqrt{2}} = |\beta_{00}\rangle$$

It's also true that

$$(Z \otimes Z)|\beta_{00}\rangle = \frac{(Z|0\rangle)(Z|0\rangle) + (Z|1\rangle)(Z|1\rangle)}{\sqrt{2}}$$

$$= \frac{(|0\rangle)(|0\rangle) + (-|1\rangle)(-|1\rangle)}{\sqrt{2}}$$

$$= \frac{|00\rangle + |11\rangle}{\sqrt{2}} = |\beta_{00}\rangle$$

Therefore, there are two stabilizing factors for the Bell state $|\beta_{00}\rangle$ are

$$\pm X \otimes X, \quad \pm Z \otimes Z$$

The letter "A" represents a set of qubits. Components of this set have a segmentation state that is defined by a type stabilizer.

$$-1kXa \otimes Zi \tag{10.11}$$

to the extent that neighbor of a. The following are possible formulas for n-qubit data aggregation state stabilizing agents:

$$S1 = X(1)Z(2)$$

$$\dots$$

$$Sj = Z(j-1)XjZj + 1 \quad j = 2, 3, \dots, n-1$$

$$Sn = Z(n-1)X(n) \tag{10.12}$$

In this context, an implementation of operator A on the jth qubit is denoted by the notation $A(j)$. Some examples of catalysts for cluster states of qubits are shown below:

$$S1 = X(1)Z(2), \quad S2 = Z(1)X(2) \tag{10.13}$$

Let's use the state's stabilizing force as an example.

$$|\psi_-\rangle = \frac{1}{2}\left[|00\rangle + |01\rangle + |10\rangle - |11\rangle \right. \tag{10.14}$$

Now

$$|\psi_-\rangle = CZ|++\rangle = \frac{1}{2}CZ(|0\rangle + |1\rangle)(|0\rangle + |1\rangle)$$

$$= \frac{1}{2}CZ(|00\rangle + |01\rangle + |10\rangle + |11\rangle)$$

$$= \frac{1}{2}(|00\rangle + |01\rangle + |10\rangle - |11\rangle)$$

We search for operations that meet our criteria to discover the stabilizers.

$$A^{(1)}B^{(2)}CZ|++\rangle = A^{(1)}B^{(2)}|\psi_-\rangle = |\psi_-\rangle$$

$CZ = CZI = CZXX$ because the Pauli operations squared to the identification. $CZXX = YYCZ$ may be shown, indicating that

$$|\psi_-\rangle = CZ|++\rangle = CZXX|++\rangle = (YY)CZ|++\rangle = YY|\psi_-\rangle$$

So YY is a stabilizer. We can also show that

$$CZ = CZXI = XZCZ$$

$$CZ = CZXI = CZIX = ZXCZ$$

This demonstrates that XZ and ZX both fulfill XZ. $|\psi_-\rangle = |\psi_-\rangle$, $ZX|\psi_-\rangle = |\psi_-\rangle$. Then,

$$CZ = CZII = IICZ$$

So, the state's stabilizing factor is $\{YY, XZ, ZX, II\}$.

10.4.1 Aside: Entanglement Witness

The number of entanglement qubits in a cluster state may be as high as n; hence, the question is: how can we tell whether or not a form with multiple qubits is entangled? An observation called an entangled witness might be used to try to address this issue. To employ a quantum superposition witness, W, we might analyze its corresponding value for a specific state. It's possible to separate the state if it is recoverable [8].

$$\langle W \rangle = \langle \psi | W | \psi \rangle > 0 \tag{10.15}$$

We may learn via the attached witness that the state is entangled from time to time. It's called "deleterious hope" when the value of the anticipation is negligible.

$$\langle W \rangle = \langle \psi | W | \psi \rangle < 0 \tag{10.16}$$

Let's take a closer look at this for two different scenarios. Three qubits are interconnected in the *GHZ* state.

$$|GHZ\rangle = \frac{|000\rangle + |111\rangle}{\sqrt{2}} \tag{10.17}$$

An entanglement witness is

$$
\begin{aligned}
W &= \frac{1}{2}I - |GHZ\rangle\langle GHZ| \\
&= \frac{1}{2}I - \frac{1}{2}(|000\rangle\langle 000| + |000\rangle\langle 111| + |111\rangle\langle 000| + |111\rangle\langle 111|) \quad (10.18)
\end{aligned}
$$

Next consider the separable state

$$|\psi\rangle = \left(\frac{|001\rangle + |111\rangle}{\sqrt{2}} \right) = \left(\frac{|00\rangle + |11\rangle}{\sqrt{2}} \right)|1\rangle$$

As a result, qubits 1 and 2 have become entangled, but qubit 3 has not. As per (10.8), the anticipated value of W for this state is something we are curious about. We now have

$$
\begin{aligned}
\langle W \rangle &= \langle \psi | W | \psi \rangle \\
&= \left(\frac{\langle 001| + \langle 111|}{\sqrt{2}} \right) W \left(\frac{|001\rangle + |111\rangle}{\sqrt{2}} \right)
\end{aligned}
$$

Now

$$
\begin{aligned}
W \left(\frac{|001\rangle + |111\rangle}{\sqrt{2}} \right) &= \left[\frac{1}{2}I - \frac{1}{2}(|000\rangle\langle 000| + |000\rangle\langle 111| + |111\rangle\langle 000| \right. \\
&\qquad \left. + |111\rangle\langle 111|) \right] \left(\frac{|001\rangle + |111\rangle}{\sqrt{2}} \right) \\
&= \left(\frac{|001\rangle + |111\rangle}{\sqrt{2}} \right) - \frac{1}{2} \left(\frac{|001\rangle + |111\rangle}{\sqrt{2}} \right)
\end{aligned}
$$

So, the expected value is

$$\langle W \rangle = \left(\frac{\langle 001| + \langle 111|}{\sqrt{2}} \right) \left[\left(\frac{|001\rangle + |111\rangle}{\sqrt{2}} \right) - \frac{1}{2} \left(\frac{|000\rangle + |111\rangle}{\sqrt{2}} \right) \right]$$

$$= \frac{\langle 001 | 001 \rangle}{\sqrt{2}} + \frac{\langle 111 | 111 \rangle}{\sqrt{2}} - \frac{\langle 111 | 111 \rangle}{\sqrt{2}} = \frac{\langle 001 | 001 \rangle}{\sqrt{2}} = \frac{1}{\sqrt{2}}$$

Since

$$\langle W \rangle = \frac{1}{\sqrt{2}} > 0$$

We are aware that the position may be divided. What about the *GHz* region? That's the case.

$$\langle W \rangle = \langle GHZ| \left(\frac{1}{2}I - |GHZ\rangle\langle GHZ| \right) |GHZ\rangle = \langle GHZ| \left(\frac{1}{2}|GHZ\rangle - |GHZ\rangle \right)$$

$$= \langle GHZ| \left(-\frac{1}{2}|GHZ\rangle \right) = -\frac{1}{2}\langle GHZ | GHZ \rangle = -\frac{1}{2} < 0$$

This shows that the *GHZ* state is intertwined, as previously thought. So far, *W* seems to be an excellent eyewitness to the connection.

10.5 Processing in Clusters

Either the *Z* eigen basis, the *X* eigen basis, or the *Y* eigen basis are all examples of how cluster state processing works [9]. To accomplish this, we will use a linear cluster, which is to say,

The middle qubit, symbolized by the edge of the circle from the left, will be the subject of measurements in the following instances. This is followed by an evaluation of the *Z* eigen basis value. The operators are written at the vertex of the structure.

- The cluster is affected in two ways by measurements in the *Z* eigen basis:
- Disconnect the qubit from the rest of the cluster by cutting all of its interconnections (edges).
- Remove the qubit. First, we've got this:

In step two, the clusters have been recreated.

It is now essential to take a completely new *X* eigen basis measurements.

The following are the two measures to take in this scenario:

- Eliminate the qubit
- Create a single logical qubit by combining the qubits that are closest to each other.

Eliminate the qubit as the first step.

The second step is to combine the qubits that are next to one other.

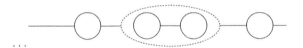

Each possible value of 0 and 1, |++ and |, is represented in the same logical qubit. When everything is said and done, we consider preprocessing through eigenvalue measurements.

Discard the offending qubit and establish connections among the other members of the cluster. We've made some progress by completing the first stage.

Now we link the two neighbors:

One more refresher: before we set up the cluster, we generate an initial product state consisting of a large number of qubits in the |+ state. As a further step, phase gates are implemented between the neighboring states. A circle or vertex may be used to represent a qubit in the |+ state in a diagram, while lines connecting circles symbolize programmable phase gates between the qubits.

Processing may be done on measurements in the Z, X, and Y axes. Once a qubit has been measured, it is no longer needed and is therefore withdrawn from the group. If the measurement was taken on the basis of Z, then the cluster's connections to that qubit would be broken. When an X-based measurement is taken, a new logical qubit is generated by using the |++, | root. When taking measurements from a Y-based perspective, it is acceptable to include all of the neighbors who were left out of the tally [10].

That's why cluster-state quantum computers rely on single-qubit observations. Since the procedures disrupt the entanglement, using a cluster state can only be done once. One-way quantum computers is a common name for this kind of machine.

References

1 Humphreys, P.C., Kalb, N., Morits, J.P.J., Schouten, R.N., Vermeulen, R.F.L., Twitchen, D.J., Markham, M., and Hanson, R. Deterministic delivery of remote entanglement on a quantum network *Nature*, 558(7709):268–273. (2018). https://doi.org/10.1038/s41586-018-0200-5.

2 Roch, N., Schwartz, M.E., Motzoi, F. et al. (2014). *Physical Review Letters* 112: 170501.

3 Narla, A., Shankar, S., Hatridge, M. et al. (2016). *Physical Review X* 6: 031036.

4 Dickel, C., Wesdorp, J.J., Langford, N.K. et al. (2018). *Physical Review B* 97: 064508.

5 C. J. Axline, L. D. Burkhart, W. Pfaff, M. Zhang, K. Chou, P. Campagne-Ibarcq, P. Reinhold, L. Frunzio, S. M. Girvin, L. Jiang, M. H. Devoret, and R. J. Schoelkopf, *Applied Physics Letters*, 109, 11, 112601 (2018). https://doi.org/10.1063/1.4962327.

6 Campagne-Ibarcq, P., Zalys-Geller, E., Narla, A., Shankar, S., Reinhold, P., Burkhart, L.D., Axline, C.J., Pfaff, W., Frunzio, L., Schoelkopf, R.J., and Devoret, M.H. Variable and Orbital-Dependent Spin-Orbit Field Orientations in a InSb Double Quantum Dot Characterized via Dispersive Gate. Vol. 8, 1–42, (2017). arXiv:1712.05854.

7 Kurpiers, P., Magnard, P., Walter, T., Royer, B., Pechal, M., Heinsoo, J., Salathé, Y., Akin, A., Storz, S., Besse, J.-C., Gasparinetti, S., Blais, A., and Wallraff, A. Deterministic quantum state transfer and generation of remote entanglement using microwave photons. *Nature* 558(7709) (2018). https://doi.org/10.1038/s41586-018-0195-y.

8 Chou, K.S., Blumoff, J.Z., Wang, C.S., Reinhold, P.C., Axline, C.J., Gao, Y.Y., Frunzio, L., Devoret, M.H., Jiang, L., and Schoelkopf, R.J. Deterministic teleportation of a quantum gate between two logical qubits. *Nature*, 561(7723): 368–373 (2018), https://doi.org/10.1038/s41586-018-0470-y.

9 Vogell, B., Vermersch, B., Northup, T.E. et al. (2017). *Quantum Science and Technology* 2: 045003.

10 Wilk, T., Webster, S.C., Kuhn, A., and Rempe, G. (2007). *Science* 317: 488.

11

Advance Quantum Computing

11.1 Introduction

Before this section, all of the algorithms in the Section 10.1 used supercomputers in a largely classical manner: in each algorithm of part I, the quantum computer's output is not a perturbation theory but a regular basis vector. As a result, the parallel computing state is seen in a way that is consistent with classical theory. These algorithms don't make use of the superposition or entanglement of sets of qubits. There is a quantum circuit that can execute the same computations at a comparable level of capability as a classical circuit. As a further step, we'll demonstrate that mathematical modeling is more effective than classical cognition. Specifically, this section focuses on real quantum algorithms, which exceed conventional algorithms in terms of performance [1].

Simple gates from quantum analogs of classical processing are included in these algorithms, as are other, more general unitary modifications that do not have a classical analog. When it comes to the geometry of n-qubit quantization alterations, they are always 2^n-dimensional complex state rotations. It was shown that all quantum transformations might be accomplished using basic gates by performing processes on nonstandard bases, whereas classical quantum operations only permute the standard basis elements. We now focus on quantum modifications that can be done quickly and how these changes help speed up specific computations. The key to creating a true quantum algorithm is to maximize the efficiency of these nonclassical fundamental unitary gates.

In the following sections, we will be discussing quantum computing using the conventional circuit model that we introduced in the area. We allow basic unitary changes with no classical equivalent, and in the same manner, we specified quantum analogs of classical computations by providing large sequences of simple quantum gates. Due to the similarities in the calculation processes, comparing the

Quantum Computing: A New Era of Computing, First Edition.
Kuldeep Singh Kaswan, Jagjit Singh Dhatterwal, Anupam Baliyan, and Shalli Rani.
© 2023 The Institute of Electrical and Electronics Engineers, Inc. Published 2023 by John Wiley & Sons, Inc.

efficiency of conventional algorithms is straightforward. While the circuit model was used to develop the first quantum algorithms, it is not the only or even the best framework to utilize when planning the structure of a quantum algorithm. Different from the taste of the algorithms used in the classic coupled inductor of quantum cryptography, the algorithms used in the various quantum computing models provide something new to the field. Some promising efforts to create quantum computers and new kinds of quantum cryptography may be seen in these models [2].

Circuit complexity, which includes the qubit count and the number of fundamental gates utilized, is a key metric of quantum algorithm effectiveness under a typical circuit model of quantum computing. In other cases, we want to know how well other components are being used, so we track the number of bits or qubits sent back and forth between two parties to complete a job or the number of incidents a function is called. For this reason, black box and oracle procedures are often used to describe these parts, which are so named because they are supposed to be impenetrable, only revealing their output when used. There are many ways of describing complications.

11.2 Computing with Superpositions

At the very least, many optimization algorithms use quantum analogs of conventional processing. Quantum algorithms often begin with the construction of a superposition state, which is then used to feed a classical circuit's quantum equivalent U_f, which computes the function f. If an algorithm were to stop here, it would have no benefit over a classical one. However, the quantum concurrency configuration leaves the system in a suitable starting place for quantum algorithm developers. With the translational concurrency setup, both Shor and Grover's algorithms begin [3].

11.2.1 The Walsh–Hadamard Transformation

One of the initial steps in many quantum algorithms is to construct a permutation of all input parameters by using the Walsh–Hadamard transformation, which is an extension of the Hadamard modernization $\frac{1}{\sqrt{2}}(|0\rangle + |1\rangle)$. All 2^n standard foundation vectors, which may be seen when n qubits in state |0 are overlaid with the encoding scheme of the numbers 0 through 2^n, [4].

$$(H \otimes H \otimes \cdots \otimes H) \mid 00 \ldots 0$$
$$= \frac{1}{\sqrt{2^n}}((|0\rangle + |1\rangle) \otimes (|0\rangle + |1\rangle) \otimes \cdots \otimes (|0\rangle + |1\rangle))$$

$$= \frac{1}{\sqrt{2^n}} (|0\ldots00\rangle + |0\ldots01\rangle + |0\ldots10$$

$$= \frac{1}{\sqrt{2^n}} \sum_{x=0}^{2^n-1} |x\rangle$$

The Walsh, or Walsh–Hadamard, transformation is the metamorphosis $W = H H H$ that appears to apply H on all the qubits in an n-qubit setup. Using $N = 2^n$, we may express this as follows:

$$W|0\rangle = \frac{1}{\sqrt{N}} \sum_{x=0}^{N-1} |x\rangle$$

Understanding the impact of W in quantum cryptography may be better understood with a different manner of expressing W [5]. This matrix W, called the n-qubit Walsh–Hadamard matrix, has entries Permodalan nasional berhad (pnb) and is of dimension 2^n in the consistent schedule, such that

$$W_{sr} = W_{rs} = \frac{1}{\sqrt{2^n}}(-1)^{r \cdot s}$$

S and R each have an odd number of common ones (r) and an even number of odd ones (s), respectively, that vary from zero to 2^n. In order to demonstrate this equality, take notice of the fact that

$$W(|r\rangle) = \sum_s W_{rs}|s\rangle$$

A resulting value of r may look like $r_{n-1}\ldots r_0$, while a resulting value of s could look like $s_{n-1}\ldots s_0$.

$$W(|r\rangle) = (H \otimes \cdots \otimes H)(|r_{n-1}\rangle \otimes \cdots \otimes |r_0\rangle)$$

$$= \frac{1}{\sqrt{2^n}} \left(|0\rangle + (-1)^{r_{n-1}}|1\rangle\right) \otimes \cdots \otimes \left(|0\rangle + (-1)^{r_0}|1\rangle\right)$$

$$= \frac{1}{\sqrt{2^n}} \sum_{s=0}^{2^n-1} (-1)^{s_{n-1}r_{n-1}}|s_{n-1}\rangle \otimes \cdots \otimes (-1)^{s_0 r_0} \mid s_0$$

$$= \frac{1}{\sqrt{2^n}} \sum_{s=0}^{2^n-1} (-1)^{s \cdot r}|s\rangle$$

11.2.2 Quantum Parallelism

For input values of type a $|x$, any linear innovation of the form $U_f = |x,y|x,y \, f(x)$ from Section 11.1. operates as follows:

$$U_f : \sum_x a_x|x,0\rangle \rightarrow \sum_x a_x|x,f(x)\rangle$$

Take into account what happens when U_f is applied to the aggregation of values between 0 and 2^n that is the result of the Walsh reinvention:

$$U_f : (W|0\rangle \otimes |0\rangle) = \frac{1}{\sqrt{N}}\sum_{x=0}^{N-1}|x\rangle|0\rangle \rightarrow \frac{1}{\sqrt{N}}\sum_{x=0}^{N-1}|x\rangle f(x)\rangle$$

All 2^n values of $f(x)$ are now interspersed with the input values x after only a single application of U_f to the superposition. This phenomenon is known as quantum concurrency. By storing an exponentially large number of computed values in a proportional amount of space, quantum concurrently circumvents the trade-off between temporal and spatial that characterizes traditional optimizations. This effect, however, is not as significant as it may appear at first [5].

To begin, the aggregation provides just a limited amount of data: the $2n$ values of f are not available separately. It is only possible to learn about a system's current state by observing it, but only one information pair, and a random one at that, can be used to project the end state onto the system. The following simple example highlights how pointless the raw combination resulting from quantum parallel processing is, without any extra adjustments, in the context of this simple example.

Example 11.1 *Combining two numbers is a breeze with the help of* T, *the controlled-controlled-not (Toffoli) gate*

You will need a single qubit register to hold the output and a concatenation of all possible x and y bit configurations as inputs. This input state is constructed using translational parallel processing in the usual manner:

$$W(|00\rangle \otimes |0\rangle) = \frac{1}{\sqrt{2}}(|0\rangle + |1\rangle) \otimes \frac{1}{\sqrt{2}}(|0\rangle + |1\rangle) \otimes |0$$

$$= \frac{1}{2}(|000\rangle + |010\rangle + |100\rangle + |110\rangle)$$

Combining these inputs via a Toffoli gate T produces

$$T(W|00\rangle \otimes |0\rangle) = \frac{1}{2}(|000\rangle + |010\rangle + |100\rangle + |111\rangle)$$

A truth table for conjunction may be constructed from this composition. It is possible to measure the truth table using the works by having and yet getting a single line of the truth table. Using quantum concurrency to compute and then measure on a conventional basis has no benefit over classical concurrency: just one result is achieved, and even worse, we have no control over which result we get [6].

11.3 Notions of Complexity

According to complexity theory, a computation's asymptotic resource require-ments, such as time or space, may be calculated. The formal computing model provided by Turing machines is often used to argue about the complexity of computational systems. To build quantum Turing machines, first David Deutsch, then Andrew Yao, then Ethan Bernstein, and ultimately Umesh Vazirani it possible to formalize quantum complexity and compare it to classical findings. A variety of additional models, such as the circuit model, may be used to express complexity concepts in both quantum and classical contexts. Most of the research on quantum algorithms has focused on the complexity of quantum circuits; thus, this book follows suit. Quantum query complexity is another prominent complexity metric used in the investigation of quantum algorithms. The difficulty of quantum communication protocols may also be assessed using a variety of other metrics [7].

There are a number of circuits in this family, and the circuit Cn is indexed by its maximum input size, which is n (bits or qubits). It is necessary to specify the set of simple gates to be considered when determining the C-complexity of a circuit. Any of the finite sets of gates introduced so far may be used, as may the infinite set of single-qubit operations and the C_{not}. With an upper bound of $O(f(n))$, the asymp-totic number of simple gates in the circuits has a complexity of $O(f(n))$. $O(f(n))$ time complexity is associated with counting the asymptotic number of simple gates in a circuit family $C = Cn$. All the simple gate families we have covered so far have the same asymptotic circuit complexity.

In models of nonuniform hardware implementation, larger input sizes need the use of other, more robust circuits. Both quantum and classical Turing machines offer a single computer that can process input of any size. Circuit complexity is harder to express than Turing machine complexity due to the nonuniformity of circuit models. This is because the complexity of constructing circuits may hide the complexity of the circuits themselves (Cn). Uniformity conditions must be implemented if we want to achieve meaningful complexity metrics, such as cir-cuit complexity measures that are comparable to Turing machine-based ones. The homogeneity requirements used by both quantum and classical circuit complexity are the same [8].

Additionally, circuits Cn within a circuit family C must operate consistently in order to meet the uniformity criteria as well. A common way to express this condition is to use the formula $g(x)$, which claims that all circuits $Cn \cdot C$ with input x yield the function $g(x)$. It is a frequent misconception that this criterion limits the $g(x)$ functions that may be calculated by a circuit family. The reason for this is because the consistency requirement need not include a function g directly; rather, it may be easily generalized (x).

Being consistent is essential. Both in a quantum and a classical circuit, the result of the circuit Cn applied to the input x of size m must be the same as the result of C_m applied to the same input. If the results from Cn's circuits are reliable, then Cn is completely compatible. This homogeneity criterion is based on the polynomial one, which is the most prevalent.

Uniformity condition: A quantum or classical circuit family $C = \{C_n\}$ is *polynomially uniform* if there exists a polynomial-time classical algorithm that generates the circuits. In other words, C is polynomially uniform if there exists a polynomial $f(n)$ and a classical program that, given n, constructs the circuit Cn in at most $O(f(n))$ steps [9]. Because of the homogeneity criterion, no circuit may have an arbitrary level of complexity. In both the conventional and quantum settings, it is widely known that the complexities of a Turing computer are proportional to the number of elements in a family of uniform and consistent circuits. Every classical function $g(x)$ that can be calculated in $O(f(n)\log f(n))$ time on a Turing machine has a family of classical circuits that are uniform and consistent, and their complexity is polynomial in $f(n)$. In contrast, a Turing machine may model a consistent collection of Boolean circuits with polynomial uniformity. Yao has shown that each conceivable computation may be carried out on a quantum Turing machine by a family of polynomial-sized quantum circuits. Every known family of quadratically uniform, dependable quantum circuits may be shown to be easily mimicked by a quantum Turing machine. Since we are only interested in discrepancies of at most a polynomial in $\log(f(n))$, we study quantum computational complexity of hardware implementation with the polynomial homogeneity criterion rather than using quantum Turing computer systems.

11.3.1 Query Complexity

Black box or oracle issues are solved by the first quantum algorithms. $f(x)$ is the output of a classical black box when x is fed into it. Like U_f, a quantum black box's output upon receiving an input from an effective implementation of theoretical entities such as black boxes is impossible to predict. Because of this, they are referred to as oracles. For example, if you want to solve an issue, all you must do is look at what comes out of a black box; you cannot see inside. When discussing black box issues, query complexity is the most prevalent sort of difficulty: how many oracle calls are necessary to solve the problem?

An efficient implementation of the black box is required to employ low-complexity black box algorithms, such as algorithms that solve black box problems with a minimal number of calls to the oracle. To put bottom constraints on a problem's circuit complexity, however, the black box technique is quite helpful. It is necessary to have an adequate level of circuit complexity if the minimum of (N) requests to the oracle are required to answer a single question (N).

Black boxes have been used to prove that the number of telephone calls to a quantum oracle necessary to solve certain issues is strictly smaller than the number of calls to a classical oracle required to solve the same problem.

The first optimization algorithms have the potential to address black box problems: such puzzles include the Deutsch–Jozsa conundrum, the Bernstein–Vazirani puzzle, and the Simon's puzzle. The most well-known finding for query complexity in unconstrained search over N things was discovered by Grover; it only takes $O(N)$ calls to a quantum black box to get what you are looking for (N). To what extent does Grover's approach's superior query complexity contribute to real-world applications [10].

11.3.2 Communication Complexity

The minimal number of bits or qubits that can only be communicated to fulfill a job is a typical complexity metric for network topologies. Some additional resources, such as the quantity of various pieces exchanged or the rate at which quantum EPR pairs may be of relevance as well, depending on the application. Depending on whether experimental or classical knowledge must be transferred, whether qubits or bits may be conveyed, and which associated components can be employed, several concepts of communicative complication exist.

We have previously seen a few instances of the effects of communication complexity. Dense coding is concerned with the number of qubits required to transmit n pieces of information as a measure of complexity. The transmission of n bits of information via conventional protocols requires n bits of data, but only $n/2$ qubits are required with quantum protocols. When it comes to EPR pairs (also known as ebits in the communications protocol environment), the number of pairs needed is $n/2$. Instead of sending qubits, as is the case with teleportation, it tries to do it using a conventional channel that can only convey bits. The basic idea is the number of bits needed to transmit n qubits' worth of subatomic particles. With the help of quantum entanglement, it is possible to transmit the state of n qubits using just 2^n bits. For every n-qubit teleport, n is the number of ebits involved.

There are no bits or qubits involved in the distributed computing protocol described, but it does need n ebits to do an enormously massive bit string computation work, bit strings of length $N = 2^n$. In order to implement a classical solution, a minimum of $N/2$ bits must be sent. We will just briefly explore network communications difficulty in this book since this is a book on quantum computing not on classical telecommunication.

11.4   A Simple Quantum Algorithm

This is the first time we can talk about a quantum algorithm. In 1985, David Deutsch demonstrated that quantum computing may outperform traditional computation using this approach. The algorithm developed by Deutsch deals with a mystery. If you want to know how many calls to the black box you need to make to get to the answer, you need a quantum algorithm that can do it with much less effort. Algorithm is too simplistic for practical usage but incorporates a few crucial features of inherently quantum computing, such as the use of non – standard work foundations and classical operations applied to combinations, which will be used in more complicated algorithms.

11.4.1   Deutsch's Problem

It is up to you to figure out whether the Boolean function f: $Z2$ $Z2$ is constant. U_f does a single invocation of the quantum algorithm developed by Deutsch (described below) to resolve the problem. In any system of equations using C_f, each input value requires its own call to a classical black box. Superposing the second qubit of input into the black box is the foundation of Deutsch's method, which uses functions such as providing. In this case, the extending is performed by the subroutine.

One bit function f may be represented by a change in time of two qubits, as we saw in Section 6.1. For this reason, when $|y = |0$, the application of U_f yields $|x|f$ (x). The algorithm U_f is applied on the two-qubit state $|+\rangle$, which consists of two values for each qubit that are overlaid to produce a single qubit $|-\rangle$. The results that we are able to achieve

$$U_f(|+\rangle|-\rangle)$$
$$= U_f\left(\frac{1}{2}(|0\rangle + |1\rangle)(|0\rangle - |1\rangle)\right)$$
$$= \frac{1}{2}(|0\rangle(|\,0 \oplus f\,(0)\rangle = |1 \oplus f(0)\rangle) + |1\rangle(|\,0 \oplus f\,(1)\rangle - |\,1 \oplus f\,(1)\rangle))$$

In other words,

$U_f(|+\rangle|-\rangle) = \frac{1}{2}\sum_{x=0}^{1}|x\rangle(|\,0 \oplus f\,(x)\rangle - |1 \oplus f(x)\rangle)$ When $f(x) = 0$, $\frac{1}{\sqrt{2}}(|0 \oplus f(x)\rangle -$
$|1 \oplus f(x)\rangle)$ becomes $\frac{1}{\sqrt{2}}(|0\rangle - |1\rangle) = |-$. When $f(x) = 1$, $\frac{1}{\sqrt{2}}(|0 \oplus f(x)\rangle - |1 \oplus f(x)\rangle)$
becomes $\frac{1}{\sqrt{2}}(|1\rangle - |0\rangle) = -1 -\rangle$. Therefore $U_f\left(\frac{1}{\sqrt{2}}\sum_{x=0}^{1}|x\rangle|-\rangle\right) = \frac{1}{\sqrt{2}}\sum_{x=0}^{1}(-1)^{f(x)}$
$|x| - f(x) |+\rangle$ is the only possible state for which (1) is a physically meaningless global phase. Because the term (1) negates one of the terms in the quantum system when f is not consistent, and the state is up to a global phase. Using the

Hadamard transformations H, we can confidently determine whether the initial qubit is $|0\rangle$ in the first instance or $|1\rangle$ in the second. If f is a constant, we can determine that with a single call to U_f. A quantum algorithm that outperforms all other algorithms is now a reality!

For those who are unfamiliar with quantum physics, it may come as a surprise to learn that this method can provide results with a high degree of accuracy. We currently understand that the first of these assumptions does not do because we research quantum analogs to classical calculations. The solution to Deutsch's dilemma demonstrates that even quantum phenomena need not be unpredictable.

11.5 Quantum Subroutines

Now we will take a look at some useful nonclassical techniques that may be performed on an optimization technique. Specific procedure is utilized in Grover's algorithm and most basic quantum algorithms, including the Deutsch–Jozsa problem, an extension of Deutsch's issue with more than one bit. Although these stored procedures are not utilized all across the manual, we explain them here to show how to deal with computational quantum mechanics in more detail.

11.5.1 The Importance of Unentangling Temporary Qubits in Quantum Subroutines

To save space in classical calculations, underline the need of uncomputing temporarily utilized bits. Even when saving space and recycling qubits is not a concern, it is critical in quantum communication to uncompute momentary qubit scans because doing so prevents entanglement between the combinatorial qubits and the momentary qubits, which might lead to calculation failure. Subroutine promises to calculate state only if it has the ability to do so. $\sum_i \alpha_i x_i|$, it is not okay I fit actually computes $\sum_i \alpha_i x_i y_i\|$ and until there is wave-particle duality between the two frequencies, discard the qubits holding $|y_i$. If, then there is no tangling. $\sum_i \alpha_i x_i y_i\|i$, which can happen only if $|y_i = |y_j$ for all i and j. In general, the states $\alpha_i|x_i|y_i$ if we have information to only one register of the second frame, which addresses quantum components, we may speak about the distinctions between these two conditions without looking at the computational repercussions. As an example, we will explain how utilizing the first state while anticipating the second might lead to unexpected results in this paragraph. To be more specific, we demonstrate that if we use the black box for V_f instead of U_f in Deutsch's issue,

$$V_f : |x, t, y\rangle \rightarrow |x, t \oplus x, y \oplus f(x)\rangle$$

Deutsch's algorithm is no longer applicable. As before, the first qubit is in the $|+\rangle$ state, while the third is in the $|$ state. Using V_f will allow you to gain.

$$V_f(|+\rangle|0\rangle|-\rangle) = V_f \left(\frac{1}{\sqrt{2}} \sum_{x=0}^{1} |x\rangle|0\rangle|-\rangle \right) = \frac{1}{\sqrt{2}} \sum_{x=0}^{1} (-1)^{f(x)} |x\rangle \, | \, x \, | -$$

The first and second qubits are now intertwined. Because of this interference, it is no longer possible to measure the first qubit after administering H. Example: The state is $(|00+|11)|$ when f is consistent and executing results in the environment

$$\frac{1}{2}(|00\rangle + |10\rangle + |01\rangle - |11\rangle)|-\rangle$$

Previously, the second and fourth terms were annulled, but this is no longer the case. The initial qubit may now be measured as either $|0\rangle$ or $|1\rangle$. A similar computation reveals that the initial qubit may be measured as either $|0\rangle$ or $|1\rangle$ when the function is not constant. This has led to the inability to differentiate between the two. When used as interference, the qubit $|t$ destroys the quantum computer's ability to do calculations quickly and accurately.

A valid uncomputed state after the computation would have allowed the method to function as intended. As an example, let's say that f is a constant. $\frac{1}{2}(|00\rangle + |10\rangle + |00\rangle - |10\rangle)$ In this situation, $(|00\rangle)|$ would be the resulting word. In order for a quantum procedure to claim to create a state $|$, it cannot generate a state that is associated with other qubits. Furthermore, any qubits used in the subroutine must not be intertwined with the other qubits after the subroutine is complete. Because of this, the following subatomic stored procedures are cautious to uncompute any supplementary qubits so that they are always in state $|0$ at the conclusion of the computation.

11.5.2 Phase Change for a Subset of Basis Vectors

Aim Change the phase of terms in a superposition $|\psi \sum a_i i=|$ depending on whether i is in a subset X of $\{0, 1,..., N-1\}$ or not. Instead, we are looking for an effective way to apply the quantum transition.

$$S_X^\phi : \sum_{x=0}^{N-1} a_x |x\rangle \rightarrow \sum_{x \in X} a_x e^{i\phi} |x\rangle + \sum_{x \notin X} a_x |x\rangle$$

An arbitrary unitary progression was discussed without consideration of efficiency. The integration of S_X would need more than $N = 2^n$ simple gates if that method were used mindlessly. An efficient implementation of the transformations S_X is shown in this section for every efficiently quantifiable subset. The S_X implementation technique allows some of the quantum cryptography; we will talk about later to surpass its classical counterparts.

Only if the Boolean expression can be used to compute memberships in X can we expect to build S_X in an effective manner. $f: Z_2{}^n \rightarrow Z_2$, where

$$f(x) = \begin{cases} 1 & \text{if } x \in X \\ 0 & \text{otherwise} \end{cases}$$

It must be a polynomial in n that can be efficiently computed. This trait is absent from most of X's subsets. The major conclusion of Chapter 6 indicates that an efficient quantum circuit exists for U_f for subsets X with this feature. S_X can be computed with a few more steps if we have an implementation of U_f like this. Uncompacting the temporary qubit's value removes any remaining entanglement with the rest of the state. Thus, we utilize the value of the momentary qubit in the phase transformation.

Since

$$T(-\phi/2)K(\phi/2) = \begin{pmatrix} 1 & 0 \\ 0 & e^{i\phi} \end{pmatrix}$$

If bit an is one, then steps (3) and (4), which introduce the single-qubit operations, shift the phase by e^i. Even though technically step (3) is superfluous since it results in a useless global phase shift; nevertheless, it does make it easier to notice that our objective has been met. Steps (3) and (4) may be omitted in favor of a single step | |, where I can be any of the qubits in register x, since adding a phase into any product term is equivalent to introducing it into any other term. In order to guarantee that register |x is in its desired state, free of the relatively short-term qubits, the interaction between |x and the qubits must be uncomputed in step (5).

For the special case = another, surprisingly straightforward approach generalizes the technique employed in the solution for Deutsch's issue to accommodate the crucial particular case =. Given U_f as described above, the transformation may be realized by computing into a temporary qubit b initialized to |=. Consider |ψ $\sum_{x \in X} a_x x = | + \sum_{x \notin X} a_x | x$, and compute

$$U_f(|\psi\rangle \otimes |-\rangle) = U_f\left(\sum_{x \in X} a_x |x\rangle \otimes |-\rangle\right) + U_f\left(\sum_{x \notin X} a_x |x\rangle \otimes |-\rangle\right)$$

$$= -\left(\sum_{x \in X} a_x |x\rangle \otimes |-\rangle\right) + \left(\sum_{x \in X} a_x |x\rangle \otimes |-\rangle\right)$$

$$= \left(S_X^\pi |\psi\rangle\right) \otimes |-\rangle$$

In Figure 11.1 superposition may be achieved using the following circuit, which modulates the n-qubit state |0 with the help of a qubit in state |1. $|\psi_X\rangle = \sum (-1)^{f(x)} |x\rangle$:

The circuit becomes more attractive if we want to execute a last Hadamard reconfiguration on the ancilla qubit so that it may be reused (Figure 11.2).

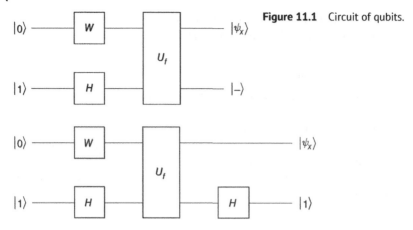

Figure 11.1 Circuit of qubits.

Figure 11.2 Structure of ancilla qubit.

Invention relationship between perceived to the straight line S_X is a reflection of the N-dimensional k-dimensional hyperplane into the higher-dimensional k-dimensional space defined by: In a hyperplane, a reflection of a vector| v perpendicular to the hyperplane becomes its antipodal|v. Each U undergoes the same alteration. Grover's approach is based on this geometric representation of S_X, which is the hyperplane corresponding to the higher-dimensional space spanned by the vectors $U|x|x$ and X.

If we apply this to the conjunction $W|0$, we get the following expression as a result:

$$\frac{1}{\sqrt{N}} \sum (-1)^{f(x)} \mid x$$

where f is a Boolean function indicating whether or not X is a member,

$$f(x) = \begin{cases} 1 & \text{if } x \in X \\ 0 & \text{otherwise} \end{cases}$$

Instead, if we are given a Boolean function f, we may write S_f as S_X, where $X = x|f(x) = 1$.

11.5.3 State-Dependent Phase Shifts

Invention redounding to when thinking about the N-dimensional hyperplane in the higher-dimensional space of k, S_X is a straight line of reflection. When a hyperplane is reflected, a vector orthogonal to the plane becomes a vector horizontal to the opposite side of the plane. No matter whatever U you choose, the translation is the same. Grover's approach is based on this geometric representation of S_X, which is the hyperplane correlating to the space of higher dimensions spanned by the vectors $U|x|x$ and X.

The outcome of applying the conjunction $W|0$ may be written as follows:

$$\approx 2\pi \frac{f(x)}{2^s} \varphi(x)$$

Constructing f can only be as efficient as f if f is expensive. Along with these two applications, a quantum circuit that conveniently implements U_f may also allow us to achieve the state-dependent frequency response in $O(s)$ steps. Unlike most functions, f can be rapidly calculated, which is a very useful property.

This section demonstrates how to optimally plan for an activity that shifts the phase of an s-conventional qubit's basis state $|x$ according to the angle $= \frac{2\pi x}{2^s} \varphi(x)$.

Let

$$P(\phi) = T(-\phi/2)K(\phi/2) = \begin{pmatrix} 1 & 0 \\ 0 & e^{i\phi} \end{pmatrix}$$

When bit 1 is set, this transformation changes the phase of the qubit; when bit 0 is set, nothing happens. It is a thing define Phase $|a[s]\rangle = $ for $i \in [0\ldots s-1]$ performs the s-qubit transformation phase:

$$|a\rangle \rightarrow \exp\left(i2\pi \frac{a}{2^s}\right)|a\rangle$$

The accompanying program incorporates the Phase program as a subroutine: transmutation of qubits Stage is the last stage.

11.5.4 State-Dependent Single-Qubit Amplitude Shifts

Each word in a permutation may be approximately represented by a single-qubit rotation $R((x))$, where the angle (x) depends on the quantum state of the other register. Fundamentally, what we're after is a transformation that sticks around for quite some time.

$$|x\rangle \otimes |b\rangle \rightarrow |x\rangle \otimes (R(\beta(x))|b\rangle)$$

where $\beta\left(\approx f(x)\frac{2\pi}{2^s}x\right)$. It is easy to compute an approximation function $f: Zn\ Zs$. with a good implementation of U_f, this change can be made in $O(s)$ time plus two calls to the function. The function takes the value in the register and multiplies it by an auxiliary translation Rot to increase the size of qubit b.

$a; |a\rangle \otimes |b\rangle \rightarrow |a\rangle \otimes \left(R\left(a\frac{2\pi}{2^s}\right)|b\rangle\right)_s$ Up to a precision of 2, the elements of the S-qubit register provide the angle that may be rotated Figure 11.3 depicts a Rot-enabled circuit, as shown. Our program nomenclature allows us to express this change in a more compact manner.

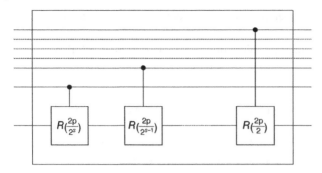

Figure 11.3 Circuit for controlled rotation.

Define for $i \in [0\ldots s, 1]|ai$ control. The software may carry out the required rotation, as defined by the function. Define $\mathrm{Rot}_f |x[k]\rangle |b[1]\rangle =$ qubit $a[s]$ an s-bit temporary register $U_f |x\rangle |a\rangle$ compute f in a Rot $|a,b$ perform rotation by $2\pi a/2s\, U_f^{-1} |x\rangle \mid a$ uncompute the value of function.

11.6   A Few Simple Quantum Algorithms

A few elementary quantum algorithms are introduced here. The first three problems are examples of what are called "black box" or "oracle" challenges, and the quantum solution excels in terms of query sophistication. With regard to the fourth problem, the quantum protocol explanation is more effective than the difficulties themselves. Although they may seem artificial, these problems have basic numerical approaches that may be shown to be more cost-effective than any possible classical methodology. Deutsch is difficult to learn. Methods like Deutsch's provide concrete answers to such problems.

11.6.1   Deutsch–Jozsa Problem

There is a quantum technique for the issue described below, which is an extension of David Deutsch's previous situation. A function f is said to be balancing if it returns 0 and 1 for an equal number of input values. It is possible to establish whether or not using either a fixed frequency or a balanced functionality Z_2 and the phenomenological oracle, we may determine whether or not f is a constant or symmetrical. To the might of x and y, with love, $uf\colon xy\,xyf\,(x)$

Phase-change procedure excludes all of the aggregation terms pertaining to basis vectors that have $f(x)$ equal to 1. The state is returned by the function.

$$|\psi\rangle = \frac{1}{\sqrt{N}} \sum_{i=0}^{N-1} (-1)^{f(i)} |i\rangle$$

In state I, a temporary qubit is used in the subroutine. That qubit must be unentangled from other qubits at the conclusion of the subroutine, as seen in Deutsch's method. The output may then be obtained by applying the Walsh transformation W to this state I.

$$||\phi\rangle = \frac{1}{N} \sum_{i=0}^{N-1} \left((-1)^{f(i)} \sum_{j=0}^{N-1} (-1)^{i \cdot j} |j\rangle \right)$$

For a fixed value of f, the $(1)f(i) = (1)f(0)$ phase transition and the state I are equivalent:

$$(-1)^{f(0)} \frac{1}{2^n} \sum_{j \in Z_2^n} \left(\sum_{j \in Z_2^n} (-1)^{i \cdot j} \right) |j\rangle = (-1)^{f(0)} \frac{1}{2^n} \sum_{j \in Z_2^n} (-1)^{i \cdot 0} |0\rangle = (-1)f(0) \mid 0$$

because, as box shows, $\sum_{i \in Z_2^n} (-1)^{i \cdot j} = 0$ for $j \neq 0$.   For f balanced

$$|\phi\rangle = \frac{1}{2^n} \sum_{j \in Z_2^n} \left(\sum_{i \in X_0} (-1)^{i \cdot j} - \sum_{i \notin X_0} (-1)^{i \cdot j} \right) |j$$

In the limit when $X_0 = x|f(x) = 0$, we have the following. For once, when $j = 0$, the amplitude is zero:

$$\sum_{j \in X_0} (-1)^{i \cdot j} - \sum_{j \notin X_0} (-1)^{i \cdot j} = 0$$

Accordingly, if f is constant, monitoring state I has likelihood 1, but monitoring state $|j$ will produce a nonzero $|j$ when the command is executed, with the same frequency.

Despite the fact that $2^{n+1} + 1$ iterations of f are required to solve the Deutsch–Jozsa problem using standard methods, one may do it using our quantum solution, which just requires one examination of U_f. Consequently, there is an exponential difference in query difficulty between this fundamental method and any plausible conventional algorithm that answers the issue with confidence. The issue can be solved with less evaluations using traditional methods, but only with a proven track record of completion.

11.6.2   Bernstein–Vazirani Problem

An unsuspecting bit string u of length n is to be valued, with only $q u$ enquiries allowed for some query string q. $O(n)$ calls to $fu(q) = q u \bmod 2$ are the best conventional algorithm. Using a computer program, a quantum method can locate u in only one call to U_{fu}: on a quantum computer, you can find u precisely with a single iteration. Deutsch–Jozsa (in superposition). Let $fu(q) = q u \bmod 2$ and then

$$U_{fu} : |q\rangle |b\rangle \mapsto |q\rangle |b \oplus f_u(q)\rangle$$

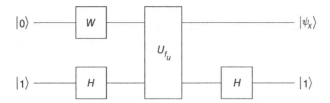

Figure 11.4 Structure of Bernstein–Vazirani problem.

The following circuit (Figure 11.4) solves this problem with certainty using only one call to U_{fu}. To understand how this circuit works, recall from that in the special case $\varphi = \pi$, the phase change subroutine can be accomplished by the circuit.

As a consequence of implementing this circuit, the following state is achieved:

$$|\psi_X\rangle = \frac{1}{\sqrt{2^n}} \sum_q (-1)^{f_u(q)} |q\rangle = \frac{1}{\sqrt{2^n}} \sum_q (-1)^{u \cdot q} \,|\, a$$

at the lowest key possible. The Walsh–Hadamard transformations W may be applied to this condition to obtain the state shown in the next couple of sentences. $|u$.

Recall that $W|x\rangle = \frac{1}{\sqrt{2^n}} \sum_z (-1)^{x \cdot z} |z\rangle$. Thus

$$W|\psi_X\rangle = W\left(\frac{1}{\sqrt{2^n}} \sum_q (-1)^{u \cdot q} |q\rangle\right)$$

$$= \frac{1}{\sqrt{2^n}} \sum_q (-1)^{u \cdot q} W|q\rangle$$

$$= \frac{1}{2^n} \sum_q (-1)^{u \cdot q} \left(\sum_z (-1)^{q \cdot z} |z\rangle\right) \tag{11.1}$$

A fact from box tells us that $(-1)^{u \cdot q + z \cdot q} = (-1)(u \oplus z) \cdot q$. The only component that remained is the $u = z$ term, as shown by Eq. (11.1), which states that the external total is zero unless when $uz = 0$ in Figure 11.5.

$$W\left(|\psi_X\rangle = \frac{1}{2^n} \sum_z \left(\sum_q (-1)^{u \cdot q + z \cdot q}\right) \neq z|u\rangle\right)$$

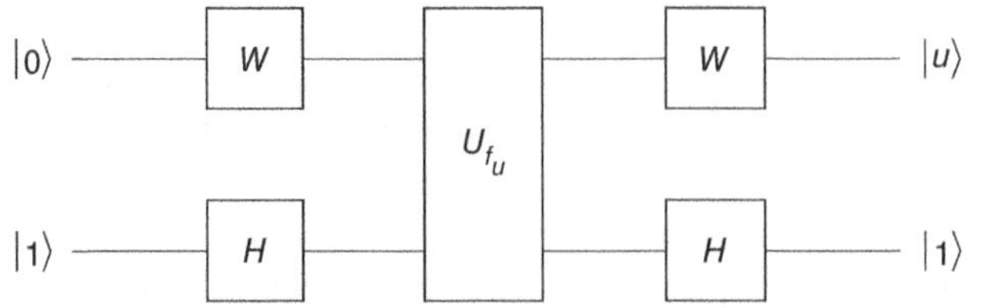

Figure 11.5 Algorithm circuitry based on the work of Bernstein and Vazirani.

Thus, the use of a consistent foundation for measurement provides $|u$ with a level of assurance. Quantum algorithms may be explained by computing on all possible inputs at once, utilizing quantum parallelism and then managing the resulting superposition effectively. The Bernstein–Vazirani algorithm may be understood from our description of this setting. The quantum superposition interpretation of algorithms may not be the most fruitful. To back up our claim, we provide a new interpretation of Mermin's original technique.

Mermin's algorithm explanations rely on the Hadamard basis. For U_{fu}, the quantum black box described by the Hadamard basis behaves as if it included a circuit with C_{not} transactions from some of the qubits to the ancilla qubit: this circuit contains a C_{not} from the ancilla to qubit I only if the ith bit of u is 1. Remember the Hadamard techniques for reverse control and endpoint qubit leadership roles (Figure 11.6):

Starting with state $|0...0|1$, the Bernstein–Vazirani algorithms work Hadamard modifications to each qubit before and after calling U_{fu}'s black box. A circuit comprising exclusively of C_{not} transactions the 1-bits in u from the supplemental qubit to the entangled particles that correspond to them is how the Bernstein–Vazirani algorithm operates. Figure 11.7 illustrates this point.

When u is set to 01101, the black box representing U_{fu} acts as if it were equipped with the following circuit, which consists of C_{not} gates for each 1-bit of u in Figure 11.8.

For $u = 01101$

C_{not}

Figure 11.6 Structure of Hadamard.

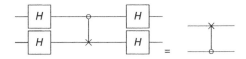

Figure 11.7 Structure of Hadamard modifications.

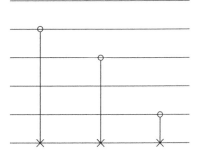

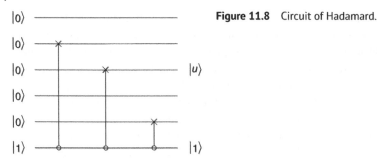

$|0\rangle$ ——————————————

$|0\rangle$ —————

$|0\rangle$ ————— $|u\rangle$

$|0\rangle$ —————

$|0\rangle$ —————

$|1\rangle$ ————— $|1\rangle$

Figure 11.8 Circuit of Hadamard.

The Bernstein–Vazirani algorithm mimics the behavior of a system built up of small circuits, one for each bit of u. When viewed in this way, the circuit guarantees that the qubits will reach the $|u$ state. You can get the right idea with this far less complicated explanation that does not include quantum superposition or "computing on all possible inputs."

11.6.3 Simon's Problem

Simon's problem: locate a hidden string when given a two-to-one function f such that $f(x) = f(x\,a)$ for all. In contrast to the $O(n)$ calls to U_f and extra $O(n^2)$ steps required by the method described by Simon, which can identify a, conventional algorithms are limited to $O(2^n/2)$. He came up with a technique for factorization that is now known as Shor's algorithm after he was inspired by Simon's algorithm, we shall see that Shor's algorithm and Simon's automated system have considerable overlap [11].

Making the superposition allows us to find a. When we take a reading from the right side of the register, we may extrapolate the value of the left register as, where $f(x_0)$ is the reading, we took from the right side. If we use the Walsh–Hadamard transform W, we get

$$W\left(\frac{1}{\sqrt{2}}(|x_0\rangle + |x_0 \oplus a\rangle)\right) = \frac{1}{\sqrt{2}}\left(\frac{1}{\sqrt{2^n}}\sum_y \left((-1)^{x_0\cdot y} + (-1)^{(x_0\oplus a)\cdot y}\right)|y\rangle\right)$$

$$= \frac{1}{\sqrt{2^{n+1}}}\sum_y (-1)^{x_0\cdot y}(1 + (-1)^{a\cdot y})|y\rangle$$

$$= \frac{2}{\sqrt{2^{n+1}}}\sum_{y\cdot a \text{ even}} (-1)^{x_0\cdot y}|y\rangle$$

If we generate a random y such that $y\cdot a = 0\bmod 2$, then the unknown bits a_i of a must satisfy the equation $y_0\,a_0\,y_{n1}\,a_{n1} = 0$. Keep going until you've found n characteristic equation arithmetic and solved them all. Every time this computation is performed, there is a 50% chance that the resulting equation will be linearly independent of the equations that came before it. After 2^n calculations, 50% of the time you'll have an independent equation. These equations can be solved for in $O(n^2)$ time steps. Finding the secret string an is expected to take $O(n)$ calls to U_f, and $O(n^2)$ steps to solve the resulting equations [12].

11.6.4 Distributed Computation

An entirely new kind of quantum algorithm is discussed in this section, one whose account for the differences is an issue. Entangling pairs may be disseminated beforehand and are not considered as qubits transferred during the computing of the problem, like dense programming and transportation, yet even after accounting for them, the savings growth rate remains exponential.

Each of Alice and Bob is provided with an N-bit number, u or v, as shown below. In order to do this, Alice must calculate n-bit number a, and Bob must calculate n-bit quantity b.

$$d_{\mathrm{H}}(u, v) = 0 \rightarrow a = b$$

$$d_{\mathrm{H}}(u, v) = N/2 \rightarrow a \neq b$$

else $\rightarrow$ no condition on a and b

When comparing two points u and v, the Hamming distance, denoted by d_{H} (u,v), is used. Alice and Bob are looking for an algorithm that would produce a and b given any two inputs, with the following properties: if $u = 0$, then $a = 0$, and for any two inputs where the distance measured between them is more than or equal to $N/2$, then $a = 0$.

Due to the fact that u and v are substantially larger than a and b, this is not an easy operation. With sufficient entanglement pairs, this problem may be solved, while a conventional solution requires communications between Alice and Bob of at least $N/2$ bits.

Let's suppose that Alice and Bob have n entangled pairs of particles (a_i, b_i) in state $+ |11$, and that Alice can connect directly a_i and Bob can access b_i. Because of this, we can represent the full 2^n-qubit state by writing $a_0, a_1, \ldots, a_n, b_0, b_1, \ldots, b_n$, where Alice controls the first n qubits and Bob controls the final n qubits.

The following is a method by which the issue may be fixed without the need for further dialogue. Alice applies the Walsh transform W to her n qubits after performing the phase change procedure described in Section 11.5.2 with $f(i) = ui$. When Bob uses $f(i) = vi$ on his n qubits, he, too, is able to execute the identical calculation. As a unit, their particles have joined the universal state.

$$|\psi\rangle = W \left(\frac{1}{\sqrt{N}} \sum_{i=0}^{N-1} (-1)^{u_i \oplus v_i} |i\rangle |i\rangle \right)$$

Alice and Bob now measure their respective part of the state to obtain results a and b. We need to show that a and b have the desired properties. a b measurement has a probability of $|x,x||2$. It is our goal to demonstrate that $H(u,v) = 2$ only holds if and only if $u = v$. The superscript in $W(1)$ denotes that W is functioning on a 1-qubit state, thus we can write down the simplified state as follows:

$$|\psi\rangle = W^{(2n)} \frac{1}{\sqrt{N}} \sum_{i=0}^{N-1} (-1)^{u_i \oplus v_i} |i\rangle |i\rangle$$

$$= \frac{1}{\sqrt{N}} \sum_{i=0}^{N-1} (-1)^{u_i \oplus v_i} (W^{(n)} |i\rangle \otimes W^{(n)} |i\rangle)$$

$$= \frac{1}{N\sqrt{N}} \sum_{i=0}^{N-1} \sum_{j=0}^{N-1} \sum_{k=0}^{N-1} (-1)^{u_i \oplus v_i} (-1)^{i \cdot j} (-1)^{i \cdot k} |jk\rangle$$

Now

$$x, x|\psi\rangle = \frac{1}{N\sqrt{N}} \sum_{i=0}^{N-1} (-1)^{u_i \oplus v_i} (-1)^{i \cdot x} (-1)^{i \cdot x}$$

$$= \frac{1}{N\sqrt{N}} \sum_{i=0}^{N-1} (-1)^{u_i \oplus v_i} \langle x, x | \psi \rangle |^2 = \frac{1}{N}$$

11.7 Comments on Quantum Parallelism

Our remarks are aimed at dispelling some of the misunderstandings about quantum parallelism's function in quantum computing. The encoding

$$\frac{1}{\sqrt{N}} \sum_{x=0}^{N-1} |x, f(x)$$

quantum operations on superpositions do exponentially more computing, according to this study $\sum_x x, 0|$.

- $f(x)$ can be computed more quickly with a classical computer than this. The next paragraph shows why this idea is incorrect, and quantum computing is so powerful. Like the exponential growth of the classical specifically, the state space corresponding to the n-qubit superposition state shows that quantum parallelism can always provide exponential gains in speed. In general, this assertion is inaccurate; however, in certain particular instances, quantum processing may yield speedups. Here, we provide a short explanation of each of the assertions [13].
- Only one input/output pair may be retrieved from the superposition formed by quantum parallelism. There is documentation that can only be retrieved to the extent of m bits from an m-qubit state, and there is no way to get more input/output pairs. The same number of U_f computations is needed to obtain all 2^n values of $f(x)$ in the classical situation, even if they all appeared in the

same fair and equitable way. A quantum computer may be able to perform in a single step any conventional process that requires 2^n steps to generate n bits of output. It is well established that no quantum technique can produce an increasing increase in speed for problems of this kind, as shown by Grover's algorithm's optimality over conventional approaches. There are other findings showing that quantum processing cannot give any speedup for various tasks. Although the notation suggests an exponential speedup, quantum parallelism and quantum processing in general do not.

- As a result, a superposition is merely one of many possible states in the place of quantum states. Given an n-qubit state space, an effective quantum algorithm cannot provide even a rough approximation of the vast majority of states. An effective quantum algorithm cannot access the overwhelming largest number of states in dynamical system. The complete state space cannot be used by quantum parallelism or effective quantum algorithms as a result.
- Even if the Bernstein–Vazirani algorithm may be described in terms of quantum parallelism, this does not necessarily imply that quantum parallelism is the most important aspect of the algorithm. The field of quantum entanglement still has a long way to go.
- When describing algorithms, how the algorithm knows how to manipulate the state produced by quantum parallelism is at the heart of the program in this context. Nontraditional programming approaches are required to do this kind of manipulation. To get you started, here are a few ideas:
- Amplifying any interesting data points at the output. The goal is to increase the amplitude of the values of interest and, hence, the likelihood that they will be measured by altering the state. This strategy is used by Grover's algorithm in Chapter 9, as well as many other roughly similar algorithms [14].
- Determine the attributes of the set of all values of $f(x)$. A quantum Fourier transformation (QFT) is used in Shor's method in order to retrieve the period of the function f to solve Deutsch–Jozsa, Bernstein–Vazirani, and Simon's problems, the algorithms use this technique.

11.8 Machine Models and Complexity Classes

Classifying complexity of the algorithm requires a vocabulary and computers capable of understanding that language. In this context, machines refer to any computer device, quantum or conventional, that runs a single algorithm counted in terms of the number of computation steps and storage cells. Each of the finite strings of elements may be represented as a subset of a language L over an alphabet. Machine M recognizes a language L if it is able to identify whether $x L$ is for each string. Depending on the equipment under consideration, we may have a better idea of what decide implies. In the case of a classical deterministic machine, the answer may be Yes, $x\,L$, no, or the machine could run indefinitely given an input x. Quantum and probabilistic machines may be able to accurately respond yes or no with a specific probability. In this article, we'll look at five different types of classical machines: those that are either deterministic, pseudo-random, randomized, probabilistic, or both (BP). Each of the classical machine retypes has a quantum equivalent (EQ, NQ, RQ, PrQ, and BQ). Quantum-limited probability of mistake machines and quantum-randomized (precise) machines are particularly interesting (BQ). Multiple resource-restricted complexity classes are defined in using this sort of machine. Now, we can more precisely explain how various robots understand a language.

One LM may be used by each kind of machine M to communicate with one another. Deterministic machines are those that always respond "yes" when given a certain set of inputs, such as "yes" or "no." The language is recognized by the deterministic machine D [15].

For all, the probability $P(D(x) = \text{True})$ is equal to zero. When presented with the same input, it is possible to construct an error-prone machine that will respond Yes or No to the question with a probability of 1/2+ or no more than 1. There are bounds on the probability of mistake, thus the LBP = $x|P(P(x) = \text{Yes})$ LBP.

For certain inputs, a computer may not be able to produce a response at all. For each machine type that we will be looking at, the criteria are shown in Table 11.1. The chance of a quantum machine recognizing a language is equal to that of a

Table 11.1 The likelihood of a machine of a certain kind responding when x is known to be a language element L, then yes.

Prefix	Kind of machine	$P(x \in L)$	$P(x \notin L)$
Classical			
D	Deterministic	1	0
N	Nondeterministic	>0	0
R	Randomized (Monte Carlo)	$> \dfrac{1}{2} + \varepsilon$	0
Pr	Probabilistic	$> \dfrac{1}{2}$	$\leq \dfrac{1}{2}$
BP	Bounded probability of error	$> \dfrac{1}{2} + \varepsilon$	$\dfrac{1}{2} - \varepsilon$
Quantum			
EQ	Quantum deterministic (exact)	$=1$	$=0$
BQ	Quantum bounded probability of error	$> \dfrac{1}{2} + \varepsilon$	$\leq \dfrac{1}{2} - \varepsilon$

Figure 11.9 Relationships of containment between several machines.

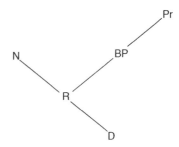

classical machine. Figure 11.9 depicts the relationships between different types of machines in terms of containment. This implies that any D machine is also a R machine by definition, for example.

This means that every sort of machine can identify any language, provided there is one that can. The list of languages that can be spoken by the machines we've created does not rely on the specific value. A Pr machine M, for example, may respond "yes" with a possibility of. EwPr machine M can be built where M is executed three times, and the response is "Yes" if and only if M has a "Yes" result two of the three times. Following that, M will assent to the stipulations of the contract.

Both conventional and quantum machines, as well as machines with a time and spatial complexity of xL, satisfy these relations. Some writers choose to stick with a simple number like 4. Because no polynomial number of repetitions can guarantee an increase in the success probability beyond a defined threshold in the first example, the scenario $P(xL) > 1/2$ differs significantly from

11.8.1 Complexity Classes

As well as considering the likelihood that a machine would provide an accurate response, complexities paper also explores how much time and space a machine expends to arrive at its conclusions. It takes a computer $O(f)$ step to identify a language L if it can respond yes or no for every string of length n and $t > O(f)$. For a computer to identify a language L in space $O(f)$, it must respond "yes" or "no" to a string of length n using at most $s(n)$ storage units (f).

The collection of languages that a certain kind of computer can recognize within a given set of resource constraints is referred to as a largely divided. Regarding the classes mTime(f) and mSpace, we specifically look at D,EQ,NR,PrBP, and R (f). if an m-type machine can identify L in time O, then L belongs to the mTime(f) difficulty category (f). A language L in location O is assigned to the difficulty class m by a machine M of type mSpace(f).

A multiplication number of resources is of special importance to us, as is smaller but still, significant available resources are only used exponentially. For instance, the class $P = \text{DTime}(nk)$ of machines that only take $O(nk)$ time to reply to an input of length n is of interest to us. Commonly used abbreviations include:

P	DTime(nk)
EQP	EQTime(nk)
NP	NTime(nk)
R	RTime(nk)
PP	PrTime(nk)
BPP	BPTime(nk)
BQP	BQTime(nk)
PSpace	DSpace(nk)
NPSpace	NSpace(nk)
EXP	DTime(kn)

Since the function f provides an upper bound on the possible runtimes, it may be safely believed that machines will always finish operating. However, machines with a high space complexity may continue to run forever in response to certain inputs. To this end, we identify the set of communications in which all m-type stopping machines in space O participate as belonging to the mH Space(f) category (f). This is because mSpace(f) = mH Space(f) (f). The circuit simulation model does not include any math. Nonstop pace classifications, for instance, need the use of quantum Turing computers in order to study their complexity [15].

11.8.2 Complexity: Known Results

Some of the confinement connections concerning quantum sophistication classes have informal justifications presented. Figure 11.10 displays the well-known link between classical and quantum time complexity classes. The relationship between BQP and NP or PP has not yet been established.

$P \subseteq \text{EQP}$ any classical polynomial-time computation may be carried out by a family of circuits with a polynomial size. Given enough time and space, every classical circuit can be turned around, and any procedure that takes polynomial time may be transformed into a mathematical model that is correct to within a constant factor.

As an alternative method of stating the same thing, BPP is superior to BQP. Each BPP computation that a machine M does may be roughly approximated by a machine M that only makes a single binary decision at each step. There are a polynomial number of choices in this tree, and each one may be represented by a bit string of length c. It is equivalent to feeding M into a random machine M when c and x are fed into a deterministic machine M d. In the case of a deterministic

Figure 11.10 Containment relation involving classical and quantum complexity classes.

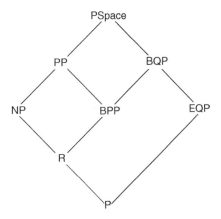

machine $M\,d$, it is possible to employ a quantum computer with a time complexity suitable for superimposing all random mistakes and choices c on $l.\ (c,x)$. When $M\,q$ is applied to x, all the possible computations of M on x are executed in parallel. A positive answer from $M\,q$ may be read with the same expectation of approval from $M\,x$.

It's not really apparent that BPP BQP should be included. The question of whether or not BPP = PSpace would be settled if it could be shown that BPP = BQP. Space in the P-quadrant equals the B-quadrant machines that operate in PSpace may take up to k steps before evaluating the results. The machine's journey, which starts at $|0 = |0$, has n stages. A computer like this can be reproduced with a surprising degree of fidelity, and if you've ever wondered how that's possible, we have excellent news: It is possible to do so in polynomial time. The state after doing Step I will be referred to as State I here. Each possible state $|i,\ I = 0$ may have an endless number of basis vectors layered on top of it. In contrast, a space polynomial in n may be used to determine the amplitude akj of a particular basis vector in the final superposition $|k$.

In each iteration, a basic quantum gate Ui may be operated with a maximum of $d|jin$ state3 quantum bits. In this paper, we show that the amplitude $|i + 1$ of the next state $|i$ is solely reliant on the magnitude ai,j of the bits being operated on by the gate to vary from $|j$, and that this is true even if the number of basis vectors is constrained to be just $2ai + 1, jdof$ basis vectors 8. Take the latest d quantum bits to be affected by the universal function $U = Ui + 1$. We will refer to x and y by their abbreviation, $x\,y$, and we'll use the symbols $2dx + y$ and let $|q$ stand for the basic elements $|r$ and $|q$ of the usual two-dimensional basis [16].

$$|\psi_{i+1}\rangle = (I^{n-d} \otimes U)\,|\,\psi_i$$
$$= \sum_i a_{ij}(I^{n-d} \otimes U)\,|\,j$$

$$= \sum_{p=0}\sum_{q=0}^{-}\overline{a}_{i,p\cdot q}|p\rangle \otimes U \mid q$$

$$= \sum_{p}\sum_{q}a_{i,p\cdot q}|p\rangle \otimes \sum_{r=0}^{2^d-1}u_{qr} \mid r$$

$$= \sum_{p}\sum_{r}\left(\sum_{q+0}^{2^d-1}u_{qr}q_{i,p\cdot q}\right)|p\rangle|r\rangle$$

It follows that each amplitude $a_{i+1,p\cdot r} = \sum_{q=0}^{2^d-1}u_{qr}a_{i,p\cdot q}$. Only the previous state's $2d$ amplitudes $a_{i,pq}$ are relevant.

We propose that $i2^d$ amplitudes must be stored in order to compute a single amplitude of state $|i$. Since we already know $|0$, it takes up no more storage space to compute the amplitude $j|0$ for each j. We just showed that the amplitude $a_i + 1, j$ may be computed from the 2D amplitudes of. Since we can only calculate this frequency and amplitude one at a time, we need to save at least two values for the $i2$-amplitude before we can compute the corresponding 2^d-amplitudes. $I + 1)2^d$ amplitude measurements must be taken and reserved for use in this process.

To get to the desired accuracy after the computation, we require a maximum precision of M at any given stage. Mistakes at each phase may add up to no more than the sum of all the errors at that step. After the final superposition, the amplitude of any basis vector may be determined in $M2^dM$ space, with M growing only linearly with the number of steps needed. Since k is assumed to be polynomial in n and d is capped at 3, computing a single value of the final state $|k$ is possible in polynomial time.

Create a random basis vector $|j$ and calculate its amplitude to verify the method. If the produced number is between 0 and 1, it is less than $|akj|$, and the outcome is $|j|$. Otherwise, empty the whole area, choose a new basis vector, and start again. If time is not an issue, iterate as many times as necessary to get a basis vector. Because of this, it is possible to implement a classical approximation of any BQP computation in polynomial time.

11.9 Quantum Fourier Transformations

When it comes to the quantum realm, QFT is the most important subroutine. It and its variants are used in several quantum algorithms that provide significant performance improvements over their conventional counterparts. As part of this discussion on extensions of the quantum Fourier transform, it is proven that the Walsh–Hadamard transformation is a generalization of the Fourier transform. As a result of its foundation in the classical discrete Fourier transformation (DFT) and its efficient implementation, the fast Fourier transform (FFT), the QFT is a powerful tool in the study of quantum mechanics (FFT). Short discussions of the classical DFT and the FFT are included before the presentation of the QFT and its amazingly efficient quantum implementation (FFT).

11.9.1 The Classical Fourier Transform

The Fourier transform with discrete values functions with discrete complex values may be transformed using the DFT, which returns another instantaneous complexity value. The discrete Fourier transform of a function $a:[0,\ldots,N-1]$ C yields a function $A:[0,\ldots,N-1]$ C defined by

$$A(x) = \frac{1}{\sqrt{N}} \sum_{k=0}^{N-1} a(k) \exp\left(2\pi i \frac{kx}{N} \right)$$

The Fourier coefficients of the DFT are the entries of the matrix representation F whose rows include the numbers 0 through $N-1$.

Example 11.2   Let the periodic function $a:[0,\ldots,N-1]$ C have some frequency u that divides N evenly. So long as the function is not constant, we have: $0 < u < N$.
This function's Fourier coefficients are

$$A(x) = \frac{1}{\sqrt{N}} \sum_{k=0}^{N-1} a(k) \exp\left(2\pi i \frac{kx}{N} \right)$$

$$= \frac{1}{\sqrt{N}} \sum_{k=0}^{N-1} \exp\left(-2\pi i \frac{uk}{N} \right) \exp\left(2\pi i \frac{kx}{N} \right)$$

$$= \frac{1}{\sqrt{N}} \sum_{k=0}^{N-1} \exp\left(2\pi i \frac{k(x-u)}{N} \right)$$

It is a well-known fact that sums of the form $\sum_{k=0}^{N-1} \exp\left(2\pi i k \frac{r}{N} \right)$ vanish unless $r = 0 \bmod N$. (We prove a more general) Since $u < N$, $A(x) = 0$ unless $x - u = 0$: only $A(u)$ will be nonzero.

The sum of partial derivatives with frequencies that are multiples of u may be determined by performing the Fourier transformation on a computationally intensive periodic function. Since the proposed technique is linear, the Fourier coefficients $A(x)$ of any constant value are the sum of the frequency components for residential and manufacturing uses. The Fourier coefficients $A(x)$ will be nonzero only if x is a multiple of $u = N/r$, assuming that N is evenly divisible by r. If r does not equally divide N, this is only a rough estimate; the highest values are at the closest multiples of $u = N/r$, and the lowest values are at the furthest multiples of u.

Counterintuitive Radon measuring implementing an FFT with N equal to a power of two, i.e. $N = 2^n$, may lead to a compact DFT representation. The key to success lies in the use of Fourier transforms to deconstruct $F(n)$ for lesser powers of 2.

The Nth root of unity is denoted by; thus, we may write. For the $N = 2^n$ dimensional Fourier transform, the elements of the $N N$ matrix $F(n)$ are simply, where we index the entries of all $N N$ matrices by $i = 0,...,N-1$ and $j = 0,...,N - 1$.

If we want to do a 2^k-dimensional Wavelet transformation, we need a $2^k \; 2^k$ matrix, which we'll refer to as $F(k)$. The matrix of identical elements, of order k. Consider $D(k)$ to be the diagonal matrix of size $2^k \; 2^k$ whose rows and columns range from $2(k+1)...i$ to position$(k+1)$. Let the permutation illustrated in Figure 11.11, in which the elements of the vector At$i+1$ moved to position $i + 2 \; k1$, consisting of I and k as indexes, be used. The elements of the $R(k) \; 2k2k$ matrix are as follows:

$$R^{(k)}_{ij} = \begin{cases} 1 & \text{if } 2i = j \\ 1 & \text{if } 2(i - 2k) + 1 = j \\ 0 & \text{otherwise} \end{cases}$$

That, as the observer may check,

$$F^{(k)} = \frac{1}{2} \begin{pmatrix} I^{(k-1)} & D^{(k-1)} \\ I^{(k-1)} & -D^{(k-1)} \end{pmatrix} \begin{pmatrix} F^{(k-1)} & 0 \\ 0 & F^{(k-1)} \end{pmatrix} R^{(k)}$$

If you're interested in seeing an implementation of the FFT based on this recursive decomposition that requires just $O(nN)$ steps, you may find one in any of the authoritative references on the topic.

Figure 11.11 The R shuffle transform shown.

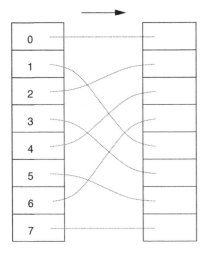

0
1
2
3
4
5
6
7

11.9.2 The Quantum Fourier Transform

Like the FFT, the QFT is a discrete Fourier transform version that operates under the assumption that $N = 2^n$. We shall refer to the amplitudes of each given quantum state as a function of x henceforth and write them as $a_x(x)$. Whereas the discrete Fourier transform of $a(x)$ contains $A(x)$ Fourier coefficients, and x is an integer between 0 and $N-1$, the quantum Fourier transform acts on a quantum state via transmitting. Immediately after the Fourier process, if the state were assessed in the standard basis, the probability that the succeeding state would be $|x|2$ would be instead of using a separate output register, U_f incorporates the output of the classical configuration into the final complex frequency and amplitude, making it fairer and more equitable than the quantum Fourier transform's extrapolation of a binary classical nonlinear function.

Applying the quantum Fourier transform to the amplitudes of a periodic function, $a(x) = ax$ with period r, yields |, where $A(x)$ is zero unless when x is greater than two. One of the basis vectors, denoted by the label $|x|$, would represent the result of a standard basis measurement performed at this time. If the period is not a power of 2 ($N = 2^n$), then it is very likely that states labeled with numbers near to multiple copies would be seen using a quantum transformation technique. The more precision required by the approximate transform; the more power is used.

In contrast to the FFT, which needs $O(nN)$ operations, the quantum Fourier transform may be completed in $O(n^2)$ operations. The quantum Fourier transform is only one example of a larger class of quantum transformations that may be implemented efficiently and effectively.

11.9.3 A Quantum Circuit for Fast Fourier Transform

We demonstrate a practical method for quickly implementing the quantum Fourier transform $U_F(n)$, defined for $N = 2^n$ as

With N equal to 2, the quantum Fourier transform is the well-known Hadamard transformation:

$$U_F^{(1)} : |0\rangle \rightarrow \frac{1}{\sqrt{2}} \sum_{x=0}^{N-1} e^0 |x\rangle = \frac{1}{\sqrt{2}}(|0\rangle + |1\rangle)$$

$$|1\rangle \rightarrow \frac{1}{\sqrt{2}} \sum_{x=0}^{N-1} e^{\pi i x} |x\rangle = \frac{1}{\sqrt{2}}(|0\rangle - |1\rangle)$$

Using the recursive decomposition,

$$U_F^{(k+1)} = \frac{1}{\sqrt{2}} \begin{pmatrix} I^{(k)} & D^{(k)} \\ I^{(k)} & -D^{(k)} \end{pmatrix} \begin{pmatrix} U_F^{(k)} & 0 \\ 0 & U_F^{(k)} \end{pmatrix} R^{(k+1)},$$

we can compute $U_F(n)$.

Each and every one of the constituent vectors is a unitary structure (the prefix multiplication factor is related to the first matrix). Whether a quantum computer can efficiently integrate these parts is still up for debate.

The procedure is as follows:

The rotation $R^{(k+1)}$ may be represented as

$$R^{(k+1)} = \sum_{i=0}^{2^k-1} |i\rangle\langle 2i| + |i+2^k\rangle\langle 2i+1|$$

To illustrate, qubit 0 is transformed into qubit k, and qubits 1 through k are inverted to take on the values 0 through $k+1$. In this case, rearranging the $k+1$ qubits are all that is needed to get the desired result. This permutation may be built using $k+1$ swap operations.

- The transformation

$$\begin{pmatrix} U_F^{(k)} & 0 \\ 0 & U_F^{(k)} \end{pmatrix} = I \otimes U_F^{(k)}$$

The quantum Fourier transform may be applied iteratively to qubits 0 through k to perform this algorithm.

- The $2k$ $2k$ diagonal matrix of phase shifts $D(k)$ may be recursively decomposed as

$$D^{(k)} = D^{(k-1)} \otimes \begin{pmatrix} 1 & 0 \\ 0 & \omega_{(k+1)} \end{pmatrix}$$

- The transformation $D(k)$ may be realized by applying to qubit I for 1 I k using this recursive decomposition. It follows that k single-qubit gates may be used to construct $D(k)$ in total.

- If $D(k)$ is implemented as described, then

$$\frac{1}{\sqrt{2}} \begin{pmatrix} I^{(k)} & D^{(k)} \\ I^{(k)} & -D^{(k)} \end{pmatrix}$$

can be implemented with only k gates.

$$\frac{1}{\sqrt{2}} \begin{pmatrix} I^{(k)} & D^{(k)} \\ I^{(k)} & -D^{(k)} \end{pmatrix} = \frac{1}{\sqrt{2}}(|0\rangle + |1\rangle)\langle 0| \otimes I^{(k)} + \frac{1}{\sqrt{2}}(|0\rangle - |1\rangle)\langle 1| \otimes D$$

$$= (H|0\rangle\langle 0|) \otimes I^{(k)} + (H|1\rangle\langle 1|) \otimes D^{(k)}$$

$$= (H \otimes I^{(k)})(|0\rangle\langle 0| \otimes I^{(k)} + |1\rangle\langle 1| \otimes D^{(k)})$$

When bit k is set to one, the transformations ($|0$ $0|I$ use $D(k)$ to affect the low-order bits that are within its control. Each of the single-qubit operations that comprise $D(k)$ may be applied to bit I, which is controlled by bit k, using a series of k randomized treatment gates, as shown in Figure 11.12.

Figure 11.12 A quantum circuit that iteratively performs the Fourier transform.

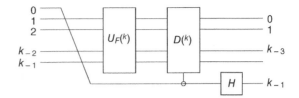

11.10 Shor's Algorithm

In 1994, Peter Shor was inspired by Simon's method to develop a limited probability polynomial time quantum algorithm for factoring integers. It has been a goal of researchers since the 1970s to find faster ways to factor numbers. The number field sieve is the most effective classical approach currently in use, and it has an input size complexity that is super-polynomial. The algorithm is given as input the number M to be factored. Since the input M is given as a string of its digits, we assume that the size of the input is $m = \log M$. Using the number field sieve takes $O(\exp[m_1/3])$ steps. The computational difficulty of factoring is crucial to the security of many cryptographic systems, including the ubiquitous RSA algorithm. The scientific community at large became fascinated by quantum computing after learning about Shor's findings.

In order to calculate the period of a function, Shor employs a factoring method. The period of a function may be determined using a well-established, classical factoring method. At one point, Shor's algorithm exploits quantum parallelism to produce a superposition over all potential values for this function. Then, it makes use of the quantum Fourier transform to efficiently generate an output with most of its amplitude concentrated in states near to multiples of the period of the function. Using the state's measurable properties, a precise calculation of the period may be made using conventional techniques. The dot is used to factor M.

- Discovering Periods: A Method of Classical Reduction
- If the order of an integer a modulo M is greater than zero, then $ar = 1 \bmod M$, and else the order is said to be infinite. A pair of integers is said to be relatively prime if it has no common prime factors. As long as a and M are almost prime, there is a bound on the order of. An example would be the expression $f(k) = ak \bmod M$. Given that $ak = ak + r \bmod M$ the order r of a modulo M equals the period f for a relatively prime M if and only if $ar = 1 \bmod M$. When r is an even number, we get the following formula: $(ar/2 + 1)(ar/2\ 1) = 0 \bmod M$. This is true only when $ar = 1 \bmod M$.
- Both $ar/2 + 1$ and $ar/2\ 1$ have nontrivial underlying themes with M as long as they are not multiples of M. If r is divisible by 2, then if $r2$, then $ar2 + 1$ and $ar/21$ probably share some nontrivial component with M.

As an aid in factoring M, the following characteristic may be used:

- Pick an integer, and the random number generator will give you the period of $f(k) = ak \bmod M$.
- Finding the greatest common divisor of $ar2 + 1$ and M is a fast and easy Euclidean approach for finding even integers.
- It is recommended to keep going with the procedure till it is finished. Calculating the period of the function $f(k) = ak \bmod M$ has replaced the formerly intractable issue of factoring M. Shor's optimization method solves the problem of determining the period of a function.
- We begin by providing a high-level summary of Shor's factoring technique. It seems that just parts 2 and 3 need quantum processing, whereas the remainder may be handled by a conventional computer.
- Randomly choose an integer a such that 0 and M. Use the Euclidean approach to determine whether a and M are relatively prime. In such case, we may have found M's missing component. If it becomes essential, the rest of the algorithm may be employed.
- Perform a quantum Fourier transform on the input superposition by calculating $f(x) = ax \bmod M$ the range $[x] = [0, 1]$, where $[n]$ is such that $[M^2 - 2^n] = [M^2 - 2M^2]$.
- Measure. It is likely that a value v will be obtained that is quite close to a multiple of.
- To get a rough estimate of the speculative duration from the known value v, classical methods may be used.
- For even values of q, the Euclidean method may be used to find a nontrivial common factor of $aq/2 + 1$ and M.
- Repeat the steps if necessary.

11.10.1 Core Quantum Phenomena

After using quantum parallelism to create the superposition $\sum_x x, f(x)|$, Shor's algorithm applies the quantum Fourier transform.

Since $f(x) = a_x \bmod M$ can be computed efficiently classically, the results of Chapter 6 imply that the transformation

$$U_f : |x\rangle 0 \to| x | f(x)$$

has a well-executed strategy. Discuss the algorithm's effectiveness. To achieve the combination, we take advantage of quantum parallel processing and U_f.

$$\frac{1}{\sqrt{2^n}} \sum_{x=0}^{2^n-1} |x\rangle |f(x)\rangle$$

If we evaluate the second register, we can simplify the analysis somewhat. How it can be done without compromising efficiency or the algorithm's results.

The state changes when the second registers return an integer number u for $f(x)$.

$$C \sum_x g(x)|x\rangle|u\rangle$$

where $g(x) = \begin{cases} 1 & \text{if } f(x) = u \\ 0 & \text{otherwise} \end{cases}$, in this case, C represents the suitable scalar. Because the second register is no longer intertwined with the first, we can simply disregard the value of u. There are various different versions of the period for which the $f(x)$ function $f(x) = ax \bmod M$ has the condition that it is $f(x) = f(y)$. Thus, the values of x remaining in the sum, those with $g(x) = 0$, varied by multiples of the period. As a result, functions g and f have a same period. We'd have the period if we could somehow add up the values of two succeeding terms. Unfortunately, the principles of quantum physics only allow us to get one random value of x from a physical quantity. Because we are unlikely to measure the same value u of $f(x)$ in two runs, restarting the procedure has no benefit. Instead, the results received from the two runs have no relationship to one another.

When the first register of this state is subjected to the quantum Fourier transform, the result is

$$U_F \left(C \sum_x g(x)|x\rangle \right) = C' \sum_c G(c)|c\rangle$$

where $G(c) = \sum_x g(x) \exp\left(\frac{2\pi i c x}{2^n} \right)$. $G(c) = 0$ unless when c is a multiple of $2^n/r$ when the period r of the function $g(x)$ is a power of two, according to the study. For periods r in which n is not equal to 2^n, amplitude is concentrated in numbers near to multiples of n. Because of this, a value near to a multiple of v may be expected to be obtained by measurement. The algorithm's quantum core has been finished. The following part looks at how v has traditionally been used to get an accurate estimate of the time period.

11.10.2 Periodic Value Measurement and Classical Extraction

Using the quantum core of Shor's algorithm, the period may be extracted from the observed value v using a conventional approach. Using the quantum Fourier transform, it is trivial to derive the period if the period r is a power of two. V is equal to j $2rn$ for some j in this situation. A fraction with the period as its remainder is most likely to be found in most cases if j and r are both reasonably prime. Rest of this section covers how to get a decent prediction for r when it is not a multiple of 2.

Because the quantum Fourier transform only offers approximation multiples of the scaling frequencies, extracting the duration from the measurements might be difficult. A decent estimation for the period may be derived from the continuing record dubbed mentioned in box when the period is not a power of 2. According to Shor's results, v is likely to fall inside some multiple of. When we attempt to retrieve the period r from the obtained by comparing v, it becomes clear why n was selected to meet M^2 2^n $2M^2$. The left inequality M^2 2^n indicates that in the high-probability situation

$$\left| \frac{v}{2^n} - \frac{j}{r} \right| < \frac{1}{2 \cdot 2^n} \leq \frac{1}{2M^2}$$

In general, the difference between two distinct fractions $\frac{p}{q}$ and $\frac{p'}{q'}$ with denominators less than M is bounded:

$$\left| \frac{p}{q} - \frac{p'}{q'} \right| = \left| \frac{pq' - p'}{qq'} \right| > \frac{1}{M^2}.$$

Thus, there is at most one fraction $\frac{p}{q}$ with denominator $q < M$ such that $\left| \frac{v}{2^n} - \frac{p}{q} \right| < \frac{1}{M^2}$. The fraction $\frac{p}{q}$. In the A continuous fraction expansion may be used to calculate the high possibility situation that v is inside. Our best estimate for the time is the denominator q of the resulting fraction. When j and r are close to prime, this assumption is right.

11.10.3 Shor's Algorithm and Its Effectiveness

In order to factor the integer $M = 21$, Shor's algorithm is shown in this stage. Since $M^2 = 441 \leq 29 < 882 = 2M^2$, take $n = 9$. Since $\log M = m = 5$, Five qubits are needed for the second register. The result is that

$$\frac{1}{\sqrt{2^9}} \sum_{x=0}^{2^9 - 1} |x\rangle f(x)$$

Having nine bits in the first register and five in the second, it has a qubit count of 14.

The second register of Eq. (8.1)'s superposition is a quantum measurement, and let's pretend $a = 11$.

$$\frac{1}{\sqrt{2^9}} \sum_{x=0}^{2^9 - 1} |x\rangle f(x)$$

results in a value of 8. The first register's state after these measurements is the graph of the function's discrete Fourier transform, which clearly displays the regularity of the result of implementing the quantum Fourier transform to this state. Since the period of f does not split 2^n, the probability density function has some dispersion around different amounts of $2^n/r$ rather than a single spike at each value.

Suppose $v = 427$ is the state measurement. We can utilize the fraction expansion of Box 8.1 to get an approximation for the period since v and $2n$ are both relative primes. The following table represents a trace of the procedure for continuing fractions:

i	ai	pi	qi	i
0	0	0	1	0.8339844
1	1	1	1	0.1990632
2	5	5	6	0.02352941
3	42	211	253	0.5

The algorithm terminates with $6 = q2 < M \leq q3$. Thus, $q = 6$ is our guess for the period of f.

Since 6 is even, $a6/2-1 = 113-1 = 1330$ and $a6/2+1 = 113+1 = 1332$ are likely to have a common factor with M. In this example, $gcd(211330) = 7$ and $gcd(211332) = 3$.

11.10.4 The Efficiency of Shor's Algorithm

As the algorithm is implemented, this section looks at how many gates or classical steps are required to accomplish each step, as well as how many times it is likely the process will be repeated.

$O(\log M) = O(m)$ steps are required for both parts 1 and 5 of the Euclidean algorithm for integers $x > y$. It is similar to the Euclidean method in that it takes $O(m)$ steps to complete the continuing fraction algorithm in part 4. As seen, the third section does not need to be included at all. In this section, we'll calculate U_f and the quantum Fourier transform. One qubit needs $O(m)$ steps to be transformed into another qubit via the quantum Fourier transform. U_f might be implemented using the technique for modular exponentiation provided, which needs $O(n^3)$ steps. Modular exponentiation, as defined by Shor, may be used to execute the transformation U_f more effectively, since it takes less time and space than the most efficient classical technique. A single iteration of Shor's algorithm takes the same amount of time as a single iteration of the method's total time complexity, which is O $(n^2 \log n \log \log n)$.

To demonstrate the efficacy of Shor's algorithm, we must also demonstrate that the portions are not repeated excessively. There are four things that may go horribly wrong:

- The period of $f(x) = ax \bmod M$ could be odd.
- Part 4 could yield M as M's factor.

- The value v obtained in part 3 might not be close enough to a multiple of $\frac{2^n}{r}$.
- A multiple $j\frac{2^n}{r}$ of $\frac{2^n}{r}$ is obtained from v, but j and r could have a common factor, in which case the denominator q is a factor of the period, not the period itself.

The classical reduction has the first two difficulties, and traditional classical reasoning limits the probability to a maximum of $1/2$. The difficulty does not occur if the period r divides 2^n. Shor shows that, in the general case, v is within $1/2$ of a multiple of $2/r$ with high probability. Taking the quantum Fourier transform as a starting point, it's easy to show that every possible solution to issue 4 is equally plausible.

$$C' \sum_{c=0}^{2^n-1} G(c)|c\rangle,$$

where

$$G(c) = \sum_{x \in X_u} \exp\left(2\pi i \frac{cx}{2^n}\right) = \sum_{y=0}^{2^n/r} \exp\left(2\pi i \frac{cry}{2^n}\right)$$

$X_u = x|f(x) = u$ in the case when $X_u = x|f(x)$. The final total is one if c is a multiple of $2^n/r$, and zero if it is not j $0,\ldots,r$ is equally probable in this instance. When j and r are relatively prime, $\gcd(r,j) = 1$, we have the period r. The famous Euler function, known to fulfill $(r)/\log r$ for any constant, gives the number of significant integers smaller than r that are relatively prime to r. Thus, we just need to repeat the portions $O(\log \log r)$ times to get a high success. However, the broader situation when r does not divide 2^n is a little more complicated but still provides a similar conclusion.

11.11 Omitting the Internal Measurement

In the equation of Shor's algorithm, the measuring of the second register of the state to determine u may be skipped. This section first explains why this evaluation may be skipped, and then provides a formal justification for why this is the case.

As a result, the state is composed of many Fourier analyses with the same period, one for every value of the $f(x)$ parameter. The Fourier transforms of these quantities are superimposed due to the linearity of quantum transitions. Because each function correlates to a different value u in the second register, the density of states of the parts does not interact with one another. The period may be determined by measuring the first register, which produces a value from one of these Fourier transformations that is near to for some j. An example of the difficulties of dealing with quantum superpositions may be seen in this argument's formalization.

In other words, we may say that X_u is equal to $[x]|f(x)] = [x]$. Eq. (8.1)'s current condition may be expressed as

$$\frac{1}{\sqrt{2^n}} \sum_{x=0}^{2^n-1} |x\rangle|f(x)\rangle = \frac{1}{\sqrt{2^n}} \sum_{u \in R} \sum_{x \in X_u} |x\rangle|u$$

$$= \frac{1}{\sqrt{2^n}} \sum_{u \in R} \left(\sum_{x=0}^{2^n-1} g_u(x)|x\rangle \right) |u\rangle$$

$F(x)$ is the function with the range R, and g_u is the u-family of functions with u as the index.

$$g_u(x) = \begin{cases} 1 & \text{if } f(x) = u \\ 0 & \text{otherwise} \end{cases}$$

They can't interact (add or cancel) with each other in the second register amplitudes. Transforms applied to previous states may be expressed in terms of the aforementioned state.

$$U_F \otimes I \left(\frac{1}{\sqrt{2^n}} \sum_{u \in R} \left(\sum_{x=0}^{2^n-1} g_u(x)|x\rangle \right) |u\rangle \right) = \frac{1}{\sqrt{2^n}} \sum_{u \in R} \left(U_F \sum_{x} g_u(x)|x\rangle \right) |u$$

$$= C' \sum_{u \in R} \left(\sum_{c=0}^{2^n-1} G_u(c)|c\rangle \right) |u\rangle$$

It's the discrete Fourier transform of $g_u(c)$ (x). This is a linear combination of every possible u in Eq. (8.3) as a consequence of this operation. Measurement of the first half of this state yields a c near to a multiple of $2^n/r$, much like how the second register was evaluated in the original process because all g_u had the same period.

11.12 Generalizations

A comparable method for the discrete logarithm issue was also included in Shor's original work. For issues that come within the broad category of hidden subgroup problems, further expansions of Shor's quantum algorithms have been shown to work. The second and third portions of this chapter assume some familiarity with group theory. There is no need for readers who are unfamiliar with group theory to spend time reading these parts; only Appendix B and the last chapter's section on recent algorithmic developments will benefit from them. There are many boxes devoted to the fundamentals of group theory.

11.12.1 The Problem of Discrete Logarithms

Diffie–Hellman, El Gamal, and elliptic curve public key encryption, for example, all rely on the traditional difficulty of the discrete logarithm issue. Factoring or the discrete logarithm issue is used in all common public key encryption and digital signature techniques. Public key encryption and digital signature techniques are critical to the security and efficiency of online transactions and communications. Is there a public key encryption system that can be constructed before quantum computers are built, such that it is safe against both classical and quantum attacks? Practical consequences will be enormous if quantum computers triumph in this race. All presently accepted public key encryption techniques will be unsafe if quantum computers become a reality.

Assume that Z_p is a collection of numbers $1,\ldots,p$ that can be multiplied by p, and that b is a generator for this collection. With regard to base B, The element $x\,Z_p$ where $b_x = b \bmod p$ is called the discrete logarithm of $y\,Z_p$ with respect to base B.

The Discrete Logarithm Problem Look for a prime p, a base $b\,Z_p$, and an arbitrary element $y\,Z_p$ such that $b_x = y \bmod p$.

This is computational complexity impossible for really large values of p. For some large finite cyclic groups G, the discrete logarithm problem may be solved classically with relative ease. One example of this hidden subgroup is the discrete logarithm issue for Abelian groups. As shown in Appendix B, a generic method for the Abelian hidden subgroup issue produces, in this particular instance, the discrete logarithm algorithm created by Shor himself in the original formulation. Hidden subgroup issues will be addressed in the next section.

11.12.2 Hidden Subgroup Issues

Many of the issues and quantum algorithms we have covered so far fall under the umbrella of the hidden subgroup framework. Familiarity with group theory is helpful for properly appreciating this concept. In Box 8.2, we see an explanation of a group and several examples of groups in action. Box 8.3 gives a comprehensive breakdown of the various categories and subcategories. Box 8.4 discusses the nature of the enigmatic subgroup of Abelian groups. Imagine G is a group for a moment. An implicit definition of a subgroup $H\,G$ exists if and only if a function f on G is constant and unique on each coset of $H\,G$. Generators of $H\,G$ may be discovered using this definition.

One of the goals is to find a polylogarithmic algorithm that requires $O([\log|G|]k)$ steps to compute a set of H generators. If given a group G, the task's difficulty depends on more than just G and F. Some group characteristics may be hard to infer from given information, while others may be obvious at a glance. It is well-known, for instance, that it is technologically challenging to determine the size of a group given its defining set of generators and relations. If f is also computationally efficient in poly-log time, then a solution should be found in poly-log time.

Although the generalized hidden subgroup issue has not been solved, a polylogarithmic limited probability quantum technique for finite abelian groups that are defined in terms of their cyclic disintegration does exist. For Abelian groups, cyclic decomposition is used.

Abelian hidden subgroup problem with finite indices Consider the cyclic decomposition $G = Z_n 0 Z_n L$ of a limited Abelian group G. Assume G has a subgroup $H G$ and that a function f on G defines H implicitly if and only if f is constant and unique on every coset of H. Identify a group of H generators.

Example 11.3 Finding a period when you're part of a secret society. The challenge of pinpointing dates might be recast as one of uncovering unseen subgroups. A periodic function f defined on ZN has a period r equal to $N2$ divided by 2. The group $H ZN$ created by r is the secret group. The period r of H may be calculated by finding the most effective common divisor (Gcd) of its integer components (h, N) (h, N).

The problem of determining a period is an example of the finite Abelian hidden subgroup problem, as are Simon's and discrete logarithms. It's not hard to see how Simon's situation may be interpreted as a hidden-group problem. The connection between the discrete optimization problem and the hidden subgroup phenomena requires some investigation.

Example 11.4 A hidden subgroup of the fractional differential equations. Finding an $x G$ such that $bx = y$ mod$p$ is the goal of solving the discrete log problem, which asks for the group with p as the prime factor, base b as G, and any element of G as the variable in question. Assume that $f(g,h) = b + Gyh$, and that $f(g,h)$ is a function. This hidden subgroup H of GG consists of all tuples of the type $f(g,h) = 1$ (mx,m). You may find the element using any of the H generators $(x,1)$. The value of x, the solution to the discrete logarithm problem, may be calculated by applying the following method to the hidden subgroup problem.

Performing a superconducting Fourier analysis is crucial to Shor's algorithm. The Walsh–Hadamard translation for the finite Abelian group, W, is used in a quantum approach to solving Simon's problem (and more broadly all finite groups). To address the hidden subgroup problem, we use the quantum Fourier transform over the Abelian group G. Fourier representations of general finite groups G exist. W, which also includes the comprehensive solution to the problem of finding hidden subgroups in finite Abelian groups, provides extensive coverage of all of these aspects. This chapter draws on more sophisticated implications from group theory than are used elsewhere in the book. The identity of the concealed subgroups of generic non-Abelian groups remains a mystery.

11.13 The Application of Grover's Algorithm It's Time to Solve Some Difficulties

In quantum computing, Grover's algorithm is second only to Shor's in terms of popularity. However, it takes a quite different stance than Shor does. Although Shor's method solves a real-world problem, it can only be applied to a subset of possible scenarios. Concerns have been raised concerning the real-world implications of Grover's technique and its many variants.

To tackle "black box" issues, Grover's method is used. Our method solves the problem with just $O(N)$ calls to the oracle, whereas the best possible classical methods need $O(N)$ calls. When compared to Shor's technique, Grover's is clearly superior. Only under certain conditions, such as when the black box can be built efficiently, and when the additional structure to the problem can be used by classical and quantum algorithms, can this query complexity advantage over the classical case translate to a speedup.

Grover's approach has been shown to have an $O(N)$ query complexity; no quantum algorithm can do better. Even more critical than the method itself is adhering to this constraint. Powerful quantum computing is severely limited. Grover's algorithm, unlike Shor's algorithm, has versions that are known to succeed with confidence, unlike Grover's algorithm. In comparison to Shor's algorithm, Grover's is much easier to understand and provides a beautiful geometric explanation.

Using amplitude amplification, Grover's method searches an unorganized set of N objects.

Any Boolean function or predicate $P : 0,\ldots,N,N\ 1\ 0,1$ that represents the problem in terms of the desired attribute is a candidate for solving the problem. The goal of this task is to identify x such that $P(x) = 1$. Similar to Simon's and Deutsch problems, Jozsa's predicate P is seen here as an opaque oracle, and the significance of the number of inquiries made to P is emphasized. If we assume that we have a black box whose output is $P(x)$, then the best classical processes will need an average of $N/2$ values, or the predicate $P(x)$ will need to be interpreted as an average (x). Similar outcomes are achievable when working with the same quantum black box.

$$\sum_x c_x |x\rangle P(x)$$

upon input of

$$\sum_x c_x |x\rangle |0\rangle,$$

An $O(N)$ call to UP is all that is needed for Grover's method to succeed in the single-solution case. Grover's approach is used repeatedly to raise $P(x) = 1$ values with growing amplitudes c_x, with the goal of guaranteeing that the process eventually yields a number x that is both fascinating and unusual. Grover's technique necessitates a computable predicate P, but it's too loosely defined to prevent traditional approaches from outperforming the quantum process in practical applications.

11.13.1 Explanation of the Superposition Technique

The starting point for Grover's method is a superposition of equals | $\psi \frac{1}{\sqrt{N}} \sum_x x =|$ The starting point for Grover's method is a superposition of equals.

1. Multiply by + to get possible results

All solution basis vectors should have their signs inverted. A second step is to invert around the mean, a modification that maps each frequency reaction A to the mean amplitude $A+$. It illustrates how the basis vector for one solution could increase in amplitude as a result of these events. Now, let's dissect this process step by step.

11.13.2 The Black Box's Initial Configuration

Without narrowing the scope too much, let $N = 2^n$ for some integer n, and let X be the state space produced by. Assume U_P is a quantum black box that serves as

$$U_P : |x, a\rangle \rightarrow |x, P(x) \oplus a\rangle$$

for all $x \in X$ and single-qubit states |a (Figure 11.13).

Let us designate the good values as $G = x|P(x)$ and the bad values as $B = x|P(x)$, and assume that the number of good states is negligible compared to the entire number of states:

$$|G| \ll N$$

Figure 11.13 Grover's approach iterates by (a) flipping the good elements' signs and (b) inverting around the mean. This is shown by using the example of a single answer.

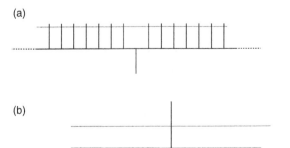

Let

$$|\psi_G\rangle = \underline{1} \sum |x\sqrt{G}_{x \in G}\||$$

be an even superposition of all the good states, and

$$|\psi_B\rangle = \underline{1} \sum |x\sqrt{B}_{x \in B}\||$$

include a neat superposition of all the undesirable ones. As a result, the superposition of all N values is a linear combination of the superpositions of $|\psi_G$ and $|\psi_B$

$$|\psi\rangle = \frac{1}{\sqrt{2^n}} \sum_{x=0}^{2^n-1} |x\rangle = g_0|\psi_G\rangle + b_0|\psi_B|$$

where $g_0 = \sqrt{|G|/N}$ and $b_0 = \sqrt{B/N}\,||$.

The repetitive application of a unitary translation lies at the heart of Grover's algorithm.

$$Q : g_i|\psi_G\rangle + b_i|\psi_B\rangle \rightarrow g_{i+1}|\psi_G\rangle + b_{i+1}\,|\,\psi_B$$

For each excellent condition, it raises and lowers the peak amplitude of g_i (and vice versa) to its maximum value. It is expected that $|b_j|\%\,|g_j|$ will have been moved to favorable states after executing Q's amplitude-amplifying transformation a sufficient number of times. An $x\,G$ result is quite likely at this point in time. Q must be applied N times, and this depends on N as well as G. Analyses are presented in great depth.

11.13.3 The Iteration Step

Constantly evolving the polarity of the positive components and inverting the average are two ways to produce the transformation Q. The execution of these two phases is described in detail in the following sections. Real amplitudes are used in both stages, thus for the sake of consistency, we'll just talk about real amplitudes here.

Changing the sign of the Good Elements π to change the sign in a superposition $\sum c_x x i \pi|$ of exactly those $|x$ such that $x \in G$, apply S_G. A sign change is simply a phase shift by $e = -1$. Section 7.4.2 showed that

$$U_P(|\psi\rangle \otimes H|1\rangle) = \left(S_G^T|\psi\rangle\right) \otimes H|1\rangle$$

By switching the positive parts' polarity, we may get

$$U_P : (g_i|\psi_G\rangle + b_i|\psi_B\rangle) \otimes H|1\rangle \rightarrow (-g_i|\psi_G\rangle + b_i|\psi_B\rangle) \otimes H|1\rangle$$

Rather than being dependent on N, the number of gates required to calculate U_P determines the sign change on the excellent elements. Inversion $a|x$ is inverted to

$(2Aa)|x$ when the averaged harmonic components of all the coordinate axes in the combination are taken into account. The change is clear to witness.

$$\sum_{i=0}^{N-1} a_i |x_i\rangle \rightarrow \sum_{i=0}^{N-1} (2A - a_i) \mid x_i$$

is performed by the unitary transformation

$$D = \begin{pmatrix} \frac{2}{N} - 1 & \frac{2}{N} & \cdots & \frac{2}{N} \\ \frac{2}{N} & \frac{2}{N} - 1 & \cdots & \frac{2}{N} \\ \cdots & \cdots & \cdots & \cdots \\ \frac{2}{N} & \frac{2}{N} & \cdots & \frac{2}{N} - 1 \end{pmatrix}$$

To perform the conversion, this section exhibits the usage of $O(n) = O(\log_2(N))$ quantum gates. You are following Grover's lead in defining where W represents where the Walsh–Hadamard eventually turns.

$$S_0^\pi = \begin{pmatrix} -1 & 0 & \cdots & 0 \\ 0 & 1 & 0 & \cdots \\ 0 & \cdots & \cdots & 0 \\ 0 & \cdots & 0 & 1 \end{pmatrix}$$

is the phase shift by π of the basis vector $|0$. To see that $D = -WS_0^\pi W$, let

$$R = \begin{pmatrix} 2 & 0 & \cdots & 0 \\ 0 & 0 & 0 & \cdots \\ 0 & \cdots & \cdots & 0 \\ 0 & \cdots & 0 & 0 \end{pmatrix}$$

Since $S_0^\pi = I - R, -W\,S_0^\pi W = W(R - I)W = WRW - I$
Since $R_{ij} = 0$ for $i \neq 0$ or $j \neq 0$,

$$_{ij} = W_{i0} R_{00} W_{0j} = \frac{2}{N}(WRW)$$

and $-W\,S_0^\pi W = WRW - I = D$

The iteration transformation is obtained by inverting the average and then altering the sign of the positive components.

$$Q = -WS_0^\pi WS_G^\pi$$

11.13.4 Various of Iterations

To identify the ideal couple of times recently to apply Q, this part analyzes the results of several applications of step Q in an iterative process that averages before and after a sign change and a reversal. The high-frequency g_i of excellent states fluctuates regularly with the number of repetitions, proving that Q is a fixed rotation. How many iterations should be used to identify a solution with high probability is an important consideration. Recurrence relations on g_i and b_i help us calculate how many iterations we should utilize to solve the problem.

The iteration $Q = \text{DSG}$ is responsible for transformations $g_i|\psi_G\rangle + b_i|\psi_B\rangle$ to $g_{i+1}|\psi_G\rangle + b_{i+1}|\psi_B\rangle$. First,

$$S_G^\pi : g_i|\psi_G\rangle + b_i \mid \psi_B \to -g_i|\psi_G\rangle + b_i|\psi_B\rangle$$

The expression $g_i|G$ adds up the amplitudes from all the i's to get the average amplitude, A_i, contributes $|B|$ amplitudes

Thus, altogether

$$A_i = \frac{\sqrt{|B|}\,b_i - \sqrt{|G|}\,g_i}{N}$$

Inversion about the average transforms

$$D : -g_i|\psi_G + b|_i\,\psi_B \to x \in G\,2A_i + \left.\frac{g_i}{|G|}\right|x + x \in B\,2A_i - \left.\frac{b_i}{|B|}\right|x$$
$$= (2A_i|\overline{G}| + g_i)|\psi_G + (2A_i|\overline{B}| - b_i)|\psi_B$$
$$= g_{i+1}|\psi_G + b_{i+1}|\psi_B$$

where

$$g_{i+1} = 2A_i\sqrt{|G|} + g_i$$
$$b_{i+1} = 2A_i\sqrt{|B|} - b_i$$

Let's call the chance that any random number between 0 and $N-1$ fulfills P the probability t. Since $1t = |B|/N$, we have $t = |G|/N$. Then

$$A_i\sqrt{|G|} = \frac{\sqrt{|B||G|}\,b_i - |G|g_i}{N} = \sqrt{t(1-t)}\,b_i - tg_i$$

$$A_i\sqrt{|B|} = \frac{|B|b_i - \sqrt{|B||G|}\,g_i}{N} = (1-t)b_i - \sqrt{t(1-t)}\,g_i$$

The recurrence relation can be written in terms of t:

$$g_{i+1} = (1 - 2t)g_i + 2\sqrt{t(1-t)}\,b_i$$
$$b_{i+1} = (1 - 2t)b_i - 2\sqrt{t(1-t)}\,g_i$$

where $g_0 = \sqrt{t}$ and $b_0 = \sqrt{1-t}$. It is easy to verify that $g_i = \sin((2i+1)\vartheta)$ $b_i = \cos((2i+1)\vartheta)$ is a solution to these equations with $\sin\theta = \sqrt{t} = \sqrt{G/N\|}$.

We can now determine the best value for Q iterations. We need to choose I so that we have a decent shot at keeping an eye on a healthy condition and finding a material that has the required property. $P = \sin((2i + 1))$, or $(2i + 1)/2$. The angle gets very tiny for $|G|\% \ N$, and therefore, the highest value of g_i will be achieved when $I >\ = |g_i$.

Success rates will decrease as the algorithm iterates. Many classic algorithms are iterative, with more iterations usually yielding better results. For $t = 1/4$, one iteration is the ideal choice, but for $t = 1/2$, it makes no difference how many times the process is repeated.

Grover's method may be considered a linear combination of $|G$ and $|B$ concerning the parameters, operating in the actual two-dimensional subspace spanned by $|G$ and $|B$ at each iteration. All that is done is switch the amplitude from $|B$ to $|G$. Here, Grover's approach is presented in a stunning geometric form. We first discuss amplitude amplification, an extension of Grover's method that necessitates this geometric graph.

11.14 Effective State Operations

Iteration operator $W|0$ is applied to $W|0$ in Grover's method at the first step. A trivial process, W translates $|0$ to every conceivable value, leading to a solution with probability $|G|/N$. W is just that – a simple algorithm. The $U|0$ analysis may be applied right away to any method U that has some amplitude in the good states, assuming we have one that offers an initial response with a higher probability than $U|0$ as this section illustrates. The iteration operator is replaced with amplitude amplification, which generalizes Grover's technique. $Q = -W \ S_0^\pi W \ S_G^\pi$ with

$$Q = -U \ S_0^\pi U^{-1} S_G^\pi$$

To get the same process of engaging as in Section 9.1.4, this part generalizes the reasoning. Allow us to refer to the subspaces G and B that are traversed by the corresponding projection operators P_G and P_B. Let's write 0 as $| = g_0|G + b_0|B$, where $|G$ and $|B$ are the Gaussian distribution coordinates of $|$ onto the negative and positive subgraphs, respectively.

$$|\psi_G\rangle = \frac{1}{g_0} P_G|\psi\rangle$$

and

$$|\psi_B\rangle = \frac{1}{b_0} P_B|\psi\rangle$$

with

$$g_0 = |P_G|\psi\rangle|$$

and

$$b_0 = |P_B|\psi\rangle|$$

We have $|G$, $|B$, g_0, and b_0 equal to one another when $U = W$. This time around, the characteristics of U, as opposed to the good states, determine g_0 and b_0, rather than the number of solutions. So long as the states $|G$ and $|B$ aren't equal superpositions of the good and terrible states, they are nonetheless genuine. The percentage by which the superposition $U|0$ generates a state that meets the precondition P is 1. Reversible method that transfers 2 $|0$ with probability to a collection of solutions in G is what the operator U may be thought of as $t = |g_0|$.

To understand the effect of $Q = -U\,S_0^\pi U^{-1} S_G^\pi$, recall from Section 7.4.2 that $S_0^\pi \varphi|$ can be

Since

$$Q|\psi_G\rangle = -U\,S_0^\pi U^{-1} S_G^\pi\ |\ \psi_G$$
$$= U\,S_0^\pi U^{-1}\ |\ \psi_G$$
$$= |\psi_G\rangle - 2\overline{g_0}U\ |\ 0$$
$$= |\psi_G\rangle - 2\overline{g_0}g_0|\psi_G\rangle - 2\overline{g_0}b_0\ |\ \psi_B$$
$$= (1 - 2t)|\psi_G\rangle - 2\sqrt{t(1 - t)}\ |\ \psi_B$$

and

$$\overline{Q}|\psi_B = -\ |\ \psi_B + 2b_0 U\ |\ 0$$
$$= -|\psi_B\rangle + 2\overline{b_0}g_0|\psi_G\rangle + 2\overline{b_0}b_0\ |\ \psi_B$$
$$= -|\psi_B\rangle + 2(1 - t)\frac{g_0}{b_0}|\psi_G\rangle + 2(1 - t)\ |\ \psi_B$$
$$= (1 - 2t)|\psi_B\rangle + 2\sqrt{t(1 - t)}|\psi_G\rangle$$

Q performs the following transformation on any real superposition of $|G$ and $|B$: $Q(g_i|\psi_G + b_i|\psi_B)\ |G$ and $|B$: $Q(g_i\ |\ \psi_G + b_i\ |\ \psi_B) = (g_i(1 - 2t) + 2b_i\sqrt{t(1 - t)})$ $|\psi_G\rangle + (b_i(1 - 2t) - 2g_i\sqrt{t(1 - t)})|\psi_B\rangle$it results in the same recurrence connection as before,

$$g_i\sin((2i + 1)\theta) \qquad g_{i+1} = (1 - 2t)g_i + 2\sqrt{t(1 - t)}b_i$$
$$b_i = \cos((2i + 1)\theta) \qquad b_{i+1} = (1 - 2t)b_i - 2\sqrt{t(1 - t)}g_i$$

with the solution for $\sin\theta = \sqrt{t} = g_0$.

g_0 is modest, therefore g_i will be at its maximum after a few repetitions. To discover a solution using the algorithm U, an average of $1/t$ iterations is required if U is successful with a statistical likelihood t. It only takes $O(1/t)$ attempts to discover a solution when using amplitude amplification. Amplification of amplitude will have no impact if U is attenuated in the happy states, then $g_0 = 0$. Furthermore, if g_0 is large, amplitude amplification cannot ameliorate the difficulty, just as no iteration of Grover's approach raises the likelihood if $t = 1/2$. The results aren't improved by using an amplitude amplification algorithm on an algorithm U that was generated by amplitude amplification.

11.14.1 2D Geometry

An argument in two-dimensional geometry and trigonometry may be used to explain the logic underlying amplifying the signal's amplitude by some factor, with consideration given to how many repetitions of the Q algorithm should be performed. In this case, we'll assume that $|G$ and $|B$ remain the same as before. This section uses Grover's method to show that the whole explanation of amplitude amplification and the subsequent revolutions in the real two-dimensional subspace can be reduced to a simple geometric statement in Figure 11.14.

$$\{|\psi G, |\psi B\}$$

The starting state $U|0 = g\,b_0|B$ has real amplitudes g_0 and b_0, as required by the definitions of $|G$ and $|B$, and therefore is in the two-dimensional real planes swept by. The closer $U|0$ is near $|B$, the lower the success probability t. Let us denote by the angle formed by $U|0$ and $|G$, as shown in Figure 11.15. As a result, the angle is

Figure 11.14 The initial state $U|0$ in the basis.

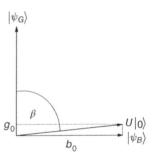

Figure 11.15 Structure of transformation variables.

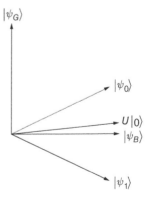

solely determined by the likelihood that a solution exists if the initial condition $U|0$ is measured. $g_0 = \cos() = G|U|0 = $ int. Here, we'll break out how Grover's method gradually moves the state in the desired direction by rotating it by a constant angle at each iteration.

By reflecting $|0$ about $|B$, the SG transformation produces the $|1$ state. Repeating this process until the desired state is very close to $|G$ allows us to optimize the amplitude of the good states. It is possible to determine the optimal number of runs and the probability of success based on the situation's fundamental geometry.

To be more precise, Grover's approach produces amplitude amplification precisely when $U = W$. To further understand the geometric significance of the SG transformation, think about it in terms of the hyperplane that is orthogonal to $|G$. To simplify this training set, we'll assume that $|B$ occupies a single dimension in the plane ($[G,|B]$). The mapping from any $|0$ state in the $|G,|B$ subspace to $|1 = SG|0$ is shown in Figure 9.3. For the transformation 1, this is also a consideration of the orthogonal hyperplane of $|0$. One may reflect on US0 U by thinking about the higher-dimensional space orthogonal to $U|0$. Its effect on $|1$ is seen in Figure 11.16. Figure 9.5 shows that the direction of the state vector has been altered by the last negative sign. The negative sign is superfluous since the quantum state is unaffected by the global phase shift. However, since we are drawing in the plane rather than projective space, it is easier to understand what is happening. In differential geometry, two reflections are said to be synchronized if and only if their axes rotate by a combined total of 360°. In this case, the angle between the two axes of reflection is where $\cos = g_0$, as in the preceding case, therefore the axes of reflection are orthogonal to $U|0$ and $|G$. The two reflections add up to a rotation by 2, and the rotation accomplishes the ultimate negation. This means that there is a 180° rotation between each Q step.

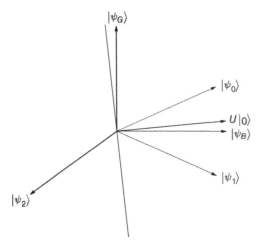

Figure 11.16 The transformation causes $|2$ to exist by reflecting $|1$ down a line that is perpendicular to $U|0$.

Let $\theta = \frac{\pi}{2} - \beta$, the angle formed by $U|0$ and $|B$, with $\sin = g_0$ as in the preceding analysis. Since the state is rotated by 2 for each Q iteration, the angle after I steps is $(2i + 1)$.

With the last minus sign, we rotate by a factor of 2, from $|2$ to $|3$.

After I steps toward the good side, the amplitude is again given by $g_i = \sin((2i + 1))$. Again, similar to what we did at the conclusion, we calculate the optimum number of iterations.

11.15 Grover's Algorithm and Its Optimality

Just as important as the algorithm itself is proof that Grover's technique is as good as any practical quantum algorithm for exhaustive search. Before Grover discovered his method, a lower bound on the query difficulty of any vast mathematical model had already been established: no quantum procedure can need less than calls to the predicate UP. Thus, Grover's method proves to be the most efficient. That's why quantum computers will never be able to compete with classical ones.

Incorrect hopes have been placed in quantum computers to provide an exponential speedup for all computations; this is due to the exponentially vast quantum state space. Quantum computers may provide exponential speedups for any parallelizable computation that only requires one result, according to a less naive notion. Optimization challenges using Grover's approach demonstrate that quantum computers will only provide a very minimal speedup compared to classical computers. This subsection details an optimality proof in the special scenario when there is just one solution x. A maximum number of oracle UP calls is established by the evidence. The reasoning may be applied to any problem with several answers.

Methods for deriving S_x from UP are shown in Sx can talk to the oracle. Every procedure using S_x can be rewritten in terms of UP, and vice versa, thanks to reversible computing, so we don't sacrifice any generality.

Each quantum search method may be seen as a cycle of unitary transformations that do not depend on x followed by a query to the oracle UP. The rationale holds even if we allow the use of additional qubits; we merely use them instead of, and the method is less efficient since N is now greater.

Important to remember: the algorithm has to work no matter which x is correct. For each x, there are transformations that can quickly find x. Whatever x may be; a fast-finding procedure is desired. An adequate probability must be returned for each possible value of x by any search technique deserving of the name. In this study, we focus primarily on quantum search algorithms that can return x with a probability of at least $p = 1/2$. Readers may check any value at their leisure.

It is possible to acquire an $O(N)$ bound by using a different constant for $0\ p\ 1$. It can be shown that the state | obtained after k steps of type $U_i S_x$ is valid.

$$|x|\psi_k^x\rangle|^2 \geq \frac{1}{2}$$

for all x, then k must be $\Omega(\sqrt{N})$. This paragraph provides a basic outline of the reasoning behind the conclusion. In order to ensure that the method works for every x, if the oracle interface is, then the outcome of performing the algorithm $U_k S_x \ldots U_1 S_x \ldots U_0 |0$ must be a state |x sufficiently near to |x that x will be acquired upon measuring device with a strong possibility. The end states of the method for different must be sufficiently far apart since two aspects of the conventional foundation |x and |y cannot be closer than a specific constant. Running the algorithm yields a different result depending on how many times S_x is called. Since the algorithms all begin in the same state, it is possible to derive a constraint on k, the number of oracle interfaces S_x calls, by bounding from above the distance between |ix and |i. This means we want to apply $U_i S_x$ to |ix 1 and $U_i S_y$ to |iy 1 to limit the rise in distance. Both |ix and |iy are compared to a state acquired by applying U_0 up through U_i with no intervening calls to S_x in order to establish this bound. As a first step, we provide a comprehensive explanation of how to leverage the inequalities derived from these concepts to demonstrate the need of making calls to the oracle.

11.15.1 Reduction to Three Inequalities

The proof considers the relation between three classes of quantum states: the desired result |x, the state of the computation |ψ_k^x after k steps, and the state $|\psi_k\rangle = U_k U_{k-1} \ldots U_1 U_0 |0$ obtained by performing the sequence of transformations U_i without consulting the oracle. The analysis simplifies if we sometimes consider, instead of|x, a phase-adjusted version of |x, namely

$|x'\ e_k^{i\theta x}\ x\ k =|$, where $e_k^{\theta x}\quad x\ \psi_k^x/x\ \psi^x =|\ |\ |\ k\ |$. The phase adjustment is chosen so that $x'_k\ \psi_k^x\ |$ is positive real for all k. Since |xk differs from |x only in a phase, whenever $|x\psi_k^x 2|\ |\ \geq \frac{1}{2}$, we have a similar inequality for |x'_k, namely

in which case $\langle x'_k\ |\ \psi_k^x\rangle \geq \frac{1}{\sqrt{2}}$.

Here, we evaluate the separation between selected pairs of these states:

$$a_{kx} = ||\psi_k^x\rangle - |x'_k\rangle$$

$$c = ||x'\rangle - |\psi\rangle|$$

$$d_{kx} = ||\psi_k^x\rangle - |\psi_k||$$

The proof provides upper and lower limits on the average or total of the squares of these distances:

$$D_k = \frac{1}{N}\sum_x d_{kx}^2, A_k = \frac{1}{N}\sum_x a_{kx}^2, C_k = \frac{1}{N}\sum_x c_{kx}^2$$

Search algorithms that may be used in a wide range of contexts must be capable of efficiently finding all potential values of x of the evidence establishing three inequalities combining D_k, A_k, and C_k. We first outline and then illustrate how the inequality suggests less limits on the use of the oracle.

To begin, the average squared distance between the final state | created after k steps and the phase-adjusted solutions state | demonstrates the need of the following inequality for achieving a success probability of | | |.

$$A_k \leq 2 - \sqrt{2}$$

Once N 4, the second inequality constraints C_k, the sum of the squared deviations between the vector $|k$ and all of the basis vectors $|j$: C_k N.

$$C_k \geq 1$$

The third inequality bounds the growth of D_k, the average squared distance between $|\psi^k{}_x$ and $|\psi_k$ as k increases:

$$D_k \leq \frac{4k^2}{N}$$

The three quantities d_{kx}, a_{kx}, and c_{kx} are related as follows:

$$d_{kx} = ||\psi_k^x\rangle - |\psi_k\rangle| = ||\psi_k^x\rangle - e^{i\theta_x^k}|x\rangle + e^{i\theta_x^k}|x\rangle - |\psi_k\rangle| \geq a_{kx} - c_{kx}$$

To relate the quantities D_{kx}, A_{kx}, and C_{kx}, we use the Cauchy–Schwarz inequality (see Box 9.1) to obtain

$$D_k = \frac{1}{N}\sum_x d_{kx}^2$$

$$\geq \frac{1}{N}\left(\sum_x a_{kx}^2 - 2\sum_x a_{kx}c_{kx} + \sum_x c_{kx}^2\right)$$

$$\geq \frac{1}{N}\sum_x a_{kx}^2 - \frac{2}{N}\sqrt{\left(\sum_x a_{kx}^2\right)\left(\sum_x c_{kx}^2\right)} + \frac{1}{N}\sum_x c_{kx}^2$$

$$\geq A_k - 2\sqrt{A_k C_k} + C_k.$$

Making use of this inequality and the three earlier ones, we bound $\dfrac{4k^2}{N}$ from below by a constant:

$$\frac{4k^2}{N} \geq D_k$$

$$\geq A_k - 2\sqrt{A_k C_k} + C_k$$

$$= \left(\sqrt{C_k} - \sqrt{A_k}\right)^2$$

$$\geq \left(1 - \sqrt{2 - \sqrt{2}}\right)^2$$

since $1 \geq 2 - \sqrt{2} \geq A_k$. Thus, for $N \geq 4$ (needed for the second inequality), and taking $q = 1 - \sqrt{2 - \sqrt{2}}$, at least $k \geq \frac{q}{2}\sqrt{N}$ iterations are required for a success probability of $|\langle x \mid \psi_k^x \rangle|^2 \geq \frac{1}{2}$ for all x. We now turn to the proofs of the three inequalities.

11.16 Amplitude Amplification using Discrete Event Randomization of Grover's Algorithm

Grover's algorithm, like Shor's, is not based on chance. It is possible to modify Grover's method in such a way that it is guaranteed to find a solution while still achieving the exponential speedup it was supposed to achieve. A more general method of de-randomizing amplitude improvement is feasible. Two solutions are suggested by Brassard, Hyer, and Tapp. The rotating angle used in the first iteration is less than in the second, while the last step in the second iteration is reduced. Each approach is broken out here for your perusal.

11.16.1 Altering Each Procedure

Consider the case when the angle used in Grover's technique or amplitude amplification is an integer. In this situation, the amplitude g_i would be 1 after a specific number of repetitions, and the algorithm would reliably return a solution. You may recall that $\sin = tg_0$ is satisfied by =. Derandomizing amplitude multiplication for algorithm U with success probability g_0 requires modifying U to achieve an algorithm U with success probability such that for fulfilling, the amount 4 12 is an integer.

We need to be certain that we can effectively construct a less enhanced U from the original U in order to make the process less productive. The key to fixing this is allowing the use of an additional qubit b. A single-qubit transformation is denoted by the notation $U B$ on a $(n + 1)$-qubit register $|s|b$, where U represents the algorithm's success probability g_0 on the register's n bits.

$$B = \sqrt{1 - \frac{g_0'}{g_0}}|0\rangle + \sqrt{\frac{g_0'}{g_0}}$$

Consider the group G to be the set of all conceivable foundation states. The reader may verify for himself that g0 is, in fact, the initial success probability when | |0|. After a given number of steps, the $U\,U\,S\,S$ and iteration operator-based amplitude amplification on a $(n+1)$-qubit state is guaranteed to work.

This tweaked method uses oracle queries to reliably acquire a solution at the expense of a single extra qubit.

11.16.2 Last Stage Variation

Though more difficult to explain in detail, this method guarantees a timely solution without the need for a second qubit. To achieve the ideal end state, it is necessary to make adjustments in the last stage. As a first step, we investigate the universal characteristics of conversions of

$$Q(\phi, \tau) = -U\, S_0^\phi U^{-1} S_G^\tau$$

where ϕ and τ are both arbitrary angles and

$$S_X^\phi |x\rangle = \begin{cases} e^{i\phi} \mid x \end{cases}$$

displayed effective methods for using S_X. To begin, we demonstrate that for each $|v$ quantum state,

$$U\, S_0^\phi U^{-1} |v\rangle = |v\rangle - (1 - e^{i\phi})\overline{\langle v \mid U \mid 0\rangle}\, U \mid 0\rangle$$

Then

$$U\, S_0^\phi U^{-1}|v\rangle = U\, S_0^\phi \left(\sum_{i=1}^{N-1} \overline{\langle v \mid U \mid i\rangle}\, |i\rangle + \overline{\langle v \mid U \mid 0\rangle}\, |0\rangle \right)$$

$$= U \left(\sum_{i=1}^{N-1} \overline{\langle v \mid U \mid i\rangle}\, |i\rangle + \overline{\langle v \mid U e^{i\phi} \mid 0\rangle}\, |0\rangle \right)$$

$$= \sum_{i=1}^{N-1} \overline{\langle v \mid U \mid i\rangle}\, U|i\rangle + e^{i\phi} \overline{\langle v \mid U \mid 0\rangle}\, U \mid 0$$

$$= |v\rangle - (1 - e^{i\phi})\overline{\langle v \mid U \mid 0\rangle}\, U \mid 0\rangle$$

Using this result, we now can see the effect of $Q(\phi, \tau) = U\, S_0^\phi U^{-1} S_G^\tau$ on any superposition $|v = g|v_G + b|v_B$ in the subspace spanned by $|v_G$ and $|v_B$. We have

$$Q(\phi, \tau)|v\rangle = g(ie^{i\tau}|v_G\rangle + e^{i\tau}(1 - e^{i\phi})\overline{\langle v_G \mid U \mid 0\rangle}\, U \mid 0\rangle)$$
$$+ b(-|v_B\rangle + (1 - e^{i\phi})\overline{\langle v_B \mid U \mid 0\rangle}\, U \mid 0\rangle)$$

$Q(\phi,\tau)|\psi = g(\phi,\tau)|\psi G + b(\phi,\tau)|\psi B$, where

$$g(\phi, \tau) = \sin((2s+1)\theta)e^{i\tau}\left((1 - e^{i\phi})g_0^2 - 1\right) + \cos((2s+1)\theta)(1 - e^{i\phi})b_0 g_0$$
$$b(\phi, \tau) = \sin((2s+1)\theta)e^{i\tau}(1 - e^{i\phi})g_0 b_0 + \cos((2s+1)\theta)\left((1 - e^{i\phi})b_0^2 - 1\right)$$

Our aim now is to show that there exist φ and τ such that if is applied as a final step, a solution is obtained with certainty.

We want evidence that may be selected so that the full amplitude of $Q(\varphi,\tau)$ is realized in the good states $b(\varphi,\tau) = 0$ or

$$(\sin((2s+1)\theta)e^{i\tau}(1 - e^{i\phi})g_0 b_0) + \cos((2s+1)\theta)\left((1 - e^{i\phi})b_0^2 - 1\right) = 0$$

or

$$e^{i\tau}(1 - e^{i\phi})g_0 \sqrt{1 - g_0^2}\sin((2s+1)\theta) = \left(1 - (1 - e^{i\phi})\left(1 - g_0^2\right)\right)\cos((2s+1)\theta)$$

since $b_0 = \sqrt{1 - g_0^2}$. Since the right-hand side equals

$$\left(g_0^2(1 - e^{i\phi}) + e^{i\phi}\right)\cos((2s+1)\theta)$$

we want ϕ and τ to satisfy

$$\cot((2s+1)\theta) = \frac{e^{i\tau}(1 - e^{i\phi})g_0\sqrt{1 - g_0^2}}{g_0^2(1 - e^{i\phi}) + e^{i\phi}} \tag{11.2}$$

Following the selection, we then choose to materialize the area to its right. Calculate the square root of the right-hand side of Eq. (11.2) to get.

$$\frac{g_0^2 b_0^2(2 - 2\cos\phi)}{g_0^4(2 - 2\cos\phi) - g_0^2(2 - 2\cos\phi) + 1}$$

The maximum value of the magnitude squared, obtained when $\cos\phi = -1$, is

$$\frac{4g_0^2 b_0^2}{4g_0^4 - 4g_0^2 + 1} = \frac{4g_0^2 b_0^2}{\left(2g_0^2 - 1\right)^2}$$

So the maximum magnitude is

$$\frac{2g_0 b_0}{2g_0^2 - 1} = \frac{2g_0 b_0}{g_0^2 - b_0^2} = \tan(2\theta)$$

where $\sin\theta = \sqrt{t} = g_0$ as before. The right-hand side of Eq. (9.5) may be any real integer between 0 and $\tan(2)$, depending on the values of and. After iteration the state has rotated to fix target value according to geometric representation. In this way, we have shown that s repetitions of Q followed by a single application of $Q(,)$ guarantees a solution.

11.16.3 Solutions: Possibly Infinite

In order to determine how many times, the transformations Q should be done, we need to know the ratio of solutions $t = |G|/N$. If you want to boost the volume, you will need to feed in the success probability $t = |g_0|2$ of $U|0$. There are two options available to us when we are in a position of ignorance. In the first approach, a different number of Q repeats is picked at random for each iteration of Grover's algorithm. Even though this approach is brief, it is quite efficient at finding the correct answer. For the second technique, quantum counting, we use the quantum Fourier transform to estimate t; this process requires $O(N)$ calls to UP.

11.16.4 Varying the Number of Iterations

Let's check out how well Grover's method works with problems that have tN solutions in a cardinality N space. When t is not known, the Grover method with a random repeating step number between 0 and is a simple approach. For large values of t, this simple method is suboptimal. As we can see, however, this simple method is applicable to the vast majority of $O(N)$ calls regardless of the value of t.

The formula should offer an average future performance for a run with I repetitions of Q, where I is a random number between 0 and 1.

$$Pr(i < r) = \frac{1}{r} \sum_{i=0}^{r-1} \sin^2(2i + 1)$$

In the same way that sin t equals t, Figure 11.17 shows a graph showing the average -future performance for various values of r. For all values of t more significant than 1%, the graph will be the same. As a side note, a graph of the Grover algorithm's success rate after precisely r iteration steps is also shown.

The graphs of these functions demonstrate the existence of a constant c such that $Pr(i < r) > c$ for all $r \geq \frac{\pi}{4}\sqrt{\frac{1}{\sqrt{t}}}$. For $\geq 1\ t \leq N$, guaranteeing at least one solution,

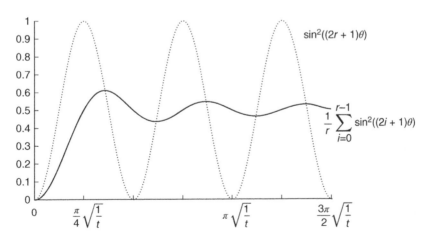

Figure 11.17 Number of iterations in Grover's approach.

if we choose $\pi/4\,N)$ c. Thus, a single run of the algorithm, where the number of iterations of Q

The average success probability $Pr(i < r)$ over runs with a random number of iterations chosen between 0 and r plotted using the conventional formula where $\sin = t$. For comparison, the dotted curve shows the chance of succeeding for a run with precisely r repetitions to get right answer, but that results must be lie between 0 and 4N $O(N)$ is the number of times the oracle will be called throughout this run. With a likelihood c, if Grover's method is run K times with the repetitions for each run selected as above, a solution will be discovered with a percentage k. There are $O(N)$ calls to an oracle for any c since Q is implemented $O(N)$ times in total.

11.16.5 Quantum Counting

While Grover's technique uses a fixed convergence rate of Q to provide an estimation of the number of solutions, quantum counting uses a variable number of rounds of Q to produce a more precise estimate of how many solutions there are in total. The similar method may be used for the amplitude augmentation algorithm to determine the successful probability $\sqrt{t}$ of $U|0$. A query complexity of $O(N)$ is also required for this method.

The process itself is straightforward to explain, but figuring out how big of a superposition you will need is more difficult. It describes the amplitude amplification algorithm. Use U and Q as specified there. Repeat Q, using $|k$ and $|$ as inputs, runs k repetitions of Q on $|$, as defined:

$$\text{Repeat } Q : |k\rangle \otimes |\psi\rangle \rightarrow |k\rangle \otimes Q^k|\psi\rangle$$

Due to its capacity to handle entanglement, this translation surpasses the traditional capabilities of repeating Q in this regard. Repeat Q is used to produce the state $U|0$ from a synthesis of all k $M = 2m$.

$$\frac{1}{\sqrt{M}} \sum_{k=0}^{M-1} |k\rangle \otimes U|0\rangle \rightarrow \frac{1}{\sqrt{M}} \sum_{k=0}^{M-1} |k\rangle \otimes (g_k|\psi_G\rangle + b_k|\psi_B\rangle)$$

where we don't worry about how M got picked just yet or a poor state $|x$ if the proper register in the consistent schedule has been measured (orthogonal to). This reduces the left register state to either 0 or $g_k|k$. Let us assume the former condition is true; the argument for the latter is similar, $b_k = \cos([2+1])$, so.

$$|\psi\rangle = C \sum_{k=0}^{M-1} \cos((2k+1)\theta)|k\rangle$$

In order to derive the corresponding quantum Fourier, transform of this condition,

$$\mathcal{F} : C \sum_{k=0}^{M-1} b_k |k\rangle \rightarrow \sum_{j=0}^{M-1} B_j |j\rangle$$

According to Section 7.8.1, for a cosine function with a period of 1, the bulk of the amplitude is concentrated in the B_j values that are somewhat close to the unique value. If we take a reading of the present condition, we may estimate by subtracting the constant $= j\, M$ from the observed value $|j$. For the ratio of solutions or the success probability of $U|0$ in the Grover's algorithm example or in the amplitude amplification case, the value $t = \sin$ is a good approximation.

We still have no clue what M should be, so that's an issue. To possibly fix this problem, you might try increasing M again and again until you have a correct number for j. We are more likely to see an integer rather than a float when M is too tiny for the context.

11.17   Implementing Grover's Algorithm with Gain Boosting

As the preface to this chapter implies, Grover's approach and its generalization, amplitude amplification, are the focus of this section. Despite seeming little in comparison to the sure this occurs speed improvement of Shor's approach, a quadratic speedup might be of practical consequence, thanks to the reduction in query complexity given by Grover's technique and amplitude amplification over-optimization technique. Although it is just a quadratic speedup compared to the standard Fourier transform, it is nonetheless seen as a significant increase. Take this as an example. Grover's technique delivering a bigger speedup is of less relevance to us than the actual world applications of these algorithms.

It is vital to think about how rapidly UP can be computed in a given real-world situation. Unless UP can be computed effectively, the $O(N)$ speedup of the search will be overshadowed by the time it takes to compute UP. Grover's method will still take $O(N)$ time to execute if UP takes $O(N)$ time to compute, which is the case for any generic P. Because the last measurement in the method breaks the superposition, it is not efficient to do several searches in the same space because UP must be computed from scratch for each search.

Furthermore, most searches in the real world occur in organized contexts, which often provide speedy classical techniques that amplitude amplification cannot improve upon. A traditional approach can find the first item in an alphabetical list of N items in $O(\log_2 N)$ time. Amplitude amplification is not going to speed up this process in any way. Since the search space for real-world search issues is seldom unstructured, Grover's method has limited practical implications. Amplitude amplification is a broad method that can be used to speed up certain heuristic classes but not others.

Grover's approach is effective at searching every possible permutation of a search space. It's common to call Grover's approach a database search algorithm, although this is inaccurate. Grover's method significantly accelerates the process of searching in an unstructured manner. Databases are so well organized that standard techniques of retrieval are efficient. Most database systems, including employment records and analytical and experimental databases (the relevant UP is computationally expensive), are not easy to compute from the first fundamentals. For instance, an alphabetical list of names is structured, but computing it is likely to be slower than adding each entry separately, an $O(N)$ time operation. Because of this, Grover's approach was never previously known as a database search algorithm. In contrast to popular assumption, Grover's approach does not speed up typical database or Internet operations since it takes more time to arrange the components in a superposition state (which is destroyed in each iteration of the search) than it does to conduct the classical search itself.

Since superposition is often linear in N, it cancels out the search method's $O(N)$ benefit. Researchers Childs et al. concluded that for ordered data, quantum computing can only improve upon optimal traditional approaches by a constant factor.

UP can be easily calculated if a complete list of all potential solutions is available, and a simple test can be run to evaluate whether a given input value, x, is a valid representation of a solution. The intensity amplification used by Grover's approach might be useful for a variety of purposes, including the precise estimation of sequence mean and other statistics, the identification of collisions in r-to-1 functions, string matching, and route integration. The appropriate UP for NP-complete problems may be used to efficiently solve that class of problems. Since the speedup provided by Grover's approach is only quadratic for amplitude amplification, problems requiring an exponential number of queries are still solved using the exponential time method. When it comes to solving NP-complete problems quickly and effectively, Grover's search is not the answer. Even if there are tried-and-true approaches to solving problems that make use of the problem's structural qualities, amplitude amplification may only help a select few of these approaches.

References

1 Wenner, J., Yin, Y., Chen, Y. et al. (2014). *Physical Review Letters* 112: 210501.
2 Reagor, M., Paik, H., Catelani, G. et al. (2013). *Applied Physics Letters* 102: 192604.

3 Girvin, S.M. (2011). *Quantum Machines: Measurement Control of Engineered Quantum Systems* (ed. M.H. Devoret, B. Huard, R.J. Schoelkopf, and L.F. Cugliandolo). Oxford University Press.

4 Chou, K.S. (2018). Teleported operations between logical qubits in circuit quantum electrodynamics. PhD thesis. Yale University.

5 Reed, M. (2013). Entanglement and quantum error correction with superconducting qubits. Phd thesis. Yale University.

6 Chu, Y., Axline, C., Wang, C. et al. (2016). *Applied Physics Letters* 109: 112601.

7 Hutchings, M., Hertzberg, J., Liu, Y. et al. (2017). *Physical Review Applied* 8: 044003.

8 Nakamura, Y., Pashkin, Y.A., and Tsai, J.S. (1999). *Nature* 398: 786.

9 Bouchiat, V., Vion, D., Joyez, P. et al. (1998). *Physica Scripta* T76: 165.

10 Bishop, L. (2010). Circuit quantum electrodynamics. PhD thesis. Yale University.

11 Gao, J., Daal, M., Vayonakis, A. et al. (2008). *Applied Physics Letters* 92: 152505.

12 Kamal, A., Clarke, J., and Devoret, M.H. (2011). *Nature Physics* 7: 311.

13 Chapman, B.J., Rosenthal, E.I., Kerckhoff, J. et al. (2017). *Physical Review X* 7: 041043.

14 Frattini, N.E., Vool, U., Shankar, S. et al. (2017). *Applied Physics Letters* 110: 222603.

15 Ristè, D., Bultink, C.C., Tiggelman, M.J. et al. (2013). *Nature Communications* 4: 1913.

16 Pop, I.M., Geerlings, K., Catelani, G. et al. (2014). *Nature* 508: 369.

12

Applications of Quantum Computing

12.1   Introduction

The term "resource" is often used when discussing entanglement in the realm of quantum entanglement and information. This is because entanglement paves the way for tasks like information transmission and storage that would be unachievable without it. In this chapter, we will look at two scenarios in which entangled may be used to do some novel tasks. The first is teleportation, which allows Alice to "send" a quantum state to her friend Bob without ever really sending anything. Using entanglement and the Einstein–Podolsky–Rosen (EPR) paradox, Alice and Bob may set up a quantum channel of communication that would enable Alice to speak with Bob in a way that seems impressive. As we will see, however, transportation can't be utilized to produce real-time communication since it needs Alice and Bob to keep up their regular communication channels [1].

As for our subsequent entanglement investigation, we will be focusing on superdense code. We have shown the potential of computing quantum information with only one qubit by inviting two classical bits to a get together.

12.2   Teleportation

Many individuals are acquainted with the concept of teleportation from reading or watching science fiction movies and television shows. The underlying idea is that you're scanned, converted to energy, and then beamed to your destination.

Using physical phenomena, we can get quite close to something extraordinary, even if it is still more likely to be discovered in fiction than in the actual world. Thanks to this method, we can move a quantum state from one spot to another without the state needing to traverse any physical distance. It would have been a disaster if Albert Einstein had been in the room to hear this. Teleportation is so

Quantum Computing: A New Era of Computing, First Edition.
Kuldeep Singh Kaswan, Jagjit Singh Dhatterwal, Anupam Baliyan, and Shalli Rani.
© 2023 The Institute of Electrical and Electronics Engineers, Inc. Published 2023 by John Wiley & Sons, Inc.

terrifying that he will be scared to death [2] if he thinks quantum superpositions are scary.

Teleportation may seem to work almost miraculously to Einstein, but may be able to take a deep breath of relief knowing that special relativity looks to step in and forbid real-time communication. Let's break this down into its basic formalities. Alice wants to transmit to Bob a quantum state of which both of them are unaware. Let's name the country where Alice plans on relocating Bob. The state is a bit:

$$|\chi\rangle = \alpha|0\rangle + \beta|1\rangle \tag{12.1}$$

When we say the state is unknown, we are implying that we have no idea what it is. For now, let's just suppose the state is normalized, in which case: $\|2 + \|2 = 1$. The process of teleportation is broken down into many stages. The first step is to create an EPR pair that is entangled.

Teleportation Step 1: Particles Entangled Between Alice and Bob

The entanglement state is the result of Alice and Bob's interactions.

$$|\beta_{00}\rangle = \frac{|0_A\rangle|0_B\rangle + |1_A\rangle|1_B\rangle}{\sqrt{2}} = \frac{|00\rangle + |11\rangle}{\sqrt{2}} \tag{12.2}$$

We have concluded that Alice is the rightful owner of the pair's first member, while Bob is the rightful owner of the pair's second member. As a result, Alice and Bob are no longer together. Alice chooses to give Bob (12.1) the state. To do this, she must allow her EPR partner to interact with it (12.2).

Teleportation Step 2: Alice Applies a CNOT Gate

First, let's take note of the system's present state. This state is the result of an EPR pair and the previously unknown state (12.1):

$$|\psi\rangle = |\chi\rangle \oplus |\beta_{00}\rangle$$

$$= (\alpha|0\rangle + \beta|1\rangle) \oplus \left(\frac{|00\rangle + |11\rangle}{\sqrt{2}}\right)$$

$$= \frac{\alpha(|000\rangle + |011\rangle) + \beta(|100\rangle + |111\rangle)}{\sqrt{2}} \tag{12.3}$$

Alice owns the top two qubits in this state, whereas Bob owns the rightmost qubit. So, Alice possesses a 01, whereas Bob has a 1 in his possession.

A CNOT gate is applied to Alice's EPR pair, the second qubit in (12.3), to begin communicating with the unprecedented extent, which is the first qubit in (12.3). An EPR pair member is the investigation's target qubit, while the control qubit is in an unknown state. Recall that the target qubit remains unchanged regardless of the value of the control qubit (0 or 1) [3].

$$|00\rangle \mapsto |00\rangle, |01\rangle \mapsto |01\rangle, |01\rangle \mapsto |10\rangle \mapsto |11\rangle, |11\rangle \mapsto |10\rangle \qquad (12.4)$$

As a result, Alice's state changes when she applies the CNOT gate to

$$\begin{aligned}
|\psi'\rangle &= U_{\text{CNOT}}|\psi\rangle \\
&= \frac{\alpha(U_{\text{CNOT}}|000\rangle + U_{\text{CNOT}}|011\rangle) + \beta(U_{\text{CNOT}}|100\rangle + U_{\text{CNOT}}|111\rangle)}{\sqrt{2}} \\
&= \frac{\alpha(|000\rangle + |011\rangle) + \beta(|110\rangle + |101\rangle)}{\sqrt{2}}
\end{aligned} \qquad (12.5)$$

Teleportation Step 3: Alice Applies a Hadamard Gate

The Hadamard gate will be applied to the first qubit by Alice next. To recap, Hadamard gates transform the operational basis states into quantum weirdness [4].

$$H|0\rangle = \frac{|0\rangle + |1\rangle}{\sqrt{2}}, \quad H|1\rangle = \frac{|0\rangle - |1\rangle}{\sqrt{2}} \qquad (12.6)$$

This is how we will modify the state (12.5) to be a little clear:

$$|\psi'\rangle = \frac{\alpha|0\rangle(|00\rangle + |11\rangle)}{\sqrt{2}} + \frac{\beta|1\rangle(|10\rangle + |01\rangle)}{\sqrt{2}} \qquad (12.7)$$

As a result, Alice changes the state to

$$\begin{aligned}
|\psi''\rangle = H|\psi'\rangle &= \frac{\alpha H|0\rangle(|00\rangle + |11\rangle)}{\sqrt{2}} + \frac{\beta H|1\rangle(|10\rangle + |01\rangle)}{\sqrt{2}} \\
&= \alpha\left(\frac{|0\rangle + |1\rangle}{\sqrt{2}}\right)\frac{|00\rangle + |11\rangle}{\sqrt{2}} + \beta\left(\frac{|0\rangle + |1\rangle}{\sqrt{2}}\right)\frac{|10\rangle + |01\rangle}{\sqrt{2}}
\end{aligned} \qquad (12.8)$$

Bob has the third qubit, so keep that in mind.

Teleportation Step 4: Alice Measures Her Pair

Alice then measures both qubits she is holding. Step one is to reorganize the state such that it is shown in terms of the possibilities associated with production on the first two qubits. These are the probable outcomes of the measurements [5]. As a result, we may write (12.8) as follows:

$$\begin{aligned}
|\psi''\rangle = \frac{1}{2}[&|00\rangle(\alpha|0\rangle + \beta|0\rangle) + |01\rangle\,|01\rangle(\alpha|1\rangle + \beta|0\rangle) + |10\rangle(\alpha|0\rangle \\
&- \beta|1\rangle) + |11\rangle(\alpha|1\rangle - \beta|0\rangle)]
\end{aligned} \qquad (12.9)$$

For if Alice takes the measures, then the state will $|\chi\rangle = \alpha|0\rangle + \beta|1\rangle$ collapse, and Bob will be in trouble because he now has in his possession the initial, unknowable state that Alice meant to give Bob. So Bob owns the state if Alice does the measuring.

He may, however, use an X gate to change this into the desired condition:

$$X(\alpha|1\rangle + \beta|0\rangle) = |10\rangle$$

Suppose Alice takes a reading. At this point, Bob has control of the $\alpha|0\rangle - \beta|1\rangle$ state. Using a Z gate, he may get the required result.

If Alice takes a reading. Bob has to use three gates, an X and a Z, this time.

$$ZX(\alpha|1\rangle - \beta|1\rangle) = \alpha ZX|1\rangle - \beta ZX|0\rangle = \alpha Z|0\rangle - \beta Z|1\rangle$$
$$= \alpha|0\rangle + \beta|1\rangle = |x\rangle \tag{12.10}$$

So how does Bob figure out what to do? What Alice has to do is call him.

Teleportation Step 5: Through a Traditional Exchange of Information, Alice Reports Her Measurements to Result to Bob.

Special relativity makes an unexpected appearance at this point in the game. This means that Alice must communicate with Bob via a method controlled by the speed of light, whether it be a phone call, an email, a radio wave, or anything else. In this stage, Alice and Bob are unable to exchange information faster than the speed of light because of this. By phoning Alice and telling Bob that she got 01, for example, Bob's X gate may be used to get the state Alice intended to send to Bob. Given that they shared an entangled EPR pair of particles, Bob was able to access that state through the classical channel.

In conclusion, local operations and classical communications (LOCC) are two pillars of quantum information transfer. Each participant must carry out two distinct actions: (i) a quantum mechanical (local unitary) operation on their own state, and (ii) the transmission of measurement data through classical telecommunication [6].

Bob will see the situation as random if classical communications are not employed.

12.3 The Peres Partial Transposition Condition

Teleportation studies are currently ongoing at this time. It may serve as a springboard for us to explore the tools of quantum computing theory [7]. To begin, we look at the Peres partial translocation requirement, which tells us whether a certain density operator reflects an entanglement state or not. It's possible to express an unlimited density matrix this way.

$$\rho_{AB} = \sum_{i,j,k,l} \rho_{ijkl} |i\rangle\langle j| \oplus |k\rangle\langle l| \tag{12.11}$$

can be partially transposed as follows:

$$\rho_{AB}^{T_B} = \sum_{i,j,k,l} \rho_{ijkl} |i\rangle\langle j| \oplus k\rangle\langle l| \tag{12.12}$$

As an example, if we're talking about a state

$$|\psi\rangle = \frac{1}{\sqrt{\alpha}} \sum_i |a_i b_i\rangle \quad \text{and} \quad \rho_{AB} = |\psi\rangle\langle\psi|$$

that is,

$$\rho_{AB} = \frac{1}{\alpha} \sum_{ij} |a_i b_i\rangle\langle a_j b_j| \tag{12.13}$$

Afterwards, we have the partial transposition as

$$\rho_{AB}^{T_B} = \frac{1}{\alpha} \sum_{ij} |a_i b_i\rangle\langle a_j b_j| \tag{12.14}$$

Just change out the second qubit. Calculating the partial transposition, for instance, of a distribution function

$$|01\rangle\langle00| \mapsto |00\rangle\langle01|, |01\rangle\langle10| \mapsto |00\rangle\langle11|, |01\rangle\langle01| \mapsto |01\rangle\langle01|$$

What is the benefit of this? If T has any deleterious eigenvectors, it is an entanglement density operator. Separability is guaranteed when all the eigenvalues are equal to 1.

Example 12.1   The Bell state is well-known.

$$|\beta_{01}\rangle = \frac{|01\rangle + |10\rangle}{\sqrt{2}}$$

is tied up. Use the Peres partial translation requirement to illustrate this point.

Solution
The density operator is

$$\rho = |\beta_{01}\rangle\langle\beta_{01}|$$
$$= \left(\frac{|01\rangle + |10\rangle}{\sqrt{2}} \right) \left(\frac{\langle01| + \langle10|}{\sqrt{2}} \right)$$
$$= \frac{1}{2}(|01\rangle\langle01| + |01\rangle\langle10| + |10\rangle\langle01| + |10\rangle\langle10|)$$

In the $|00\rangle, |01\rangle, |10\rangle, |11\rangle$ on what the matrix form of this density operator is

When the B qubits in each phrase are switched, the partial transposition may be calculated. Hence

$$\rho^{T_B} = \frac{1}{2}(|01\rangle\langle01| + |00\rangle\langle11| + |11\rangle\langle00| + |10\rangle\langle10|)$$

The matrix representation of

The eigenvalues of ρ^{T_B} are $\left\{ \frac{-1}{2}, \frac{1}{2}, \frac{1}{2}, \frac{1}{2} \right\}$. This is an entangled state, as shown by the existence of a negative eigenvalue. Even while the eigenvalues of a matrix are not affected by the underlying basis, the term referring of the transformation T_B itself is reliant on the underlying basis.

Example 12.2 For this illustration, let's imagine a state that may exist independently from any other.

$$|\psi\rangle = \left(\frac{|0\rangle - |1\rangle}{\sqrt{2}} \right) \otimes \left(\frac{|0\rangle - |1\rangle}{\sqrt{2}} \right) = \frac{|00\rangle - |01\rangle - |10\rangle + |11\rangle}{2}$$

Prove this by demonstrating that it satisfies the Peres partial transposition requirement.

Solution

The density operator is

$$\rho = |\psi\rangle\langle\psi|$$

$$= \left(\frac{|00\rangle - |01\rangle - |10\rangle + |11\rangle}{2} \right) \left(\frac{\langle 00| - \langle 01| - \langle 10| + \langle 11|}{2} \right)$$

$$= \frac{1}{4} (|00\rangle\langle 00| - |00\rangle\langle 01| - |00\rangle\langle 10| + |00\rangle\langle 11| - |01\rangle\langle 00| + |01\rangle\langle 01|$$

$$+ |01\rangle\langle 10| - |01\rangle\langle 11| - |10\rangle\langle 00| + |10\rangle\langle 01| + |10\rangle\langle 10| - |10\rangle\langle 11|)$$

$$+ |11\rangle\langle 00| - |11\rangle\langle 01| - |11\rangle\langle 10| + |11\rangle\langle 11|)$$

The partial transpose is

$$\rho^{T_B} = \frac{1}{4} (|00\rangle\langle 00| - |01\rangle\langle 00| - |00\rangle\langle 10| + |01\rangle\langle 10| - |00\rangle\langle 01| + |01\rangle\langle 01|$$

$$+ |00\rangle\langle 11| - |01\rangle\langle 11|) - |10\rangle\langle 00| + |11\rangle\langle 00| + |10\rangle\langle 10| - |11\rangle\langle 10|)$$

$$+ |10\rangle\langle 01| - |11\rangle\langle 01| - |10\rangle\langle 11| + |11\rangle\langle 11|)$$

In this instance, both operators are the same. So

$$\rho^{T_B} = \frac{1}{4} \begin{pmatrix} 1 & -1 & -1 & 1 \\ -1 & 1 & 1 & -1 \\ -1 & 1 & 1 & -1 \\ 1 & -1 & -1 & 1 \end{pmatrix}$$

The eigenvalues of T_B are 1, 0, 0, 0. The Peres partial transposition condition demonstrates that this is a separate state since all I 0.

We have Bob and Charlie, two quantum states with unknown parameters that may be simultaneously teleported by Alice. Let's say Alice wishes to send the current state to someone else.

$$|\emptyset_1\rangle = \alpha_1|0\rangle + \beta_1|1\rangle \tag{12.15}$$

to Bob and the state

$$|\emptyset_2\rangle = \alpha_2|0\rangle + \beta_2|1\rangle \tag{12.16}$$

Sending Charlie warm wishes. Alice must be holding two sets that are joined together, which she shares with Bob and Charlie:

$$|\beta_{A_1B}\rangle = \frac{|00\rangle_{A_1B} + |11\rangle_{A_1B}}{\sqrt{2}}$$

$$|\beta_{A_2B}\rangle = \frac{|00\rangle_{A_2B} + |11\rangle_{A_2B}}{\sqrt{2}} \tag{12.17}$$

The current condition of Alice, Bob, and Charlie's interconnected system is

$$|\psi\rangle = (\alpha_1\alpha_2|00\rangle + \alpha_1\beta_2|01\rangle + \alpha_2\beta_1|10\rangle + \beta_1\beta_2|11\rangle)$$

$$\otimes \frac{1}{2}(|0000\rangle + |0101\rangle + |1010\rangle + |1111\rangle)$$

$$|\psi\rangle = (\alpha_1\alpha_2|00\rangle + \alpha_1\beta_2|01\rangle + \alpha_2\beta_1|10\rangle + \beta_1\beta_2|00\rangle) \tag{12.18}$$

Specifically, the first and third qubits of this formula indicate the ambiguity between Alice and Bob, whereas the second and fourth qubits denote the quantum states between Alice and Charlie.

The unitary transformation is used to teleport both states (12.17) and (12.18) simultaneously [8] the qubits belonging to Bob and Charlie. The quantum connection is now "locked." What was the previous state (12.18) becomes what is now

$$|\psi'\rangle = (\alpha_1\alpha_2|00\rangle + \alpha_1\beta_2|01\rangle + \alpha_2\beta_1|10\rangle + \beta_1\beta_2|00\rangle)$$

$$\oplus \frac{1}{2\sqrt{2}}(|0000\rangle + |0101\rangle + |0011\rangle + |0110\rangle + |1000\rangle$$

$$- |1011\rangle + |1101\rangle - |1110\rangle) \tag{12.19}$$

The Bell basis is used next by Alice to quantify her qubits. Pauli matrices I, X, Y, and Z are used to conduct local unitary manipulations on Bob and Charlie's results based on classical communication. However, they lack the necessary states. By performing the inverse of (12.19), namely, they must "unlock" the quantum channel.

$$U_{BC^\dagger} = \frac{1}{\sqrt{2}}\begin{pmatrix} 1 & 0 & 0 & 1 \\ 0 & 1 & 1 & 0 \\ 1 & 0 & 0 & -1 \\ 0 & 1 & -1 & 0 \end{pmatrix} \tag{12.20}$$

Example 12.3 When the channel is secured, Alice and Bob's initial state (12.20) is entangled, but the state they communicate after the connection is locked (12.21) is a product of their original condition.

Solution
Before locking the system, we first write down the density matrix. We take a look at the current situation.

$$|\psi\rangle = (\alpha_1\alpha_2|00\rangle + \alpha_1\beta_2|01\rangle + \alpha_2\beta_1|10\rangle + \beta_1\beta_2|11\rangle)$$

$$\otimes \frac{1}{2}(|0000\rangle + |0101\rangle + |1010\rangle + |1111\rangle)$$

The second term is all that matters to us:

$$|\phi\rangle = \frac{1}{2}(|0000\rangle + |0101\rangle + |1010\rangle + |1111\rangle)$$

The density operator is

$$\rho = |\phi\rangle\langle\phi|$$

$$= \frac{1}{4} (|0000\rangle\langle0000| + |0000\rangle\langle0101| + |0000\rangle\langle1010| + |0000\rangle\langle1111|$$

$$+ |0101\rangle\langle0000| + |0101\rangle\langle0101| + |0101\rangle\langle1010| + |0101\rangle\langle1111|$$

$$+ |1010\rangle\langle0000| + |1010\rangle\langle0101| + |1010\rangle\langle1010| + |1010\rangle\langle1111|$$

$$+ |1111\rangle\langle0000| + |1111\rangle\langle0101| + |1111\rangle\langle1010| + |1111\rangle\langle1111|)$$

In order to determine the concentration operators describing the combined state of Alice and Bob, we must first compute the partial tracing over the Alice–Charlie states. Both of the other qubits have arrived (A_2, C). Therefore, we engage in numerical analysis [9].

$$\rho_{A_1B} = \langle00 | \rho | 00\rangle_{A_2C} + \langle01 | \rho | 01\rangle_{A_2C}$$

$$+ \langle10 | \rho | 10\rangle_{A_2C} + \langle11 | \rho | 11\rangle_{A_2C}$$

Thus, the minimized density operator is established.

$$\rho_{A_1B} = \frac{1}{2}(|00\rangle\langle00| + |00\rangle\langle11| + |11\rangle\langle00| + |11\rangle\langle11|)$$

$$= \frac{1}{2}\begin{pmatrix} 1 & 0 & 0 & 1 \\ 0 & 0 & 0 & 0 \\ 0 & 0 & 0 & 0 \\ 1 & 0 & 0 & 1 \end{pmatrix}$$

The partial transposition has been computed, and it is

$$\rho^{T_B}{}_{A_1B} = \frac{1}{2}(|00\rangle\langle00| + |01\rangle\langle10| + |10\rangle\langle01| + |11\rangle\langle11|)$$

$$= \frac{1}{2}\begin{pmatrix} 1 & 0 & 0 & 0 \\ 0 & 0 & 1 & 0 \\ 0 & 1 & 0 & 0 \\ 0 & 0 & 0 & 1 \end{pmatrix}$$

The eigenvalues of this matrix are $\left\{\frac{-1}{2}, \frac{1}{2}, \frac{1}{2}, \frac{1}{2}\right\}$. Alice and Bob are in an entangled state together before they lock, as shown by one of the eigenvalues, which is $\frac{-1}{2} < 0$.

After locking, the state is defined as (12.23). To be specific, the second term in the tensor product is of interest.

$$|\phi_L\rangle = \frac{1}{2\sqrt{2}}(|0000\rangle + |0101\rangle + |0011\rangle + |0110\rangle$$
$$+ |1000\rangle - |1011\rangle + |1101\rangle - |1110\rangle))$$

Density matrices are represented by

$$\rho_L = |\phi_L\rangle\langle\phi_L|$$

Compiling this matrix is a time-consuming endeavor. You will have to take my word for it that there are 64 words in the expansion. Once we have traced out the A_2C qubits (the second and fifth qubits) and included the Alice–Charlie components, we get the reduced density operator:

$$\rho'_L = \frac{1}{4}(|00\rangle\langle00| + |00\rangle\langle10| + |01\rangle\langle01| - |01\rangle\langle11| + |10\rangle\langle00|$$
$$+ |10\rangle\langle10| - |11\rangle\langle01| + |11\rangle\langle11|)$$
$$= \frac{1}{4}\begin{pmatrix} 1 & 0 & 1 & 0 \\ 0 & 1 & 0 & -1 \\ 1 & 0 & 1 & 0 \\ 0 & -1 & 0 & 1 \end{pmatrix} \tag{12.21}$$

The partial transposition yields the same matrices as the full transposition. In this case, we have. Since each I 0, we infer that the state may be divided into distinct halves. As a result, the connection between Alice and Bob was severed during the locking process.

12.4 Expansion of Transportation

We can entangle two entities that have never communicated before in an intriguing expansion of transportation. Even if the particles are light years away, this is theoretically feasible [10].

Two EPR pairs are needed to begin entangled switching. There are four distinct qubits, each with a unique identifier. This means that while Bob has qubits 2 and 3, Alice has qubits 1 and 4. Qubits 1 and 2 are intertwined in the Bell state.

$$|\beta_{00}\rangle_{12} = \frac{|00\rangle_{12} + |11\rangle_{12}}{\sqrt{2}} \tag{12.22}$$

Similar entanglement exists between qubits 3 and 4:

$$|\beta_{00}\rangle_{34} = \frac{|00\rangle_{34} + |11\rangle_{34}}{\sqrt{2}} \tag{12.23}$$

The product of these two states is

$$|\beta_{00}\rangle_{12}|\beta_{00}\rangle_{34} = \left(\frac{|00\rangle_{12} + |11\rangle_{12}}{\sqrt{2}}\right)\left(\frac{|00\rangle_{34} + |11\rangle_{34}}{\sqrt{2}}\right)$$

$$= \frac{1}{2}(|00\rangle_{12}|00\rangle_{34} + |00\rangle_{12}|11\rangle_{34} + |11\rangle_{12}|00\rangle_{34} + |11\rangle_{12}|11\rangle_{34})$$

Let's get started with some basic algebra. There are two qubits in each term that may be written as a single qubit: qubits 1 and 4 together, and qubits 2 and 3.

$$|\beta_{00}\rangle_{12}|\beta_{00}\rangle_{34} = \frac{1}{2}(|00\rangle_{14}|00\rangle_{23} + |01\rangle_{14}|01\rangle_{23} + |10\rangle_{14}|10\rangle_{23} + |11\rangle_{12}|11\rangle_{34})$$

12.5 Entanglement Swapping

Notice that

$$|\beta_{00}\rangle_{14}|\beta_{00}\rangle_{23} = \left(\frac{|00\rangle_{14} + |11\rangle_{14}}{\sqrt{2}}\right)\left(\frac{|00\rangle_{23} + |11\rangle_{23}}{\sqrt{2}}\right)$$

$$= \frac{1}{2}(|00\rangle_{14}|00\rangle_{23} + |00\rangle_{14}|11\rangle_{23} + |11\rangle_{14}|00\rangle_{23} + |11\rangle_{14}|11\rangle_{23})$$

Some $|\beta_{00}\rangle_{12}|\beta_{00}\rangle_{34}$ of these terms are not present in the product; however, by subtracting them we get

$$|\beta_{00}\rangle_{12}|\beta_{00}\rangle_{34} = \frac{1}{2}\left(|00\rangle_{14}|00\rangle_{23} + |01\rangle_{14}|01\rangle_{23} + |10\rangle_{14}|10\rangle_{23} + |11\rangle_{12}|11\rangle_{34}\right.$$

$$+ |00\rangle_{14}|11\rangle_{23} + |11\rangle_{14}|00\rangle_{23} - |00\rangle_{14}|11\rangle_{23} - |11\rangle_{14}\,|00\rangle_{23})$$

$$= \frac{1}{2}\left(|\beta_{00}\rangle_{14}|\beta_{00}\rangle_{23} + |01\rangle_{14}|01\rangle_{23} + |10\rangle_{14}|10\rangle_{23}\right.$$

$$- |00\rangle_{14}|11\rangle_{23} - |11\rangle_{14}\,|00\rangle_{23})$$

There are similar algebraic strategies that may be applied on the other terms to demonstrate

$$|\beta_{00}\rangle_{12}|\beta_{00}\rangle_{34} = \frac{1}{2}\left(|\beta_{00}\rangle_{14}|\beta_{00}\rangle_{23} + |\beta_{10}\rangle_{14}|\beta_{10}\rangle_{23} + |\beta_{01}\rangle_{14}|\beta_{01}\rangle_{23}\right.$$

$$+ |\beta_{11}\rangle_{14}\,|\beta_{11}\rangle_{23})$$

In addition to particles 1 and 4, Alice possesses them. Particles 1 and 4 are now subjected to a Bell state measurement by Alice. It is conceivable, of course, to get other outcomes, both of which have a chance of being true. Regarding the outcome of Alice's assessment, Bob's system will fall into one of the Bell curves. Particles 2 and 3 are now intertwined.

What we need to do is go back and look at the procedure. There is a new linked state involving Alice and Bob. Particles 1 through 4 are all connected to one another through quantum entanglement. Pieces 1 and 4 belong to Alice, whereas pieces 2 and 3 are Bob's. While Bob carefully flies to a new place with Alice's nanoparticles, Alice does a Bell state standard measurement on them. When Bob's system's state collapses, the connections between particles 2 and 3 get tangled. Just what is it that has been sent over here? A counterargument may be that the link has been severed because of the distance. This procedure will work even if particles 2 and 3 have never interacted. You may imagine the potential significance if Charlie were to steal particle 3 and go somewhere else before the measurement was taken. By measuring Bell states, Alice creates an entanglement pair that Bob and Charlie may use to exchange information about their internal states.

12.6 Superdense Coding

Alice and Bob have reseparated and need to communicate by sending Bob some knowledge. Bob has requested that Alice needs to convey two classical pieces of information but can only use a single qubit. In order to accomplish this remarkable feat, she used a method known as superheated plasma coding. Once again, the simulation begins with Alice and Bob sharing an entangled pair of particles. We also settled on a code: $xy = 00, 01, 10,$ or 11 for the Bell states in a typical bit string. At first, it will be determined by the state.

$$|\psi\rangle = \frac{|00\rangle + |11\rangle}{\sqrt{2}} \tag{12.24}$$

Suppose that Alice has one qubit while Bob has the other. This time, Alice sends Bob her qubit to convey the knowledge. Once she has decided which bit strings she wants to transmit to Bob, Alice uses a single-qubit gate of her choice to manipulate the qubit. Even if she's sending Bob a bit of string, she should not worry about Alice's qubit. As a result, we refer to this initial condition as the Bell state (12.25).

$$|\beta_{00}\rangle = \frac{|00\rangle + |11\rangle}{\sqrt{2}} \tag{12.25}$$

Suppose Alice's qubit was X gated before being sent on its path.

$$(X \otimes I)|\psi\rangle = \frac{|10\rangle + |01\rangle}{\sqrt{2}} = |\beta_{01}\rangle \tag{12.26}$$

The state (12.27) if Alice uses a Z gate on her qubit before sending it to Bob, the state of the qubit will be changed.

$$(Z \otimes I)|\psi\rangle = \frac{|00\rangle - |11\rangle}{\sqrt{2}} = |\beta_{10}\rangle \tag{12.27}$$

Finally, notice that if Alice applies the iY gate, the state is

$$(iY \otimes I)|\psi\rangle = \frac{|01\rangle - |10\rangle}{\sqrt{2}} = |\beta_{11}\rangle \tag{12.28}$$

As soon as Bob $|\beta_{00}\rangle$, $|\beta_{01}\rangle$, $|\beta_{10}\rangle$, or $|\beta_{11}\rangle$ receives Alice's qubit, bob do measurements in the Bell basis to identify are among. Consequently, he gets a 00, 01, 10, or 11 string, the conventional two-bit values.

Example 12.4 A W state is a three-qubit state of the form

$$|W_n\rangle = \frac{1}{\sqrt{2+2n}}(|100\rangle + \sqrt{n}e^{i\gamma}|010\rangle + \sqrt{n+1}e^{i\delta}|001\rangle) \tag{12.29}$$

Consider the particular case of $|W_1\rangle = \frac{1}{2}(|100\rangle + |010\rangle + \sqrt{2}|001\rangle)$. Demonstrate that if Alice has qubits 1, Bob has qubits 2 and 3, and Alice sends Bob her qubit via localized unitary operations, Bob will get two classical bits.

Solution
The state of Alice's qubit is sent to Bob together with the first qubit if she changes nothing to it between sending it and receiving it.

$$|W_1\rangle = \frac{1}{2}(|100\rangle + |010\rangle + \sqrt{2}|001\rangle) = |\psi_{00}\rangle \tag{12.30}$$

Under his control or surveillance Let's pretend for a moment that Alice uses the X gate. If the state does

$$X \otimes I \otimes I|W_1\rangle = \frac{1}{2}(|000\rangle + |110\rangle + \sqrt{2}|101\rangle) = |\psi_{01}\rangle \tag{12.31}$$

If instead Alice applies iY , we have

$$iY \otimes I \otimes I|W_1\rangle = \frac{1}{2}(-|100\rangle + |010\rangle + \sqrt{2}|001\rangle) = |\psi_{10}\rangle \tag{12.32}$$

Under his control or surveillance Let's pretend for a moment that Alice uses the X gate. If the state does

$$Z \otimes I \otimes I|W_1\rangle = \frac{1}{2}(|000\rangle - |110\rangle + \sqrt{2}|101\rangle) = |\psi_{11}\rangle \tag{12.33}$$

The two states are entirely orthogonal to one another. Specifically, consider the example

$$\begin{aligned}\langle\psi_{00} \mid \psi_{01}\rangle &= \frac{1}{4}((\langle100| + \langle010| + \sqrt{2}\langle001|)(|000\rangle + |110\rangle + \sqrt{2}|101\rangle)) \\ &= \frac{1}{4}(\langle1 \mid 0\rangle\langle0 \mid 0\rangle\langle0 \mid 0\rangle + \langle0 \mid 1\rangle\langle1 \mid 1\rangle\langle0 \mid 1\rangle \\ &\quad + 2\langle0 \mid 1\rangle\langle0 \mid 0\rangle\langle1 \mid 1\rangle) \\ &= 0\end{aligned}$$

As a result, once Alice transmits Bob's first qubit, Bob may do a separation of the states using a projective measurement of three qubits. Once Bob has the correct data, may decode it using the predetermined method to retrieve back the two standard bits 00, 01, 10, and 11. $|\psi_{00}\rangle$, $|\psi_{01}\rangle$, $|\psi_{10}\rangle$, or $|\psi_{11}\rangle$, respectively.

References

1 Geerlings, K., Shankar, S., Edwards, E. et al. (2012). *Applied Physics Letters* 100: 192601.

2 Megrant, A., Neill, C., Barends, R. et al. (2012). *Applied Physics Letters* 100: 113510.

3 Houck, A.A., Schuster, D.I., Gambetta, J.M. et al. (2007). *Nature* 449: 328.

4 Hatridge, M., Shankar, S., Mirrahimi, M. et al. (2013). *Science* 339: 178.

5 Reed, M.D., DiCarlo, L., Johnson, B.R. et al. (2010). *Physical Review Letters* 105: 173601.

6 Steck, D.A. *Quantum and Atom Optics*. http://steck.us/teaching; revision 0.10.2, 16 October 2015.

7 Khalil, M.S., Stoutimore, M.J.A., Wellstood, F.C., and Osborn, K.D. (2012). *Journal of Applied Physics* 111: 54510.

8 Gao, J. (2008). *The Physics of Superconducting Microwave Resonators*. PhD thesis. California Institute of Technology.

9 Padamsee, H. (2001). *Superconductor Science and Technology* 14: 1–32.

10 Pappas, D.P., Vissers, M.R., Wisbey, D.S. et al. (2011). *IEEE Transactions on Applied Superconductivity* 21: 871.

Index

Quantum Computing: A New Era of Computing, First Edition.
Kuldeep Singh Kaswan, Jagjit Singh Dhatterwal, Anupam Baliyan, and Shalli Rani.
© 2023 The Institute of Electrical and Electronics Engineers, Inc. Published 2023 by John Wiley & Sons, Inc.

Printed and bound by CPI Group (UK) Ltd, Croydon, CR0 4YY

27/10/2024

14580668-0002